IN THE

CITY *of*

BIKES

ALSO BY PETE JORDAN

Dishwasher: One Man's Quest to Wash Dishes in All Fifty States

~The Story of the Amsterdam Cyclist~

IN THE CITY *of* BIKES

PETE JORDAN

HARPER ● PERENNIAL

NEW YORK • LONDON • TORONTO • SYDNEY • NEW DELHI • AUCKLAND

HARPER ● PERENNIAL

Portions of this book previously appeared (in different form) in the *Amsterdam Weekly*, *Oek*, and *Het Parool*.

HarperCollins books may be purchased for educational, business, or sales promotional use. For information please write: Special Markets Department, HarperCollins Publishers, 10 East 53rd Street, New York, NY 10022.

FIRST EDITION

Designed by Michael Correy

Library of Congress Cataloging-in-Publication Data
Jordan, Pete.
In the city of bikes : the story of the Amsterdam cyclist / Pete Jordan.
p. cm.
ISBN 978-0-06-199520-0
1. Cycling—Netherlands—Amsterdam. 2. Amsterdam
(Netherlands)—Description and travel. I. Title.
GV1046.N442J67 2013
796.609492'352—dc23
2012032105

13 14 15 16 17 OV/RRD 10 9 8 7 6 5 4 3 2 1

For Ferris,
and in memory of my mom

Contents

Author's Note

A note on the usage of some place-names (streets, canals, etc.) in Amsterdam that have not been translated from the Dutch in the text. Among some of the place-names that the reader will encounter:

- *straat*: street
- *gracht*: canal
- *plein*: square
- *steeg*: alley
- *weg*: way
- *dijk*: dike

Also, throughout this book, the name "Holland" is used interchangeably with "the Netherlands," as is "Hollanders" for "Dutch/Netherlanders." Since the provinces of North and South Holland (home to the nation's three most populous cities: Amsterdam, Rotterdam and The Hague) comprise only two of the Netherlands' twelve provinces, many citizens of the non-Holland provinces rightly take offense at the term Holland being used to denote the entire nation. I've chosen to use the term liberally, partly because so many Dutch people already refer to the nation as Holland, partly because many quotations from Dutch sources in the book use the term to describe the nation and partly because of any chauvinism I myself may possess as a resident of North Holland.

1

Even a Man from America Can See a Few Things: The Arrival

Welkom in Amsterdam," the flight attendant said upon our landing. From the airport, a 20-minute train trip brought me to Central Station. Then, with my duffel bag slung over my left shoulder, I stepped onto the streets of continental Europe for the very first time. Two minutes later—and two blocks away on Spuistraat—I was busy gaping at 17th-century, gable-roofed buildings that leaned so severely they appeared ready to spill into the street, when suddenly a bike bell rang out: *Brringg! Brringg!*

Though I clearly heard the bell, I didn't react to it. Why should I? I was walking on the sidewalk.

Then, from behind, a bicycle slammed into me. Under the weight of my duffel bag, I stumbled a few steps forward before righting myself. I turned and saw a young brunette cyclist in a short skirt. She looked awfully cute. She also looked mighty pissed—at me. She scowled, then muttered "Klootzak!" and sped off.

Huh? Why was *she* upset? *She* was the one riding carelessly on the sidewalk. *I* was the injured party here!

I was still pondering this ignoble welcome to Amsterdam when I heard the frantic ringing of another bike bell: *Brringg! Brringg! Brringg!*

I turned around. A sneering cyclist was barreling right toward me. *Ack!* My body clenched; I braced for a second collision. Fortunately, this time, no bike struck me. The sneerer had managed to skillfully swerve around me. As I watched him pedal on, I thought, This sidewalk is a dangerous place to walk! Then it dawned on me, this was no simple pedestrian sidewalk; it was a separated-from-the-street *bike path*. I had no idea such a thing even existed. A smile came over my face. This was brilliant! How *civilized*!

Seconds before a third cyclist could target me, I stepped off the asphalt path onto the brick-lined sidewalk and watched one bike after another zoom by. A window washer cycled by with a 15-foot ladder dangling over his shoulder as casually as if it was a purse. Another cyclist passed with a dining room table somehow perched behind him. Several young couples rode by on single bikes, the men pedaling and the women—sidesaddle on the rear racks—lounging languidly as if kicking back on recliners.

THE YEAR WAS 2002 and at the age of 35, I was already a bike nut who had lived and cycled in cities all over America. Just two years before, I'd convinced my sweetheart, Amy Joy, to move with me to Pittsburgh, Pennsylvania, telling her it was where I wanted to live for the rest of my life. I'd been lured there by the cheap housing prices and funky old neighborhoods, but I'd failed to consider one aspect of Pittsburgh living: cycling.

Soon after arriving in Pittsburgh, I began working as a dishwasher at a local café. It was autumn, and I regularly saw other people on bikes in traffic, jostling with cars. They weren't great in number but were numerous enough to help me believe I could comfortably settle forever in Pittsburgh. But as winter dawned, my daily 30-minute commutes to work grew chillier, more challenging and increasingly more lonely. I saw fewer and fewer fellow cyclists until, finally, several days passed during which I saw none. I grew despondent and, at the same time, became even more determined to spot other bikers.

Then, early one December morning, while riding to work, I saw them: in the snow, weaving back and forth across each other, lay *two bicycle-tire tracks*. My heart began thumping. Somewhere up ahead, just out of view, someone else was cycling. I wasn't alone after all!

As I sped to catch up to them, my hope for Pittsburgh surged. For minutes, I raced in the mystery cyclist's tracks across the shuttered Nabisco factory parking lot and through some alleyways. Remarkable! He or she was following my same route! Who could it be? A coworker? If so, then we could commute together. Maybe we could even . . .

Suddenly, mid-fantasy, I stopped pedaling.

My bike slowed to a halt.

My chin dropped.

Ugh.

Could I have been any more foolish? These weren't the tracks of someone up ahead. They were *my* tracks—the ones I'd made while riding home from work the night before.

I then questioned how I could possibly spend the rest of my life in a place inhospitable to cyclists. Hope for Pittsburgh ebbed.

Months later, Amy Joy and I left Pittsburgh for good and arrived back in Portland, Oregon—the place where we had met and the city widely praised as America's cycling capital. Early on my first morning back in town, while sitting on the front steps of our rental at NE 20th and Couch, I was pleased to watch a cyclist ride past. A minute later, another whizzed by. Soon they were zipping by from all directions. In a 30-minute span, I counted 19 people on bikes. *Nineteen!* After having searched in vain for evidence of fellow cycling life in Pittsburgh, I was now so elated I rushed inside to tell Amy Joy.

"Nineteen cyclists!" I said, shaking her awake.

"Huh?"

"I just counted 19 cyclists in the past half hour!"

"Oh," she responded before falling back to sleep.

Now, while standing in the middle of Amsterdam, I recalled that event from just one year earlier. And I had to laugh. Portland? *Nineteen* in 30 minutes? Ha! I was now seeing 19 cyclists just about every *30 seconds*.

AS I TRUDGED along the streets of Amsterdam that buzzed with bike traffic, I couldn't take my eyes off the bikers. Later, I would find a passage from a 1933 guidebook to Amsterdam that perfectly described the type of captivation a newcomer like me was experiencing:

> [T]he odd gaps between going from one place to the next
> may be profitably filled in by making first-hand studies
> of the noble art of trick bicycle-riding. Those who are not
> absolutely perfect, get killed off very young. The survivors

thereupon develop a perfection in the difficult technique of balancing which will fill your soul with deep envy. Sit you down on the Leidse Plein or on the Rembrandt Plein and let the show pass by you while you are supposed to be writing postal cards to the dear family in Ithaca, NY. You won't write many, for you will be forever clutching your companion's hand and shouting, "Look at that girl carrying a potted palm on her shoulders!" or again, "Look at that family with five kids tucked away between the frame!" All very harmless and pleasant and the cost, again, is negligible.

That's exactly how *I* felt, except, I had no companion with me whose hand I could clutch to share my amazement. Amy Joy wouldn't be joining me in Amsterdam until a month and a half later.

What I really wanted her to see was the impressive number of kids riding as passengers. Many of them rode behind their parents in rear seats, the kind I'd seen used in the United States. Other kids rode in large wooden boxes on elongated cargo bikes, contraptions I'd never seen in America. Some infants rode in little seats between their parents and the handlebars, complete with little windshields. Babies rode in slings strapped to their parents' chests. One girl stood on the rear rack of her mother's bike while holding on to her mom's shoulders—like a little trick rodeo rider preening atop her horse. This was all new to me.

Despite all these crowds, I found the city startlingly quiet. The narrow streets and the roadways along the canals carried far less motorized traffic than their congested counterparts in American city centers. This tranquility, though, was compromised by an ever-present clamor created by the army of creaky bikes. Scraping fenders *clunk-clunk-clunked*. Loose chain guards continually *kerchunked*. And countless rusty chains—apparently last oiled when they'd exited the bike factory decades earlier—shrieked desperate pleas for grease.

These bikes were nothing like the sleek and polished mountain bikes and racing bikes and cruisers I was accustomed to seeing on the streets of America. Back home, I'd always felt like an outcast on my beloved fifth-hand clunkers. More than once, I'd been rudely dismissed by a bike shop mechanic who'd deemed an old two-wheeler of mine unworthy of repair. But now I found myself in a city inundated by kindred spirits on beat-up old bikes, many of which were held together in part by string, twine, yarn, wires, rubber bands, inner tubes, shoelaces, masking tape, duct tape, etc. The cyclists appeared utterly unconcerned with the status of their rides. Suit-and-tie-clad businessmen rode unabashedly on broken-down workhorses—women's models, no less. In fact, with so many well dressed Amsterdammers riding crappy wheels, it seemed that the chicer one's threads, the shabbier—and noisier—his or her bike.

Yet, no matter the condition of their bikes, every cyclist appeared happy and satisfied. They moved with fluidity and sophistication. They stepped on and off their moving bikes with the gracefulness of ballerinas. At busy intersections, columns of bikers threaded past one another effortlessly. Such universal comfort and elegance on such basic, crappy bikes: it seemed the basis of an egalitarian society.

FOR SEVERAL HOURS, as I wandered aimlessly, I scrutinized the bikers with a nervous longing. I walked the length of Vondelpark and then, beyond the far end of the park, I entered a tiny bike shop. A row of a dozen ratty-looking, secondhand bikes, each sporting a handwritten price tag, stood along one wall. Straightaway I located the cheapest bike: a single-speed, Union-brand men's model. It cost 80 euros—roughly a hundred dollars at the time, which was double the most I'd ever paid for a bike. Over the years, bikes had usually come into my possession as hand-me-downs or throwaways or as little unwanted street orphans in need of a home. But despite the cost, I was now desperate to join the action. I needed a bike, and this one appeared roadworthy; that was plenty enough for me.

The only other person in the shop was a mechanic who was busy replacing the brake pads on a three-speed. "I'll take this one," I told him.

The mechanic wiped his greasy hands on a rag, walked over and asked, "You don't want to try it out first?"

Too impatient to hit the streets, I answered, "No."

I quickly counted out the cash and handed it over.

"Do you want a lock, too?" the mechanic asked.

I patted my duffel bag and said, "I already have one."

"Just one?"

"Yeah."

"And you're going to lock it outside at night?"

"Yeah, I guess so."

"In Amsterdam, you're going to need more than one."

He stressed that I should lock both wheels and that the frame should be locked to a fixed object. I took his advice and bought a second lock.

Before leaving the shop, I mentioned to the mechanic that someone had slammed into me that morning; I repeated as best I could the woman's utterance. "What's that mean?" I asked.

"You were walking in the bike lane?"

"Yeah."

He laughed and said, "She called you an asshole."

I walked the bike outside. Since the consensus color of the frame—drawing from the paint, rust and dirt—was brown, I wasted no time in christening it "Brownie." I threw one leg over Brownie's top tube, plopped my butt on the seat and placed my right foot on the right pedal. My helmet remained buried in the bottom of my duffel bag. Of the thousands of cyclists I'd seen so far that day, I had yet to see one wearing a helmet. So I decided to go native by going helmet-less.

A couple of cyclists rode past. I didn't move. Then another rode by. Still I didn't budge. My heart, I realized, was racing.

I found myself too nervous to embark. I'd presumed that riding a bike in Amsterdam would come effortlessly. After all, I'd cycled in Los Angeles, New York and dozens of other cities in between, always riding as a second-class road user on streets dominated by cars. But here bicycles ruled the streets; yet I was intimidated. The Dutch cyclists rode with such poise and confidence, I doubted whether I could fit in or if I could avoid causing havoc. I didn't really know where in the city I was or even what some of the traffic signs meant. To help explain it all to me, I wished I had a guide—be it a person or a book.

Travel guides to Amsterdam and Holland—particularly those published in the 1940s and '50s—warned tourists of Dutch cyclists. "The visitor must . . . be careful of the countless cyclists whose agility and speed are stupefying," cautioned one guidebook. Another counseled: "You'll think the Lord has unloosed a plague of cycles upon Holland for some national sin."

For the motorized tourist in Holland, a 1945 guide advised, "Don't be frightened of . . . reckless cyclists." Ten years later, another guidebook suggested, "You will need discipline in traffic, adroitness and a certain amount of courage . . . to thread your way through a host of bicyclists." More direct was the recommendation from a 1949 travel book on how motorists should handle biking Amsterdammers: "If you feel like cursing them, we hope you will manage to keep your temper."

Even taxi passengers received tips. A 1950 guide titled *All the Best in Holland* stated:

> Taxi drivers seem always able to weave an intricate pattern in
> and through the mad needling of bicycles. They plunge into
> seemingly impenetrable masses of them and, like the Red
> Sea before the wand of Moses, the cycles open up a miraculous path. Close your eyes. Don't look. You'll reach your
> destination safely, without leaving a trail of casualties.

This same book also strongly advised pedestrians to "steer a straight course" at traffic intersections in order to best cope with the cyclists. It explained:

> When walking on or across streets in Holland *never halt or
> change your pace abruptly!* This caution is of utmost importance,
> since disregard of it may cause a severe bump with some cyclist.
> Holland's bike-pushers plot their swift and silent courses on the
> assumption that the pedestrian will keep going where he seems
> to be going, that he will not strike off at a sudden, whimsical
> tangent, that he will not stop in the middle of the street to see if
> he left his traveler's checks back in the room.

In 1959, one visitor to Amsterdam noted, "It is the daring 'foreigner' who would board a bicycle and attempt to keep pace with these Hollanders who weave in and out of traffic at 'breaking-the-sound-barrier' speeds."

Seated on my new bike, I went ahead and dared myself—and then took off.

BROWNIE WAS LUMBERING and sluggish, a reluctant mule in need of prodding. (I wouldn't discover all the oily sand packed into the enclosed chain guard until weeks later.) But after about a hundred feet of riding, he proved manageable. When I pedaled, his wheels turned; when I braked, he slowed. That was more than could be said of some bikes I'd owned, so I was more than satisfied.

Having no destination, Brownie and I simply started following the guy who happened to be riding ahead of us in the bike lane. When he turned left, so did we. When he turned right, we did, too. And when absentminded tourists wandered onto the bike path, I followed my leader's example by aggressively ringing my bell and muttering at them the first word in my Dutch biking vocabulary: "Klootzak."

All afternoon Brownie and I rode in the summer sunshine. Gradually, my confidence grew, especially when I realized Brownie must already have logged thousands of hours on these streets. Along canals, over bridges, though alleys and parks, we obediently pursued one cyclist after another. That is, when we could keep up. When three ten-year-old boys left us in their dust, I blamed the weight of my duffel bag. When an elderly woman left us for dead, I blamed jet lag. Ultimately, though, I was forced to suppress my machismo and admit that the tempo of many of the town's cyclists was simply faster than my own pedaling lollygag. My pace never hindered my progress, though, for each time one person pulled away, some other nearby laggard was on hand for me to trail instead. And slowly but surely, with each turn of the crank and with each new guide followed, I got into the groove of the city's cycling rhythm.

For some reason, many of these unwitting guides were women. And there were so many women—beauties made even more beautiful because they were on bikes. Unlike bike riders in America, who so often ride hunched over their handlebars, "The Amsterdammer sits upright on his bicycle as if he's sitting in an uncomfortable chair at home," noted an English tourist in 1954. "In a busy street filled with traffic, it's as if all the cyclists are paying each other a visit, yet they're riding." These Amsterdam women were riding so tall in the saddle, regally atop their thrones, that the tips of their shoes were barely able to touch the ground.

Without a doubt, on this lone July day in Amsterdam, I saw more stunning women on bicycles than I had seen in my entire 35 years in the United States. Some women were riding in long skirts hiked up to their knees. Others were riding in short skirts hiked up to their thighs. And a few rode in miniskirts hiked up so unbelievably far, one could hardly justify calling them skirts.

Dutifully, I gaped at them while not knowing my reaction was actually rather customary among American males. Almost a century earlier, in 1911, a tourist from Kansas had commented: "Perhaps it will be thought that I am going too far in my investigation, but the Dutch ladies ride bicycles so generally that even a man from America can see a few things, no matter how hard he tries to look the other way and comes near getting run over." A Yank in Amsterdam in 1929 wrote: "There seem to be as many of the fair sex riding as there are men, and they wear short skirts—as short as they wear them anywhere—so it is a real sight to watch the bicycle parade."

In 1965, a 50-year-old American marriage counselor, after spending time in the Netherlands, noted, "Nowhere else in the world have I seen so many women and girls with such shapely, truly feminine legs as in Holland. And the Dutch *know* that. They like to show their legs. It's due to the bikes. Massage can do a lot, but cycling makes the leg just perfect."

Of his visit to Amsterdam, a New Yorker wrote in 1972: "At first you cannot refrain from looking out of the corners of your eyes at the rounded knees and shapely legs of those blond goddesses who quickly pedal past you, as though galloping on a winged Pegasus. Soon, however, the superabundance of thighs exposed by the breeze immunizes you to their effect."

But here in my first hours in the city, I wasn't yet immunized. One American who might have been, though, was Walter H. Waggoner, the 39-year-old Holland bureau chief for the *New York Times*, who, in 1957, wrote:

> The foreigner . . . may have a picture of rain-soaked, frost-bitten squinting faces under a tangle of wind-whipped hair. This contributes to a notion abroad that Dutch girls are what one American resident has described as "not very appetizing."
>
> The description is untrue. They just do not look appetizing, because they always are fighting the weather on their bicycles in a way that produces, on the most comely, the leathery, the buffeted look of a veteran sea captain.

If these were sea captains I was seeing, then I was ready to sign up and ship out.

The sight of all these dreamboats on bikes made me eager to see among them my own belle, Amy Joy. Now I was already picturing her in Amsterdam riding in her flowery orange dress or in her flowery green dress or in her black polka-dot dress. Really, though, it wouldn't matter what she wore. In America, she'd always been ravishing on a bike. In Amsterdam, she'd be nothing less than a goddess.

ONE WOMAN I found myself trailing was dolled up in a tight, sleeveless gown and stilettos, looking as if she was heading to a ball. Even more enchanting than her outfit was the rattletrap bike she was riding. Its front wheel weaved somewhat, but the back wheel was out of control. It wobbled so severely, each revolution looked as if it could be its last before completely falling off. Watching the tail end of her bicycle sway from side to side made me loopy. Finally, when I could stand it no more, I veered off and commenced trailing a guy who was rolling a cigarette as he pedaled. Though I was now spared the nausea, I was left wondering if Miss Partygoer ever reached her festive destination before her bike collapsed.

A couple of blocks later, after my latest guide had finished rolling his cigarette and begun smoking it, I caught a glimpse of a woman biking through an intersection. At first I thought I'd noticed something unusual about her, something peculiar about her midsection. Then I quickly dismissed the notion. Impossible, I thought. Still, I wasn't sure. So I raced through the intersection, labored to catch up, then tucked in right behind her. From this vantage point, though, I still couldn't confirm what I thought I'd seen. So I pedaled yet harder and pulled alongside her.

Then I looked over.

Sheesh! I thought.

Either she was cycling to the beach with a beach ball stuffed under her shirt—or she was extremely pregnant. I dismissed the former as implausible. But the latter? Inconceivable.

So I looked over again. Now it was undeniable; that was no ball. Of all the various methods for transporting kids on bikes in Amsterdam that I'd witnessed so far, this woman was employing the most basic one of all: *in her belly.*

I continued staring at her ready-to-burst abdomen, wondering if she was leading me to the maternity ward. When the expectant mother caught me gawking, she shot me a look that seemed to say, *What, you've never seen a pregnant woman on a bike before?*

In reply, my expression hopefully conveyed, *No, I never have!*

Mother and fetus then accelerated, leaving me flabbergasted in their wake.

I'd already suspected that this place was magical. My lefty heart was already warmed by what little I knew about Dutch culture, like governmental toleration of soft-drug usage and legalized gay marriage (both of which were unknown in the United States at the time). But there was something about the sight of a pregnant woman cycling so casually that made me really swoon. In America I'd witnessed motorists verbally attack cyclists who had the temerity to ride with child passengers, calling them bad parents for endangering their children. And maybe those motorists had a point. In fact, I could not imagine allowing a child to roam the streets of an American city by bike the way I did as a kid in the 1970s. But here, children were everywhere on bikes— alone or with their parents. That conveyed to me a lot about this city. And that this society provided streets safe enough to cycle without helmets made a big impression. Yet the icing on the cake was a people who provided an environment secure enough for a *pregnant* woman to cycle. It seemed to me the pinnacle of a humane culture.

Before my introductory Amsterdam bike ride ended that day, I saw a second and then a third cycling preggers.

I'D COME TO Amsterdam knowing almost nothing about the city's—or country's—history or culture or society. If I'd been asked to point to Holland on a map of Europe, my finger probably would've landed somewhere on Scandinavia. What I knew about the country could have fit in a thimble. Dutch masters? Weren't those cigars or something? Famous Hollanders? I couldn't have named a single one—not a politician nor a monarch, not a sports figure nor a musician. If I'd been asked to name a Dutch painter, I couldn't even have come up with Van Gogh or Rembrandt. Anne Frank? I was vaguely familiar with her tragic story of hiding from the Nazis and her subsequent death, but if someone had told me she'd hidden in Brussels or Copenhagen, I'd have nodded in agreement, oblivious to the truth.

I had just spent the previous decade absorbed with exploring America and gave scant thought to what lay beyond its borders. About Holland, mostly I'd just heard that the Dutch loved bikes. So, as an older, returning college student, I'd come to Amsterdam to study Dutch urban planning for five months at the University of Amsterdam. That first night, I settled into the university-provided studio apartment on Spaarndammerstraat.

On my second morning in Europe, I began my intensive, monthlong, five-morning-a-week Dutch language course. When not in class, I explored the city by bike, day and night.

Though I was a newlywed, I was falling for a new sweetheart.

I was fully enraptured with Amsterdam, but even more powerful was the prospect of sharing Amsterdam with Amy Joy. On my third afternoon in the city, I sat in the sun on a bench in Vondelpark and fantasized about cycling side by side with my wife while she held my wrist or forearm (the way I was seeing cycling lovers do in the park) or with her seated on the back of Brownie (another standard among the local couples). Also exciting was picturing her riding in this city with a big, round belly. Yet most thrilling of all was imagining Amy Joy cycling with our own future little tyke as a passenger.

As the endless line of cyclists streamed by, I sat on the bench and handwrote a letter to Amy Joy. I described my new perspective: how terribly stressed I now realized I'd been while cycling all those years in America compared to how incredibly relaxed I had become in Amsterdam. I described to her how comfortable this city felt and the utter "coziness" of my new surroundings. The letter concluded: "It's so absolutely amazing to ride a bike here. Maybe we should just live in Amsterdam forever. What do you think?"

This proposition was little more than wishful thinking, not unlike a kid at Disneyland asking her parents if she could stay and live in Sleeping Beauty's castle. But to Amy Joy, the thought of being at home in Amsterdam was already real. Her response to my letter was so enthusiastic that it couldn't wait for airmail. Just hours after receiving and reading my proposal, Amy Joy—the girl from Mississippi who'd never before set foot in Europe, much less Amsterdam—replied by e-mail: "Living there forever sounds wonderful! I've already started telling my friends, 'Goodbye, I'm moving to Amsterdam. . . .'"

2
Lucky Few: The 1890s

Nine months before I arrived in Amsterdam, in a used bookstore in San Francisco, I stumbled upon a 1963 book titled *Cities* by the landscape architect Lawrence Halprin. The book contained hundreds of photos of engaging and interesting urban spaces from around the world. While I scanned these images of streets, plazas and waterfronts, one picture in particular struck me. The photographer had captured a swarm of cyclists moving as one through an intersection in Amsterdam. Sidewalk café patrons sit facing the street as the parade of cyclists breezes past, flanking a lone automobile. For more than ten years, I had roamed around the United States, exploring big cities and small towns seeking the place where I felt most comfortable, somewhere I could call home for the rest of my life. Ultimately, I'd never found a place that had ticked all the boxes. But now, while staring at this one photo, I was mesmerized.

I bought the book, took it home, ripped out the photo and taped it to the wall beside my bed. For the next few days, when going to sleep and upon awakening, I counted the cyclists. Each time, the tally ended with the same incredible total: 60. Sixty people on their bikes. They weren't radicals shouting slogans or Lance Armstrong wannabes on Treks. They weren't children playing on toy bikes or deadbeats on the only means of transport they could afford. Judging from their attire (coats and ties, purses dangling from handlebars) and their demeanors (matter-of-fact, not harried), they appeared to be just 60 individuals commuting home from work or school on a simple, yet effective, form of transportation.

While the photo portrayed my ideal locale, I had no idea if 21st-century Amsterdam resembled the Amsterdam of the photo. But even if that photographed street nowadays had only a fraction of the cyclists in the picture, I figured Amsterdam would still be a far greater bike town than anywhere in America. As an urban planning student, I needed to get there, to be there, to learn from the best how to build a city for bikes.

AS KIDS GROWING up in the post-hippie/pre-yuppie Haight-Ashbury district of 1970s San Francisco, none of my older brothers or sisters owned bikes. My parents simply couldn't afford such luxuries. Other kids on our block had their own wheels, though, and anytime I could cadge a spin on one of those, no matter how briefly, the moment was special. In fact, it was so special that when I was eight years old, I began delivering newspapers in order to earn the money to buy a bike of my own. After working two months as a paperboy, I saved exactly enough for a $45 bicycle I saw in a toy store advertisement.

My new bike was puke-green and had its name—"Dill Pickle"—written in script across the chain guard. Though I stood out as much as a guy on a hot-pink bike sporting the name

"Princess," when my bike and I took to the streets of my neighborhood, no eight-year-old could've ever worn a broader smile. My kooky-colored bike with its dopey name was the butt of endless razzing from friends and strangers alike. But none of that mattered. Despite its look and moniker, the Dill Pickle was *my* bike and it provided me the freedom to travel beyond my block and explore the city. I no longer had to wait for the bus or be chauffeured in my parents' station wagon; I could just *go.*

Countless hours were spent riding with my friends through Golden Gate Park out to Ocean Beach or up and over the hills to the video game and pinball parlors at Fisherman's Wharf. Sometimes we even cycled outside the city, down to a friend's cousin's house in suburban South San Francisco.

By the end of its first year, my Dill Pickle had aged considerably. Spokes were missing; the handlebars were bent from a collision with a wall; dents and scratches pitted the frame. Admittedly, I didn't take especially good care of the Pickle and, eventually, rode the poor thing into an early grave. We were unable to even celebrate a second anniversary together.

A long string of other low-budget bikes followed. Some I bought secondhand from friends. One I found abandoned and covered with ivy in Golden Gate Park. Another I found rusting on the rooftop of a neighboring apartment building. Unbothered by their homely looks, I always fell for junkers and granny bikes—ones that weren't embarrassed by their broken-in appearances. Maybe they didn't always have the keenest brakes or the best tread tires, but those bikes seemed to be glad just to be ridden at all—and I always happily obliged them.

During my senior year of high school, the driver's education teacher sought me out to inform me I was one of only two students from my class of 200 who hadn't taken his course. While my peers treated obtaining a driver's license as a vital—almost universal—rite of passage, I was uninterested in cars. My classmates eagerly became motorists, while I remained a devoted cyclist.

As I grew older, bike riding continued to fascinate me far more than car driving. Bikes were so much cheaper to own and operate, were far simpler to repair and maintain, and with no license or insurance required, they certainly required far less responsibility. Most important, no matter what clunky, crappy old bike I ever owned, each remained a delight to ride.

I cycled around towns and cities across the nation. Some places—Davis, California; Portland, Oregon; Madison, Wisconsin—were easy to ride in. Other places—Los Angeles, Houston, Atlanta—were tougher. Yet no matter where in the nation I happened to be, I joyfully cycled, regardless of the place's bikeability.

AFTER MORE THAN a decade of incessant rambling, trying to see and experience as much of America as possible, I began studying urban planning at San Francisco State University in the fall of 2001. My interest focused on learning how cities could best be organized in ways that limited car usage, increased mass transit ridership and added facilities for pedestrians and cyclists.

At school, inspired by what I was learning, I'd leave class feeling extremely motivated. But then, just after stepping outside and unlocking my bike, I'd face an urban-planning nightmare: 19th Avenue, San Francisco's busiest—and one of its most dangerous—streets. On just about an annual basis, pedestrians had been killed at the four-way intersection in front of the campus.

A major reason why I liked to cycle was that I found it far less nerve-racking than driving. However, on the bike, I didn't yet realize how very stressed I really was. In fact, despite the fact that San Francisco was the birthplace of the Critical Mass bike activist movement, the city was often challenging for me to navigate by bike. The hills weren't the problem, though; the other road users were. Almost daily, on my commute to and from campus, I encountered some sort of altercation. Most were minor: motorists cutting me off, people thoughtlessly opening car doors in my path, etc. But other times the infractions were more severe: drivers blowing through stop signs or barreling along in the bike lanes.

Though the city's population was more or less the same as during my Dill Pickle days in the 1970s, the number of automobiles in the city had doubled in that time. And as a cyclist, I felt squeezed out, pushed to the margins, alone.

A COUPLE OF days after having discovered the 1950s Amsterdam cycling photo, I walked into my university's Study Abroad office. Applying to study urban planning—in English—at the University of Amsterdam turned out to be far easier than I'd expected. I was duly accepted into the program.

The plan was set: Amy Joy and I would marry in June 2002. I'd leave for Amsterdam in July. She'd follow me seven weeks later. I'd study Dutch urban planning through the fall semester and learn all I could about how to help make American cities more accommodating and less perilous for cyclists. Then, in December, we'd return to San Francisco.

At least, that had been the plan when I'd left the States.

ONCE I WAS in Amsterdam, all the papers I wrote in my urban planning courses focused on some aspect of Amsterdam cycling. I quickly learned that the level of cycling was much lower than it had been when the 1950s photo was snapped. This made me even more curious about the history of Amsterdam cycling, especially in the period from the 1920s to the 1970s. Unfortunately, there wasn't much readily available information on this subject in English or in Dutch. For example, the only book concerning Amsterdam cycling history, written in the 1970s, devoted a scant page and a half to the story of the city's bikers during the five years Amsterdam was occupied by the Nazis. So in order to learn the full story myself, I began digging through libraries and archives.

AT THE VERY beginning of the 1890s, bicycles—with their high mounts, giant front wheels and solid tires—were just the playthings of hard-core enthusiasts. But that changed quickly in both America and Europe with the advent of the "safety bike" and its low mount, diamond frame, two wheels of equal size and—most important—pneumatic tires. (As an Amsterdammer of that era testified: "The pneumatic tire came along, which made it possible—even alluring—for anyone to become a bicycle rider.") In 1890, there were only about 150,000 bikes in all of the United States, but by the end of the decade, Americans were buying more than a million "safeties" annually. It was the bicycle's "golden age."

In the decades-long development that resulted in the safety bike, the various innovations occurred primarily in France, Great Britain, Germany and the United States. Despite its later reputation as a "cycling nation," the Netherlands actually contributed no major developments to the bicycle.

In the United States, due to the mass manufacture of bikes, cheap models flooded the market. At the same time, in Holland, while some Dutch bike manufacturers existed, they didn't mass-produce bikes on the American scale. Dutch bicycles, therefore, remained expensive. Also pricey were the many American bikes imported into the Netherlands. Comparing one Dutch bike to the American bikes, an American visitor in 1897 observed: "In Amsterdam . . . the 'Wilhelmina,' called after Holland's Queen and of home manufacture, is 'not in it,' as the boys say. Why? Because they are not as durable as the Yankee importation."

AFTER AMSTERDAM GREATLY expanded in the 17th century, the new streets became the envy of foreigners. One Englishman visiting Amsterdam in 1641 remarked: "[T]he Streets so exactly straite, even, & uniforme that nothing can be more pleasing." In 1691, another Englishman commented: "Certainly Amsterdam is one of the Beautifullest Cities in the World . . . their Streets . . . Paved so neatly, as is to be found no where else in any Country."

The cobblestoned streets that had once marveled 17th century visitors greatly irritated bikers at the turn of the 20th century. In 1900, one cyclist, riding from Central Station to Dam Square, claimed that the Damrak's wet cobblestones (or, as he called them, "the lumpy heads of little children") caused the rider to "bob up and down and about like a rudderless ship."

In 1898, another cyclist described the paving on Nieuwezijds Voorburgwal as "nothing less than a mountainous landscape that a Lilliputian would regard as a delightful, undulating terrain. A bicycle wheel doesn't take up much space, but the cyclist on this street who finds a path wide enough to ride on without jolting is a trick-rider of the highest order."

A woman in 1902 found Leidseplein to be particularly rough for cycling, saying, "Really, when I sit there shaking—bumpity, bumpity, bop! (with 'bop!' I fly off my seat)—I'm left feeling completely foolish. I fancy that someone from the sixteenth century would think they were seeing a new sort of torture device."

"Even the sturdiest bicycles are not equipped for such medieval conditions," complained an Amsterdam cyclist in 1906. "The bicycle repairmen will attest to how great the damage is that is inflicted on bicycles due to poor paving."

THE ONE PLACE in Amsterdam that provided the city's cyclists with solace was Vondelpark. In the 1860s and '70s, the lanes of the park had been laid out specifically to promote promenading, whether on foot, on horseback or in a buggy. By the 1890s, those same lanes became so enormously popular for cycling that various attempts to ban cycling in the park never stuck. In 1897, two pedestrians noted a typical spring Sunday morning in Vondelpark. "Wherever you look, you see bicycles, bicycles and yet more bicycles," they wrote. "We also then heard a couple of little scalawags justifiably singing, 'Everyone on the bike! Everyone on the bike!'"*

---

* Just as the 1890s biking craze in the United States was exemplified by that era's hit song "Daisy Bell" ("But you'd look sweet / upon the seat / of a bicycle built for two"), the hit song "Allemaal op de fiets" ("Everyone on the Bike") exemplified the craze in the Netherlands.

But because the safety bike was a rather recent phenomenon, Amsterdammers in the 1890s weren't accustomed to cycling since childhood (unlike the generations that followed). Lacking basic biking skills—like balance—many adults were far from proficient riders. The two aforementioned Vondelpark strollers reported seeing cyclists crash into each other and slam into pedestrians. Of the riders on rental bikes, they said, "We saw one of them lose his balance and land in the middle of the path and create a dam in the stream [of cyclists] that irresistibly pushed onward."

Many of these neophytes came to Vondelpark specifically to learn to cycle. One Amsterdammer of the era later recalled:

In the streets and on the squares and especially in Vondelpark, very often you could see the most clownish feats executed by the giving and receiving of cycling instructions. The student—fearful and awkward, trying to master that difficult balance—was helped by the instructor who—panting and gasping—held on to the bike's seat post while trotting alongside and pushing. The student could ride independently for a bit but then, upon the realization that he or she was no longer being helped, fell over.

A teacher from an outdoor cycling school recounted how, first, he would hold on to the frame of the student's bike,

And then just run alongside until my tongue hung to my shoes. There were ladies who, at the slightest wobble or just when I'd let go, would begin to yell and others who, after a near-crash, would immediately throw in the towel. Conversely, there was also an "old young lady"—a little, slight, wilted type—that had not the least bit of fear, who insisted on riding "free," took nasty spills and—laughing—tried again.

SUCH WAS THE demand for biking instruction that a number of impressive indoor cycling schools emerged around town. In 1895, for example, on Frederiksplein, within the great hall of the Paleis voor Volksvlijt (Palace of the People), a large cycling school and velodrome complex opened. In 1897, at the new Simplex bike factory on Overtoom, a bike-riding school opened up on the fourth floor of the complex (from which 237 students graduated within its first three months). Just a few blocks away, on Nassaukade, another bike manufacturer—Fongers—opened its own riding school.

The most conspicuous of these establishments, though, was the Velox. When it opened in July 1898 on Hobbemakade in a grand, new edifice that stood among the Museumplein's other grand, new buildings—the Rijksmuseum, the Stedelijk Museum, the Concertgebouw—a reporter wrote: "'Cyclist School' is too modest a name. A better name for the large, sturdily-built and splendidly-furnished building would be: 'Cyclist Palace.'" Its main attraction—a 16,000-square-foot, wooden-floored riding hall—was purported to be the largest hall in the nation. Other amenities included a gallery overlooking the main hall, sitting rooms, changing rooms, a restaurant, a bike shop showroom and a basement repair shop. The facilities were said to be "extremely practical and pleasant. In such an enormous building, one feels immediately at ease and at home."

The Velox could be used for "figure cycling" (akin to figure skating) and by cycling clubs or individuals who wished to bike in comfort during wet and/or cold weather. But the Velox's main function was cycling education. At its grand opening, the Velox's commissioner proclaimed it to be "a school for beginners but also an academy for trained cyclists." Beginners first learned how to sit properly on a stationary bike. Then they progressed to wearing a harness that hung from above and kept them safely upright. Men learned how to steer with one hand while properly tipping their hats with the other. Women learned how to mount and dismount a bike in the utmost ladylike manner. One woman who had attended a cycling school in Amsterdam in the 1890s later recalled, "We practiced for weeks on end, just as if it was a horseback riding lesson. The first trip to Vondelpark was quite an event; we had purchased special cycling-gowns & our friends regarded us as heroes."

SINCE BIKES WERE expensive, lessons costly, proper riding attire expected and leisure time required for riding—all of which the city's large working class typically couldn't afford—cycling in Amsterdam during the 1890s "golden age" was largely restricted to the "lucky few," the affluent. Yet when it came to, arguably, the luckiest of them all—the wealthiest young woman in the country—cycling was strictly forbidden. Princess Wilhelmina was ten years old in 1890 when, upon the death of her father King Willem III, she became queen. But because Wilhelmina was still a minor, her mother, Emma, would rule as queen regent until Wilhelmina turned 18 in 1898.

In May 1897, while Emma and Wilhelmina were vacationing in Vienna, Austria, the 16-year-old girl became so captivated by the cycling she encountered there, she purchased an "excellent" bike and had it shipped back to Holland. Once home, Wilhelmina tried to take her new bike for a spin on the grounds of Het Loo Palace. When Emma discovered what her daughter was up to, she was aghast. The queen regent—who deemed bicycle riding highly inappropriate for a monarch—immediately forbade Wilhelmina from cycling.

Just as any parent's unpopular command could frustrate any teenager, the edict frustrated the teen queen. Wilhelmina, though, had a recourse unavailable to any other Dutch teenager: she pleaded her case before the Raad van State (Council of State), the body of statesmen that settled, among other things, disputes concerning the crown. In Wilhelmina's argument, she named other female European monarchs and royals who biked. They cycled, so why couldn't she? After deliberating, the council concluded that, for Wilhelmina, riding a bicycle was incompatible with reigning over more than 50 million subjects (90 percent of whom lived in the Dutch East Indies). In its ruling, the council's president stated:

> The precedents cited in favor of the contrary opinion are not to the point. In no other case was the person who used the bicycle as a mode of locomotion so precious to her subjects, in no other instance was the life and health of the Royal bicyclist so necessary to the welfare of such a large number of subjects as in this. Therefore, we humbly implore your gracious Majesty not to expose your precious life to this danger, how so ever slight it may seem.

This decision, one duchess said, cost Wilhelmina "many a tear." Even so, the young queen accepted it. "She sighed like a biker and obeyed like a Monarch," is how one foreign news account of the affair put it. As a consolation, Emma presented Wilhelmina with a gift: a buggy drawn by four Shetland ponies.

Within weeks, the tale of the queen who'd been prohibited from cycling ran in newspapers from Australia to America. The *New York Tribune* joked that a conspiracy was at the root of this "savage persecution" of Wilhelmina:

> The purport of it is, of course, entirely clear. It is to drive Her Majesty to abdicate her throne. And, indeed, no more potent measure could have been devised. For what right-thinking girl of seventeen would hesitate between a throne and a bicycle? But surely some milder course could have been pursued, some less atrocious proposition made. A simple revolution, with force of arms, would have been preferable to this.

Curiously, the Dutch press initially remained mum on the subject. It wasn't until after the foreign press had reported on the ruling that several Dutch periodicals finally published brief pieces about Wilhelmina's bike ban, the editors admitting they'd only learned of the matter through the foreign newspapers.

Despite the setback, Wilhelmina remained patient. After she finally ascended to the throne on her 18th birthday in August 1898, it was said that one of her first acts as a ruling monarch was to learn to ride her bike.

WHILE THE 1890s bicycling golden age had transpired on a much smaller scale in Holland than it had in the United States, unlike in America, bike riding didn't immediately become passé with the dawning of the automobile age (more about that in chapter 6). Even so, during the first two decades of the 20th century, the new transportation rage in Amsterdam wasn't the bicycle or the car; it was another relatively new mode of transit: the electric tram. During this period, the city's tram network greatly expanded and ridership shot through the roof.

But the modes of transport that continued to dominate the city's street traffic were *not* new. One was the pushcart, from which goods (fruit, vegetables, bread, clothes, etc.) were sold or transported. "Back then, it wasn't the cyclist who created chaos in traffic through his undisciplined driving," stated an eyewitness to that era; "it was the man who pushed the pushcart!"

Another major component of Amsterdam traffic, one that—it was said at the time—formed "the principal traffic hindrance on the roadway" was the pedestrian. Read one account in 1906:

If there is one category of people who still need to be educated on matters of traffic, then those are the pedestrians. Not conscious that they are in a busy traffic corridor, nor taking into account all that is moving around them, they go on their way with their heads in the clouds. They ignore sidewalks, preferring the middle of the street. Yes, indeed! They cross without looking. . . . Entire families socialize in the streets.

One eyewitness of the era spoke of "that peculiarity that repeatedly surprises foreigners: Amsterdam's pedestrians prefer to walk in the roadway." A visiting Englishwoman found this custom to be "so funny."

The pedestrians had, for centuries, constituted the bulk of Amsterdam's street traffic, making traffic regulation largely unnecessary (however, one-way traffic for carts had been mandated in some of the city's alleys as early as 1595). But in the early years of the 20th century, when the older, slower modes of transport (pedestrians/pushcarts/horse-drawn vehicles) mixed with the modern, faster modes (trams/bikes/cars), disorder arose, particularly at the intersections.

In 1906, action was finally taken to bring order to the street traffic when Amsterdam mayor Wilhelmus Frederik van Leeuwen implemented a broad plan that prohibited bike riding and car driving on 49 streets in the city center. While some of the affected streets made the list for reasons obvious to all (for example, various narrow, medieval alleyways), the inclusion of streets that served as major cycling thoroughfares (for example, Haarlemmerdijk, Leidsestraat and Utrechtsestraat) infuriated cyclists. Of the mayor's plan, one skeptical bike rider wrote:

Wonderful! But it won't work. In the genus *Amsterdammers*, there is a wretched spirit that opposes any type of regulation. The police have always encountered opposition to the implementation of what is now law. As much as possible, people try to slyly circumvent that which is not allowed.

Immediately after the ban went into effect, irate cyclists flooded the newspapers with letters that decried the rule as "ridiculous," "repressive" and even "terrorism." The letter-writing campaign succeeded; within three months, the ban was scuppered.

In 1912, another major attempt was made to tame the city's traffic. Assigned the unenviable task of serving as the very first agent in the police department's newly established traffic brigade was Gerrit Brinkman. At noon on his first day on the job—December 3, 1912—Brinkman positioned himself on Nieuwezijds Voorburgwal at the spot between the Royal Palace, the main post office and the Nieuwe Kerk. His mission: disentangle the crush of traffic that squeezed through that irregular-shaped intersection. Brinkman commenced gesturing to the mob of pushcart pushers, trams drivers, horse-and-cart drivers, motorists, cyclists, motorcyclists and pedestrians to keep them moving. This attempt, though, produced an unexpected result: the more Brinkman gesticulated, the more people puzzled over his intentions.

"The Amsterdammer enjoys watching his cops," Brinkman later recalled, "so you'll understand the attention I got when I went and stood in the middle of the street."

People stopped to gawk at the character waving his arms and pointing his fingers; they wondered why a policeman would involve himself with the traffic. The throng of curiosity-seekers became so great that eventually traffic ground to a standstill. After two frustrating—and entirely fruitless—hours, Brinkman finally concluded that the best way to unravel the traffic jam was to remove its biggest impediment: *himself*! So he abandoned his post and took refuge around the corner, in an alley.

At 4 p.m., the brave pioneer ventured back into the intersection, where he tried again to execute his duties. This time the result was even worse. "In less than no time," Brinkman recalled, "the traffic was again completely blocked."

The following day, Amsterdam's first traffic cop gave it one more shot by taking up a post around the corner on Dam Square. With this attempt, he had more success. "Maybe the people were wiser due to the newspapers, or their curiosity had been already satiated. In any event, it appeared that they understood that they shouldn't stand in the way of traffic."

Though Amsterdammers would consistently be drawn to spectacles surrounding any new form of traffic regulation, they did slowly grow accustomed to the sight of policemen directing traffic. Within a year, it was said that the Amsterdam cyclist was surprised to see "his absolute independence truncated" by the new traffic cops. "Where the authorities provide good direction, in general, the traffic is noticeably well-organized," reported one newspaper in 1918, before adding, "However, at places where the traffic is not controlled, absolute anarchy reigns."

In the ensuing century (right up to the present day), the term "anarchy" would be often employed to describe traffic conditions in Amsterdam. But the author who used the term in 1918 probably had little idea what was in store for the street traffic. The city stood on the brink of an era of cycling that would far surpass that of the "golden age."

3
Piggy Hunters: The Bike Thievery

ven though Amy Joy wouldn't be joining me till weeks later, within an hour of reading her letter that proclaimed she wanted to live in Amsterdam forever, I purchased a second-hand bike for her. It was a classic *omafiets* (granny bike): old, black, heavy and meant to be ridden upright. A more typically Dutch bike didn't exist. To personalize it *and* to save her the grief I'd already suffered when trying to locate my parked bike among hundreds of others, with a black Sharpie I inscribed her initials in bold letters on the white strip of the back fender—AJJ: Amy Joy Jordan.

A couple of nights later, I was riding AJJ while accompanying Jessica—a fellow San Franciscan/urban planning student/bike nut—to a late-night french fries stand that opened onto Damstraat. Right in front of the place, Jessica parked—but didn't lock—her bike. Likewise, I parked Amy Joy's bike and—for whatever reason (gullibility? stupidity?)—I followed Jessica's lead and didn't lock up.

Jessica got her *frites* and sat on a stool not ten feet from our bikes. I drifted over from the bikes and stood next to her. As Jessica ate and talked, I looked over at AJJ. It was still standing on the sidewalk. I glanced at Jessica, then back at AJJ. It was still there. Another glance at Jessica, then back at the bike. Still there. Glanced at Jessica, back at AJJ. Not there.

"Bike's gone!" I yelped.

Out on the sidewalk, we looked up and down the narrow street. The sidewalks were filled with pedestrians, the street with some bike traffic, but AJJ and the thief had already—somehow—disappeared.

Argh! How could I have been *so naïve?* How could I have been *such an idiot?* Ever since the bike mechanic had warned me, I'd been hypervigilant both with my own bike and with AJJ. I hadn't stepped away from either one without first securing it with two locks, one of the locks securing the bike to a fixed object: a rack, a bridge railing, *something.* That hypervigilance was all for naught now that I'd essentially placed a sign on AJJ that read: FREE BIKE.

"I bet if we go down to the bridge, we'll find the thief selling it," Jessica said.

I sat on the rear rack of Jessica's bike and brooded while she sped us along a canal. A couple of blocks later, we came to a bridge alongside the Grimburgwal canal, just outside some university buildings.

This nondescript bridge—similar to dozens of other bridges in the city and with a span less than 25 feet long—stands where the Oudezijds Achterburgwal and the Grimburgwal canals meet. A bridge has spanned this spot since the 14th century; just a few steps away, Rembrandt once stood and sketched the Grimburgwal canal. While known in city records as the Gasthuisbrug (Hospital Bridge, in reference to the hospitals that had stood beside it for centuries), to many Amsterdammers it was notorious as "the Grimburgwal bridge," "the bike bridge" or simply "*the* bridge," for at the time, it was home to the city's main open-air stolen-bike bazaar.

I'd first learned about the bridge from the orientation paperwork I'd received from the university that cautioned students against purchasing stolen bikes there. This official warning, though, only served as a seductive advertisement: a number of my fellow foreign exchange classmates had already flocked to the bridge to buy incredibly inexpensive bikes. In her two weeks so far in Amsterdam, Jessica had already lost two bikes to thieves. After both thefts, she'd bought a replacement here.

On the bridge, we stepped off Jessica's bike. No one was in sight. At first it appeared that, at this late hour, no peddlers were on duty. But then, about thirty seconds after our arrival, out from the shadows, a figure appeared. As he pedaled slowly toward us on a black *omafiets*, my spirits lifted in hope that he was riding AJJ. The man was hunched, scruffy and of an indeterminate age. He looked like one of the stumbling, heroin-addicted zombies on the nearby Zeedijk that I'd slalomed through a few times on Brownie. Among the junkie population, bikes served essentially as a currency: steal a bike, sell it, score drugs. If a dope fiend was lucky, he could manage all three steps within a matter of blocks *and* minutes.

As the junkie on the junker bike neared, Jessica advised, "Be sure to haggle with him 'cause he's desperate to get any money."

While slowly riding past us, he mumbled, "Fiets te koop." Bike for sale.

The bike wasn't AJJ. I shook my head at him.

Paying a thief for returning a bike wasn't an unknown phenomenon—or a new one. In 1940, for example, one Amsterdammer observed: "The bicycle has . . . one disadvantage: on average, it's stolen once every five years. Then again, one generally has the opportunity of buying back his own bike. Although, by then, it's usually painted beyond recognition, or it's beat to hell. But that labor needs to be paid for as well."

No sooner had the thief passed than, from the other direction, a second decrepit figure inched forward on a bike. My spirits lifted again. As he approached, he muttered, "Fiets kopen?" Wanna buy a bike?

This bike was also not AJJ. I shook my head again.

Then I thought, What the hell's the plan here? Pay some slimeball a reward for him returning the bike he just stole from me? Not likely. Fight the dirtbag to get the bike back? Even less probable. Go to the police? They'd only shrug. Actually, if anything, it could be *me* the cops might reprimand, since, in Amsterdam, it's illegal to *not* lock one's bike.

After only a few minutes of standing on the bridge, I felt scuzzy. Sure, here I could easily and cheaply buy a replacement for AJJ. But by doing so, I'd just be creating further incentive for the thief to steal another bike. Not wanting to contribute to the demand side of the bike thievery loop, I asked Jessica for a lift home.

The route from the bridge back to my apartment took us past the building where Anne Frank and her family had hidden from the Nazis. Not even Amsterdam's—if not the world's—poster girl for innocence was immune to this issue. As described in her famous diary, one afternoon in April 1942, before she had gone into hiding, Anne discovered that, from in front of her apartment building, her bike had been pinched. When we reached my block, I was relieved to see Brownie standing right where I'd left him hours earlier: locked in the rack directly in front of my apartment building. Still shaken by the loss of AJJ, I unlocked Brownie and lugged him up the narrow, steep stairwell to my apartment, where he safely spent the night beside my bed.

AMSTERDAM'S BICYCLE THEFT problem dates to decades before Anne Frank lost her bike to a *zwijntjesjager* (piggy hunter—a century-old Amsterdam term for a bike thief). In fact, as early as 1904, bike thievery in Amsterdam was decried as a plague of the new, modern century. By the beginning of the 1920s, when the number of cyclists in Amsterdam began to rapidly escalate to the point where the city had become internationally recognized as a bicycle capital, the number of bike thefts also rapidly escalated, earning the city a corresponding reputation as a bicycle theft capital. Since many Amsterdammers at the time didn't bother to lock their two-wheelers, bike-thieving was hardly an arduous task. Such a crime disgusted one newspaper commentator who, in 1923, wrote:

> To me it would be too effortless. Grabbing a bike left unattended, jumping on it and riding away is so easy, so innocently infantile, that you don't even need to be a thief to do it. A clever burglary I can appreciate. A bicycle thief is a sluggard in his profession. He'll never amount to much.

To combat the *zwijntjesjagers*, undercover detectives periodically took up posts in the area around the main post office on Nieuwezijds Voorburgwal, the vicinity of a number of banks and offices. Due to the high concentration of white-collar workers in the area, a "choice selection of bicycles" stood leaning against the walls of buildings. Detectives would act as if they were waiting for a tram or they would sit on a stoop, smoking a pipe, pretending to look jobless. All the while, they eyed the crowds, trying to spot a *zwijntjesjager* casing the bikes, which usually didn't take very long.

Despite the capture of bike thieves, though, bike thefts continued, which led Amsterdam's police to conclude that undercover stakeouts wasted manpower. They determined that this crime could better be combated if the bicycles were made more difficult to steal. So in 1928, Article 156A was added to the city's criminal code, which read: "It is forbidden to leave a bicycle unattended on or along a public street unless it is adequately secured by means of a reliable lock." Many bike owners, though, blatantly ignored this new law. In 1933, for example, Amsterdam police cited 1,834 cyclists for not locking their bikes. The following year—in the midst of the Great Depression—the newspaper *De Telegraaf* denounced as "immoral" those who still left their bikes unlocked.

> Because in times like these, there are many who could
> use a bike and "opportunity makes the thief." One doesn't
> leave his wristwatch on his front steps or his wallet on the
> windowsill. Just the same, you shouldn't leave your bike
> unguarded. That can lead to great disappointment, creates
> lots of police work and has provided many a young man the
> chance to earn a prison sentence.

The piggy hunters' hunting grounds extended beyond the city limits. For example, around this time, officials in Haarlem—12 miles due west of Amsterdam—noticed that on days when a stiff westerly wind blew, bike thefts in their city increased. Haarlem's police determined that on such days, when a bike theft was reported right away, if they drove quickly enough out on the road to Amsterdam, they were oftentimes able to catch up to the culprit: a *zwijntjesjager* who had reached Haarlem earlier in the day by train and who now, with the wind at his back, was speeding home to the capital on the stolen bike.

In 1937 alone, more than 10,000 bikes—about 30 per day—were swiped in Amsterdam. But as alarming as the 1930s figures were, they would pale in comparison to those for the first half of the 1940s, when the Nazis occupied the city. In 1940, for example, it was estimated that thieves were stealing 50 to 60 bikes per day. That year, one newspaper reported:

> There is no other city in the Netherlands where so many
> bicycles are stolen each day as in Amsterdam! Nowhere else
> in the world are people so careless with their two-wheeled
> property. Day and night, thousands of bikes stand on the
> public streets for the taking.

By early 1942, the problem had already become, as one account put it at the time, "a criminal epidemic of unprecedented proportions." The situation became vastly more dire when, on a massive scale, the Germans began confiscating bikes—both officially and illicitly—from Amsterdammers. (See chapters 10 and 11.)

In the few years immediately after World War II, bike thieving in the city actually subsided, but by the 1950s, bikes were again being stolen in record numbers. An Amsterdam bike thief could sell a brand-new, 200-guilder one to a fence—the middleman between thieves and buyers—for 40 to 50 guilders. Or, instead, the *zwijntjesjager* could pedal it to outlying towns like Weesp or Zaandam, where a bike could fetch 100 guilders from a farmer. An Amsterdam policeman estimated that a typical bike thief could survive on stealing one bike per week.

According to the "code of honor" among Amsterdam thieves of the postwar years, the *zwijntjesjager* was disdained by his fellow robbers. Stealing a bike that some working stiff needed in order to get to work? "Could he honestly call himself a thief?" scoffed one disgusted burglar to a cop.

In the 1950s, the most popular spot in the city for bike thefts was the same as it had been in the 1920s, as one police detective professed: "Regardless of the day of the year, if I stand in front of the main post office on Nieuwenzijds Voorburgwal for an hour, I'll come upon at least one [thief] sizing up the bikes. I can fully guarantee that." Likewise, the most popular spot for buying and selling of stolen bikes also remained the same: the Waterlooplein flea market. Even guides on tour boats in the mid-1950s described Waterlooplein to tourists as the place "where Amsterdammers are able to buy back their stolen bikes."

The city's professional *zwijntjesjagers* were joined in the 1950s by a new breed of bike thief. Unlike the professional—whose incentive was, of course, quick cash—this new-fashioned thief, the "joyrider" (the Dutch used this English term), didn't seek financial gain. When in need of a bike, the joyrider simply grabbed the first bike he found that had either a flimsy lock or no lock at all. According to the police, the accomplices to the joyriders were the "nonchalants"—those bicycle owners who (still) never bothered to lock their bikes, yet who would, in the words of one policeman, "weep and wail" if their bike was pinched. Of the bikes reported stolen in 1957, 58 percent of them hadn't been locked.

Many joyriders were youths seeking a thrill ride; others were adults in need of ad hoc transport. A late-night clubgoer heading home after the trams had stopped running or a sailor returning to his ship in the harbor would just hop on a random bike to make the journey. A single, dedicated joyrider could bedevil scads of bike owners. Police cited the case of an Amsterdam-West man who cycled every day to his city center job site—despite not owning a bike. Each morning this man just grabbed the first unlocked bike he found. After work, to get home, he did the same again.

By the 1970s, yet another strain of bike thievery had taken hold. Late at night, organized gangs moved through the city, plucking bikes not locked to fixed objects and tossing them into a delivery van or trailer. While this tactic was known to be employed in the 1930s and the 1950s, it was now more popular than ever. One Amsterdammer of the time noted, "Bicycle thieves . . . have reached such a degree of efficiency that . . . each night every street is inspected and swept clean." After the bikes were hauled away, locks would be cut and removed and then, often, the cycles would be shipped out of the city and sold elsewhere in the Netherlands. "The entire northern part of [the Dutch province of] Overijssel rides on bikes that were stolen in Amsterdam," claimed one Amsterdam cop in the mid-1970s.

The writer Gerben Hellinga, like many other Amsterdammers, was a repeat victim of bike pilfering. In 1972, he pondered the fate of his latest bike—a woman's model that was actually too small for him.

But when you lose around ten bikes a year to theft, the size of a bike no longer plays a role. If the tires are decent and the brakes work, then you're more than satisfied. . . .

If it gets swiped, I don't know what I'll do. A hundred feet away is a police station. . . . Not one complaint about the increasing bike thievery has ever been successfully lodged there. Their advice: You should just buy a better lock.

"I've done that, sir, but they come poaching here at night with large delivery vans. They throw the bikes in. They cut the locks with bolt cutters."

"We're closed at night, so we can't do anything about it. You should just take your bike indoors."

Closed at night? Here there's prostitution, a car crash almost every night and many drunken fights. But the [police] have no time for that at night. That's when they're taking a break from writing parking tickets.

Alas, at the time, despite the rash of bike thefts, the city's police department had no special unit to fight it. In fact, in 1976, Amsterdam's head police commissioner, Theo Sanders, acknowledged that his force simply couldn't "devote any attention" to bicycle thievery. "I'll admit, it's indeed depressing," Sanders said. "But we just don't have the means to combat it. If we were to do so, then we'd lose our grasp on the major cases." With such lax police enforcement, the stealing of bikes became so commonplace in the 1970s that one contemporary observer claimed: "Whoever lives in a city like Amsterdam who can say he's never had a bike stolen from him, is someone who's never had a bike."

IN 1972, WHEN Amsterdam reigned as a mecca for countercultural youth, the *Living Guide to Amsterdam*—a guidebook written by and for American and British hippies (or, as the authors termed themselves, "foreign freaks")—recommended renting or buying a bike while in town. That tip, though, was accompanied by a warning: "In Amsterdam there is an invisible subculture of bicycle liberators. . . . Even if you lock it you'll average to have one stolen, lock and all, every two or three months if you're around the center a lot."

Such thefts were increasingly being committed by a certain segment of the "freak" population. Despite the exploits of the organized gangs in the 1970s, according to the police, those responsible for most of the bike thefts were yet another new type of bike thief, one that would beleaguer the city for decades to come: the junkie. The era of free love and soft-drug highs of the late 1960s and early 1970s gave way to a period of hard-drug lows as many young people and others became addicted to a drug that had recently been introduced in Amsterdam: heroin. The next fix for many a junkie was often just a bike theft away. He'd pinch a bike, then try to peddle it to a fence on Waterlooplein or to a student at the then-new hot bike hotspot: the Grimburgwal bridge. With cash in hand, the addict would go purchase the requisite drugs. When he needed to fund his next fix, he simply snatched another bike.

Like his predecessor—the 1950s joyrider—a single, committed junkie bike thief could wreak havoc on the city's residents. For example, in the 1980s, a 32-year-old Amsterdam addict named Piet told a reporter that in the previous eight years, to support his heroin habit, he had nabbed three bikes a day—for a total of nearly *nine thousand* bikes. Piet usually stole bikes from wherever there was a large congregation of them—Central Station, shops, schools, cafés—and he targeted newer ones that could bring in top dollar. "Often I'll nick bikes to order," Piet said. "During the

Tour de France, you can't find enough racing bikes, the demand is so great."

Finding customers for his wares was never strenuous for Piet. By his calculation, 10 percent of the public didn't buy stolen bikes on principle, and 30 percent didn't buy them because they were "chicken-hearted." But the rest of the populace—the majority— willingly bought hot bikes, especially if Piet fed them some yarn about his girlfriend no longer needing it because she had recently attained a driver's license. "It's a nothing story," Piet admitted, "but people want to believe it."

According to Piet, the business of bike filching was demand driven. "As soon as I can no longer unload bikes, of course I'll be done with stealing," he said. "But I'm in no danger of that happening. People are hypocrites. They'll condemn theft, but they'll still buy a new bike for less than fifty dollars though it's obvious that the bike is hot."

Another junkie bike thief who was very active in the 1980s, Chiel van Zelst, later recounted his experiences in his memoir *100,000 Bike Valves*. When Van Zelst hunted for bikes, he traveled fully prepared with wrench, Phillips-head screwdriver, flat-head screwdriver, bike lightbulbs, wire cutters, crowbar, inner tube patches and—last but not least—his most vital resource: bolt cutters. According to Van Zelst, to steal a bike, one couldn't dillydally.

> There's only one way to do it: jacket open, bolt cutters out, apply and cut. With your right hand, smoothly slide the cut lock into your pocket and then slip the bolt cutters back into your jacket with your left hand. The chain goes around your neck and, in one sleek move, get on the bike. Out of

the corner of your eye check your surroundings and then, without panicking, ride away. That's how it works.

Unlike the 1920s commentator who despised *zwijntjesjagers* for their lack of craftsmanship or the 1950s burglar who refused to even recognize them as proper thieves, Van Zelst expressed pride in his vocation. "It's a beautiful profession," he wrote, "a noble profession that requires brains."

After stealing a bike, Van Zelst would immediately attend to minor repairs: tightening a loose kickstand, fixing a flat tire, adjusting a seat to an average height or even screwing in a new lightbulb. "A light on your bike—that's nicer than a teddy bear." Then it was time to sell the bike, which, for Van Zelst, often meant heading straight to the students on the Grimburgwal bridge.

They always stood waiting on the bridge like Indians with their hands forming a visor on their foreheads. You saw them waiting in little groups of three, the most eager one in front. "Is that bike for sale? Is that bike for sale?"

They stood there fighting over who had seen the bike first. If you didn't jump off the bike in time, they'd pull it out from under your ass.

A gang of wild chicks were clinging to your bike. A little pack of wolf girls. "I saw it first!" . . . I make a sale and then take . . . an order for later. "Great, then I'll see you here on the bridge at seven o'clock." I split. I was selling them like hotcakes.

AS BAD AS it already had been, quite incredibly, Amsterdam's bike-thieving problem grew worse in the 1990s. Early in that decade, the standard price for a stolen bike sold on the street had stood at about $30. But by 1997, $30 was a price of the past, according to one bike thief with five years' experience in vending on the bridge. By then, the standard price had plummeted to about $15 a pop. And even so, sellers could be bargained down even further, depending on the shoddiness of the bike and/or the desperation of the junkie. (In an article advising incoming freshmen on bike-buying at Grimburgwal, a student newspaper noted, "A minimum price does not exist.") According to the five-year-veteran thief, the prices had dropped because "there are too many sellers now. It's very competitive." "It used to be enough to steal just one bike per day," complained another junkie. "But now the market is completely spoiled and to earn enough money, I need to steal five bikes a day." Yet another junkie said he typically sold three or four bikes a day on the bridge, which, if all went well for him, would bring in about $40, just enough cash to score a bit more than a gram of cocaine.

With the lower prices forcing addicts to steal more bikes in order to earn enough to score their drugs, by the late 1990s, police estimated that the number of bikes heisted annually in Amsterdam rose to around 180,000—more than 20 bikes an hour, every hour of the day, every day of the year. Of course, the exact figure (or even a credible estimate) was extremely difficult to calculate, since so few bike theft victims reported the crime to cops. (For example, police estimated that 1,000 bikes had been stolen in 1991 within the immediate vicinity of the Grimburgwal bridge, yet only *eleven* of those thefts were ever officially reported.) While the actual citywide bike theft total remained unknown, whatever the exact figure, it was undoubtedly astronomical. Joep Huffener, the bicycle coordinator within the city government at the time, felt the 180,000 figure was inaccurately high. "But even if it's a hundred and fifty thousand," Huffener stated, "that's still far too many."

Junkies in the 1990s sold hot bikes in other spots of the city as well (for example, on Spuistraat, in Vondelpark, in front of Central Station, on Koningsplein),* but according to Henk Visser, a university employee who monitored the activities on the Grimburgwal bridge, "The market here is the best." Visser noted that, on the bridge each day, hundreds of bikes were sold by a "hard core" of about 40 to 50 junkies. "In good weather," he said, "they sprout from the ground like weeds."

One person who probably prayed for bad weather was the 79-year-old resident of an apartment that faced the Grimburgwal bridge. According to a 1999 news report:

[He] seldom casually leans out the window of his living
room. He prefers to go the whole day with the curtains
closed. The reason: the junkies who sell bikes on the bridge
in front of his apartment are driving him crazy. . . . [He] is
thoroughly worried about it, but he no longer dares to ask
the junkies to scram. The times when he's done just that, he's
been verbally abused. So now he walks past quietly out of
fear of getting a rock through his window.

---

* One thief who sold bikes at night on Koningsplein explained the trade there: "On weekends, after they leave the pub or disco, a lot of people prefer buying a stolen bike for $13 over taking a taxi home. Sometimes they stand in line for a bike."

On the bridge, college students provided a steady customer base for the thieves. August and September formed a traditional busy season as many students purchased their back-to-school bikes. Few, if any, students were unaware of what transpired on Grimburgwal; according to a poll, 97 percent of university students who attended classes in the buildings near the bridge reported having been offered a bike for sale there. Purchasing stolen goods was, of course, illegal, but by then, among students, buying a purloined bike had become an accepted form of criminality. Not only was it common, but it was said that for some students, it was mandatory: initiation rituals of some student organizations required hazed freshmen to each purchase a stolen bike.

In 1997, after purchasing a bike on the bridge, when a fourth-year psychology student was asked if she had any qualms about buying hot bikes, she replied, "No, not anymore. When my tenth bike was stolen, I was completely fed up." Empathy was expressed by one Grimburgwal thief who said, "It's logical that people buy a bike here. They're tired of their bikes being constantly stolen." Indeed, the stolen bike market was quite a peculiar economy, since each theft created a potential customer—a cyclist in need of a bike. With the increase in bike thefts in the 1990s, a broader group of (frustrated) cyclists also elected to buy stolen bikes. "It used to be only students," noted one junkie thief. "Now, it's also middle-class types, you know, with regular jobs."

Even tourists purchased bikes on the bridge, since they were cheaper than rentals. "How they know about it, I have no idea," said one puzzled patrolman who worked the Grimburgwal beat, referring to some Portuguese tourists who'd turned up on the bridge looking to score bikes. (Actually, foreign visitors were tipped off by canal boat guides and sightseeing literature.)

Meanwhile, the bike in Amsterdam had become—in the words of one repeat customer of stolen bikes—a "disposable object." If a bike broke down—a tire flattened, a chain snapped—many cyclists found it more convenient, cheaper and/or faster to just ditch the busted one and buy a stolen replacement. Jaap Molenaar, the owner of a bike shop near the Grimburgwal bridge, witnessed firsthand this glib attitude toward the value of bikes. Of those who walked into his shop with a bike in need of fixing, he said, "If a repair costs more than ten dollars, then six times a day, we hear: 'Then I'll go buy a new one.'" After once surveilling the action on the bridge, Molenaar commented, "It's a real market. They sell more bikes there in an evening than we do in a week." He admitted, though, that his shop still profited from the trade; buyers of stolen bikes often turned up at his shop to buy—of all things—locks for their new bikes.

In 2000, Amsterdam's then mayor, Schelto Patijn, stated: "Let me be clear: bike thievery is an unsolvable problem. It's impossible for us to station an undercover policeman on every bridge." In regard to this type of acceptance of bike thieving, a few months prior to AJJ's fateful night, the municipal official in charge of overseeing bike theft said, "The mentality of the Amsterdammer must change." It was this municipal mentality that I'd faced—far too naïvely—the night I'd foolishly stepped away from an unlocked bike.

THE MORNING AFTER AJJ was stolen, at the beginning of my Dutch class, I told my classmates and our teacher about the events of the night before. The teacher chuckled at what he deemed the most stereotypical baptism to Amsterdam living. When I asked him how many bikes he'd lost to thieves, he estimated that, over the previous twenty years, it'd been about one bike a year. The statistic sounded extraordinary. In the weeks that followed, though, other Amsterdammers repeated to me roughly that same one-bike-per-year statistic.

I'd arrived in Amsterdam determined to not lose *any* bike to thieves. Now I was already well on track to being yet another bike-a-year dupe. If I could just get AJJ back, I figured I could roll back my stat to zero and become a hero to my wife for recapturing her bike (which she wasn't even yet aware had been stolen).

After class, I pedaled straight over to the bridge. There I squatted on the rear rack of Brownie and ate my lunch. Within a few minutes, first one junkie, then another—neither of them a dopehead from the night before—cruised slowly past on bikes. Each whispered a sales pitch at me. Neither dude had AJJ for sale, so when I finished my sandwich, I rode off.

That afternoon I cycled all over the city, scanning the rear fender of each bike I trailed and each parked bike I passed. I was desperate to see my wife's initials, but again I had no such luck.

After that, every day for weeks, any chance I had, I checked in at the Grimburgwal bridge or I browsed the rear fenders of thousands of bikes. If I hadn't already appreciated how many bikes inhabited Amsterdam, while trying to scrutinize each one, I now did. Looking for a needle in a haystack would have been much easier. A haystack might contain millions of stalks of straw, but it doesn't spread out over 50 square miles and its stalks aren't constantly fluctuating.

Nevertheless, I remained determined to rectify the theft. I kept looking.

4
King of the Street: The 1920s

I f I wasn't hanging out by the Grimburgwal bridge or riding up, down and all about town, then I was usually sitting outside somewhere watching the cyclists and noting their rituals, customs, looks and features. Of all my cyclist-watching hangouts, my favorite came to be a bench at the Weteringcircuit intersection. There, I once saw two cyclists slam into each other and fall to the ground. Neither had been expressly at fault—or actually, maybe both had been *entirely* at fault. One guy had been riding against traffic; the other had ignored a red light. As they picked themselves up, neither uttered a word. Incredibly, no one muttered, "Sorry, dude" or screamed, "Klootzaak!" Each man—without looking at the other—simply mounted his respective bike and pedaled off.

At the beginning of the 1920s, when the number of cyclists in Amsterdam began to rapidly escalate, this new phenomenon was probably most noticeable at this very intersection. "That endless, unbroken row of three, four cyclists riding beside each other along the whole length of Weteringschans," wrote an eyewitness in 1922, "makes crossing the street deadly!"

The year before, Ernst Polak, a portraitist who proudly claimed to "belong to the people who cross Amsterdam daily by bicycle," noted a drawback to this new cycling sensation. "Raw and rough is how this riding occurs. And it degenerates into speeding, weaving and slipping through—perilous to pedestrians and fellow cyclists. Nowadays, the vast majority rides in Amsterdam in a manner that defies all description." Weteringschans specifically, Polak claimed, was "a speedway during the hours when school lets out or at the end of the workday."

A couple of blocks east, at Frederiksplein, Polak declared:

It's simply beastly the way people cycle there. Literally, not a day goes by that I don't hear or see someone crash to the asphalt, then stand up again, straighten his bike a bit, dust himself off a little, dispute with bystanders, tussle among the colliding parties sometimes and then ride off again, perhaps at a slower pace.

As a cyclist-watcher in the 21st century, I was witnessing scenes that, in many ways, differed little from those of the early 1920s. This shouldn't have been surprising, though; the Amsterdam cyclists' current reputation for being headstrong, careless, carefree and domineering became firmly established in the boom years of the early 1920s.

DURING MUCH OF the first two decades of the 20th century, the bicycle as a mode of everyday transport remained largely unaffordable to a great many Amsterdammers. But that changed immediately after the end of the First World War—a war that the Netherlands sat out as a neutral party. Not long after Holland's warring neighbors signed the armistice on November 11, 1918, an economic slump in defeated Germany led to hyperinflation of that country's currency, the mark. With Germans looking to earn stable Dutch guilders, German-made bikes—now incredible bargains when purchased with Dutch currency—quickly flooded Holland. In 1919, fearing that this new trend would adversely affect their own businesses, the organization representing Dutch bike manufacturers sent a letter to the German envoy in The Hague that protested what they felt were unfair trade practices and beseeched the German government to curtail the onslaught of cheap exports. The letter, in part, read:

In the past couple of months, along the entire eastern border of the Netherlands . . . German bicycles of all sorts of makes—Adler, Brennabor, Cito, Diamant, Excelsior, Göricke, Victoria, etc.—have been shipped from German border towns . . . into the Netherlands and sold here for a song. At the moment, this is so intense that dealers in hardwares, manufacturers, mailmen, fishmongers, affluents and other residents of Dutch border towns have spent all their spare cash on the purchase of German bicycles and have filled all available space—sheds, attics, basements and even living rooms and bedrooms—with them. Moreover, many of these so-called import/export houses that have shot up like mushrooms since the armistice have gotten involved in the sale of German bicycles. Some of these firms have received them by the truckload and sold them, in part, directly from the truck, one by one to the public.

It didn't take long before these cut-rate bikes reached Amsterdam. In 1920 and 1921, when most bikes sold in Holland were imports, more than 90 percent of the imports came from Germany. At the same time, the average price of a new bicycle in the Netherlands dropped steadily each year, from 129 guilders in 1919 to 61 guilders in 1925.

As one form of transportation dropped in price, the cost of alternative transportation skyrocketed. In 1919 and 1920, over the course of just a few months, the basic fare on Amsterdam's extensive tram network rose from 5 cents to 10 cents to 12½ cents to 15 cents. Each fare increase caused a reduction in ridership and income, which—in turn—led to another fare increase to cover the lost income. This caused a further reduction in ridership—and so the cycle went. Floor Wibaut—the government official who oversaw Amsterdam's public transit agency—blamed the drop in tram ridership on "the abnormal increase of bicycle traffic." Indeed, for a commuter struggling to cough up a higher tram fare, an investment in a bike could pay for itself within a few years in terms of money saved on fares. One Amsterdammer reckoned that he had spent 450 hours annually commuting by tram. "But on the bike, I do it in a third of the time," he said. "I save at least eighty guilders per year and gain [300 hours] in which to rest up and spend those eighty guilders."

Throughout the 1920s, the average price of new bikes in the Netherlands continued to fall, which made them even more affordable to the masses. "The time that a bicycle was something only accessible to wealthy lads . . . is long gone," one Dutch commentator noted in 1923. "Whether he spent ten guilders or two hundred guilders for it, to a Dutchman, the bicycle is a part of

his life, something which has intertwined with his daily needs."
The bike was also no longer largely limited to sport or leisure usage, as it had been in the 1890s. As one local put it in the 1920s:
"One now goes everywhere by bike: to the office, to school, to
the factory, to college, to the tennis court, to the beach, to every-
place that one wants to reach quickly."

This dramatic increase in bike riding occurred, of course, in
a city—and nation—that was well suited for two-wheeled commuting. Built atop wetlands, Amsterdam was pancake flat and
possessed no hindering inclines aside from those on little canal bridges or (former) dikes. Also, the city was compact; any
destination within its limits was an easy trek. And while the
relatively mild climate also accommodated cycling, in inclem-
ent weather—rain, snow or even heat—a cyclist could still, in a
pinch, spring for a tram ride.

The lower classes weren't the only ones cycling more frequently; the well-heeled now used the bike for more than just
promenading in Vondelpark in their Sunday best. "The bicycle no longer demands special clothing," reported a handbook on proper female etiquette published in Amsterdam in
the 1920s. "As long as it is not a formal gown, everything is
suitable on the bike." According to a companion handbook for
men, societal mores also relaxed with respect to male cycling
attire: "Presently, one bicycles in whatever suit he happens to
be wearing."

As for the fashion regarding the bicycles themselves, very
little variation existed; at the time, about 95 percent of all bikes
in Holland were painted solid black. This prompted one Dutchman, in 1924, to ask:

Why is that so? With our neighbors to the south, the Belgians, and their neighbors, the French, one sees all sorts of colors, from lilac to bright yellow, from stone gray to sky blue. Even white and entirely nickel-plated bicycles are to be seen there. There are even beautiful little bikes with colors that are too glaring. It's true! The prim-and-proper black bicycle, not striped or nickel-plated, seems to me too dull a color.

The bicycle's popularity grew to the point where, in 1928, one Dutchman could claim: "The Netherlands is preeminently a cycling nation." And that cycling nation was headed by a cycling sovereign. In addition to a great passion for horseback riding, Queen Wilhelmina remained fond of cycling. And whereas Wilhelmina had been forbidden to cycle as a teenager, in early 1925, her only child, Princess Juliana, learned to ride a bike at the age of 15. During the next few summers, the queen and the teen princess cycled together regularly. Sometimes they'd be driven from Soestdijk Palace and dropped off in the countryside. From there, they'd cycle on local roads back to the palace. Or, from The Hague, the two would cycle on the hard sand of the North Sea coast up to the fishing village of Katwijk, where a waiting car and driver would return them to The Hague.

If indeed the Netherlands had become preeminently a cycling nation, then, in turn, its capital—Amsterdam—had become preeminently a cycling city. "The Amsterdam cyclist . . . feels he is the king of the street," wrote one local in 1926. "The cyclist rules the streets of the capital. He is an attraction for the foreigners who must think that cycle and cyclist are cast from a single mold."

Indeed, few, if any, foreign visitors to the city in the 1920s neglected to notice the new legion. An Italian, upon visiting Amsterdam, wrote: "On the brick-paved streets glide the automobiles, the carriages but, most of all, the bicycles, which are as numerous as the frogs in the canals." An English visitor wrote: "While the traveler in Holland may run little risk from the deadly avalanche, . . . at any moment he may be crushed to pulp in the streets of Amsterdam beneath the relentless wheels of a hundred bicycles." At the beginning of the decade, a bowled-over American declared Amsterdam to be "the city of a million bicycles." Though his calculation was off by about 900,000 when he made his claim, his quote would be parroted with civic pride by the Amsterdam press throughout the decade.

NOT EVERYONE IN Amsterdam, though, was enchanted by this growth spurt of cyclists. One such dissenter was Social-Democrat Party city councilman Zeeger Gulden. At a city council meeting in November 1923, during a discussion about lifting the ban on dance halls, Gulden tried to steer the discourse toward his own pet peeve: the "misery" caused by reckless cycling. Gulden proposed an outright ban on cycling in the city center between 8 a.m. and 7 p.m. Though Gulden acknowledged that such a ban wouldn't be well received in some circles, he entreated the mayor and *wethouders* to deliberate his plan. Yet when Gulden concluded his speech, his appeal was met with resounding indifference; the council immediately resumed discussing the dance hall ban (which, one councilman argued, should be lifted because in the evenings Amsterdam offered few "public entertainments" for American and British tourists to enjoy).

The "traffic anarchism" that had so vexed Gulden was

often blamed throughout the 1920s on one particular group of cyclists—high school girls—who "often ride very carelessly," as one newspaperman put it. In 1921, another newspaper reporter wrote:

> It happens repeatedly—perhaps 90 times out of 100—that at dangerous intersections, cyclists ride through despite the traffic policeman's signal for them to stop. . . .
>
> According to our Mister Bakker, chief of the traffic police, most of the blame for accidents lies with the cyclists who often ride in the most inconsiderate ways. Cyclists aren't alert. They try to slip through every little opening and they don't bother to dismount when required.
>
> Typically, it's mostly young ladies who are the worst violators of traffic regulations. They ride over the speed limits and ignore the traffic policemen's directions with an air of, "You won't dare ticket me."

Actually, in May 1922, Amsterdam's traffic police *did* dare to ticket cyclists—even the young ladies among them—by setting a speed trap on Utrechtsestraat, one of the streets with a new, meager cycling speed limit of 12 kilometers (*seven and a half* miles) per hour. When a suspected speeding cyclist passed a stationed plainclothes policeman, the cop threw up his hand. A second plainclothes cop, 100 meters farther on, clicked a stopwatch and timed the cyclist ("as if it counted for a world record," quipped one dissenter). If the cyclist crossed that hundred meters within 30 seconds, the second cop signaled to a third cop, standing farther up the street, who would stop and cite the cyclist. In this manner, more than 100 cyclists a day were ticketed.

The speed limit was widely regarded as far too low, even by 1922 standards. One newspaper called the speed trap "a ridiculous enterprise." Another newspaper—which called this "scandal" an "unnecessary annoyance"—argued that cycling faster than this terribly low speed limit posed no threat to the public and that, besides, thorough enforcement was "absolutely impossible."

In any case, over the course of a few months, the bike speed traps lost their effectiveness. Cyclists had quickly learned to look out for them—a gathered crowd watching the theatrics provided an obvious tip-off. "Every cyclist on Utrechtsestraat knows where the police trap is," one policeman was forced to admit. "Once past it, he lets loose and speeds up again."

IN THE 1920s, probably no street in Amsterdam was more affected by the increase in cyclists than Leidsestraat, the narrow shopping street that was home to many of the city's most "respectable establishments." Because it served as the most direct route for a great many commuters between the city center and neighborhoods south and west of Vondelpark, Leidsestraat was also a hectic thoroughfare. Every day, like a performance whose audience was also its stars, a great mass of persons and vehicles—trams, pedestrians, autos, pushcarts, motorcycles, horse-drawn carts and bicycles—all squeezed into a street that had a building-to-building width narrower than some sidewalks in Paris. This startling spectacle was performed much to the frustration of many of its participants. With a scant 30-foot-wide roadway and narrow sidewalks, Leidsestraat simply couldn't safely and comfortably accommodate all who returned day after day for encore presentations.

Of the perils of Leidsestraat cycling, in 1928, one newspaper joked: "Leidsestraat is for cyclists what the English Channel is for swimmers: not all cyclists survive a trip through Leidsestraat—just as most Channel swimmers don't succeed." Other users of the street swore the cyclists themselves were the menace. Pedestrians, for example, found it difficult and hazardous to cross against the constant stream of passing bikes. The head of a Leidsestraat pharmacy claimed that several times a week pedestrians injured by cyclists were helped into his shop. "What is more dangerous these days?" *Het Volk* newspaper asked in 1920. "Strolling through Leidsestraat or doing a loop-de-loop in a flying machine?" Motorists, too, felt thwarted by the cyclists. In 1926, *De Telegraaf* reported that one motorist ("red with rage") complained that driving down Leidsestraat meant having "cyclists surround your car in front, behind and to the sides."

Ultimately, imposing a speed limit on Leidsestraat did little to fix the street's congestion problem. "The Leidsestraat issue is a puzzle in the Amsterdam of these times," wrote one newspaperman in 1927. "A *very* tricky puzzle." To solve this conundrum, throughout the first half of the 20th century, a great many other ideas were floated, including widening the street, establishing a *minimum* speed on the street, constructing a parallel street just south of Leidsestraat and filling in various nearby canals for the use of trams and cyclists.

The most persistent idea, though—one that had been and would be floated for decades—was banning cyclists from Leidsestraat. Such bans actually already existed on other streets. For example, cyclists had long been forbidden from riding on the (even narrower) Nieuwendijk and Kalverstraat shopping streets. On the main street in the Jewish quarter, Jodenbreestraat (its name meaning "Jewish

Broad Street"), cycling had been banned on Fridays after 3 p.m.—the hours just before and during the start of the Jewish Sabbath. And, of course, as mentioned in chapter 2, cycling had already been banned on Leidsestraat for several weeks in 1906.

In 1927, Mayor Willem de Vlugt claimed Leidsestraat's function as a traffic corridor threatened its character as a shopping street. "[The] cyclist has become a nightmare to the shopkeepers in the city center," claimed *De Telegraaf*. The mayor asserted that the street's upscale businesses would be forced to either relocate or shut down, leaving the storefronts to become occupied by "fly-by-night stores and sinister shops." De Vlugt therefore proposed a law to partially ban cyclists from Leidsestraat. Since it was argued that cyclists hindered women who came by car to shop on the street, and since, as one advocate of the ban put it, "Bicycle riders are generally not buyers," the mayor's proposal was to ban cycling on the street between 2 and 5 p.m.—the hours when "most ladies go shopping." This proposal was heartily endorsed by many of the street's tonier shops, led by the posh Metz & Co. department store.*

Banning bike riders from one of the most heavily cycled streets just so the well-to-do could shop in peace? That thought struck a nerve with one cyclist who penned a fiery letter to the editor:

I have but one bit of advice for Amsterdam's cyclists: Unite before it's too late! . . .

---

*These days, the timeworn, hand-painted wooden sign riveted to the outer wall of the former Metz & Co. building that reads KINDLY REQUESTED—PLACE NO BICYCLES HERE serves almost as a memorial to that store's anti-cyclist legacy. While it's possibly the oldest existing no-bike-parking sign posted in the city, just like many of its newer contemporaries, it's routinely ignored by cyclists.

The world has now turned upside down: many thousands of Amsterdammers—who seek out the cycling vivacity and the asphalt on Leidsestraat—are impeding the shopping of a couple dozen of their fellow female citizens. . . .

Despite all our democratic airs, a delusion is now developing in the heads of our authorities and of ourselves. And just as a swamp produces mosquitoes, this delusion will produce a nuisance: the idea that ten cyclists are less important than a single motorist. . . .

Therefore, cyclists of Amsterdam, unite. Apart from your other associations, unite into one union with a single purpose: to protect the traffic interests of Amsterdam's cycling citizens. It's about time! . . . If the cyclists don't do something about it, soon—as the pariahs of the roadway—they'll simply be consigned to the streets that are lifeless and poorly-paved. Then, as in no other city in the world, the masses will be impeded just because their large presence in certain parts of the city makes shopping less pleasurable for those who are the most well-off.

Ultimately, the cyclists did not rise up and organize. (Unfortunately for them, that wouldn't happen for another half century.) Nevertheless, on this occasion they were spared. Because no satisfactory alternative routes were shown to be available to the thousands of cyclists who would have been affected by the ban, and because the measure was viewed as little more than a Band-Aid for all that ailed the street, a majority of the city council voted against the afternoon bike ban. For the tens of thousands who cycled Leidsestraat each day, the show would go on.

BY 1925, SOME of Amsterdam's first bike lanes had been laid on Van Woustraat, Rijnstraat and Amsteldijk. This development, though, wasn't necessarily beneficial for cyclists, since—as they complained—slow-moving pushcarts and horse-drawn vehicles often clogged the new bike lanes. Since no law prohibited other road users from using these lanes, the traffic police were powerless to free them up for the cyclists.

By now, traffic police were familiar sights throughout the city. These officers, however, weren't always successful when using just their hand signals to indicate which road user was to stop and which was to proceed. While a traffic cop could halt traffic approaching from one direction, as soon as he turned his back, often some—if not many—of those he'd just stopped (particularly the cyclists) would begin creeping through the intersection.

One intersection in particular where this behavior was common was the very one that housed my favorite bike-viewing bench. As one journalist described in 1922: "Whoever takes a look at the Weteringschans/Nieuwe Vijzelgracht intersection between 5 and 6 p.m. will see that the vast majority of cyclists disregard the gestures of the traffic policeman." The need to curtail such behavior led to what Gerrit Brinkman—the city's first traffic cop, who would once again witness history—called "*the* great event" of 1925. On September 28 of that year, in the middle of the Weteringschans/Nieuwe Vijzelgracht intersection, a traffic cop stood holding the city's first stop sign. The word "Stop" was written in white letters against a red background on a board perched atop a pole that the cop could swivel. This device allowed the officer to keep certain traffic at a standstill while gesturing for the cross traffic to advance.

The new contraption was an instant hit, if not as an instrument of traffic regulation, then certainly as a prop for street theater. "On Weteringschans, where the first sign is now displayed, dozens of people stand and stare. At what? They're not sure themselves," reported *Het Algemeen Handelsblad*. "If fifteen of these signs appeared in the city, then in fifteen places the onlookers would be more curious than ducks in a ditch, staring at signs that always remain the same."

Over the following weeks, as new stop signs materialized on Dam Square, Leidseplein, Stadhouderskade and elsewhere, the onlookers still had those ducks in a ditch beat in the curiosity department. A full month after the stop sign's debut in Amsterdam, a report on the unveiling of yet another one noted a great hindrance caused by "the crowds that constantly remained watching the turning of the stop sign." Actually, the traffic police welcomed the crowds, which helped boost awareness of the new intersection regulation. Nevertheless, some road users remained ignorant of the fact that when stopping for a stop sign, they were expected to stay behind a certain orange-yellow line. So additional traffic cops had to be stationed at some intersections with orders to hold back the transgressors. "Naturally, these are mainly cyclists," observed one reporter, "who behave like naughty, stubborn children."

ANOTHER DEVELOPMENT ELICITED an even stronger reaction from cyclists. In 1923, *De Kampioen* magazine predicted, "A bicycle tax in the Netherlands would be the most unpopular tax ever levied." Despite the premonition, the following year the Dutch parliament passed a bike tax law that took effect on August 1, 1924. A three-guilder-per-bike tax (later reduced to two and a half guilders) was to be paid annually. As forewarned, the added levy greatly irritated cyclists who—after having already purchased their bikes—were now required to remit an additional fee, year after year. Many cyclists were also irked because, unlike a previous bike tax (in effect from 1899 to 1919), which had been linked to the bike owner's income level, under this new flat tax, a dishwasher paid the same fee for his dilapidated third-hand bike as a bank director did for his lavish new one.

Bike owners paid the tax at the post office and, in return, received a small copper plate imprinted with the current tax year, to be affixed to the bike's head tube and replaced annually.

Immediately after the law took effect, Amsterdam's petty criminals began regarding this new source of state income as their own new source of personal income. Thieves pried tax plates from bikes and counterfeiters produced fakes. Amsterdam's bustling Waterlooplein flea market—already notorious as an open-air emporium for stolen bikes—became equally renowned as "the market for stolen tax plates." In the 1930s, at the Zwanenburgwal canal end of Waterlooplein (just a few feet from Rembrandt's house), fences paid thieves 75 cents ("no more, no less") for stolen tax plates and resold them to citizens at the fixed price of one and a half guilders.

A cyclist caught riding without a current tax plate was liable for a fine of at least three guilders and the cost of a new tax plate. Initially, to enforce the law, plainclothes tax agents stood along busier cycling routes during rush hours—Leidsestraat, Nieuwezijds Voorburgwal, the Rijksmuseum passageway, the ferry landings—hunting tax dodgers. These "eagle-eyed" officials were acclaimed for their ability to eyeball, from among the deluge of bikes, the lone one lacking a current tax plate.

The tax agent was accompanied by a policeman, since, as one observer put it in 1926, "many an Amsterdammer on a bike—a bit perturbed to be summoned [to stop] by a non-uniformed civil servant—would want to ride on." The sight of the assisting policeman usually, though not always, induced the scofflaw to stop.

The issuing of a citation to an offending cyclist became, according to one account at the time, "clearly an utmost and intriguing 'amusement' for many along the street, with the exception of, naturally, the victim—the one who'd 'been had.'" Just as when traffic policemen enforced cycling speed limits or operated new stop signs, the onlookers themselves provided a tip-off. "In Amsterdam, it's not so difficult to know when [tax plates] are being inspected," a columnist noted. "There's usually a crowd milling about and one would have to be very disoriented to not understand what's happening there."* One person who clearly *did* understand was a young man who, upon sighting the commotion ahead, quickly dismounted and with his unlicensed bike in hand (according to a witness standing beside the authorities) "crept slowly past us, like a thief in the night."

An offender's bike could be confiscated and taken to East India House, the early 17th century building that had long served as the headquarters for the Dutch East India Company and that now housed the tax agency. The bikes stood in the building's interior courtyard waiting for their owners to pay the appropriate

---

*Among those lingerers who claimed to enjoy this "bit of fun" was an onlooker who remarked that it was "surprising how many people in a big city—a busy, working city like Amsterdam, no less—still always have time to spare if there's some little thing happening on the street."

fees. So many confiscated two-wheelers filled the courtyard, it looked like—said one eyewitness—"a bicycle auction."

Responsibility for enforcement of the bike tax law eventually transferred from tax agents to the traffic police. One Amsterdam traffic cop, who spent years upholding this law, would later admit, "Seldom did the police have to enforce a law that was *more* unpopular with the public." Ultimately, this detested tax would be abolished by the unlikeliest of groups—one that possessed no love for Amsterdam's cyclists and which Amsterdam's cyclists, in turn, would abhor far more than the bike tax itself . . .

5

It Made My Head Swim: The Elephants, Centaurs, Punks and Nuns

On one warm summer night in 2002, a few weeks after my arrival in Amsterdam, I went to a party hosted by some fellow students. Upon entering the apartment, I grabbed a bottle of Heineken. But after a quick look at the other attendees, as a 35-year-old I immediately felt too old for the scene. So I left with the beer—and Brownie and I headed home. It was late; the streets were almost devoid of traffic. Three blocks from my apartment on Spaarndammerstraat, I rode into a small intersection. A cop car, approaching from my left, did the same. Just as we were about to collide, we both screeched to a halt.

Just nine seconds earlier, I'd looked up at the larger-than-life-size statue of Ferdinand Domela Nieuwenhuis—the father of Dutch anarchism. The image and proximity of Domela Nieuwenhuis, with his clenched fist raised defiantly, might have emboldened me.

"Hey!" I said. "I've got the right-of-way." As proof, I pointed down at the shark's teeth—the three triangle-shaped tiles on the bike path whose tips pointed in the direction from which I'd just come.

The cop in the passenger seat leaned his head out of the window and said, "No, *we* have the right-of-way."

Up to that moment, like a moron, I'd been reading the shark's teeth completely backward, thinking that when they pointed *at* me *I* had the right-of-way. It was remarkable that this was my first close call.

Now, though, I realized I was in a horrible position. Here, I had failed to yield to a squad car, had mouthed off about it, was holding a beer in my hand and had been cycling without lights. Obviously, I was screwed.

My mind flashed to a month earlier, to a night in Portland when I'd gone out biking with Amy Joy and three friends. All but our friend Jim had lights on his or her bike. Just minutes after we set out, while we were cycling west on North Killingsworth Street, a police cruiser flashed its lights and pulled us over. While the cop issued Jim a citation, the rest of us patiently waited. When the officer finished with Jim, he then walked over to me and asked to see my ID.

"I've *got* lights on my bike," I told him. That didn't matter; he wanted my ID. Reluctantly, I handed it over. When the cop noticed my San Francisco address, he asked, "So what are you doing in Portland?" I was puzzled. A friend was cycling without lights; now *I* had to account for my interstate movements? The cop was putting me on the spot under the flimsiest of pretenses: for associating with a nonlighted cyclist.

Though, in the end, nothing came of the incident with the Portland cop (he called in my name and I "checked out"), that scenario raced through my mind as I faced these two Amsterdam police officers. These guys didn't need any flimsy pretenses; they had enough credible reasons to grill me or cite me or even—*gulp*—arrest me. Yet they did none of the above. In fact, they didn't even ask a single question. Instead, the nondriving cop just said to me, "Go home." As they drove away, I was left stunned.*

My initial ignorance of the correct way to read the shark's teeth stemmed from my having trailed behind too many cyclists who had failed to properly heed them by yielding to the cross traffic. Sometimes, though, when one is following cyclists, *obeying* the traffic laws could be hazardous. For example, one morning on my way to school, I was near the rear of a long line of cyclists as we all waited at a red light on Frederiksplein. When the light turned green, dozens of cyclists moved on through the intersection. As I pedaled forward, the light turned yellow. I slowed down, and when I stopped, a bike slammed into Brownie's back wheel. The rider muttered at me, "Mafkees!" *Freak!* Then, along with seven or eight other cyclists, he zipped past me, past the red light and through the intersection.

My curiosity piqued, I walked Brownie over to the sidewalk and—for the next 45 minutes—I watched. Each time the light turned red, a great snake of undeterred cyclists continued moving forward, almost as if they were pulled by those in front and—concurrently—pushed by others from behind. Meanwhile, the motorists in the cross traffic waited patiently until the bikers had cleared the intersection before proceeding. That morning, the

---

*A few years later, after consuming five beers during a night out, a 32-year-old Amsterdammer was arrested on Leidseplein for drunk cycling. "If you're going to hunt down drunken cyclists," the perplexed man complained to a reporter the next day, "you'll arrest half the city every Saturday night." A police spokesman clarified, "We're not starting a witch hunt. This man just had rotten luck."

record number of cyclists that entered the intersection during a single red signal was 27.

It became obvious to me that, for many Amsterdam bikers, green meant "go," yellow also meant "go," and while red didn't necessarily mean "go," by no means did it mean "stop."

IN THE 1990S, one of the few cyclists in the city who rigidly obeyed the traffic laws was Mayor Schelto Patijn. Patijn—who hailed from The Hague and had never lived in Amsterdam until his appointment as mayor of the city in 1994—would, within his first year in office, become renowned as "the cyclist who stops for red lights." Throughout his six-and-a-half-year tenure, during which Patijn's strict adherence to traffic signals became a running theme of his mayoralty (and for which he said he was called an "idiot"), Patijn acknowledged that his behavior was uncommon. "Often, I stand like a nervous Nellie at a red light," he said in 1998. "Even the people I'm cycling with ride right through. I find it extremely annoying." Of the "age-old anarchy" of Amsterdam street traffic, Patijn said even cycling through a green light could be "really truly scary" since, from the cross street, red-light-running cyclists would "slam into you, . . . say, 'Watch out!' and give you the finger."

In January 2000, in the mayor's annual New Year's Day speech, Patijn complained about "the insane fact that ninety percent of cyclists in Amsterdam ride without lights or ride through red lights."* That same day, in his own speech, Police Chief Jelle

---

*Patijn's figure might have sounded like hyperbole, but, as far as cycling without lights goes, he wasn't far off the mark; from the tabulations I made during my first winter in Amsterdam, of 1,000 nighttime cyclists, 79 percent rode without (working) headlights.

Kuiper grumbled, "Cyclists behave like anarchists in traffic." Of the ubiquity of red-light runners, a few weeks later a spokesperson for the police department commented, "It's not just the youth. Go stand by any traffic light. No one stops. Even mothers with children don't. They don't give a damn about anyone. It's downright antisocial."

Not all authority figures were exemplary cyclists like Patijn, though. For example, in September 2002 (just a few weeks after my late-night encounter with the Amsterdam police), Piet Hein Donner—who was born in Amsterdam and had spent six years studying law in the city—was sworn in as the nation's minister of justice. For Donner, a Christian Democratic politician who regularly biked to work, his new position demanded of him new responsibilities. "Because I realize that I'm the minister," the nation's top law official admitted, "I can no longer ride through red lights on my bike."* Years later, Amsterdam's retired head police commissioner, Joop van Riessen, bragged about the manner in which he cycled through the city. "I do everything that's not allowed," Van Riessen said. "While others wait patiently for a red light, I tear right through."

Such ambivalence toward the traffic laws had long been a well-known trademark of the city's cyclists. In 1932, for example, the chief of traffic police, Claas Bakker—the man in charge of enforcing the traffic laws on Amsterdam's streets—admitted that the city's average cyclist was "no pure, innocent angel." In the mid-1970s, a sociologist who had tagged along with police officers noted: "An almost universal phenomenon in Amsterdam

---

*Soon after taking office, Donner's bike was stolen out of the Ministry of Justice's bicycle garage.

is the contempt that cyclists have for the law; many young people cycle without lights or consider themselves exempt from observing traffic lights. The policemen's attitude to this was usually one of weary indulgence."

One 24-year-old police inspector in the city in the 1970s said:

A real Amsterdammer likes to joke around. For example, he'll call a policeman "chief." But that same Amsterdammer can also be troublesome. In Haarlem, if you say, "Hey, get off and walk" to a cyclist without lights, he'll get off and walk. But in Amsterdam, they pretend not to hear you. And unless you chase them down, they won't cooperate.

One police official who *was* particularly bothered by the behavior of the cyclists was Amsterdam police chief Jelle Kuiper. Not long after he was sworn in as the top cop in 1997, due to his focus on "minor criminality" it was said of Kuiper: "He wants to go down in history as the man who got Amsterdammers to stop for red lights again." But after six years at the helm of the police department, such history was still waiting to be written; in 2003, Kuiper complained about how the cyclists rode at night without lights on their bikes and with complete disregard for traffic signals. "I call them anarchists," he said, "because, as a matter of principle, they rush to ignore all the rules that are there to protect them." The way cyclists barged through the city without restraint, Kuiper claimed, made them "just like **elephants**."

When Kuiper spat out this particular epithet, he was probably unaware that he'd just ensured his name *would* go down in history, after all—though probably not in the way he had envisioned. His name entered the history books (well, this one, anyway) for using a zoomorphic term to describe Amsterdam cyclists. By comparing them to elephants, Kuiper unwittingly contributed to the long list of members of the animal kingdom that the cyclists have been likened to, especially when being demonized.

Likening Amsterdam's cyclists to beasts has a long history. For example, when emphasizing the enormous number of bikers in the city, commentators have noted that they traveled "in droves like **buffalo**" (1932), formed "a splendid army of industrious **worker ants**" (1934) and yet still maintained their individuality when moving "like **salmon** going upstream" (1970). Two days after she had visited Amsterdam in 1935, the English author Virginia Woolf wrote in her diary of how "the cyclists go in flocks like **starlings**, gathering together, skimming in & out."

The Czech writer Karel Čapek (the man who introduced the word *robot* to the world) was captivated by the numerous cyclists he encountered in the Dutch capital. In 1933, he wrote:

And then those bicycles. I have seen various things in my time, but never have I seen so many bicycles as, for instance, in Amsterdam; they are no mere bicycles, but a sort of collective entity; shoals, droves, colonies of bicycles, which rather suggest teeming of bacteria or the swarming of infusoria or the eddying of flies. The best part of it is when a policeman holds up the stream of bicycles to let pedestrians get across the street, and then magnanimously leaves the road open once more; a regular swarm of cyclists dashes forward, headed by a number of speed champions, and away they pedal, with the queer unanimity of **dancing gnats**.

Observers also used such animal kingdom analogies when describing the talents of the cyclists. In 1938, one writer noted that the Amsterdam cyclist "shoots through the bustle of the big city with the smooth movements of a **tropical fish**." In 1972, an Englishman who lived in Amsterdam lamented the decline in the number of cyclists:

> They used to swarm everywhere, ridden with dash, initiative and terrible confidence. It was a dance of death and for the inexperienced motorist to be caught in Amsterdam's rush hour was the sternest of tests. They seemed to avoid cars as **flies** avoid a swat; it was as if air pressure forced them out of your way.

In 1972, an American wrote: "The Dutchman is a **modern centaur** who was born with half his body human and the other half a bicycle; he possesses two feet and two wheels, a mouth for talking and a horn for making his fellow beings move aside."

Mostly, though, zoomorphic terms have been reserved for demonizing the cyclists. In 1931, for example, an Amsterdam professor decried them as the "**bacteria of the street** who prove themselves to be the least disciplined in the field of traffic." In 1935, an Amsterdam newspaper writer wrote: "They don't belong in traffic. They are as bad as a plague. While other countries have their **locusts**, earthquakes and famines, the Netherlands has its cyclists." In 1956, another Amsterdam news writer opined, "No, the **black sheep** of the street traffic isn't the scooter rider (though he does have some pretty dark spots); it's the cyclist."

Often, such zoomorphic terms were used by pedestrians. In the 1890s, one Amsterdammer and his wife were walking on the Omval dike when a pack of thirty cyclists suddenly besieged them. "Like **lurking hyenas**," the man wrote, "they came up on us from behind and forced us off the road." In 1956, a visitor from Chicago wrote:

> It is quite possible that all the bicycles in the world are not in Amsterdam, but you'll never be able to convince me. . . . To an American pedestrian accustomed to negotiating Michigan Ave. or State St. against traffic, this city is a fearsome thing. I'd rather breast rush hour on the Outer Drive than attempt to cross some intersections here. For the cycles take after you like **hornets**.

The most vicious remarks have come, naturally, from motorists. According to a 1934 news report, motorists dismissed Amsterdam's cyclists as little more than "**street fleas**," while, in 1958, it was said that the motorists regarded them "as **overgrown vermin** that must die a natural death." And in 1963, a local newspaper claimed: "In the jungle of Amsterdam traffic, the cyclist is the **big game**. . . . During rush hour, every cyclist sees each car as a large dangerous animal that's ready to pounce on him." After dodging scooters and buses wore them down, the cyclists then "become easy prey for the cars."

In Albert Camus' 1956 novel *The Fall*—set in a café on Amsterdam's Zeedijk—the book's narrator states that Holland is "a dream of gold and smoke—smokier by day, more gilded by night" in which the people were "dreamily riding their black bicycles with high handlebars, **melancholy swans** drifting restlessly through the land, by the seas, along the canals."

While Police Chief Kuiper intended his elephant analogy to be an insult, I found it to be apt and inoffensive. I was no more insulted than if he'd called me a flea or a locust or a black sheep. In fact, after mulling it over, I began appreciating the elephant moniker and wore it with pride. Watch out! I'd think while whizzing through the city. Elephant stomping through!

Eventually, though, after studying Amsterdam's cyclists as intensively as any zoologist has ever studied animal life, I came to regard these creatures as a different sort of pest. Due to their resiliency and their tenacity, I viewed them as indestructible **cockroaches**. In spite of all they have endured over the past century, the city remains overridden with them.

AMSTERDAM ADDED ANOTHER cockroach, er, cyclist the day Amy Joy finally arrived. Since she'd requested that I not pick her up from the airport on bikes (my surprise foiled), we rode the train into town. Still, I was eager for her to experience the city in the way I already had for seven weeks. Outside our apartment building, I presented Amy Joy with AJJ's replacement. This one was also an old, black *omafiets*; its name—AJJ II—was written in black on the rear fender.

I gave Amy Joy the keys to her bike's two locks, a bike map of Amsterdam and a little 24-page booklet I'd written for her about cycling in the city. Each page covered a different topic and provided her with advice I'd gleaned from my head start as an Amsterdam cyclist, such as:

- "Always keep right and always presume someone faster is going to overtake you because no matter how fast you're riding someone *will* overtake you."

- "In Portland, where it's the norm to greet others with a hello or a nod, in Amsterdam you should forego such niceties. Here, if you try greeting every cyclist you encounter, you'll be regarded the same way as someone walking through midtown Manhattan greeting each pedestrian: you'll be thought a kook."
- "Unlike in Portland, where bells are novelties that are rung in delight, here, they are essentials that are rung in alarm and/or anger."
- "If it starts to rain, just pull over and wait under an awning or a tree with other cyclists. It probably won't last long. Or you can go native and ride with an umbrella."
- "With so many bikes everywhere, always take careful note of where you park AJJ II. I wrote your initials on your bike to help facilitate this task for you."
- "If the bike racks seem crowded, don't be shy, shove on in. Unlike in America, it's not taboo for your bike to touch another parked bike."
- "When locking a bike to a bridge railing, ensure that the keys don't slip and fall into the water (as I've already witnessed)."
- "Use hand signals so others can anticipate your intentions, but avoid using that dopey American-style crooked left arm signal. If you're turning right, just point right. Turning left? Point left. Stopping mid-block? Point down and to the side. These need not be grand gestures. Often the best signaling is done with little more than a faint flicker from a limp arm/hand/finger."
- "Since I've been in Amsterdam, I've been able to enjoy many aspects of cycling here. One thing I have not been able to do yet is bike with my sweetheart. But now that

you're here, I'm so excited to ride around town with you among all the thousands of other cyclists while I hold your wrist or you hold mine."

AFTER SPENDING A couple of hours resting up from her transatlantic flight and settling into (that is, reorganizing) our studio apartment, Amy Joy donned her flowery green dress and we went for a ride. Almost immediately, my wife noticed the numerous couples sharing single bikes by riding double or "dinking" (to use the Australian term introduced to us by an Australian pal of Amy Joy's). Such passengers almost always rode perched on the rear racks that are standard on Dutch bikes. In Dutch, these racks are called *baggagedraggers*—"baggage carriers." Quite often, though, the baggage they carry is human.

In a study I conducted of 1,000 dinking pairs (teenaged and older), among male/female combos, 94 percent of the time the woman was the passenger. In other words, for every case of a woman dinking a man, there were seventeen men dinking women (and, for that matter, eleven women dinking women and four men dinking men).

While most male passengers (54 percent) rode astride the rack, almost all female passengers (93 percent) rode sidesaddle. And among those sidesaddlers, a vast majority of them (83 percent) sat facing left—that is, facing traffic. This is most likely due to right-footedness, since a similar percentage of the populace (81 percent) is right-footed. When boarding an embarking bike, the passenger typically performs a little dance: first, a couple of stutter steps, then a tiny leap with the butt landing on the rear rack. To get airborne, a right-footed passenger leads with her right foot and pushes off with her left foot. Right-footed riders end up facing left and left-footed riders facing right.

Like a lot of Amsterdam cycling practices, dinking, naturally, was nothing new. In 1954, one foreign observer noted the effectiveness of back racks serving as seats. "Many a young Dutchman uses this seat to give a ride to his girlfriend," he wrote. "More likely than not she will seat herself sidewise, and will keep in excellent balance without holding to the bicycle or even touching the coat of the man who moves the pedals." Another foreigner of the time noted: "Girls, in theater dress and high heels, sit side-saddle fashion as nonchalantly as you please on the narrow rear mudguard [*sic*] while their escorts pedal furiously to keep up with the rushing traffic."

In 1958, an Englishman living in Amsterdam—who found dinking to be a "typical Dutch courtesy"—was particularly impressed when he saw one "very chivalrous young man" who was dinking two girlfriends: one on the back rack and one on the top tube. "Although this isn't fair to the innertube, not to mention to the one pedaling," he commented, "it is permitted by law."

The legality of dinking was (and is) notable to many foreigners because dinking was (and is) illegal in many other European countries. Because of this, in 1956 one Dutch newspaper felt compelled to warn its readers to *not* ride double when vacationing in antidinking lands such as Germany, France, Britain, Spain, Italy, Belgium, Luxemburg, Austria, Switzerland, Norway, Denmark and Sweden.*

During World War II, when the Nazis occupied the Netherlands, dinking played a vital role. The Dutch Resistance needed to shuttle to safety Allied soldiers—downed airmen or POW

---

*Another typical aspect of Dutch cycling that was (and is) striking to many foreigners due to its illegality in other countries: coaster (or back pedal) brakes.

camp escapees. Transporting an American, British or Canadian soldier by bike, though, wasn't necessarily an easy feat, as one member of the Resistance recounted:

> We were astonished to discover that many Allied soldiers could not ride a bike and we had to teach them how to before we could move them. . . . [I]t would be most unusual to see a Dutchman fall off his bicycle, and such an event would have aroused the suspicion of any German who happened to witness it. This was an extra problem we could have done without. . . . [T]hey were warned not to talk during the journey in case someone overheard them speaking English. They promised faithfully but, when they fell off, of course they automatically swore in English!

When there wasn't enough time to teach an Allied soldier how to ride a bike, Resistance couriers (almost always women since they sparked less suspicion from the Germans) would have to dink the soldier on the back of her bike. The sight of a woman dinking a man, of course, would have looked queer since, as a Resistance courier recalled, "A Dutchman would never let a girl do the work. It would have been unheard of." To avoid arousing suspicion, a courier dinking an Allied soldier had to follow back roads through the countryside, which made the trip longer and more arduous than if the soldier had known how to cycle in the first place.*

---

*Even after the war, in the 1950s, the American GIs on leave from posts in Germany who visited Amsterdam still didn't fare much better on bikes. At the time, the owner of one Amsterdam bike rental shop noted, "Those American guys are terrible cyclists. . . . Often, after riding for only half an hour, they return the bikes with pained looks on their faces from saddle soreness!"

A few days after her arrival, Amy Joy—enamored of the romance she saw in dinking—asked me to dink her on the back of my bike. I told her it would be my honor. After some initial fumbling on both our parts, Amy Joy eventually settled sidesaddle on Brownie's rear rack. We cycled for a few blocks as she hugged me around my waist and rested her head against my back. But then on the Haarlemmersluis, I misjudged the distance between us and a pole in the middle of the bike path. Amy Joy's knee slammed into the pole. After many cries of pain from her and many pledges of apologies from me, from then on we stuck to riding side by side, each on his or her own bike.

Side-by-side riding, of course, has its own charms. Many Amsterdam couples ride hand in hand, or with a hand on the other's shoulder or pushing gently on the other's lower back. But most typical was one cyclist holding the wrist of the other, who had two hands on his or her own handlebars. I'd never seen such a gesture in the States and was quite flattered when the first time, while riding, Amy Joy took me by my wrist.

ONE DAY, ON Marnixstraat, Amy Joy and I were following a frail-looking elderly couple. They looked so terribly sweet riding together (the woman holding the man by the wrist); it made me picture Amy Joy and me still cycling together in Amsterdam when we were their age. I reached over and took hold of Amy Joy's forearm. She smiled at me. This idyllic little scene was disrupted when, in tandem, the older couple each looked back over a shoulder and then darted left. They narrowly missed a #10 tram coming from behind. The tram driver rang his bell: *Dong! Dong!* Approaching from the other direction, another tram also nearly ran them down: *Dong! Dong!*

After the two trams passed, we saw the couple still riding side by side as they crossed a bridge in the distance, the woman's hand still on the man's wrist. At first, I chalked up their moment of madness to senility. But then, noting that they seemed completely unfazed, I realized age may have actually favored them. It's possible that over the course of decades, they'd cycled that same route thousands of times. Maybe they'd done this very maneuver so often, they could do it flawlessly. If indeed one needs 10,000 hours of practice in his or her field before becoming an expert, it's possible this agile couple had already reached that threshold of expertise.

In 1972, a Portuguese man who had been living in Amsterdam for 16 years commented:

Whoever is not used to it—and I shall never get used to it—fears for the life of the elderly ladies who navigate through traffic on bikes dating from the First World War. At intersections or in dangerous situations, they come to a standstill by means of a remarkable maneuver in which they slide forward from the saddle and, at the same time, lean backwards to brace themselves as the friction of their shoes against the pavement functions as a brake. Unfortunately, no simple description can give an impression of the virtuosity, the astonishing steadiness and the steering ability with which these women propel themselves. What they—in their twilight years—exhibit in the middle of the street would, in any other country, be considered a circus act.

SEEING SO MANY old folks on bikes fueled my enthusiasm for our newfound plan to stay in Amsterdam forever. Elderly cyclists have long been notable to visitors, who often express amazement at the diversity of the city's cycling population. In countless guidebooks, travel articles, news reports, memoirs, etc., dating from 1920 to the present day, the most popular way for writers to describe the broadness of cycling in Amsterdam has been to create a list of a cross section of society they saw on bikes. In order to provide the most thorough overview of how *all* elements of Amsterdam society cycle, I culled scores of such lists to create a master list.

On bikes, in and around Amsterdam, visitors reported seeing in various combinations: mothers with babies in wicker baskets and fat grandmothers, toddlers and urchins; beer-bellied magistrates and town patriarchs; schoolgirls, schoolboys, shop girls, errand boys, peasant girls, butcher's boys, baker's boys; members of Parliament and cabinet ministers with bowler hats; soldiers, sailors, generals and veterans; pastors, priests, monks and nuns; delivery boys on three-wheelers and office boys eating their sandwiches; bank managers, bank directors and bank presidents; furriers and fur-coated women; mill hands and farmers in wooden shoes; lawyers and judges, doctors and nurses, veterinarians and pharmacists, engineers and scientists; preppies and punks; barber's assistants and cat litter boys;* authorities and subordinates, millionaires and the unemployed, aristocrats and beggars, bosses in top hats and the most humble scrubwomen; teenage boys with girlfriends balancing sidesaddle on the back and teenage girls with boyfriends balancing splay-legged over the handlebars; courting couples and bridal pairs; the humblest

---

*These young men, working for a 1930s business enterprise, rode large cargo bikes to customers' homes, where they replaced soiled cat litter with fresh litter.

citizens and average Joes; people eating snacks and people taking their dogs for a ride; tradesmen and dockworkers, sewer workers and chimney sweeps, policemen and hawkers, undertakers and railroad engineers, mechanics with their tools and painters carrying open buckets of paint; university students with their books and young men reading their newspapers or playing chess*; movie theater ticket takers and funeral attendees in high hats; ladies on shopping expeditions and elegant gentlemen going for tea; tweedy dowagers and take-straight gents with their attaché cases; office clerks and city clerks, typists and stenographers; shy schoolteachers and retired high school headmasters; Orthodox Jewish boys in yarmulkes and Islamic women in chadors; businessmen politely tipping their hats to passersby and prominent directors of large concerns who own one or more cars; black boys in soccer jerseys and pretty lasses who could be models; dreadheaded design consultants and melancholy cello players; pale Turkish grocers carrying full crates of bottled beer and coffee-colored Indonesian women carrying full sacks of market vegetables; tourists and prostitutes "and just about everyone else."

Many of these lists were composed from a staple of four main categories of Amsterdam cyclists:

- **Businesspeople**: with "their briefcases dangling from the handlebars" and "in pressed white shirts and ties."
- **Females**: in "plumed hats," "woolen berets," "long full

---

*The line about chess-playing cyclists comes from the 1957 edition of Eugene Fodor's guide to the Low Countries. That same year, a writer for the *Atlantic* magazine, while listing his own cross section of Amsterdam cyclists, joked, "Fodor's guidebook, *Benelux*, which I found the most useful guide to Holland, reports that even blind men in the Netherlands get around on bicycles, led by their Seeing Eye dogs."

skirts," "frumpy dresses," "a chic dress, silk stockings," "low-cut cocktail dresses" and "miniskirts and four-inch platform shoes."

- **The elderly**: old ladies who "pedal like mad," who "race along as skillfully as schoolboys," "with long-stemmed gladiolas pinioned under one arm" and "with the sensible purse"; old men "with their wool trousers tucked into their socks," "in a Prince Albert coat, wearing wooden shoes and a stovepipe hat of Lincoln vintage" and one who "straddles his bike as a horseman sits his mount, stately and dignified."

- **Nuns**: in a "black veil dangling to her waist," "aged nuns," "nuns with flowing habits," "pedal[ing] to her hospital," "troupes of nuns"—nuns, nuns and ever more nuns.

Indeed, within seconds of any bike excursion I made or cyclist-spotting I undertook, I saw no shortage of cycling business-people, women or elderly—sometimes all at once. (An older businesswoman? *Check!*) But the most-often cited type of cyclist listed, the nun, eluded me. Nuns were mentioned in so many testimonials, they would have seemed the *easiest* to spot. Yet as I rode around and cyclist-spotted around town, no matter how hard I tried, no matter how thoroughly I searched, every other sort of Amsterdammer was spotted on a bike *except* for nuns.

I mentioned my frustration about my lack of cycling-nun-spotting to Amy Joy a few weeks after her arrival. She casually replied, "I've seen nuns on bikes here."

"Really?" I asked, with equal parts suspicion and jealousy. "*Nun-zuh?* Plural?"

"Yeah," she replied. "A few different times."

Her report made me even more frustrated—and determined to bag a cycling nun of my own.

ONE MORNING, DURING my first winter in Amsterdam, I left for class an hour earlier than necessary so Brownie and I could meander along the way. When it began to rain lightly, we sought shelter in the passageway of the Rijksmuseum—the national art museum—which is perhaps the most unique urban bike path on earth. The street-level tunnel, lined with columns and vaulted ceilings, led straight through the cathedral-like building and directly under the spot where Rembrandt's masterpiece *The Night Watch* hung. Due to its incredible acoustics, the tunnel had long served as a performance space for street musicians; sometimes I stopped to listen to Tuvan throat singers or Jamaican steel drummers. As early as the 1930s, harmonica players performed there. "This is the best place to play in Europe," a Russian saxophonist once professed. "Covent Garden in London is also okay, but it's better here." While I waited out the rain, several schoolchildren, riding as passengers on their parents' bikes, exploited the passageway's acoustics by joining their parents in hooting, hollering and singing as they passed by. I watched with envy, envisioning the day I could do the same with my own offspring as passenger.

After a couple of minutes, the rain began to let up. Brownie and I exited the passageway. A few feet farther on, we approached the Weteringschans/Spiegelgracht intersection. Here, glove- and scarf-clad cyclists were coming from and going in all directions. Watching the cyclists weave and zoom through each other's paths made me woozy. When I reached the intersection, instead of weaving and zooming myself, I pulled over and stopped. The horde of cyclists was so overwhelming—so mesmerizing—I had to count them.

When the hands on the Rijksmuseum clock tower struck 7:55, I began counting with the intention of continuing for half an hour. For each cyclist spotted, I scratched a single hash mark in my notebook. After only two minutes, though, this method proved inadequate. The cyclists were appearing faster than I could mark hashes. So, instead, I began tallying the bikers in batches of five; each fivesome earned one hash mark. While this method wasn't foolproof (some folks still slipped by untallied), it was much more efficient.

An American so overawed by the cyclists that he's driven to counting? This wasn't without precedent. In 1954, a Texan, after declaring "it seems impossible to count" the city's cyclists, nevertheless gave it a shot. In a four-minute span, during the afternoon rush hour along a "business street," he counted 201 passing cyclists (and 21 cars). Four years before that, a tourist from Michigan had had a go at it. "I counted a hundred so fast," he reported, "it made my head swim and I quit."

My head was also swimming as I struggled to keep count, but I was determined not to quit. When the winter air began numbing my fingers, in between hash marks I blew into my cupped hands. When my toes started numbing, I danced back and forth from foot to foot—and kept counting. Eventually, though, the elements got the best of me. At exactly 8:15— ten minutes short of the intended half-hour mark—my blood needed to get circulating through my body again. I caved in, gave up, jumped on Brownie and pedaled through the inter-section.

When I reached the warmth of my classroom, I tallied the hash marks. In just 20 minutes I had counted 927 cyclists.

A FEW DAYS later, Amy Joy and I attended a birthday party for one of my Dutch classmates in his apartment. We were the only foreigners in attendance. Throughout the evening, any Hollander I met eventually asked why I'd moved to Amsterdam. Each time, I recounted the tale of the dark, cold, wet morning when I'd ridden around town and through the Rijksmuseum and then had spontaneously counted 927 cyclists in just 20 minutes.

"Oh?" said the aunt of our host when it was her turn to hear my explanation. "Is that a lot or something?"

"*A lot?*" I said. "That's massive!"

The aunt looked puzzled. "You left America to live here because of that?"

"Yeah," I said. What could be a more obvious reason?

The woman shook her head, then muttered, "I don't understand."

She wasn't alone. That evening, several others reacted similarly to my 927-cyclists-in-20-minutes reason for emigrating. To the Dutch, the bike is so everyday, so normal, so deeply ingrained that trying to explain its remarkableness to a Hollander proved pointless.

That evening at the party, after receiving the umpteenth blank-stare response to my story, I realized how others saw me. I was like an immigrant to the United States who had pulled over on a freeway shoulder during rush-hour traffic; marveled at all the cars; and then later professed to Americans his love for their country on account of freeway traffic.

"All these cars!" he'd proclaim. "This is awesome! This is the country for me!"

If any immigrant had ever professed such a thing to me, I'd think he was nuts. Now, I realized, no matter how passionately I recited the 927 figure, a Hollander didn't understand me *better*; he or she only regarded me as nuttier.

After the party, Amy Joy and I cycled home. When we reached our apartment building, I left her at the front door. Then I went for a late-night ride while I ruminated about my inability to explain my passion for urban cycling to Amsterdammers. Thirty minutes later, while lost in thought on a bike path on Herengracht, I found myself riding behind a slow-moving pair of wrist-holding cyclists. I managed to maneuver around them, only to meet the tail end of another pack of slowpokes. I rang my bell and wormed my way through them till my path was again blocked. Looking ahead, I saw a long line of dawdling cyclists in front of me. I was stuck.

It was past midnight. What the hell were all these people doing out on their bikes? Why were they all moving so unhurriedly? And why were they in my way?

That's when it struck me: *It's the middle of winter; it's past midnight—and I'm stuck in a bicycle traffic jam.*

My haste vanished. I decelerated, accepted the pace of the others and appreciated the rest of my ride home.

From then on, whenever anyone asked why I had immigrated to Holland, I didn't hesitate to reply: "So I can be stuck in a bicycle traffic jam at midnight."

6

A Matter of Individual Expression: The Land of the Automobile vs. the Land of the Bicycle

During my rides around Amsterdam, some things continued to puzzle me. Why had cycling taken off in the Netherlands in a way it hadn't in the United States? And likewise, why had the automobile taken off in the States decades earlier than it had in the Netherlands? In order to answer these questions, I pored over scores of accounts of Americans in the "nation of cyclists" and of Hollanders in "the land of the automobile" from the first decades of the 20th century. Viewing the two countries through the eyes of visitors from the other nation provided some very keen insights.

For example, in 1923, an American scholar of Holland wrote:

> If a referendum were held among the Dutch on the question what modern invention has been most instrumental in changing the aspects of their social life during Queen Wilhelmina's reign, nine out of ten would cast their ballot for the bicycle. Not for the telephone, nor for plumbing, nor for the automobile.

If such a referendum had been conducted among Americans of that era, the results would have differed markedly. Their ballots, most certainly, would have been cast for a modern invention that was widely and rapidly changing aspects of *American* social life: the automobile. While bicycle sales and usage were skyrocketing in Amsterdam and Holland in the 1920s, a similar phenomenon was transpiring in the United States—albeit with the car.

In the late 1890s, at the peak of America's golden age of cycling, Americans were purchasing upward of 1.2 million bikes annually. But then, almost as suddenly as enthusiasm for the bicycle had soared, interest in it plummeted as Americans quickly disparaged cycling as merely a fad that had run its course. By 1902, bike sales dropped to less than a quarter of what they had been just a few years earlier. The League of American Wheelmen, a cycling advocacy group that in 1898 had more than 100,000 dues-paying members, had fewer than 9,000 members by 1902. "The bicycle fantasy has passed," one American magazine reported that same year, "but it has been succeeded by even a stronger movement, that of automobiling."

In 1906, the Dutchman Henri Meijer wrote about America:

In all places where, years ago, thousands of American bicycles were being built but where the fires of the bicycle blacksmiths were gradually extinguished—in Cleveland, Boston, Kenosha, Buffalo, Pittsburgh, Milwaukee, Chicago, Springfield, Indianapolis, Middletown, Hartford, Topeka, St. Louis, Lansing, Detroit—there, these days, the automated metalworking machines drone and groan a song of resurrection and reborn energy.

The same manufacturers who had been producing bikes or bike parts—such as Henry Ford or the Dodge brothers—were now producing cars or car parts. As Meijer put it: "There is no factory in the New World that does not believe in the permanence of automobilism."

Almost unanimously, Dutch tourists, emigrants and reporters in America were flabbergasted by the number of cars they encountered there. And just as American visitors have long illustrated the staggering level of bicycle usage in Holland by citing cross sections of those who cycle (particularly stressing those with *high* status and/or incomes), Dutch visitors illustrated the staggering level of car usage in America by citing cross sections of those who drove (particularly stressing those with *low* status and/or incomes). For example, Dutch visitors in the 1910s, 1920s and 1930s recounted seeing car owners in the United States who were gardeners, house painters, piano teachers, laundrymen, farmers, office clerks, longshoremen, shopgirls, bricklayers, college students, carpenters, high school teachers, porters, civil servants, road workers, housekeepers, stenographers, factory workers, journalists, deliverymen, assistant secretaries, shopkeepers, prison employees, preachers and "every businessman of little importance." "Often you can see children—that is boys or girls of sixteen or seventeen years—fly through the city in large autos," observed one Dutchman in Michigan. "It is shocking sometimes, but here people are not surprised by this." Of the young drivers, another wrote, "Just as easily as a little boy or girl in Holland learns to ride a bike, here they learn to drive a car."

"Every ordinary person has one," wrote a Dutchman of car usage in Washington, D.C., in 1921. Decades before the civil rights movement, African-Americans were noted for driving "with pride." One Dutchwoman, while being driven through the Jewish Lower East Side in the mid-1920s (which she described as "unbelievably filthy"), wrote that it was to her "great surprise" to see in this impoverished neighborhood "rows of little Fords and Chevrolets lining both sides of the streets just like everywhere else" in New York. That the indigent also owned cars greatly excited one visiting Dutch socialist leader. "Ripe and unripe both drive motorcars," he wrote. "There is no better leveling device in this miraculous country."

What seemed to impress Dutch tourists even more than seeing members of the American working class driving cars was seeing behind the wheel their *own* countrymen—emigrants from Holland: skilled tradesmen in Chicago, farmers on the Great Plains, furniture factory workers in the Dutch enclaves of Grand Rapids and Holland, Michigan. Of one young Hollander who had been in the United States for only three months, it was said he "drove his plucky little Ford 'Tin Lizzy' every day and acted like a big shot all the while."

In Los Angeles, a Dutch visitor observed (decades before it had become a cliché), "Almost nobody walks here." A Dutch immigrant in Iowa in 1920, while noting that many farmers owned two or three cars, commented, "Whatever else an American does, he doesn't walk. It is certainly a rarity to encounter a pedestrian on the road." One Dutch tourist discovered this the hard way when, on her first morning in America, she strolled from her hosts' home in suburban New Jersey. Before long, she came upon a large thoroughfare, where, as the lone pedestrian among so many passing cars, she stuck out like a sore thumb. Immediately "almost every motorist" pulled over and offered her a ride. Shaken by the sudden attention her walking had garnered, she cut short her excursion and hastened back to the house.

What most puzzled many Hollanders in America—more than the great number of cars or the lack of pedestrians—was the absolute dearth of bikes. "A bicycle here is as rare as a rickshaw in the Netherlands," observed one Dutch visitor. Another wrote, "In America, the bicycle has become a prehistoric means of transportation." They were also stunned to discover that—unlike Amsterdam's narrow, brick- and cobblestone-paved streets—streets in American cities were wide, asphalt-paved and "without treacherous twists and curves." These sleek American roadways were absolutely ideal for cycling, so where were the cyclists? One Dutch tourist in Manhattan in 1927 managed to spot a few of these rarities, though each was cycling—to the tourist's amazement—on the *sidewalk*. In 1931, a Dutch emigrant living in New York remarked that sidewalk cycling was actually "very common and permitted. Even a policeman won't give chase since the cyclist is safer there than among the busy traffic."*

WHEN I READ in a European magazine that Henry Ford's ideal . . . was for every American to have his own car, I laughed," wrote an Amsterdammer during his trip to the States in 1919. "After what I've seen in Washington and Buffalo and New York, I'm no longer laughing." "Good heavens," exclaimed a Dutchwoman immediately after she'd stepped off an ocean liner returning from America. "Have there always been *so* few cars in Holland?"

Whether it was a Hollander in America or an American in Holland, both sets of observers arrived at the same conclusion: America

---

*For decades afterward, into the 1960s, other Hollanders noted not only the scarcity of cyclists in Manhattan but also this phenomenon of sidewalk cycling.

was a nation of motorists and Holland was not. By the middle of
the 1920s, when the number of automobiles on the planet reached
25 million, 20 million of them—an incredible 80 percent—were
in America. In California, there was already one car for every 3.3
people, while in the United States as a whole, there was one car for
every 6 people (or, roughly speaking, one per family). On the other
hand, in Canada, the rate was one car for every 13 people; in France,
one car for every 53 people; the United Kingdom, one for every 55.
In the Netherlands, the figure was one car for every 185 people—a
rate of car ownership *less than one-thirtieth* of America's. In fact, at
the time, the Ford plants in America were churning out more cars
each day than existed in all of Amsterdam. Meanwhile, there was
one bicycle for every 3.25 people in Holland yet only one for every
seventy in the United States.

So why did the level of car ownership in Amsterdam/the
Netherlands pale in comparison to that in America? And why
did the level of bike ownership in America pale in comparison to
that in Amsterdam/the Netherlands? A number of factors contributed. Among them:

- **The difference in the price of a car**

The large-scale production model—as championed by Henry
Ford—helped drive the sticker price of new cars in America
down to a level where they were affordable to a great deal of the
populace. In 1916, a Dutch emigrant in Grand Rapids wrote
home to a cousin that cars "are so ridiculously cheap here that
almost everyone can afford one. For $350 you can have a dandy
car for five persons." In 1926, another Dutchman in America,
who was surprised by the low price of cars, remarked, "[T]he

purchase of a little Ford costs not much more than double what we pay for a bicycle."

Holland wasn't populous enough to support a large-scale auto industry. Its largest manufacturer—Spijker (located in Amsterdam)—produced, at its peak in the early 1920s, fewer cars *per year* than the Ford plants in America were producing *per hour*. Without any large-scale domestic auto industry, most cars had to be imported, which greatly increased their retail price. As a result, new cars in Holland were far more expensive than ones in the United States.

For those Americans who couldn't afford a brand-new car, an inexpensive used one was usually easily obtainable. In 1930, one enthusiastic Dutchman living in New York commented: "The sale of secondhand autos is *so* beautifully organized that one can get a working car at almost any price."

A huge secondhand market existed not only because there were so many cars in the States but also because there was so much turnover in car ownership as many Americans eagerly "traded up." Of America's burgeoning used car market, the French academic André Siegfried observed in 1927: "The American is fickle and quickly tires of a thing after he has bought it." In Holland, without a large pool of cars to begin with, and without an American-style yearning to continually trade up, the used car market remained minuscule, leaving those who couldn't afford a new car with little opportunity to purchase a secondhand one.

- **The difference in access to easy credit**

A key reason why so many Americans could afford to purchase a car—new or used—was that a credit plan (with payments as low as five dollars a week) was simple to attain. In Holland, such easy credit was rare. Without access to credit, the already high price of a new car remained out of reach for even middle-income earners.

- **The difference in the price of gasoline**

Mass petroleum deposits and low (or even, in some states, nonexistent) gasoline taxes in the United States made fuel relatively cheap and affordable to American car owners. In contrast, mass petroleum deposits had yet to be discovered in Holland, and the tax on gasoline was much higher than in the States. "While there is already complaining about the high prices of gasoline in America . . . ," noted one Dutchman just before World War I, "the distress is even greater in other countries. For example, here and in Germany, gasoline prices are more than twice as high as in America." In the early decades of the 20th century, gasoline in Holland was generally about *three times* as expensive as gasoline in the United States (a comparative ratio that, by the way, exists to this day). Such expensive fuel was beyond the means of a great many Hollanders.

- **The difference in the availability of parking**

During the car boom in the United States, free curbside parking along the streets of American cities and towns was treated practically as a universal right—all to the bewilderment of the Dutch. An Amsterdammer visiting Washington, D.C., in 1921 was amazed when his host drove him to the White House, to the Capitol, to the barbershop, and at each stop they simply left the car alongside the street. He further marveled that a "young lady, when she goes to buy a little box of safety pins, can leave her car unattended in front of the store."

A seemingly pedestrian concept like curbside parking made such a huge impression because, unlike in the United States (and much of the rest of Europe), leaving a car unattended on the streets of Amsterdam was downright illegal. At all times, unattended cars in the city had to be housed in public parking facilities (for a fee) or in one's own home garage (often a converted stable). Such restrictions not only made car ownership an expensive undertaking but also made cars impractical for running simple errands like going to the store for safety pins. Amsterdam's rigid curbside parking restrictions weren't relaxed until December 1921 (though a ban on overnight curbside parking remained in effect for more than a decade).*

- **The difference in the need for a chauffeur**

A Dutchman in Philadelphia in 1910 found it "striking" how many female college students not only had cars but were also their own drivers. While Americans typically drove their own cars, the common car owner in Amsterdam, due largely to the parking restrictions, was chauffeured. In the morning, the driver would deliver the car owner to his workplace and then take the car to a nearby paid garage or return it to the home garage. At lunchtime or at the end of the workday, the driver would pick up the car owner. If a car owner wished to shop in the city center,

---

*Street parking in America baffled other Dutch tourists, though for a different reason. In 1916, upon seeing "innumerable" cars parked on the streets of Detroit "for as far as the eye can see," one of them wrote, "It's a riddle to me how, in America—where people are not always so very fussy about property rights (not only the watch of a sauntering Hollander gets swiped, but even in the middle of the day, the furnishings of a house are known to nimbly disappear)— hands are kept off these . . . automobiles."

the chauffeur would drop her off in front of the store while he remained outside with the car. Under such conditions, car ownership was limited to—as one Amsterdammer put it—"those who can afford the luxury of employing a chauffeur twenty-four hours a day just so they can ride in the car for maybe half an hour."

- **The difference in the amount of physical space—and how that physical space was regarded**

The area of the contiguous United States is about two hundred times larger than that of the Netherlands. Not only is America a large country spatially, but in many ways Americans held to a frontier mentality, treating physical space as if it was an unlimited commodity. A great deal of space could easily be devoted to the needs of the car (such as wide roadways, curbside parking, blacktop parking lots, etc.). A Dutchman in Los Angeles in 1929 found it remarkable not only that almost every house in that city had its own garage but also that many people left their cars outdoors on a mysterious plot of the residential property. The concept of a *driveway* was so foreign to the Hollander, he puzzled over what to call it in Dutch.

In the Netherlands, space had been so limited that for a millennium, the Dutch had been constructing dikes to reclaim land from the sea. This scant, hard-won land wasn't so quickly allocated to—or wasted on—parking lots or sprawl development.

- **The difference in how distances were regarded**

Before the arrival of the car, the average American was already far more accustomed to traveling long distances by land than was the average Hollander. When the car arrived on the scene, it enabled Americans to cross these distances with far more ease.

That Americans so readily drove such long distances dumbfounded the Dutch. For example, one tourist in the 1920s was amazed when her American hosts invited her on an overnight car trip from New York City to Niagara Falls, more than 400 miles away. As she noted, the distance was longer than the trek from Amsterdam to Paris. In Holland, traveling such a stretch just to spend the night would have been unimaginable. But as the Dutch woman put it, "An American thinks nothing of it." Another Dutch visitor, while attending a dinner party in New Jersey in the 1930s, was shocked when she learned some of the other guests lived "rather far away." This made the Americans laugh at her concept of "far." People who live 20 miles apart, she then noted, "think of themselves as neighbors!" In 1930, a Dutchman who had moved to a rural locale 40 miles north of New York City was astounded that so many people from his area commuted to work in Manhattan. "Nobody finds this crazy," he remarked. "On the contrary, there are many who commute from even farther away."

In the country where 400 miles wasn't considered a long distance or 40 miles a long commute, driving was the norm. On the other hand, in the country that was only about 250 miles long at its longest and where "everything is cozily close together or accessible by bike" (as the Dutchman living north of Manhattan put it), cycling was the norm.

- **The difference in urban street widths**

These days, it's easy to presume that the relatively wide streets of American cities resulted from urban planners catering to the needs of the automobile. But actually, the existence of many such wide streets predated the rise of the car. For example, planners laid out Salt Lake City in the 1840s on a grid pattern with incredibly broad streets that were said to have been specifically made wide enough to enable an ox-drawn wagon to make a mid-block U-turn. The grid patterns of Manhattan, Chicago, San Francisco, etc.—all planned decades before the invention of the automobile—included streets so wide, they easily accommodated cars when the time came.

In the 1920s, one Dutch tourist was so startled by the major streets of American cities that he compared them to Amsterdam's Weteringschans. This was wide by that city's standards but nothing, he said, compared to New York's Park Avenue or Boston's Commonwealth Avenue, with their landscaped median strips and four to six lanes of traffic. At the time, Amsterdam was still very much a city of narrow streets set in irregular patterns and intertwined with numerous canals and bridges.

In short, American-style, sprawling, wide, grid-patterned streets suited automobiles; Dutch-style, compact, narrow, irregularly patterned streets suited bikes.

• The difference in the physical size of urban areas

In 1937, when one Dutch tourist arrived at downtown Chicago's La Salle train station, she was picked up by her hosts and driven to their home in the Dutch neighborhood of Roseland. The home happened to stand along the same street as the train station—La Salle Street. "Almost without stopping . . . , we drove down that one endless street," she recounted. When they finally reached the house, she was baffled that they were still in Chicago despite being about 12 miles from the city center.

"In the neighborhood where I'm staying, I'm as far from downtown as Haarlem is from Leiden." (Those two Dutch cities were separated by miles of flower bulb farms.) When she learned that some streets ran as long as 25 miles within the city limits of Chicago, she was stunned. Even in Holland's largest metropolis—Amsterdam—only a handful of streets ran for more than a mile.

"With rare exception, bicycles are unknown here," the visitor to Chicago reported, "so one always has to make use of another form of transport." For many in such a large urban area, that form of transport was a car. Meanwhile, since Amsterdam's physical size was not much larger than it had been in the 17th century, trips across the compact city could be made far more easily by foot, tram or bike.

- ## The difference in the pace of traffic (and of life)

Tourists and emigrants to both countries agreed that the tempo of street life differed between America and Holland. A Californian living in the Netherlands in 1934 noted:

The Dutch life is beautifully attuned to the deliberate pace of bicycle riding. It has the same calm and slow rhythm which allows the Hollander time off for coffee in the middle of the morning, for tea in the afternoon, and tea again in the evening. . . . To a Dutchman a bicycle becomes a matter of individual expression, almost a part of the body, controlled subconsciously and leaving him free to meditation. There is no noise, no smell of gasoline, so he can notice little things like birds and flowers, which the automobilized American leaves in the roar and dust.

An American who cycled across the Netherlands also noticed this contrast in pace. "To a Dutchman nothing is more inconceivable than haste," he wrote in 1928. "Even a bicycle can break speed limits. Mine did, and my conduct was under grave suspicion until the fact that I was an American became known."

On the other hand, an American observed in 1923: "Speed, rush, impatience are the features of American life that strike the Hollander most when he visits [the United States]." A Dutch immigrant living in a small town in Michigan wrote home: "Everything, quick, quick! If it doesn't go quickly, it's no good. And so everything here flies along. Autos here are as common as bikes in the Netherlands."

In short, in the nation where haste was valued, a car was suitable; in the nation where it wasn't, a bike did just fine.

• The difference in the necessity of a car

One Dutch tourist in New Jersey, upon seeing out-of-town factories surrounded by massive parking lots filled with cars, was confounded that so many workers would choose to drive to work. Then it dawned on her: the workers hadn't *chosen* to do so. With the factory located far from residential districts and without suitable public transit, driving was their *only* option for getting to work. In many of America's new sprawling developments (for example, suburban residential areas), car ownership wasn't a luxury, it was practically mandatory.

From Amsterdam, rail connections to points throughout the rest of the country were excellent; many other Dutch population centers—Rotterdam, The Hague, Utrecht, Haarlem—could be reached by train within an hour or so. In the Netherlands—home to compact cities, efficient public transportation networks and very few American-style out-of-town developments—car ownership was hardly a necessity.

- **The difference in traffic safety**

In 1930, one American proclaimed, "In many parts of America bicycling has become, because of the prevalence of the motor car, . . . dangerous to life and limb." The rapid increase of car ownership in the United States enabled motorists to dominate the road and disregard the safety of the cyclists. Each increase in the number of cars only further discouraged cycling. In turn, with fewer cyclists on the road, cars became ever more dominant.

In Holland, on the other hand, an Amsterdam cyclist predicted in 1898: "When our brothers, sisters and children start cycling, then we'll begin thinking differently about cyclists in general." Indeed, as more took to cycling, they became relatively safer in traffic with regard to cars. In 1927, a tourist in Holland noted, "[M]otor cars are not yet sufficiently numerous to make cycling in a city equivalent to suicide." And in 1936, a Detroit suburbanite, after biking in Amsterdam, expressed shock: "The motorists here respect the cyclists!" The rapid increase in the number of bikes and the dominance of the cyclists on the road discouraged car driving, which in turn helped to further increase the number of cyclists.

- **The difference in perspectives on bike riding and car owning**

After the bicycle's golden age in the 1890s, "America got so new-rich and arrogant," one Californian of the era stated, " . . . that it turned up its parvenu nose at bicycles." Another American claimed that after the populace had taken to cars, cycling was then confined to "telegraph messengers, schoolboys and eccentrics." In 1923, a Dutch reporter in New York observed, "The average American feels complete for the first time when he's sitting behind a steering wheel." Then such a driver "immediately assumes an air of piteous contempt" toward anyone who didn't drive.

American children could fool around with bikes, but as they aged, their bicycles were expected to be shed along with their dolls and teddy bears as they matured into full-fledged motorists. This entrenched stigma toward cycling was expressed when two young men from Southern California—in Amsterdam for the 1928 Olympic Games—caught sight of the cyclists. "It seems so funny to see grown-up folks peddling [sic] along on bicycles," the two remarked, "but they think nothing of it."

In 1912, a Dutchman in Washington, D.C., experienced this stigma firsthand when he asked various Americans about the possibility of cycling the city's streets with his wife. The response, he said:

People strongly advised against it. Such an attempt in the year 1912 would be tantamount to a revolution. In the past few years, so few respectable people have been sighted on a bicycle, that one runs the risk of earning sudden newspaper headlines that few would wish for. It sounds odd: the land of liberty, yet such a fear of being ridiculed.

While Americans derided cycling, they revered the car as the ultimate possession. As a Dutch immigrant in Michigan noted,

"Anyone here who does not have an auto is not highly regarded. Thus we also are not much because we don't have a car." In 1920, a Hollander in Boston wrote in a Dutch newspaper about how amusing it was to watch Americans make a "quick, covert glance" when sizing up someone based on his or her car.

> A good American knows the brand names—and the prices!—by heart. Then they check whether the car is new or old and whether the occupants are making do with blankets or are wrapped in thick fur coats and the lickety-split judgment is made. . . . Everything depends upon it: the faster the speed, the larger the vehicle, the higher the price signifies the greater the purchasing power and social prestige of the owner. Perhaps, dear reader, you'll think: "That's the same as with us." But surely these things play an even greater role here than with us. The passion to outdo each other is fiercer and the shame of being outdone more distressing.

Of the American motorist, one such driver in the 1920s observed: "He must look prosperous even if he isn't." In such a status-conscious society, it was impossible to look prosperous riding on something widely disregarded as a mere toy.

Meanwhile, in Holland, where a more Calvinistic ethic reigned, the display of one's wealth was largely disparaged. So, without any great pressure to portray an image of wealth via material possessions, all walks of Dutch society could—and did—cycle comfortably, free from ridicule.

• **The difference between spendthrifts and cheapskates**

When the influential Spanish philosopher José Ortega y Gasset visited Amsterdam in the 1930s, his first impression was like that of so many foreign visitors: streets filled with "the abundance of bicycles." But while this marvel generally impressed and/or amused other foreigners, it disgusted Ortega y Gasset. Cycling in a Dutch city, he wrote, "is stupidly dangerous, is unreasonably fatiguing and is woefully unsightly." In particular, the Spaniard found the sight of bare-legged female cyclists to be "vulgar."* According to Ortega y Gasset, all this cycling pointed "to certain deep secrets that operate in the Dutch soul."

Ortega y Gasset's greatest distaste for Dutch cycling, though, centered on the reason he felt so many Hollanders cycled: in order to satisfy their "enthusiasm for frugality." The Spaniard argued that, to the Dutchman, thrift was "more important than beauty or comfort." And he believed this thrift inhibited the Dutch from becoming car owners.

The question must be asked: Was Ortega y Gasset's argument valid? *Was* the level of car ownership so much lower in Holland than in North America and other Western European nations because the Dutch were simply *too cheap* to buy cars? Though the Dutch had long had a reputation abroad as penny-pinchers, any of the reasons stated above would probably trump the "too cheap" standpoint. Owning and operating a car in Holland was

*More specifically, he wrote:
> We'd rather not speak about the pain felt when witnessing female cyclists and their frequent and vain struggles with their skirts as they tried to prevent shameful spectacles. The tourist who wanders through the streets, and who is respectfully interested in the new humanity that he encounters without the least erotic feelings, is somewhat frustrated when he's so inconveniently confronted with the sight of a female thigh.

simply far more expensive, and far less essential, than it was in other Western nations.

But even if Dutch thriftiness *did* contribute to a preference for bikes over cars, was that—as Ortega y Gasset so vehemently proclaimed—a bad thing? Actually, what Ortega y Gasset regarded unfavorably as tightfistedness was most likely just a case of simple practicality.*

WHILE CAR OWNERSHIP was expensive and superfluous to most Hollanders, owning a car could also be expensive and superfluous to many Americans, yet that didn't prevent the latter from succumbing to the societal pressure to buy wheels. This enormous peer pressure was noted by the aforementioned Dutchman who had been strongly dissuaded from cycling in Washington, D.C., in 1912. He wrote:

> It's a question of uniformity, not of liberty. The principle of uniformity here is stronger than that of liberty. Everyone is expected to do what everyone else does. The smallest deviation from this law will be punished through the tacit disapproval by the combined humanity. He who doesn't want to believe this should try wearing a straw hat or a high hat in the "off season," or go strolling in a green tie while knowing that purple is in vogue.

*After Ortega y Gasset's notions were reprinted in a Dutch newspaper in 1936, one Dutchman penned a letter to the editor urging his countrymen to shrug off the Spaniard's attacks. "Let us not be intimidated by a foreigner. The next thing you know, a Frenchman will come along and ridicule us for not painting our lips."

In June 1925, the *Atlantic* magazine published an article titled "Confessions of an Automobilist," written by William Ashdown, a small-town banker whose bank specialized in car loans. Up front, he confessed, "I am careful and I am thrifty—at least I was until I became a motorist." Ashdown witnessed firsthand the epidemic of Americans of all income levels purchasing cars that stretched their budgets. He concluded:

> The avalanche of automobile-owners is not a good omen. It signifies that the people are living either up to their means or beyond them; that the old margin of safety no longer obtains; that the expense account must constantly increase. The race to outdo the other fellow is a mad race indeed. The ease with which a car can be purchased on the time-payment plan is all too easy a road to ruin. The habit of thrift can never be acquired through so wasteful a medium as an automobile. Instead, the habit of spending must be acquired, for with the constant demand for fuel, oil, and repairs, together with the heavy depreciation, the automobile stands unique as the most extravagant piece of machinery ever devised for the pleasure of man.

As Ashdown predicted, America's spree of buying on credit in the 1920s served as a bad omen; it foreshadowed the stock market crash and the Depression that followed. Yet despite his own sage insight, Ashdown remained a red-blooded American; he ended his 1925 article about the madness of mass car ownership by admitting: "But—I still drive one myself. I must keep up with the procession."

7
Problem Children: The 1930s

Seven months after arriving in Amsterdam, Amy Joy and I had to give up our apartment; it was slated for renovations. So we moved from Spaarndammerstraat to the city center. Our new place was a cramped studio apartment (we showered hovering over the toilet) on Spuistraat—the very street where the cyclist had slammed into me on my first day in Amsterdam. Despite its small size, our new digs had one amazing feature: three large windows that overlooked the street's heavily used bike path. Sitting in the window for hours on end, I watched the cycling parade pass by day and night, as I continued my field research.

The new apartment was also on the same street as the university building where I took my Dutch courses. In fact, the school building was so close, it probably would have taken only 90 seconds or so to walk the distance. The first time I stepped outside our new apartment building to head to class, I looked down the street at my destination. Then I looked across the street at my locked bike. Cycling such a short distance, of course, would be absolutely silly. I figured I'd probably spend more time unlocking and locking Brownie than actually riding him. Nevertheless, I stood frozen, my eyes fixed on the bike. It felt so unnatural to not just go and hop on him. So I convinced myself that I was running late for class. I crossed the street, grabbed Brownie and—for 20 seconds—rode down the block. From then on, the question of whether to commute to class by foot or by Brownie remained a no-brainer.

Of course, I wasn't the first person ever struck by such a fever. In 1930, one newspaper columnist illustrated the magnitude of what he termed Amsterdam's "cyclomania" by describing an office boy he knew who had been dispatched to post a letter. The closest place to send mail was at the nearby Spui Square tram stop.* But instead of just walking there, the office boy, gripped by this cyclomania, walked three minutes in the other direction to the cycle garage, where he retrieved his bike. Then, due to various traffic circumstances, he rode a roundabout route for six minutes to the tram stop. The errand that would've taken him three minutes on foot took him, by bike, nine minutes. But time mattered not to the youngster. The errand had allowed him to cycle, and that was far more important. And I could relate.

I hadn't thought it could be possible, but living in Amsterdam had made me even more pathological about cycling. Any excuse to ride, any reason to get on the bike, I eagerly grabbed. Amy Joy needed something from the market? Boom! Brownie and I were off to the store. Laundry needed washing? Bam! I was out the door to the laundromat. And even then, with the laundry bag strapped to my back, I often found myself cycling past

---

*At the time, mailboxes were affixed to the backsides of Amsterdam's trams, which tempted—or even dared—some risk takers to post mail while cycling. The last of the tram mailboxes were removed in 1971.

one laundromat after another, pedaling farther and farther from home just so I could ride and ride some more.

THE AMSTERDAM CYCLING explosion that commenced in the 1920s mushroomed in the 1930s. "The bicycle rage in the capital," noted one magazine writer in 1934, "has burst into a fury." Steadily, the number of bikes in the city grew annually by about 10,000. The origin of these new bikes was different, though. Whereas at the beginning of the 1920s, few new bikes sold in the Netherlands were of Dutch origins, throughout the 1920s the number of bike manufacturers in the country rose dramatically, as did their market share of bikes sold. By the early 1930s, virtually every new bike sold in the country—more than 99 percent—had been produced in the Netherlands.

Though Holland was gripped at the time by the worldwide Great Depression (or, as the Dutch call it, the "Crisis Years"), the poor economy had little adverse effect on the number of people cycling. In fact, as a means of transport that was relatively cheap (the average price of a new bike in Holland dropped steadily each year from 1919 till 1936, when it bottomed out at 27 guilders), the economic crisis actually helped to increase cycling. Some cyclists who'd fallen on hard times caught a break; unemployed heads of households were exempt from paying the annual bicycle tax. But tax plates for the unemployed came with a catch: a punched hole, which served as a rather public—and undesirable—pronouncement of the bike's owner's jobless status.

Not only did the number of bikes increase, but so, too, did the frequency of how often those bikes were ridden. The number of fair-weather cyclists—people who idled their bikes during rain,

snow or low temperatures—noticeably decreased. As the chief of
the traffic police pointed out in 1932, "How many people used
to put their bikes in storage once the bad weather began in October? Now that's no longer the case. Just one look at the traffic
during the winter months will convince you of this."

Adults weren't the only ones swept up in the bicycle rage.
Because the average price of a bike had dropped so low, many
parents could then afford bikes for their kids. The sight of children cycling quickly became the norm across the city. "If there
really is anything in all this talk about evolution," wrote one
Dutchman in 1933, "another century will see the Dutch children
coming into this world on tiny bicycles." Indeed, by this time
children were well accustomed from a very early age to riding on
bikes, if only as passengers. "As soon as they dare, mothers strap
their babies into a little seat on the bicycle and whiz away into
the thickest traffic," wrote one visitor to Amsterdam in 1934.
"Tiny children sit easily behind their parents, or in front, kan-
garoo fashion, experiencing no fright even in the most exciting
congestion."

In the mid-1930s, it was said that any six-year-old Amsterdammer without his or her own bike was considered "somewhat
backward." And so many youths were taught (by family members) how to cycle at such a young age that the city's bike-riding
schools suffered. With few adults left who didn't already know
how to cycle, one by one the cycling schools had folded. The
grand Velox cycling complex had already long since closed its
doors, back in 1904.* Fongers, the last remaining major cycling

---

*Afterward, the Velox building served as an art gallery and a boxing gym
before it was renovated and reopened in 1912 as the Zuiderbad swimming
pool—a name and function it retains more than a century later.

school, managed to hang on until 1936 before finally shutting down.

That an entire generation of the city's youths was being raised as cyclists—and not as tram passengers exclusively—terrified the director of the municipal public transit agency. "Considering it psychologically," he declared in 1934, "the tram will lose out in the long run because adolescents are unaccustomed to riding it!" Indeed, tram service was greatly affected by the continued growing popularity of the bicycle. As one observer put it: "The cyclists of Amsterdam are the Masters of the roadway and rule the traffic. The tram must comply with their wishes." At the time, it was said that a trip across the city that took fifteen minutes to make by bike took half an hour by tram. Trams rode at a "snail's pace" not only because they had to stop for passengers but also because they had to stop for anyone wishing to post mail. "Meanwhile," a reporter wrote, "the cheery, swift-pedaling cyclists race past."

At the beginning of the decade, a peak number of tram lines—25—crisscrossed the city (including the #22 line, which did nothing but circle Central Station). Within a couple of years, though, five lines were discontinued, due in no small part to Amsterdammers' growing preference for the tram's "pesky competitor"—the bicycle.

IN 1934, WITHIN the span of four months, Queen Wilhelmina's mother died, and then the queen's husband died. The loss of these two monumental figures in Wilhelmina's life seemed to have left her with a sense of liberation: shortly after those deaths, Queen Wilhelmina, now in her mid-50s, was more frequently spotted on her bike. But in contrast to her previous cycling outings—on royal grounds or along country lanes—Wilhelmina now regularly took to the streets of The Hague and cycled among the masses like any ordinary citizen.

According to a member of her staff, Wilhelmina cycled not only for the health benefits and as an expression of her simplicity but also as "a sign of her sincere desire to show herself as a true-blue Dutchwoman." That bond with the public was noted by an American reporter in 1938, who wrote: "Wearing a gray sweater and a battered felt hat, she rides a bicycle through the shaded streets of The Hague, indistinguishable from the least of her subjects, more truly at one with the people than any other monarch."

This "lady on the bicycle" was a curious figure to the international media, particularly to the American and British press. A queen cycling among her subjects challenged the image Yanks and Brits held of the stodgy propriety expected of royalty (as reflected by the pompous British monarchy). An American magazine reported:

Sitting very straight on her bicycle, an elderly lady—clad in a worn raincoat and a shapeless hat—was pedaling gravely down the Noordeinde, one of The Hague's busiest streets. Other cyclists paid no particular attention to her. At the modest white façade of the Royal Palace she turned into the gateway. Two policemen on the sidewalk and a sentry at the door stiffened to attention, and as she dismounted one of them stepped forward to help her. Imperiously she waved him aside, lifted the bicycle herself and put it into its rack. Adjusting her hat with one hand, her fur boa with the other—a gesture that reminded us of Tugboat Annie—she stalked with long strides into the building. It was Her Majesty, Queen Wilhelmina of the Netherlands.

When in Amsterdam, during her annual several-week stay at the Royal Palace on Dam Square, Wilhelmina wasn't known to cycle. Cycling in The Hague was one thing; cycling in the capital another. Nevertheless, she still got kicks from making excursions into civilian life. She'd leave the palace incognito to wander among Kalverstraat shoppers or to ride with tram commuters. Once, she left the palace on her own and made a beeline for the post office across the street to buy charitable postage stamps. Though a traffic cop commanded the disguised sovereign to wait before crossing, like the Amsterdammers she was trying to impersonate, Wilhelmina ignored his instructions, stepped off the curb—and was nearly run down by a cyclist.

THE CONTINUED GROWTH of cycling in 1930s Amsterdam occurred without the government assistance that many municipal bodies worldwide now employ to encourage urban biking. Unlike their modern-day counterparts, city authorities of the time didn't promote programs like "Bike to Work Day." They didn't offer tax incentives for purchasing a bike or for commuting by bike. They didn't even install sidewalk bike racks. In fact, Amsterdam's bike boom occurred largely despite city officials' indifference toward improving conditions for cyclists.

Although a terrific network of bike paths across the Dutch countryside accommodated touring cyclists, a great many of Amsterdam's streets—paved with bricks and cobblestones—remained obstacles for bike commuters. Some of the streets that had been asphalted weren't paved this way for the convenience of the cyclists but rather to help minimize a noise nuisance: the incessant rattling of cars and trucks. Only in the new residential districts constructed in the west of the city were some boulevards necessarily laid out with separated bike paths. In older parts of the city, bike lanes and separated bike paths remained rarities. And even where bike lanes *did* exist, they weren't always beneficial for cycling. For example, the Van Woustraat bike lanes, which in 1925 had been clogged with slow-moving pushcarts and horse-drawn traffic, were in 1937, according to one cyclist, clogged with "parked busses, cars with chicken coops, milk wagons, food scrap collector's carts, heating oil carts, vegetable trucks and bread carts."

While city officials did little to address the needs of cyclists, they did act on behalf of the small minority of residents who were motorists. In 1936, for example, the city council considered a measure to fill in part of the Rokin canal (just a few feet south of Dam Square) in order to accommodate cars. In the late 1800s and early 1900s, dozens of canals had been filled in for a variety of reasons, including to rid the city of the stench of trash-filled waters and to give the city "a more modern and worldly appearance." Now, in the 1930s, there was pressure to fill in canals with the aim of creating parking spaces for cars. When the council debated the question of converting the Rokin canal into a parking lot, Councilman Sol Mok gave an impassioned dissenting speech, which he ended by decrying the measure as an "attempt to Americanize a part of the city on behalf of the automobile traffic." The motion passed, though, and the canal was soon filled; for decades afterward, cars parked atop it.

WITH REGARD TO one Amsterdam street—Museumstraat—the *inaction* of municipal authorities actually benefited the city's bike riders. In the early 1880s, a new building—projected to be the largest in the nation—was set to rise on the edge of the city to house the national museum, the Rijksmuseum. Because the new building was going to be so imposing, as part of the deal in which the city provided land cheaply for its construction, the municipal government asked that it be built with a roadway leading through it to accommodate traffic between the city center and the planned residential neighborhoods to the south. In accordance with this agreement, architect Pierre Cuypers designed a passageway through the center of the museum that would be as lavish as the rest of the ornate building. The tunnel—lined with two rows of twelve columns each that supported brick-lined, vaulted ceilings—was decorated with mosaics, reliefs and uplifting texts like "Cheeky chattering is useless and idle" and "Art is long, life short." Halfway through, on either side, light shone in from the arched, glassed openings that looked into the museum's two interior courtyards.

As intended, after this unique street opened in September 1896, it served as a vital traffic artery between the city center and the new neighborhoods of the Museum Quarter, the Vondelpark area and beyond. But the passageway had been designed at a time when non-foot traffic consisted of horse-drawn vehicles. By the 1920s automobiles and trucks dominated the tunnel's roadway—much to the trepidation and frustration of the cyclists. The terrific acoustics (which would later make the corridor a favored haunt of busking musicians) created a nerve-racking echo chamber for the clamor of automobile engines and horns. One Amsterdam cyclist, in 1920, appealed for more oversight of the "helter-skelter-driven cars" in the passageway that threatened cyclists and caused accidents. In 1925, another cyclist foisted upon the chief of police the following dream:

> Seated on a bike, you go for a ride under the Rijksmuseum. In that dark passageway, wild-howling monsters with two shimmering eyes come toward you. You retreat to the side and—gasping—you pedal toward the gleam of light yonder that signifies exit and salvation. Roaring behind you are new monstrosities who, with unbridled speed, are breathing down your neck. The behemoths draw closer and closer. In your dream, with a heart that threatens to burst, you pant to the yonder lighted point—to no avail. The monster shows no mercy; it wants past you, or over you. Its voice fills the vaults with such raucous shrieks of hunger that, up in the middle gallery above you, out of fear, d'Hondecoeter's pheasants flee from the canvas and flutter like bats into the *Schuttersmaaltijd.*[*]
>
>   Listen, right behind you! Beside you! You slip . . . you fall . . .

Upon waking from such a nightmare, the author was convinced the police chief would immediately take action to curtail the excesses of the motorized traffic in the passageway.

Rijksmuseum officials also detested the cars and trucks that passed through the museum. In addition to the noise that

---

[*]The "bird pieces" of Melchior d'Hondecoeter (1636–95) and the *Schutters- maaltijd* (*Banquet of the Amsterdam Civic Guard in Celebration of the Peace of Münster*) by Bartholomeus van der Helst (1613–70) hung in the gallery directly above the passageway.

reverberated into the galleries, the heavy, rumbling vehicles shook the building. As a result, inside the passageway, walls cracked, the ceiling crumbled, columns were dislodged, the glass of the light fixtures jostled and broke. In the gallery above, terrazzo floors cracked. And—partly because motor vehicles regularly crashed into the sides of the narrow, arched portals while entering or exiting the corridor—the façades above the portals developed deep fissures.

While cyclists called for motorized traffic under the museum to be tamed by a lowered speed limit, Frederik Schmidt-Degener, the director of the Rijksmuseum, wished to ban *all* through traffic—including cyclists—and annex the tunnel into the museum proper. As it was, at the ground level the passageway split the museum in two. The longtime museum director dreamed of not only converting the passageway into a grand, traffic-free entrance to the museum (which the building lacked) but also of using the space as a gift shop, a restaurant, a lecture hall and/or a reception hall.

But because the passageway was a public right-of-way, any alterations to its function required the approval of the city government. In 1928, when museum director Schmidt-Degener requested a total traffic ban, Mayor de Vlugt replied that, in regard to the cyclists who would be affected, such a ban would be "met by great opposition and [would] be regarded as an unpopular deed." While the city government resisted the call for a complete closure of the passageway, it did agree to ban cars and trucks. This prohibition went into effect on November 3, 1931. On that morning, it was noted that while the motor vehicles had to circumnavigate the building, "the cyclists jauntily chose their path: straightforward through the archway." Soon thereafter,

Schmidt-Degener professed that the galleries of the museum, now freed from the "years-long abuse" of rumbling traffic, had become "a place of tranquility." And because its roadway became solely the domain of the cyclists, the resplendent Rijksmuseum passageway was suddenly transformed into, arguably, the world's most remarkable bicycle path.

For several days in July 1936, the passageway was closed to bike and pedestrian traffic and converted into a reception area for the opening night of the museum's "Old Art Exhibition." Persian rugs covered the corridor's roadway, Gobelin tapestries hung from between the columns and the space was decorated with an abundance of flowers and palms. Musicians played "soft music." Many of the nearly 1,000 reception attendees—dressed in formal attire—were greatly impressed by the "architecturally exceptional, lovely space." It was said that many of those in attendance that night fantasized: "If only this could be incorporated into the museum once and for all!" One who shared—if not championed—that fantasy was director Schmidt-Degener, whose long-held desire to annex the space was finally realized, if only fleetingly. Days after the reception, the space reverted back to a throughway for cyclists and pedestrians, which led Schmidt-Degener to complain that the passageway's

> charming architecture isn't getting its due. When the cor-
> ridor was closed off . . . its three sections—in a harmonic
> composition of columns and arches—made an impression of
> awe and veneration. Presently, the passageway is a gather-
> ing place for rubbish, a play area for screaming youth and a
> raceway for cyclists.

Two weeks after the reception, Schmidt-Degener penned a letter to the nation's minister of education, art and science arguing that—because several Amsterdam *wethouders* had warmed to the idea of permanently incorporating the passageway into the museum—they should "strike now while the iron is hot" in order to "make the long-cherished desire a reality." Schmidt-Degener argued that by banishing the cyclists from the passageway and incorporating it into the building itself, the result would create "a majestic entrance to our national collections—as a reception area of the greatest magnitude—that would place our most notable government institution at the forefront among European museums."

This latest plea to ban the cyclists from the building—like those that came before it and many that would follow—fell upon deaf ears. The passageway would remain the dominion of the cyclists for decades to come.

ONE PRESSING ISSUE that the city faced in the 1930s was where to store all these hundreds of thousands of bikes. At the time, the sidewalk bike rack was a virtually unknown entity. Many cyclists simply parked their bikes anywhere possible. And since the typical bike lacked a kickstand, any stationary object became fair game for cyclists to lean their two-wheelers against.

In 1935, a visitor to Amsterdam noted, "Clumps of cycles round the trees and lampposts outside the Royal Palace are typical of the scenes in the capital." The previous year, a newspaper account reported: "Glittering bikes and gloomy bikes, fancy bikes and ordinary bikes, men's bikes and women's bikes: there is almost no spot in Amsterdam that is lacking a resting bicycle." The outer walls of many residential and commercial buildings supported rows of bikes three, four or five deep. Near the Grimburgwal bridge, the great number of bicycles that coagulated at the entrance to the municipal university were said to haunt the place like a "threatening ghost" since it was impossible to wade through them without a bike part snagging and ripping one's clothing.

In the city's residential districts, bikes cluttered the sidewalks because their owners simply had no other place to park them. A great many people lived in buildings where the only access to their apartments was via narrow, steep stairwells. These typically Dutch staircases, with their ladderlike grades, were hardly suitable for hauling weighty bikes up and down on a regular basis. Even more unsuitable for daily bike parking were the storage units in many such apartment buildings: high up in the attics.

All those bikes left out on the sidewalks not only hampered the pedestrian passageway but also provided thieves with easy pickings. Anyone who wanted to ensure that their bike would still be waiting for them in the morning was left to simply lock the bike and then hope and pray a thief didn't pinch it during the night.

In 1932, one newspaper reporter illustrated the problem of bike parking by describing an apartment-dwelling family of four whose only option for the safekeeping of their bikes was to hang them in the stairwell. The reporter went on:

> We are the nation of cyclists. You have horse people;
> Americans are a car people; the Norwegians live on skis.
> The Dutchman is seated on a bicycle, yet has no storage
> space for his steel steed. The Netherlands is a land of the art
> of construction; we modernized international architecture.

But we've forgotten our bikes. Would the Arabian forget his mustang? Henry Ford his little Ford?

This great need for bicycle storage eventually sparked a new enterprise, one that took off in the 1930s: the cycle garage. Throughout many residential districts, small private garages popped up in ground-floor storefront locations. Here, a rack to securely store one's bike could be rented by the month. For many bike owners, the cycle garages were godsends. "Without bike thieves, the cycle garages would have few customers. Without the cycle garages, the bike thieves would have no rest," wrote one satisfied bike owner in 1934. "The man who first came up with the idea to store bikes for pay was simply a genius and he deserves a bust in a bicycle museum."

Some office buildings and bank buildings contained large cycle garages that could house hundreds of employees' bikes during the workday. Though Central Station also had large cycle garages, Amsterdam's main train station—already legendary as the nation's greatest bike magnet—was plagued in the 1930s by the unceasing problem of too many bikes and not enough accommodations for them all. It was an issue that would persist for decades.

IF SCHOOLCHILDREN ON bikes were the sheep of Amsterdam's street traffic, then, as one newspaper writer put it, the wolves were the *fietsjongens*—the bike boys. These young men—usually 14 to 20 years old, often clad in white cloth jackets—delivered goods by bike. Some used transport bikes that had a heavy-duty frame with a rack over the front wheel that usually supported a huge rectangular wicker basket for carrying goods. Others rode on three-wheeled, elongated *bakfietsen*, which had a large wooden box in front for carrying cargo. Production of three-wheeled *bakfietsen* more than tripled between 1929 and 1933, the mid-1930s being the peak years of their manufacture.

Just about any business enterprise that needed commodities to be transported across town employed *fietsjongens*: florists' delivery boys rode with "ceremonious floral pieces or airy bouquets in slender vases"; delicatessen delivery boys rode with "baskets full of fruit and canned preserves"; laundry delivery boys rode with stacks of folded laundry. But especially notable—and notorious— among the *fietsjongens* were the *slagersjongens* (butcher's boys) and *bakkersjongens* (baker's boys), or as one observer of the era called them, "the cannibals of the roadway." Due to their frenetic riding, *fietsjongens* were regarded as "very powerful kings—albeit with anarchistic principles."

In the pages of the city's newspapers, letters to the editor often complained about the potential dangers caused by, for example, "the young man [cycling] through the heart of the city, hauling on his shoulder four hollow zinc pipes, each twelve to fifteen feet long," "a shop servant with a divan on his back . . . pedaling along Weteringschans" or *bakkersjongens* riding with "four, five, six cake boxes stacked atop one another." One writer spoke of *fietsjongens* hauling "flower pots, hat boxes, suitcases, or floor lamps . . . who, with both hands in their pockets, whistle as they cut off a car. They have a contempt for death like a soldier who has grown old in the trenches. . . . Silently they sneak up on [pedestrians] from behind and then shoot right past them with a one-centimeter clearance." About the "much-maligned, fast-riding butcher boy," one Amsterdammer conceded in 1932, "It's true he misses you by the width of a hair, but that's just enough to keep you out of the hospital."

In addition to couriers, tradesmen were also noteworthy for their use of bikes; many cycled with their tools and supplies to their job sites. Window washers rode with ladders and pails, bricklayers rode with buckets of mortar and house painters rode with pails of paint.* When the English author Aldous Huxley visited Amsterdam, he was greatly impressed by the skill displayed by the cycling delivery boys and tradesmen. Huxley wrote:

> Messenger boys think nothing of taking two cubic meters
> of parcels. Dairymen do their rounds on bicycles specially
> constructed to accommodate two hundred-quart bottles of
> milk in a tray between the two wheels. I have seen nursery
> gardeners carrying four palms and a dozen of potted chrys-
> anthemums on their handle-bars. . . . The most daring feats
> of the circus and the music hall are part of the quotidian
> routine in Amsterdam.

ONE FOREIGNER, WHO became confounded while watching the traffic scene in Amsterdam in 1930, threw up his hands and exclaimed to a Dutchman, "You people do everything— and I mean *everything*—on the bicycle!" By "everything," the

---

*Later, in 1964, a United Press International wire story describing Amsterdam's cycling tradesmen ran in several American newspapers. Published during the very period when civil rights workers were being lynched in the American South, the article contained this repulsive line: "The cyclist who is black with soot and has a rope around his neck is not on the way to a lynching party—he's a chimney sweep."

Dutchman understood the foreigner to mean that Amsterdammers "made love" on their bikes. In fact, during the 1930s, it wasn't hard to miss the many cyclists who were flirting, courting, wooing, spooning and canoodling on the city's streets. "Naturally," remarked one concerned member of Parliament about embracing cyclists, "their thoughts are then on things other than the bike or the threat of the cars."

The physical contact of such lovemaking took a variety of forms; observers reported seeing:

- "courting couples . . . pedaling along, arm in arm, on bicycles, toward a blissful future" (1933).
- "a pretty young girl riding beside her escort and coyly holding on to the handlebars of his bicycle" (1934).
- "lovers (the girl resting her hand on the man's arm)" (1935).
- "couples holding hands riding nonchalantly" (1936).
- "the male party riding with his right hand on the handlebars of the girl's bicycle [and] a kiss passing from one bike to the other" (1937).
- "a maid and a youth, holding each other by the pinkies and pedaling merrily" (1938).

The American author of a 1928 guidebook to Holland recalled seeing a cyclist in a "frock coat" who was "a round little person in a black swallow-tail, with a derby cocked rakishly over one eye . . . riding along beside his lady-love and they were holding hands." The author proclaimed the sight "delicate and inspiring." Such passionate cycling apparently didn't always involve two human sweethearts. In 1939, an Amsterdammer wrote: "The life's motto of Dutch men appears to be: 'My bicycle is my best friend.' . . . Even the love for a woman comes in second place for a Dutchman. If he must walk with her, the bicycle often goes along between them, scraping the shinbones of each."

Flirting on a bike was the subject of a diary entry when, in June 1942, thirteen-year-old Anne Frank, not yet in hiding, described her own technique:

> As soon as a boy asks if he can cycle home with me and we start talking, nine times out of ten I can be sure he'll immediately fall head over heels in love and simply won't let me out of his sight. Of course, in time, the infatuation dies down, especially since I ignore his passionate glances and cheerfully pedal onward. If it ever gets so bad that they start babbling about "asking Father's permission," I swerve slightly on my bike and my satchel falls. For the sake of propriety, the young man gets off and hands the bag to me, by which time I've changed the subject.

Vondelpark, naturally, was a favored location for lovey-dovey cycling, though it was also practiced on virtually every street in the city, much to the disdain of some. One such sourpuss was city councilman Zeeger Gulden, the man who had unsuccessfully proposed a ban on cycling in the city center in 1923. At a 1933 council meeting, Gulden railed against "courting cyclists who ride hand in hand," who, he argued, were so distracted by their lovemaking that their inattentiveness to their surroundings obstructed traffic and posed dangers not only to themselves but also to those around them. In all sincerity, Gulden proposed the police "put an end to this evil." Gulden's colleagues on the council responded immediately—with laughter. One shouted: "Let the sun shine in the water!"—a Dutch expression that teasingly accused Gulden of being envious. Straightaway, the mayor dismissed Gulden's proposal. Outlaw cyclist hand-holding in Amsterdam? The notion was preposterous.

Gulden may have been heartened when, in the mid-1930s, the nation was swept by a sudden boom in the sale of tandem bikes. More couples were now cruising less obtrusively by pedaling together on single bikes. The tandem craze was in full effect when Crown Princess Juliana—the only heir to Queen Wilhelmina—became engaged in September 1936. Soon afterward, news photographer Simon Smit requested that Princess Juliana and her betrothed, Prince Bernhard, allow him to photograph the couple riding a tandem around the grounds of The Hague's Noordeinde Palace. Juliana and Bernhard agreed. From a bike shop a few blocks from the palace, Smit rented a Gazelle tandem for 50 cents an hour. Naturally, as future monarch, Juliana rode in front, steered and sat higher in the saddle than her fiancé. The resulting photos of the happy, confident cycling couple ran on the front pages of Dutch newspapers the following day and in newspapers around the world in the days thereafter. The publicity of the love match was said to have raised the spirits of the Dutch populace during the Great Depression.

After the photo shoot, Prince Bernhard presumed the tandem was an engagement gift from the citizens of The Hague and tried to keep it. Smit, already eager to return the tandem to the bike shop before he had to pay an additional hour's rental, pleaded with Bernhard to give it back. The future husband of the future queen grew visibly disappointed by the situation. Then—and only with some reluctance—Bernhard finally relinquished the bike.[*]

IF THERE WAS a single day of the year when courtship by bicycle was most common, it was "Bulb Sunday"—the first warm and sunny Sunday of the spring blossoming season. On Bulb Sundays throughout the 1920s and '30s, enormous processions of Amsterdammers streamed westward from the city bound for Holland's famed flower bulb fields.

Many traveled by foot, by train or by car to the bulb fields, but the most popular manner in which the pilgrimage was made was by bike. In 1931, one reporter observed preparations in Amsterdam on the morning of Bulb Sunday: "In fashionable quarters and in old, narrow back streets alike, they polish up their 250,000 bicycles, old bikes and brand new ones; they pump up their 500,000 tires and hastily patch up old inner tubes which gave out at the last moment." Unlike those on foot, cyclists could reach a wider range of fields. And unlike those in cars, cyclists could bypass the traffic congestion and access narrow paths between the fields.

One Bulb Sunday observer claimed that the "courting couples cycling side-by-side, chatting and cooing" were "poets of the

---

[*]Prince Bernhard's greediness further came to light in the 1970s when it was revealed that—while married to one of the richest women in the world—he had accepted more than $1 million in bribes from Lockheed to influence the Dutch government's purchase of military aircraft from that company. A popular joke of the time went: A man parks his bike in front of the Soestdijk Palace. A guard immediately tells him, "Sir, you shouldn't park your bike here." "Why not?" asks the man. "Because Prince Bernhard is coming," replies the guard. "It's all right," the man says, "I locked my bike."

street and—like the true beacons of humanity—proclaimers of spring." In addition to lovebirds, entire families and social organizations (boy scouts, college sororities, church groups, etc.) paraded to the fields with "flags on the handlebars, bike bags packed full with provisions." Men rode with their jackets strapped to the rear racks, their pant legs rolled up. Women rode in airy, short-sleeved dresses, "many with bare legs." Boys pedaled in short pants "to make it easier for their legs to move." Girls wore summer clothes, even sweat suits. Dogs rode in wicker baskets. People sang joyfully as they cycled. "Everyone is gay," wrote one observer in 1938, "everyone eager for the first glimpse of the lovely fields of color." Another described 1934's Bulb Sunday as a "battlefield of human hordes versus the millions of flowers."

Along the way, hundreds of vendors lined the roads and bike paths selling cut hyacinths, daffodils, crocuses and tulips. The real cash crop was the bulbs themselves (at the time, Holland annually shipped to the United States more than *a hundred million* tulip bulbs). The flowers that sprouted before the bulb harvest were treated as a negligible by-product and sold to passersby for mere pennies. Children sat along the roadside threading string through daffodil heads to create garlands. "And whenever a bicycle . . . approached," wrote one witness, "up like a shot went a hand—or a little hand—and waved, and the flowers waved with it." Peddlers—crying out their bargain prices—also used long poles to hold out the garlands to cyclists rushing past. And if a cyclist "wanted nothing from the first ten flower sellers, then—inwardly enticed by the eleventh and twelfth—he or she bought something from the twentieth."

Other popular roadside hawkers were those pushing ice-cream cones, lemonade, orangeade and admissions to lookout towers—wooden structures that offered bird's-eye views of the patchwork of red/blue/white/orange/yellow/purple-hued fields and from where the spectator was "bombarded with more beauty than the human eye could cope with." Just among the various fields of red tulips, observers reported seeing shades of "soft-red," "wine-red," "glowing-red," "bright-red," "burning-red" and "blood-red." One Bulb Sunday celebrant said a field of white hyacinths looked like "a pasture overflowing with snow, like in the Alps of Switzerland." In addition to the feast for the eyes was the feast for the nose. "The intoxicating fumes of the flower fields," wrote one journalist, created an "affectionate atmosphere for the courting couples." Or, as another observer unabashedly asserted: it was an "orgy of color and scent."

Upon reaching their destinations, revelers picnicked, frolicked and lounged among the flowers. And though the blooms themselves were a popular tourist attraction (tour buses and express trains arrived from as far as Belgium, Germany and France; American cars with American license plates were even spotted), a still more rousing sight appeared at the day's end, when the processions of "dusty, hot, and happy" cyclists returned to Amsterdam. Jovial decorations adorned every bicycle (and if we're to believe numerous testimonials from the 1920s and '30s, it was *every* bicycle). The vivid flowers wrapped around handlebars, entwined frames and wove through spokes. Wicker baskets fastened to handlebars sagged under the weight of so many blossoms. Cyclists' hats were trimmed with flowers, their heads crowned with wreaths. Garlands dangled from necks; sashes were strapped across chests. Small boys were "literally festooned" with flowers. "But the most beautiful," wrote one reporter, "were the girls, their arms full of flowers, their faces glowing in the spring sunshine."

THE HECTIC TRAFFIC in the flower region so exasperated one 1933 Bulb Sunday cyclist, she declared, "It's just like Leidseplein here." At the time, one could not invoke a hustle and bustle any better than by declaring it akin to Leidseplein—the square at the heart of Amsterdam's entertainment district. If it wasn't already immediately obvious that Leidseplein was teeming with traffic, then it was made clear when, in October 1930, the city conducted a massive and thorough traffic count.

On two weekdays, almost 3,000 high school and college students were posted at about 250 intersections throughout the city. From 6:30 a.m. till 6:30 p.m., they counted the number of people who passed each spot via foot, tram, car, motorcycle or bike. "Good Lord," exclaimed one traffic enumerator with my dream job, "is there anyone left in Amsterdam who doesn't cycle?"

During that twelve-hour stretch, almost 30,000 cyclists were tallied passing through the tiny intersection where Leidsestraat meets Leidseplein. Incredibly, between 8:45 and 9:00 a.m., some 1,100 cyclists squeezed through that space smaller than half a tennis court; for 15 minutes straight, enumerators had noted one cyclist every .82 seconds.

So when it came time for Amsterdam to install its first traffic signal, the lively Leidseplein was an obvious choice of locale. On the morning of Monday, October 17, 1932, at the central Leidseplein intersection where Kleine Gartmanplantsoen meets Marnixstraat, and with Mayor Willem de Vlugt and Police Chief H. J. Versteeg presiding, the signals commenced operation. One traffic cop stood in the intersection directing traffic while, on the sidewalk, two others operated "a secretive green switchboard box" to control the traffic lights by hand. Other traffic cops explained the meaning of the lights' colors to those waiting in cars and on bikes.

Since the new signals stood in front of the Stadsschouwburg—Amsterdam's municipal theater—*De Telegraaf* treated the news like a theatrical opening: "This morning was the first performance of the famous play 'Green-Yellow-Red.' . . . The troupe that performed was large and the number of roles innumerable. In general, it can be said the production was a success and that the lighting most satisfactory."

Gerrit Brinkman, Amsterdam's first traffic cop, from twenty years earlier, was once again present for a grand day out—as were many others. Though traffic lights were by then already commonplace in American cities, on this day in Amsterdam they were all the rage. So many pedestrians lined the sidewalks and so many motorists repeatedly drove back and forth through the intersection, Brinkman reported, that it made him "think back to my first day on the job in 1912."

Some in the Leidseplein crowd, though, felt duped by the extravaganza. "Amsterdammers who had taken to the streets . . . were nastily disappointed by the appearance of an army of tax officers accompanied by policemen," wrote one eyewitness. The bicycles of the many "unsuspecting cyclists" were scrutinized; those without a current tax plate were impounded. "First they lure you to the city center under false pretenses," complained one cyclist, "and then they pinch your bike!"

In the following months and years, traffic lights were installed at other intersections around the city. One newspaper claimed "a slight improvement" could be discerned in cycling behavior because now, instead of operating stop signs, "the traffic police have been freed up to pay more attention to the misconduct of His Majesty, The Cyclist." Ultimately, though, cyclists proved casual in obeying the lights. In 1936, one journalist asserted,

"It's a recognized fact that cycling Amsterdam still doesn't fully respect the traffic lights." Many cyclists started through the intersection as soon as the cross street's light turned yellow; others disregarded the red signal altogether. On November 17, 1936, after a police crackdown, one hundred cyclists were tried en masse for running red lights. All were found guilty and each fined five guilders.*

IN 1937, AFTER the launch of a civic campaign to reduce car honking in Amsterdam, C. A. Castrikum—a taxi driver with 28 years of experience—wrote a letter to the newspaper *Het Volk* contending that the motorists weren't responsible for the honking. The guilty parties, Castrikum argued, were the targets of their honking: the cyclists. He claimed it was "hard to imagine there's a city . . . where there's such a disorderly mob as the cyclists here in Amsterdam. . . . Stop at a traffic light and in no time you're surrounded by the cyclists who should yield to you when the light changes. But instead, they remain in front of you for as long as possible, preventing you from passing." Concurring with Castrikum was an Amsterdammer who wrote in 1938 that the cyclist "has done more for the spreading of foul language among motorists than all the greasy sparkplugs and flat tires combined."

Several years earlier, the newspaper *Het Algemeen Handelsblad* had complained about cyclists' refusal to ride as far to the right

---

*Amsterdam's cyclists were even more lawless when it came to a new traffic code that mandated each bicycle have a rear light. In July 1938, six months after the national law had taken effect, *De Telegraaf* reported that fully half of all bikes in Amsterdam still lacked a rear light. The newspaper condemned this "dangerous and equally ridiculous situation" as "intolerable."

of the roadway as possible. An editor further griped: "Also, when high schools or factories or workplaces let out, the cyclists ride in fours, fives or sixes beside each other without regard to the cars behind them." The newspaper's call for the enactment of new traffic laws to curb such undesirable road behavior was, ultimately, in vain. In 1930, *Het Algemeen Handelsblad* was left to concede: "Proper traffic discipline like there is in many major foreign cities will, in Amsterdam, with its intense bicycle traffic, never be possible." In 1937, chief of traffic police Claas Bakker—the man in charge of overseeing the conduct of cyclists on the city's streets—lamented that Amsterdam "has, among the cities of the world, its unique problem: you know it, the [cyclists]. They are our problem children."

If these problem children bothered and irked their fellow Amsterdammers—particularly those who drove—then they completely distressed and infuriated foreigners who dared to drive in the city. Throughout the 1920s and '30s, so many visiting motorists reacted with alarm to Dutch cyclists that one journalist at the time joked: "A story goes that a foreign tourist spent two full days in our country . . . without making a single remark about the number of cyclists that he came across everywhere he went. Of course, no one believes it."

One French tourist in the 1930s noted that Dutch cities provided "unexpected complications" for driving, such as canals and bridges and "the millions of cyclists about whose actions, at any moment, no one can be certain." This led him to proclaim that he who could successfully drive in a city in Holland could drive absolutely anywhere. While another Frenchman, in 1928, called Amsterdam's cyclists "the nightmare of the motorists," a Swiss driver, stuck in traffic among a long queue of Dutch cyclists in

1929, was at such an utter loss, he muttered repeatedly to his Dutch passenger: "Dreadful . . . dreadful . . ."

An Englishman who visited Amsterdam noted:

> The bicycle rules the road in Holland. I have talked to browbeaten automobile owners who assured me that a cyclist can do no wrong. I do know that there are few things in the way of human emotion to equal the look of scorn and indignation on the face of a Dutch cyclist if an automobile gets in his way.

Of course, among all foreign motorists, those who were most affected by the cyclists were the über-motorists: the Americans. For example, in 1928, one American wrote:

> [T]raffic in Holland . . . is as completely dominated by [the bicycle] as in America it is dominated by the automobile. . . . [T]he Dutch cyclist is even more indifferent to the rights of others than is the American taxi driver.
>
> With that superb stolidity for which the Dutch have always been famous, the bicyclers in that country even extend their scorn to automobiles. They know that they have the right-of-way, and that even though motorists may dearly wish to run them down, they dare not do so. With an almost American desire of wishing to show their independence, the cyclists will ride in the middle of a narrow road and pay no more attention to the honking of the motorist behind than would our own country people in buggies in the old days before flivvers had become universal.

When the top dog of the Masonic Lodge of America, John Henry Cowles, visited Amsterdam in the summer of 1935, he remarked:

It took us two days to cease remarking about the thousands of wheels, rushing hither and thither, apparently oblivious to the autos. The chauffeurs must look out for the cyclists, who dodge in and out with no thought of the morrow. It is enough to scare an American into hysterics.

In 1938, an American journalist recalled his Dutch adventure:

Most vivid recollection of that country was the city of Amsterdam at half past five of a summer's evening. The streets were a mass of whirring wheels accompanied by a symphony of tinkering bells, as thousands of working people started for home over two wheels each. . . . [W]e tried to thread our way through the maze of cyclists that day. Our American driver's annoyance was audible as bicycles took the right-of-way at every turn.

To be fair, though, not *all* Americans of the period felt annoyed, hysterical or scorned upon encountering the city's cyclists. In 1937, Sarah Williams Bosman, an American who resided in Amsterdam, sent a letter to the *New York Times* praising European living. She wrote:

In America I had my own car. In Amsterdam I have never missed it. I have my bicycle. Revisiting America I could not help but notice the enormous amount of automobile traffic.

It was as much as my life was worth, I felt, to cross a street. I prefer dodging the bicycles of Amsterdam.

In any case, no matter the nationality of the motorist—Dutch, French, Swiss, English or American—in the decade that followed, the 1940s, a different nationality of drivers would descend upon Amsterdam, one whose outspoken reaction to the cyclists would far surpass any that preceded them. These foreigners would become the motorists most irritated—if not enraged—by the cyclists of Amsterdam. And those bitter feelings would be reciprocated . . .

8

Which One's the Wrench?: The Settling Down

By the end of my first year in Amsterdam, I had completed my schooling and—thanks to my Irish grandparents— had gained Irish citizenship. As an Irishman, I could legally remain living in Amsterdam. By now, though, Amy Joy was in the country illegally. In order to make her legit, I needed to have legal employment; any job would do. My job prospects appeared bleak, though. No employer in Amsterdam needed an inexperienced urban planner whose Dutch was far from fluent. So, in order to help make our dream a reality, I took the first job I found, as a janitor.

The job was at two locations. One was a janitor's worst nightmare: a concrete plant. From my perspective, it was little more than a dust factory. Any surface I wiped clean was—within seconds—coated again in dust. The other job site was a depot for garbage trucks and street-sweeping machines. Many of the garbagemen and street sweepers were immigrants from Turkey, Morocco and Ghana. Mine was the ultimate bottom-rung immigrant job: I cleaned up after the immigrants who cleaned the city.

During those first days of employment, my work pace

became the subject of much discussion at both my workplaces. Concerned parties were eager to point out that I was working much too fast. In America, I was so often admonished for being a sluggish worker; now, in Amsterdam, I was rebuked for working *too hard*. I was happy to accept the advice of these concerned folks and soon adopted a far more relaxed working tempo. The new pace allowed me time to gather up copies of the Dutch newspapers that the garbagemen had brought back to the lunchroom and take them to my broom closet, which afforded me just enough space to sit and pore over the newspapers. Each day I huddled in my closet for hours, with my Dutch-English dictionary at hand, and searched through the newspapers for articles on my three topics of interest: Amsterdam cycling, Amsterdam city planning and Amsterdam history. In this regard, I had success most days. If my luck was really good, I'd strike gold: a single article that covered all three topics.

The photos of bicyclists responding to weather conditions became another favorite. For example, if it had been rainy, a newspaper was apt to publish a shot of a cyclist riding with an umbrella. If there had been a real downpour? Then a photo of cyclists lifting their legs as their bikes waded through a deep puddle sufficed. Windy? Cyclists on foot struggling to push their bikes into the wind. Hot? Cyclists splashing over a bridge being cooled by water. Chilly? Cyclists so bundled up only their eyes are visible. Snowy? Snow-covered cyclists trudging through snowfall. Icy? Cyclists wiping out on black ice.* *Extremely* icy? A picture of discarded bikes lying atop a frozen canal.

---

*It always feels creepy to see this kind of wipeout photo: the photographer must stand near the icy spot in question and, instead of warning cyclists, wait for a biker to slip and crash so that the moment can be captured on camera.

After my first week on the job, many of the dozens of people at both job sites that I regularly came into contact with expressed curiosity about why an American would be working as a janitor in Amsterdam. Each time, I smiled and gave my now standard reply: "Zo ik midden in de nacht in een fietsfile terecht kan komen." "So I can be stuck in a bicycle traffic jam at midnight." This only created confusion, and not clarification. The questioners expected to hear me say something about a job or a relationship and were confused when I'd say that I moved to the city because of bicycles. To them, bicycles were as natural as air or water—and hardly anything special.

EACH DAY, WHEN I got off work in mid-afternoon, I tooled around the city on my bike, keeping an eye out for cycling nuns, checking in on the *zwijntjesjagers* at the Grimburgwal bridge or enjoying a late lunch at the very top of the three-story Central Station bike garage. Oftentimes I sought out any neighborhoods I hadn't yet been to in my quest to photograph all of the city's 200 or so bike shops.

We had no TV or Internet access in our apartment. So in order to try to improve my Dutch, as well as to better understand this culture I was living in, I started going to the movie theaters to watch Dutch films once or twice a week. Mostly, however, I paid attention to how cycling was portrayed in these films. Rarely was I disappointed, since pretty much every Dutch film I saw contained some sort of cycling scene. For example, in *Turks Fruit* (*Turkish Delight*)—considered the greatest Dutch film ever (in both commercial and critical terms)—after the lead couple get married at the old city hall on Oudezijds Voorburgwal, they joyously set off on the groom's bike with the bride seated on the rear rack. Riding across Dam Square and then, later, down Vijzelgracht, the two swerve back and forth through traffic, much to the annoyance of a driver who is desperately trying to pass them. The frustrated driver repeatedly honks his horn and calls them idiots, all to the delight of the blissful couple. Eventually the dinking pair cycle straight through an open door into a liquor store. Within a year, I watched more than a hundred Dutch films. When any Netherlander learned this, he or she usually first expressed disbelief and then sympathy, saying this figure was about a hundred more than the number of Dutch films he'd ever seen.

I also spent my postwork afternoons sitting and watching the cyclists while carefully tallying any number of their noteworthy characteristics. For example, intrigued by the fact that so many Amsterdammers ate while cycling, I kept track of their tastes. The most popular food item consumed, by far, was apples; they outnumbered the second-place item, ice-cream cones, three-to-one. These were followed by (in descending order of popularity) sandwiches, croissants, ice-cream bars, Popsicles and bananas. While the frozen treats were a staple in the warmer months, by no means did they drop out of the cycling diet during the colder months.

As for drinking, among 200 cyclists who were in the act of swilling either beer or water while riding, beer edged out as the favorite beverage (104 versus 96). And among chairs being transported on bikes, folding chairs were tops, while bar stools made a surprisingly strong second-place showing, followed by plastic patio chairs, dining table chairs and rocking chairs.

Even more fascinating to me was breaking down the cyclists' characteristics by gender. Some features of Amsterdam bike riding in which females dominated:

- Cycling with an open umbrella. Among 1,000 umbrella holders, 61 percent (606 total) were women. (Among those tallied were one woman and one man who each, separately, cycled with umbrellas on warm, sunny days.)
- Cycling while talking into a cell phone. Among 1,000 cell phone chatterers, 57 percent (572 total) were females.
- Cycling with children as passengers. Among 1,000 child haulers, 72 percent (716 total) were women. (However, on the weekends, the percentage of men hauling kids on bikes greatly increased.)
- Cycling with decorative plastic flowers attached to a bike. Among 1,000 florally enriched bikes, 91 percent (908 total) were pedaled by females. Of the few bikes adorned with actual cut flowers, a majority were, interestingly, ridden by men. Were the bikes of these men decorated by female spouses/lovers (as, more than once, Amy Joy had done to my own bike in the past)? Or were these men bringing flowers to their loved ones?
- Cycling with dogs as passengers. Among 1,000 dog chauffeurs, 63 percent (632 total) were female. Dogs generally sat in baskets or even perched on the rear rack, though some smaller dogs rode tucked into a cyclist's zipped-up jacket with only their heads peeking out the top. (While far fewer cats were transported by bike, of the 30 people spotted cycling with felines in cat carriers, 18 were male.)

Males, on the other hand, dominated other facets of bike riding in Amsterdam, including:

- Cycling while smoking. Among 1,000 cigarette puffers, 69 percent (688 total) were male. While some of these smokers were indeed inhaling marijuana or hashish, from the best I could estimate (via smell, the look of filters, etc.), the vast majority were smoking straight tobacco.
- Cycling with two bikes at the same time. Among 500 riders guiding a second bike, 87 percent (435 total) were male.
- Cycling with a hard plastic crate of beer bottles. Among 100 cyclists either hauling full bottles or returning empties back to the store, 96 were men.
- Cycling with a ladder. Among 30 cyclists carrying a ladder, 90 percent (27 total) were men.
- Cycling with an arm in a sling. Among 50 cyclists with an arm in a sling, 86 percent of them (43 total) were men. (And, for what it's worth, among the slung arms, 70 percent of them were the left one.)

In a nutshell, then, to view the differences between the genders purely through the prism of Amsterdam cycling, just picture a woman cycling with an open umbrella while talking on a cell phone and with kids and dogs as passengers, plastic flowers adorning her bike. Meanwhile, picture a man cycling with his left arm in a sling while smoking, guiding a second bike, hauling a ladder and carrying a crate of beer bottles.

The most gender-neutral characteristic noted: the carrying of ironing boards. Of the 16 people spotted with an ironing board, 8 were female, 8 male. Far from being an ironer myself, the meaning of these stats is unclear. Further study on this topic is required.

ONE WORKDAY MORNING, I stepped outside at 5:50 and saw, in the dark, two dudes lurking by the racks across the street. At first they seemed to be searching for something where forty or so bikes stood parked. But then, as I crossed the street, I realized they weren't merely lurking, they were *inspecting*. They were hunting for bikes to steal!

"Wegwezen!" I barked. *Scram!*

Neither *zwijntjesjager* flinched or even acknowledged my presence. As I neared, I saw that one of them was hunched over *my* bike. Instinctively, I stomped my foot at him trying to shoo him away as if he were a pesky pigeon who was interested in my sandwich. In reply to my stomp, the *zwijntjesjager* looked up at me and emitted a dismissive hiss. Then, just as casually as if he'd had as much right to Brownie as I had, he resumed inspecting the bike's two locks. Apparently, my locks passed (*failed?*) his test because he then moved on down the row, grabbing, jiggling and scrutinizing the locks of other bikes, searching for the weakest link.

I stood dumbstruck. The duo operated with complete impunity despite my presence or the fact that we were standing beside—of all places—a police station. The cops, though, were no fools; just a few feet away stood the locked door that led to their secured bike garage. For the rest of us chumps without indoor parking facilities, our poor bikes were left to be savaged by these vultures.

Before the scavengers could change their minds and pounce on Brownie, I unlocked him and rode off to work. That afternoon, on my way home, I bought a third lock. If my bike appeared too burdensome, I hoped the lock would increase his chances of surviving nights spent alone on the streets. With this latest expenditure, I had now paid more for his locks than I had for Brownie himself. And the combined load of these mighty locks felt as if they outweighed that which they protected.

ALL THE WHILE, I continued my search for AJJ. In this regard, I was greatly inspired one morning in my janitor's closet when I read an article about a bike—stolen 24 years earlier, in 1979—that had been recovered in Amsterdam a few days before. The police found it when they caught a thief in the act of stealing it again. There's no telling how many times that bicycle had been stolen and restolen in the intervening two and a half decades. "The bike was in a pretty good condition, considering," said an Amsterdam police spokesman. "It's still rideable, so it must have been a good one." Its original owner—who now lived in Germany—came to Amsterdam to reclaim it. I fantasized of someday enjoying a similar joyous reunification between AJJ and myself.

Then again, another news item around this time reminded me to remain more vigilant than ever about Brownie's security. After a taxi had struck a 58-year-old cyclist on Van Baerlestraat, a trauma helicopter had rushed the biker to the hospital. During all the commotion, while the man was lying unconscious in the street, some lowlife came along and made off with the injured man's bike.

AFTER WE HAD moved to our third Amsterdam apartment (this one in Westerpark), Amy Joy moped through the front door one afternoon. Her bike had a flat tire and she asked me to fix it.

"Why not fix it yourself?" I asked.

"I've never fixed a flat before," she replied.

I figured she had to be joking. In the five years I'd known Amy Joy, she'd cycled religiously. And never, in all that time, had she asked me to fix a flat for her. Then again, I realized, I'd never seen *her* do it herself.

I told my wife that instead of fixing it for her, I'd walk her through the process. After Amy Joy hauled the bike up to the apartment, I began the lesson.

"First," I said, "take the wrench and loosen—"

"Wait," she said while rummaging through our little toolbox. "Which one's the wrench?"

I pointed at it.

"Now use it to unscrew that nut."

"Uh," she said, "the *nut*?"

The lesson progressed at a snail's pace. But eventually, after Amy Joy had removed the Dutch-style chain tensioners and the Dutch-style chain guard (a whole affair in itself), she removed the rear wheel, removed the tire, located the hole on the inner tube and patched it. Then I walked her through the reassembly. The project took nearly two hours to complete, about five times as long as if I'd done it on my own.

Three weeks later, after a day of nannying, Amy Joy arrived home with a big smile on her face.

"I finally know what I want to do with my life!" she announced. "I'm going to become a . . . *bike mechanic*!"

Amy Joy explained that earlier that day, her bike had suffered another flat tire. She had walked it to a bike shop on Lauriergracht. While sitting in the shop and waiting for the tire to be patched, she learned the place was actually a 25-year-old non-profit whose mission was to teach bike mechanics. Her interest piqued, Amy Joy arranged with the mechanic to return in two months to start training.

Nothing in my wife's job history—supermarket janitor, preschool assistant, hotel desk clerk, bookstore cashier, community theater house manager, nanny—indicated any interest in any mechanical trade. Her most recent career decision, announced just a few weeks prior, was to become a professional torch singer. She'd posted SINGER SEEKS PIANIST flyers around town. No one had responded.

Nevertheless, two months later, true to her word, Amy Joy returned to De Fietsenmaker—The Bike Mechanic—where she spent her first day fixing one flat tire after another. That afternoon, she returned home proud to announce that she could now fix a flat on her own.

After her second day of training, Amy Joy expressed to me that she really enjoyed repairing bikes. "In fact," she said, "I want to own my own shop someday, one where we live in an apartment above it."

The following week, I stopped by De Fietsenmaker to pick up Amy Joy. I stepped inside the discreet storefront into a narrow shop crammed with old bicycles. Bike parts hung strewn across the walls and cluttered upon shelves. The worn wooden floor was stained with years of grease and oil. The place looked a mess.

At the rear of the shop, Amy Joy was loosening the rear axle bolts on a bike that was suspended from the ceiling. Old bike inner tubes as well as metal cables kept the bike in place. Amy Joy's hands were coated with grease; she sang as she worked.

Jos—Amy Joy's teacher/boss—said to me, "She's a very good student." We stood and watched her ease the rear wheel off a bike. He added, "She learns fast."

"Yeah, she sure seems to like it," I said. "She even says she wants to open her own shop."

Jos said he had trained dozens of people to repair bikes, many of whom had also expressed such a desire to open their own shops.

"None of them ever actually did it," he said. "But Amy . . . I believe Amy can."

A few weeks later, on my way home from work, a shard of glass punctured Brownie's rear tire. I walked the bike home, slunk into our fourth apartment (back again on Spuistraat) and told Amy Joy about my tire.

"I'll patch it for you!" she said.

I hauled Brownie upstairs; Amy Joy got out the toolbox.

"Time me," she said.

"Okay," I said. "Go!"

Without removing the wheel from the frame, Amy Joy pulled the inner tube out from the tire, found and removed the offending shard of glass from the tire, located the tiny hole, applied first the glue and then the rubber patch, replaced the inner tube and tire, and pumped in air.

"Done!" she shouted.

I checked the clock.

"Six minutes and thirty-seven seconds!" I said.

"Pretty good, huh?" she asked.

It was three times faster (and took three times less effort) than if I had done it. I was indeed impressed. The student was now the master.

9

We Were True Libertines: The First
Two Years of the Occupation

On one May 4—Remembrance Day in Holland—I stood with a group of about 50 people on the sidewalk just up the street from our Spuistraat apartment, waiting for a ceremony to begin. The others in the crowd were mostly male, in their twenties and drinking cans of Grolsch. Many of them were dressed in T-shirts, cutoff cargo pants and bike-racing caps; their bike shoes *click-clacked* on the brick sidewalk. Periodically, one or two of them would slip across the street to a little shop and reemerge with more cans of beer.

Just a few hundred yards from us, another Remembrance Day crowd was assembled on Dam Square—the heart of the city. There the scene was as formal as this one was informal. On Dam Square, thousands of people—among them the queen, the prime minister, the mayor and many other dignitaries—were on hand to participate in a huge memorial service. With great pomp and sobriety, and before a national television audience of millions, the notables would soon lay wreaths at the base of the War Memorial—the large, phallus-like travertine monument that presides over the square.

Another difference between these two gatherings was that more bikes were in attendance at the smaller gathering than at the bigger one. Ahead of the larger commemoration, municipal workers had swept Dam Square clean of parked bicycles, May 4 being the one day of the year the square isn't littered with bikes. But here, at the far smaller gathering, in rows of threes and fours, dozens of bikes leaned against the small hotel beside us. Most of them were fixed-gear bikes—a peculiar sight, since fixies aren't anywhere near as popular in Amsterdam as they are in so many American cities. Most of those gathered were bike messengers, another population that, surprisingly, there are fewer of in Amsterdam than in many American cities, given that the era when the city teemed with butcher's boys and baker's boys on bikes had long since passed. The group gathered around a small granite monument that stood on the sidewalk and that, during the rest of the year, usually only served as a stable object for parked bikes to lean against. This evening, though, it was the center of attention. A plaque atop it read:

> *On this spot on May 4, 1945,*
> *the last courier of the Resistance,*
> *Annick van Hardeveld,*
> *was murdered by the German occupying forces.*
> *She was 21 years old.*
> *This plaque is a tribute to all who*
> *fight against injustice and oppression.*

While commemorations were taking place throughout the city and across the country, most of those here were gathered to pay respects to one of their own—a fellow bike messenger. I, too, was present to pay my respects to the fallen messenger. I was also there to pay my respects to *all* of Amsterdam's wartime cyclists. Though the bicycle had already served a tremendously important role in the lives of Amsterdammers throughout the 1920s and '30s, these heroes and heroines took on great significance during the five-year-long Nazi occupation of the city.

DURING THE FIRST World War, Holland had successfully preserved its neutrality while its neighbors had battled viciously not far from the Dutch borders. Soon after that war ended, the Dutch army established a new regiment comprising nearly 3,000 cyclists. Their motto: "Swift and Nimble—Composed and Dignified." These troops drilled and conducted maneuvers on their bikes. Within the regiment, each company of 100 to 150 troops had its own bicycle mechanic—a corporal. Even so, every soldier of the regiment maintained his own bike. He cared for it as meticulously as he did his rifle; at inspection, his bike was expected to be spotless, right down to the links of the chain.

Like other army regiments, the Cyclists Regiment had its own military band, though with a twist: its musicians performed while riding. The horn and reed players rode with special handlebar extensions that allowed them to steer their bikes with their elbows. The drummers rode with their drums mounted on their bikes. According to one account:

> [T]he surprising spectacle of the Cyclists Regiment's music corps—an almost acrobatic display— . . . arouses a general admiration. Bike riding and music playing appear to go well together. The band rode and played bravely and casually—a

sweet pleasure to see and hear! At no time did the drummers lose the dauntless tempo.

The troops of the Cyclists Regiment even sang their own anthem, titled "Song of the Cyclists." Its first two verses went:

> *We bike sometimes for ten hours, on tires as soft as silk*
> *Of all the military units, we're the fastest there's to be*
> *Our bikes roll over field and path, they are our best friends*
> *Nighttime doesn't trouble us, nor does the wind or the rain.*
>
> *And when our bike seats pain us, we are all right with it*
> *'Cause behind us with the medicine, comes the cycling medic*
> *He has a box with fine salve, you rub it on nice and thick*
> *Afterward you feel like a knight, like your rear was made of tin.*

WITH TURBULENCE BREWING throughout Europe in the late 1930s, the Dutch hoped to, once again, sit out any armed conflict. So while the Nazis prepared neighboring Germany for battle by producing thousands of tanks, the Dutch, incredibly, possessed not a single one. Holland's military was far from prepared for modern warfare. But it can't be said that the Dutch did absolutely nothing to ready themselves for the possibility of an armed conflict. In fact, as part of the country's mobilization effort, on March 1, 1939, the Dutch army added a second Cyclists Regiment. When newsreel footage of a performance by the Cyclists Regiment's music corps was shown in a movie theater in Germany, a Dutchman in attendance said the scene "sparked off laughter in the crowd."

In March 1939, as Adolf Hitler and Benito Mussolini prepared to wreak havoc across Europe, one Amsterdam pundit suggested a rather simple solution for avoiding conflict. "Our queen rides a bike," he stated, "and do you know a calmer people in Europe? What could be better for international politics than if each of those hot-headed gentlemen were gifted a bicycle? Then the world would quickly be freed from all its misery."

Unfortunately, a spin on a bike likely would have done little to pacify Hitler, especially since, at the time, he was strongly advocating the mass motorization of Germany. A German traffic law enacted in 1934 affirmed the promotion of the motor vehicle to be "the declared objective of the Führer." Hitler was the proud overseer of the construction of the Autobahn—the world's first freeway system and ultimate bicycle-less roadway.* He was also a huge proponent of the Volkswagen—the "People's Car"—the reasonably priced car created for the German working class. "Ultimately, we want to get to the point that America has already reached," Hitler proclaimed in 1937; "that is: one car for every five people." The target to build up to 7 million Volkswagens (which would increase the number of cars in the country by tenfold) astounded a journalist at the Dutch newspaper *Het Vaderland*. Germany's rate of car ownership, wrote the reporter, would then be on par with the staggering rate of bike ownership in Holland. "Germany will be teeming with cars." Of course, all those freeways, cars and car factories weren't simply intended to stimulate Sunday drives; they would also fulfill important military functions in time of war.

---

*Anton Mussert, the head of the Dutch fascist political party—the NSB— had a keen interest in highway construction as well. In 1931, Mussert, an engineer by trade, published a book of his roadway designs. But whereas the fascist Hitler gave little or no consideration to the bike with regard to road schemes, the fascist Mussert remained ever the Dutchman: his sketches for highways included adjacent bike paths.

IN THE SPRING of 1940, especially good weather drew Amsterdam's cyclists to the bulb fields on a string of Sundays. That year's best-attended trek, though, happened on a Thursday—May 2—Ascension Day. According to one eyewitness on that national holiday: "The great amusement . . . of the cyclists trimmed with lively garlands of flowers, who rode in a single peloton stretching from Haarlem to Amsterdam, made an unforgettable impression." But such delights for Amsterdam's cyclists would prove to be short-lived: days later, the Germans attacked.

Germany's all-out invasion of Holland commenced on May 10. Among the Dutch defenses, the 5,600 troops of the two Cyclists Regiments were spread along the front lines at strategic locations. Early on May 11, Cyclist Roelof Keppel paused from the fighting to pen a letter to his wife and children. "Cyclists have a dangerous job," he wrote. "They seek danger and they find it." The following day, gunfire from an enemy aircraft killed Keppel.

Troops on bikes versus troops in tanks and planes? "The Cyclists put up a tough resistance," a Cyclists Regiment sergeant later recalled. Even so, he had to admit: "What we couldn't do—what the whole army couldn't do—was repel those thousands of tanks . . . and the superior number of airplanes. That was the Blitzkrieg. All of Europe was unprepared for that."

The war between the two nations was woefully lopsided. Within days, Queen Wilhelmina and the leaders of the Dutch government fled across the North Sea to London. The crushing blow came on May 14 when the Luftwaffe bombed Rotterdam, reducing the city's center to rubble and ashes. Less than a week after the invasion had begun (and after the deaths of almost 5,000 Dutch civilians and military personnel—including 77 members of the Cyclists Regiments), Holland capitulated.

Though Amsterdam itself was spared major fighting, for the next five years many of its citizens would suffer terribly under the heels of those they called the *moffen*.[*]

ON THE AFTERNOON of May 15, the first vehicles of the conquerors entered Amsterdam. Arriving from the southeast, the German 207th Infantry Division crossed the Amstel River over the Berlage Bridge. The bulk of the convoy drove down Apollolaan and continued west to the city of Haarlem along the very stretch that, barely two weeks before, had carried the streams of joyous, adorned cyclists back from the bulb fields. After crossing the Amstel, a smaller contigent of Germans immediately turned right and followed the river along the Amsteldijk, heading for Dam Square and city hall.

The following day, at Hitler's command, the German troops conducted a more proper march of conquest. Amsterdam's traffic police closed off streets along the designated route. The long convoy consisted of motorcycles (many with sidecars), trucks, Panzer III and Panzer IV tanks, halftracks towing anti-aircraft guns and Mercedes-Benz sedans bearing officers. Amsterdam hadn't witnessed such a grand display since Napoleon strutted into town with his army 129 years earlier. Huge crowds of onlookers lined the route: Haarlemmerweg, Nassaukade, Rozengracht, Dam Square, Rokin, Rembrandtplein, Utrechtsestraat, Stadhouderskade, Amsteldijk and Weesperzijde.

---

[*]*Mof* (plural: *moffen*)—by far the most popular pejorative term for "German" used by the Dutch during World War II—was akin to the wartime English terms *kraut*, *Hun* or *Jerry*. One Dutchman of the time explained that the term, "while not translatable, is very far from being a term of endearment."

While the momentous procession commemorated the military victory, it also—if only for a few hours—subdued Amsterdam's cyclists. By now, there were 300,000 bicycles in Amsterdam—more than ten times the number of the city's motorized vehicles (cars, trucks, motorcycles). Yet on this day, the Germans—unlike any foreign motorists before them—weren't subjected to the customary bossiness of Amsterdam's bikers. The cyclists stood aside, their bikes in hand, as they watched their occupier swagger.

In the ensuing days, life on the city's streets was relatively uneventful, as if the military truce signed between the two countries extended to their road users. "The Netherland people bicycle along the avenues of their beautiful cities," noted one foreign reporter, "and their manner betrays little of what has passed." A German radio announcer broadcast to a German audience: "We are now in Amsterdam. In front of the Royal Palace, there is a veritable concert of bicycle bells, and the cyclists perform amazing acrobatics in the traffic. Two women kiss each other as they pass by without getting off."

If life initially appeared normal for Amsterdam's bike riders, it was anything but normal for its car owners. Straightaway, the Nazis pillaged the Dutch gasoline reserves and strictly rationed what little gasoline remained for public consumption. Within days after the capitulation, so many motorists switched to cycling that sales more than doubled at some bike shops, while the number of orders from bicycle manufacturers ran "fantastically high." (That year, 1940, Dutch factories would produce a record number of bikes: almost half a million.)

This sharp increase in cycling had a noticeable effect on Amsterdam's street traffic. Weeks after the invasion, one newspaper reported:

And now, due to the circumstances of the times, the army of cyclists has grown even larger. Even those who were driving a car just a few months ago now have to mount their bikes. They now cycle to the theater and the Concertgebouw. The bicycle is more popular than ever.

A journalist reported:

The city is populated with swarms of cyclists. To motorists, these cyclists used to be a thorn in the side because they hindered traffic by swerving from left to right and back again—often while riding three abreast. But now that most motorists have become cyclists themselves, they act as if they've never even touched the steering wheel of a car.

One car owner professed:

For 32 years, I had not sat on a bike. But now, with the car in the stable, I have tried it once again. I rode off as easily as if it had been 32 hours ago. And now, every evening, I pedal home on my new little bike and then again, after dinner, for another hour or so. I had almost forgotten a bike could provide so much pleasure.

Parked bikes replaced parked cars during workdays on Beursplein, the square in front of the Amsterdam Stock Exchange. Privately owned cars weren't the only motor vehicles idled. For example, mail trucks—long notorious for recklessly racing through the streets—were replaced by bikes, as one newspaper noted:

The "people murderers"—as they were popularly called—will disappear. Until some other time, they'll go to the garage. The cyclists won't mourn them; they'll be spared much angst. . . . Let us hope that the drivers demoted to cyclists cause fewer calamities on their two-wheelers than they had with their raging four-wheelers.

Though taxis also ceased to operate, a new mode of transport soon sprang up in their place: the *fietstaxi*, or pedicab. Though such a vehicle is a familiar sight these days in Amsterdam (not to mention American urban tourist spots like Manhattan, San Francisco, etc.), in 1940 they were an entirely new phenomenon in the Dutch capital. The pedal-powered rickshaw consisted of a two-wheeled, two-seater cab that was hitched to the rear of an everyday bike. By early June, three were in operation in Amsterdam. One sarcastic observer noted, "Drivers worked diligently with their feet to transport their clients at the breakneck speed of ten miles per hour."

Despite their slow pace, the pedicabs proved a wartime sensation; in June, bridal couples were no longer being chauffeured in luxury cars but in pedicabs. By October, 24 of them were servicing the city. That month, at one Saturday evening performance of *Peer Gynt* at the Stadsschouwburg, 20 pedicabs stood in the dark on blacked-out Leidseplein waiting to chauffeur home theatergoers. By the end of 1940, several different companies were operating a total of at least 60 pedicabs, each a visible reminder of changing times in Amsterdam.

THOUGH THE NAZIS had initially motored into the Dutch capital without experiencing the traditional treatment from the cyclists, almost immediately the occupiers became acquainted with two-wheeled Amsterdam's true nature. Dutch bicycle behavior contrasted greatly with that of the German cyclist. Back in Nazi Germany, the motorist was unquestionably the master on the streets. A German sense of orderliness and a strict adherence to Nazi law kept the cyclist subdued. One Dutchman, while riding a bike in prewar Germany, discovered firsthand the glaring difference between cycling there and cycling in Holland. Of the cycling conditions in Germany, he wrote:

> The motorist, who always keeps as far to the right as possible, can and will cut it extremely close when passing a cyclist. . . . So watch out and pay attention—not to the beautiful scenery, but to where you ride and to how you ride. As a result, here, we can't ride beside each other nonchalantly, chatting pleasantly, with an arm akimbo or linked arm-in-arm with another. No, cycling is serious business here. We ride single file and we don't talk.

In contrast, a German who was in Holland just after Hitler had come to power was terribly impressed with how Dutch cyclists, through their courageous and daring riding, defended "with great doggedness" their right to the roadway. "In Germany, this right has long since been lost," he noted. "In Holland, this right has remained as a consequence of a true democracy."*

---

*Another (though far earlier) example of the difference between cycling in the two countries was the bike touring done by a 14-year-old Franklin Delano Roosevelt with his tutor in the summer of 1896. After cycling through many little towns between Amsterdam and The Hague without hassle, they biked in the German Rhineland, where, in a single day, they were arrested four times: for picking cherries, taking bikes into a train station, riding over a goose and cycling after dark.

Now German motorists—who had long ruled the streets of their country—were in the Netherlands as the invaders, the occupiers, the victors. They'd crushed Holland in just *five* days; across the continent, German forces were storming from one victory to the next. These motoring soldiers certainly possessed a sense of invincibility. Yet when the soldiers were motoring through Amsterdam, the cyclists didn't give them the respect they felt they deserved. Just four days after the Germans' motorized parade through the city, the chief of police reported that the German authorities had already complained that "the general public of Amsterdam is very poor at heeding the decreed traffic regulations. . . . The cyclists are especially warned to always keep to the right."

Three months after the invasion, a German with an "important position" in his nation's traffic police agency was asked what he felt was the problem with Dutch traffic regulation. His answer: the cyclists. First, he argued, the occurrence of "six, seven or eight cyclists riding beside each other on the roadway needs to be combated." He added:

> The second weak spot of Dutch traffic is the manner in
> which the cyclists give signals, or better said, don't give sig-
> nals. Signaling is often neglected and when it does happen,
> it is done carelessly. The motorist approaching from behind is
> no mind reader. . . . At the moment, there are many German
> drivers on the road who are not familiar with the peculiari-
> ties and quirks of the Dutch cyclists and who, moreover,
> have privileges as military drivers.

A Dutch newspaper reported:

It is fully understandable that, oftentimes, the German occupation authorities become exasperated by those throngs and
clouds of cyclists that pose so many problems to the rushing
military vehicles. Our Dutch troops had been used to them
since childhood and were prepared for them. But, of course,
foreigners cannot be expected to easily feel at home in, for
them, such unaccustomed conditions.

In Germany, where motorists never had to yield to cyclists,
cyclists were always expected to yield to cars. In Holland, on the
other hand, at unregulated intersections (of which there were—
and still are—a countless number in Amsterdam), the Vehicular
Code since 1927 had mandated that whoever approached the intersection from the right—be they cyclist or motorist—had the
right-of-way (as is the case presently). Therefore, in Amsterdam,
the German motorist approaching from the left expected to have
the right-of-way, while the cyclist approaching from the right
expected the same for himself.

The rights of the military traffic, the Germans believed,
trumped any local traffic ordinances. Amsterdam's cyclists
clearly felt otherwise. No matter the bulk or the velocity of the
German vehicles, no matter the urgency or impatience of the
German drivers, Amsterdammers continued cycling in the familiar manner that motorists—both foreign and domestic—had
condemned for years. Many cycled fast and carelessly. Others
cycled slowly and blithely. Couples, of course, rode side by side,
holding hands. The Germans had vanquished the Dutch military and toppled the Dutch government; that was indisputable.
But the invaders had not overthrown the kings and queens of
Amsterdam's streets.

Not long after the capitulation, traffic policemen began roaming the city in cars that each had a large loudspeaker mounted atop it. Trailing behind cyclists, the police boomed admonishments at two-wheeled misbehavers, instructing them to adhere to the rules of the road, such as keeping to the right. Ultimately, the loudspeaker campaign changed little in the way the free spirits cycled. Of the type of riding done in the summer of 1940, one Amsterdam biker boasted later that year: "We were true libertines, true traffic anarchists, true individualists of the cyclery."

MEANWHILE, IN THE English countryside just outside London where she had established residence, Queen Wilhelmina eagerly wished to cycle "like an ordinary person." The queen felt that purchasing a new bike while in England would be wasteful as she still had a decent bike back home at her palace in The Hague. Therefore, Wilhelmina instructed her personal secretary to procure for her a trustworthy secondhand bike. The secretary protested that a secondhand bike wouldn't be as reliable as a new one. Wilhelmina remained unmoved. Even when informed that a new bike actually wouldn't cost much more, the queen didn't budge. She also refused to reconsider when her secretary argued that Her Majesty's bike back in The Hague was certainly a goner.

"If the conditions there are like that," Wilhelmina stated, "then a secondhand bike will be good enough for me."

At the nearby bicycle shop in Maidenhead, the queen's secretary purchased the bike. But, unbeknownst to Wilhelmina, the bike was in fact new and cost £25. The queen's secretary had covertly instructed the bike mechanic to replace the pedals and handlebars with used parts. When the queen was presented with her new purchase, she was informed it was secondhand. Wilhelmina was immediately charmed by the bike, and when she asked its price, she was told, "Ten pounds, Madam."

"You see!" Wilhelmina exclaimed. "That's much cheaper than a new one!"

And so, throughout the rest of the war, when not meeting with the Dutch government in exile, receiving members of the Dutch Resistance or broadcasting inspirational radio speeches to her countrymen in occupied Holland, Queen Wilhelmina—now in her sixties—could be spotted on the country roads outside London, riding her good-as-new bike.

IN THE FALL of 1940, as the number of daylight hours dwindled, the multitude of Amsterdam cyclists was forced to ride during darkened rush hours, now pitch black due to the Germans' blackout mandates. Streetlights were turned off; bicycle headlights had to be completely covered by "blackout paper" (with the exception of a tiny one-by-three-centimeter rectangular cutout that allowed a sliver of light to escape). By December, the Dutch electronics firm Philips had introduced a government-approved, specially dimmed bulb for bike lights.

While the resulting darkness on the streets helped conceal the city from British bombers, it also created a myriad of problems for anyone out before sunrise or after sunset. While cyclists collided with one another, those trying to keep to the right-hand side of the street crashed into curbs, parked cars, trees, etc. Accidentally biking or walking into a canal—already a high risk—was now an even greater possibility. For example, on the evening of November 2 alone, emergency workers responded to

18 cases of people falling into canals. Three of those incidents were fatal, including one involving a 23-year-old nurse on Jacob Catskade who had been on her way to visit a patient. Cycling in the darkness, the nurse veered off the street and into the water. In November 1940, 125 people drowned in canals nationwide, compared to 40 drowning deaths the previous November. "If a pedestrian does not fall into a canal," one foreigner observed, "he is likely to stumble against a parked bicycle. If you've ever barked your shins on bicycle pedals, you can imagine the situation in a blacked-out land where there are 4,000,000 bicycles."

In the autumn of 1940, one description of the street scene read:

It seems as though the legion of cyclists that moves through the streets of Amsterdam morning and evening has suddenly doubled. Never before has there been such a swarm of racing, swirling, zigzagging cyclists on the major streets leading to the heart of the city. . . .

In the morning, tens of thousands of cyclists make their way to the city center, not with the easy pace of a tourist passing a cherry orchard, but with haste. . . . The dimmed, yellow streetlights are still burning. The city is still a cheerless, dark gray as the shop girls, the factory and warehouse workers and the office personnel all get on this so utterly Dutch means of transportation and begin their morning bike ride. With metronomic regularity, the ferry over the IJ waterway discharges surges of cyclists by the hundreds. The major arteries from the West (Overtoom, Rozengracht, Kinkerstraat), from the South (Van Woustraat and Ferdinand Bolstraat) and from the East (Sarphatistraat), become busier every minute.

At the major intersections leading to the city center, the result is a crashing wave of cyclists. Then comes the worst: everyone has to find his own way through. And thus fortune favors the bold because the traffic lights are not yet operating. At the corner of Stadhouderskade and Ferdinand Bolstraat, at the intersection of Weteringschans and Vijzelgracht, by the Rijksmuseum, on Leidsestraat, it is bedlam. . . .

And at the end of the workday, between half past five and six o'clock, it is exactly the same.

THE GROWING CONFLICT between the Dutch cyclists and the German motorists peaked that fall. On September 28, 1940, the mayors of Dutch cities received orders passed down from Hanns Albin Rauter, an Austrian who headed both the SS in the Netherlands and the nation's (Dutch and German) police forces. According to Rauter, cyclists were now expected to: ride as far to the right as possible, ride no more than two abreast, always use hand signals and—apparently most crucial to the Nazis—always yield to the German vehicles. Any cyclist caught not heeding these rules could be fined. In addition, Rauter, a quintessential Nazi (a sinister-looking scar ran across his right cheek), introduced a new form of punishment: valve removal. Dutch bike tire valves—unlike the American-style Schrader valves or the French-style Presta valves—could be disassembled. Without the valves, the tires would deflate and the cyclist would be left to seek out a bike shop—either on foot or by riding on the airless tires—to replace the valves.

Three weeks after issuing his decree, Rauter grew even more aggravated by the cyclists. In a stern letter to the Dutch secretary-general of internal affairs, Rauter snarled that he continued to receive complaints about the "undisciplined behavior of the cyclists." Due to a "lack of vigorousness" by the Dutch police, Rauter argued, the cyclists were riding "according to their own free will and not according to the rules and regulations." If the Dutch police proved incapable of constraining the cyclists, Rauter threatened to have German police step in to do so.

In mid-November, Claas Bakker—Amsterdam's long-standing chief of traffic police—publicly announced a crackdown against the disobedient cyclists (or, as one newspaper writer described them that week, "the shameless louts, the bitchy vixens, the thick-skinned blockheads"). Bakker—whose sympathies to the occupiers would soon help him to be named head commissioner of the police—declared:

> There are so many bikes and so few cars these days, so why
> is this measure necessary? The German authorities have
> decreed it to clear the way for military traffic. The number
> of bicycles in Amsterdam is estimated to have increased by
> 15,000. . . . And during rush hours, 180,000 of them cross
> through the city! . . . The new rules will cause certain delays
> to the cyclists, but nothing can be done about that. My only
> advice: cyclists should depart from home five or ten minutes
> earlier.

In addition, the Germans demanded an end to one particular Amsterdam pastime. "Cyclists may not hold on to each other while riding," Bakker reported, "even if they are recently engaged." Thus cyclist hand-holding—a proposed ban on which had elicited only laughter from the city council a few years before—had become so vexing to the dour Nazis, they proscribed it. One German tourist in wartime Amsterdam had noticed the enchanted air of couples cycling together—the women holding tight to the men's forearms. Even this tourist had warned, "It would be bad if, as with us, the Dutchman was forbidden to ride side by side. He'd be even angrier than if you had confiscated his cheese."

Within a few days of the announced crackdown, Bakker said, "We have now yanked out some 900 valves from bicycles. But no matter how annoying it is for people, we shall continue with it as long the regulations are not observed!"

A couple of weeks into the clampdown, the valves of 2,500 bikes had been yanked. Exactly how many lovers defied the hand-holding ban is unknown, but in general, the cyclists' conduct had not greatly changed. So Bakker then warned:

> We will have to act even more stringently, because the problem is that thousands and thousands [of cyclists] need to kick the habit—one we have always tolerated—of enjoying equal rights with other street traffic. . . .
>
> We live in the middle of a war zone and if people will just consider the consequences of that, then we are a step further. The automobile traffic must have absolute priority. And the understandable haste of the military vehicles compels us to say it is in the cyclists' own interests that we impose a much more sober regimen; to wit: they should keep to the right with painful precision and they should not ride more than two abreast.

As punishment for defying the blackout rules, there was an "added surprise." In addition to a fine, the bicycle belonging to anyone caught riding without the proper blackout lighting would be impounded for 24 hours. "This measure was only very recently introduced," stated Bakker, "yet the Traffic Bureau's garages on Overtoom have already received more bikes to store than they can hold."

Yet another measure was also added: just as Rauter had threatened, German traffic police—of stocky build, wearing helmets and snazzy Nazi uniforms (that reportedly made the Amsterdam traffic police uniforms look "awfully nineteenth-century-ish")—stood lookout at hectic intersections and on busy streets supervising the cyclists' behavior.

Loudspeaker cars, monetary fines, tire deflations, bike impoundments, German traffic cops—the Nazis were desperate to impose their authority on Amsterdam's bike riders. Yet despite all the steps taken, and judging by the reaction of the authorities, the cyclists remained undaunted.

IN MID-DECEMBER 1940, rather uncharacteristically, Rauter repealed one of his own edicts. In order to "reduce the premature wear and tear of tires," he now forbade the police from removing bike valves (while also forbidding officials from publicly revealing this order). Apparently valve extractions had resulted in cyclists carelessly and/or defiantly riding on flats, which needlessly ruined the tires. That Rauter now concerned himself with the minutiae of the condition of the tires of the cyclists he so loathed spoke volumes about the state of the nation's tire supply—and of their vital importance.

In early 1941, it was said that upon greeting one another, the Dutch would ask: "How are your bike tires? Can you still get by on them?" Production of bicycle tires in the country had ground to a halt because raw rubber from the Dutch East Indies could no longer reach Holland. With heightened demand and a dwindling supply, cyclists were riding on tires that were becoming increasingly threadbare. In March 1941, the national government implemented a rationing system for bike tires. (By then, many food items were already being officially rationed.) A myriad of rules determined eligibility for purchasing new bike tires. The most important qualification was that one must live more than three miles from his or her place of work or study and have limited access to train, tram or bus service. Given that Amsterdam was both compact and had an extensive public transit network, this rule disqualified a great many Amsterdammers from receiving tire replacement.

"To get a new tire was a most intricate business and generally, after an avalanche of red tape, one's application was rejected, without the possibility of protest," wrote one wartime observer. And even if one's application was successful, possession of a ration voucher didn't always guarantee receiving a new tire.

In April 1941, the Propaganda Office of the Department of Commerce ran a newspaper advertisement titled: "We must go easy on our bike tires!" It asked: "A Dutchman without a bicycle? This is not a hypothetical now with so few tires available." The ad implored cyclists to nurse their tires by, among other things, not riding on low air, not riding onto or off of curbs and not skidding. The ad's tagline: "He who doesn't spare his tires, doesn't deserve his bike!"

A couple of months later, in the summer of 1941, the tire rationing candidates were restricted even further. Instead of being required to live more than three miles from work or school, one now needed to live more than three miles from the nearest public transit stop—an impossibility in Amsterdam. In announcing the rule change, one newspaper gave an example of how to reduce wear on tires:

> People repeatedly ride their bikes back and forth along the
> beach boulevards at our seaside resorts. It's clear many of
> them want to bike to the sea. But once there, they need not
> continue cycling back and forth. They can stroll. They can sit
> or lie on the beach and enjoy the sun.

With tires becoming a rarer commodity, the price of bikes "began to rise in value like the shares of a suddenly productive gold mine." Even bike rentals, once a lucrative practice for bicycle shops, now became a chancy affair as some unscrupulous customers would swap the decent tires from their rented bikes with threadbare replacements.

THE LACK OF available tires inevitably contributed to an increase in bike thefts; some thieves took more interest in the tires than in the bike itself. Of one case, Dutch police reported that two stolen secondhand tires and two stolen secondhand inner tubes were sold first for a gold watch and then sold again for twenty packs of shag cigarettes.

One newspaper reported:

> The bicycle is currently a very costly possession. It seems as
> if the army of parasites—which lusts after the high prices
> stolen bicycles and tires can now fetch—grows by the day.
> Presently, no bike is safe. . . . From day to day, [bike thieves]

dupe dozens of people, without showing the least awareness
of the fact that among their victims there may be many for
whom the bicycle is a necessity for getting to work and earning a living for a family.

Another newspaper reported:

There used to be many people who carelessly left their bicycles on the street thinking that such outdoor parking was
safe. These people have learned the errors of their ways since
the guild of the *zwijntjesjagers*—as bicycle thieves are still
called—display great courage and are very active, leaving no
bike at peace.

Actually, not all Amsterdammers learned the errors of their
ways, as bikes continued to be left unattended and ripe for
thieves. The best prevention against bike thefts, concluded civic
authorities, was to store bicycles indoors at night. So, in May
1941, the Amsterdam police pronounced: "It is hereby forbidden to park two-wheeled bicycles in public places or leave them
standing unattended between a half-hour after sunset and a
half-hour before sunrise." The maximum punishments for failure to heed this new law: a 300-guilder fine and/or a two-month
jail sentence.

Soon thereafter, the Amsterdam police launched another
anti-bike-theft campaign. On the morning of August 18, 1941,
on Leidseplein, the police began impounding unlocked bikes.
Rightful owners could recover their bikes after paying a fine.
"Within the first hours, a large number of bikes were already
taken away," read a news report that day. "Among these were

bikes laden with baskets of bread or meat." In the following days, unsecured bikes were also gathered on Utrechtsestraat and Frederiksplein.

The police campaigns against unlocked bikes and bikes left outdoors overnight, though, seemed to have little effect. In November, one newspaper reported:

> The custom has shown that the many cyclists of Amsterdam care little or nothing for the [nighttime parking] regulation. Many bicycles, often not even locked, are parked against houses and trees. Apart from the fact that these bicycles create hazards in the darkness for the public on the streets, they also make it extremely easy for bicycle thieves—and the number of bike thefts has increased alarmingly.

As a result, the police then began confiscating parked bicycles from the streets at night.

The extent of the bike theft problem during the first years of the occupation could probably be best illustrated by an incident that occurred in June 1942. Blonk Ford, an Amsterdam police detective who specialized in catching *zwijntjesjagers*, exited the courthouse after testifying at a trial only to find . . . his bike had been stolen.

AMSTERDAM'S CYCLISTS RECEIVED some rare good news on April 24, 1941, when the Reich's commissioner—Hitler's top man in Holland, the Austrian Arthur Seyss-Inquart—announced an end to the 17-year-old (and ever-maligned) annual bicycle tax. Nazi propaganda boasted that this was "proof that the occupying government strives . . . as much as possible to ameliorate the living conditions of the Dutch people."

For several years, the Dutch fascist political party—the NSB—had campaigned against the bike tax by claiming the flat two-and-a-half-guilder-per-bike annual levy more heavily burdened working stiffs, especially those with large families. Anti-bike-tax rhetoric hadn't been enough to win the party many followers, though; in the last pre-occupation parliamentary election, the NSB had garnered a mere 4 percent of the vote. But since then, the Nazis had outlawed all Dutch political parties except for the NSB. Anton Mussert, head of the NSB, declared to Seyss-Inquart that the bike tax was "an antisocial measure that . . . kept the people enslaved." So, the Nazis tossed the NSB a bone by scrapping the bike tax in hopes that the resulting propaganda would help to warm the Dutch populace to the Germans.

Afterward, the NSB distributed flyers and stickers that crowed of the elimination of the bike tax that they had "fought against in vain during the democratic regime." The Nazis, in an internal report, noted that the repeal was well received. Indeed, one newspaper embraced the news by publishing a photo of three smiling cyclists holding a sign that read:

ALL OF HOLLAND IS HAPPY.

NOW AGAIN WE CYCLE FREE.

WHILE THE NAZIS felt magnanimous about the bike tax repeal, they had even stronger feelings about another bike issue in Holland. When the pedicab had emerged at the beginning of the occupation, one Amsterdam newspaper had proudly claimed that this "Dutch rickshaw" really did make Hollanders the "Chinese of Europe" (a term that had long been used as a slur against the Dutch). While the present-day tourist-shuttling pedicabs of Amsterdam seem rather innocuous (except when their lumbering, wide frames hinder cyclists stuck behind them), during the occupation, many Amsterdammers regarded the pedicab as an ingenious and essential addition to the city's transportation system. On the contrary, though, the Nazis and their collaborators found the pedicab neither innocuous nor ingenious. In fact, they deemed it to be downright offensive.

In the spring of 1941, an article titled "Modern Slavery: The Germanic People Debased" appeared in *Volk en Vaderland*, the NSB's weekly newspaper. It read:

> There are races and peoples who are not demeaned when they are used as draft animals. We think of the Chinese rickshaw companies and the Chinese coolies. . . . That these coolies are treated like draft animals by their passengers is well-known. However, the coolie does not feel degraded, neither through this disgraceful and beastly toil, nor by being treated like a dog. To him, the self-confidence that lives in the Germanic worker is completely unknown. Thus, rickshaw enterprises are only feasible in countries where coolies are readily available. And so we have always found it inconceivable to have, in our county, the rickshaw. We were wrong.
>
> In Amsterdam and other cities, this vehicle has been introduced. Dutch entrepreneurs have managed to hitch a little cart to workmen (who are eager to earn a meal) in order

to lead around those who have money, yet have no desire to walk, enabling them to spare the soles of their shoes.

Of course, the Chinese coolie walks and the Dutch worker bikes. But it boils down to the same thing: their labor is abused. It is ridiculous to see two fat gentlemen sitting untroubled in the little cab while a young fellow makes every effort to ensure the 450-pound load that dangles behind him arrives on time for lunch or cocktails. It is worse than ridiculous. It is a humiliation for the workingman; an indignity that is intolerable in a Germanic community. . . .

The pedicab must disappear from Dutch streets. The Germanic laborer demands honorable work. He does not shy from hard work, but he wants work that is in keeping with his virtue as a person, as a laborer and as the possessor of the most beautiful thing that Providence has bestowed in order to make life possible: the Germanic capacity for work. This gift from God should no longer be hawked by slick salesmen and, as a consequence, be destroyed by folks who are too lazy to walk. . . . Therefore, down with the rickshaw!

And who did the fascist author of this article blame for the supposed horrors of the pedicab? Not surprisingly, it was the Jews. "The Dutch worker should no longer be victimized by Jewish morals," the author argued. "That time is over."

Several days later, Rauter, that hater of hand-holding cyclists, issued Proclamation 20 of 1941, which banned pedicabs. One Dutch newspaper reported:

The Germans argued for the enactment of this ban on the grounds that, these days, the "bike-taxi" is not in accordance

with the healthy and natural sense of morality of the Northern European people. Men who work as "bike-coolies" perform humiliating services. If one wishes to remark that this
will cause unemployment among those who will be deprived
of the opportunity to earn a living this way, then, according to the explanation from the Germans, just the opposite
could be said: nowadays these men can find sufficient and
improved labor here in this country or in Germany.

The message was clear. Any pedicab driver who groused about
losing his job was welcome to find more suitable work at job sites
where the openings were unlimited: the German slave-labor
camps.

Responding to the glaring irony that Nazis—of all
people—were complaining about the use of slave labor, the
underground newspaper *Vrij Nederland* took a satirical view of
these "delicate souls" who had suddenly expressed "a wealth of
humanitarian and ethical tendencies" toward pedicab drivers.

[The pedicab drivers] would be better off working at air-
fields, manufacturing munitions or clobbering Jews. This
sort of labor—which directly or indirectly helps promote the
New Order—is honorable. . . . And such honorable work
simply cannot be achieved by driving a pedicab. Therefore,
down with the pedicab!

After the ban went into effect, many of the cabs were detached
from the bikes and attached to horses, creating a fleet of so-called
pony taxis. Nevertheless, one could still be taxied across Amsterdam by bike, since the pedicab ban didn't affect another sort

of bike taxi service that had also appeared soon after the Nazi invasion: the tandem taxi. This form of public transport couldn't have been more elementary. "The chauffeur does the pedaling," as one observer put it, "while the 'boss' on the back seat relaxes a little by freewheeling, or lending just a helping 'foot' when the road goes uphill." Or, as another observer put it, "[I]f so desired, the passenger could loaf."

One tandem taxi passenger, a German visitor to Amsterdam, recalled his experience:

> When the train arrived late at night in Amsterdam's Central Station, the last tram had long since gone to bed. In the darkness, I stood rather helplessly with my two heavy suitcases. A voice called to me: "Bicycle-taxi?!" . . . A properly dressed gentleman picked up the suitcases; his was the voice that had called. He led me to a tandem and asked me to hold the bike while, with lots of cord, he fastened the suitcases on the rack. Then he mounted his two-seat bicycle and invited me to also saddle up. Along the quiet canals, the noiseless journey through the sleeping capital on the Amstel River was broken only by the soft hum of the bike's generator light. Due to the weight on its rear, the tandem swayed. The cyclist balanced the movement by pedaling more vigorously. The rhythm of his feet was the rhythm of my own. Finally, we arrived at our destination. The fare was double that of a taxi trip the same distance in Berlin— and that was without being charged for my own labor.

ON DECEMBER 9, 1941, two days after the bombing of Pearl Harbor and the day before Germany declared war on the United

States, the Germans effectively declared war on another group: the cyclists of Amsterdam. It was the second autumn of the occupation. Again, rush hours were occurring during blacked-out hours. And again, Nazi motorists striving to navigate their vehicles through the throngs of the cyclists were suffering fits. Despite the various crackdown efforts initiated the previous autumn, the cyclists were still reigning royally on the streets.

At their wits' end, the Nazis enacted new traffic laws with the intention of aligning Dutch traffic regulation to that of Germany. For cyclists, this meant a host of new laws. Riding without hands on the handlebars or without feet on the pedals was now prohibited, as were riding alongside vehicles (especially trams) and holding on to vehicles. Cyclists were also expected to ride in a "snake pattern" (riding beside the curb and snaking around any parked cars they encountered). A child passenger could no longer ride on a back rack or a bike's frame but had to sit in a proper child's seat. And anyone over the age of ten was prohibited from riding as a passenger on a one-seat bicycle. Thus, dinking—every bit as popular as cyclist hand-holding had been—was banned!

The most noteworthy interdiction, though, involved the Nazis' biggest irritation: cyclists could no longer ride more than two abreast. And where space was tight, they had to ride single-file. If three or four (or more) rode side by side (by side . . .), the outermost cyclist(s) would be fined.

"The occasional disorderly conduct of cyclists will be curbed with the help of the new regulations," reported one newspaper. "More discipline will be expected of them."

Initially only warnings were issued. But then, after December 22, violators were fined. Immediately after the war, one observer recalled:

During the occupation, the Germans . . . meddled with the traffic. They tried, among other things, to get the cyclists to ride nicely alongside each other, two by two. Although it was announced with much pomposity, it was a needless measure because the auto traffic was already so significantly reduced by the German thievery.

Even so, as far as inconveniences went, this latest "needless" crackdown on Amsterdam's cyclists would pale in comparison to the tribulations that awaited in the following year.

10

Smash Your Bikes to Bits, Slice Your Tires to Pieces: The Mass Bike Confiscation

At the beginning of 1942, a new cabaret variety show—with songs performed in Dutch, Yiddish and Hebrew—enjoyed an "enormous success" at the Theater van de Lach (Theater of Laughter) on Plantage Middenlaan. The show's title act was a rendition of the old hit song "Allemaal op de fiets" ("Everyone on the Bike"). The singing of that "ode to the bicycle," a reviewer wrote, took the crowd back to the turn-of-the-century "glory days." That the show's Jewish audience longed for a better era is understandable given that, at the time, the Nazis were increasingly ostracizing them via restrictive laws and measures. Even admission to this show was segregated: Jews only.

A few months later, on May 21, 1942, Reich's Commissioner Seyss-Inquart decreed that Jews had to register their bikes with the government. This was not, Seyss-Inquart insisted, a first step toward confiscation. Even so, that same week, a brief article in the Dutch fascist newspaper *De Misthoorn* stoked contempt for the Jewish ownership of bikes. The entire article read:

If you spend a beautiful Sunday visiting the Gooi area or one
of the many other beautiful expanses of our land, then you
will find a good deal of the bike paths are clogged with noisy
Jews who, in this way, spoil our enjoyment. To make matters
worse, there are thousands of our fellow countrymen who
desperately need a bicycle for their work and, in these times,
cannot attain one. For example, think of newspaper deliver-
ers, debt collectors, etc.! It is intolerable that the Jews are
still riding around for pleasure on their luxurious bikes while
those people who need a means of transport for their work
must do without. Take away the bikes from these Yids and
distribute them to the Dutch who are eligible for them!

A month later, on June 22, the head of the SS in the Netherlands, Rauter (already on a roll with his anticyclist measures),
banned all Jews in the country outside of Amsterdam from owning, renting or borrowing bicycles. The nation's 60,000 non-
Amsterdam Jews had to turn in their bikes by 1 p.m. on June
24—fewer than 48 hours after Rauter had made his pronouncement. Failure to heed this edict was punishable by up to six
months imprisonment and/or a fine up to 1,000 guilders.

On the 24th, a Jew living outside Amsterdam wrote in a letter:

Today we have entered the cycle-less age. . . . In Amsterdam—so I read in the newspaper—the Jews can still cycle.
What a privilege! At least we no longer have to fear that our
bicycles will be stolen. That is some balm for the nerves. In
the desert, we also had to do without bicycles—for forty long
years.

A few days later, a teenaged Jewish girl in The Hague recorded in her diary:

Last Wednesday we all had to turn in our bicycles. A mob scene. Long lines. Lots of friends and acquaintances, of course. It was like a social event. I had to wait from eleven-thirty till two o'clock. Jews are not allowed to cycle anymore. What a mean, dirty trick. Even that they take away from you!

Though Jews in the capital were not yet forbidden from owning bikes, Jewish Amsterdammers took precautions. On June 24, Anne Frank reported in her diary, "Father gave Mother's [bike] to some Christian acquaintances for safekeeping." Apparently many other Jews had hidden their bikes or had given them to non-Jews for safekeeping since the 60,000 non-Amsterdam Jews turned in only 6,500 men's bikes and 3,500 women's bikes. One internal Nazi report stated: "It does not appear that the campaign against the bikes of the Jews will reach the goal of 18,000 bicycles." The low quantity of bikes received wasn't the only matter that disappointed the Germans. The author of another internal report complained, "The condition of the delivered bikes is so bad that, at best, only 1,000 usable bikes are now available."

Within a week, Rauter proclaimed more restrictions. Jews were now not allowed to: be outdoors between 8 p.m. and 6 a.m., socialize in the homes or yards of non-Jews, shop in non-Jewish stores outside the hours of 3 and 5 p.m., have goods delivered to their homes or use public telephones. They were also "forbidden from making use of all public and private means of transport." Thus Jews weren't allowed to ride trains or trams; even the rudimentary tandem taxis were off-limits.

A week later, an Amsterdam Jew wrote in a letter:

This week, they've stolen my bicycle. . . . The worst things in the world are happening now. As you know, we can no longer ride the tram here. Yet another nuisance now that my bike is gone.

In her diary, Anne Frank wrote:

It's sweltering. Everyone is panting and broiling, and in this heat I have to walk everywhere. Only now do I see how wonderful a tram is, especially an open one, but that pleasure has been taken away from us Jews. For us, hoofing it is good enough.

Walking was now the only option available to Anne, since two months earlier, her bike had been stolen.

Nevertheless, despite the frustration and debasement caused by these latest regulations, they were, unfortunately, mere inconveniences compared to the destiny that awaited the vast majority of Dutch Jews. At the beginning of July, the Nazis ordered young Jewish adults to report to work camps. In response, on July 6, the Frank family went into hiding. Anne's sister, Margot, cycled from home to the hiding place, while Anne and her parents crossed the city on foot, in the rain.

On Monday, July 20, 1942, the bikes of Amsterdam's Jews were decreed confiscated, to be turned in by 7 p.m. the following day. At that time, much of non-Jewish Amsterdam was up in arms. But it wasn't the fate of the Jews' bikes or even the mounting persecution of the Jews themselves that so riled the city's gentile majority. Instead, non-Jewish Amsterdammers became outraged about something else: the fate of their own bikes.

ON JULY 9, 1942, General Friedrich Christiansen, commander of the German army in Holland, sent a letter to Reich's Commissioner Seyss-Inquart titled "Confiscation of Bicycles." In the letter, Christiansen explained that bikes were needed to increase the mobility of the German troops. Apparently, the Nazis suspected that an Allied invasion along the North Sea coast was imminent. Therefore, Christiansen requested that Seyss-Inquart, as the head of the Nazi government in Holland, deliver 50,000 men's bikes to the army "as soon as possible—at the latest, within 8–14 days."

Seyss-Inquart, in turn, delegated the task of rounding up the bikes to two Dutch government officials: Secretaries-General K. J. Frederiks and Hans Hirschfeld. Yet, for whatever reason, Seyss-Inquart didn't do this until July 18—*nine days* after Christiansen had set an 8- to 14-day deadline. In the meantime, Christiansen ordered an additional 50,000 bikes to be delivered to the armed forces in early August.

The secretaries-general quickly devised a plan in which the mayors of the nation's 144 municipalities with populations of 10,000 or more would be ordered to turn over to the German army the number of men's bikes equivalent to 0.9 percent of that city's population (as per January 1, 1941). For The Hague, this meant 4,000 bikes; Utrecht: 3,000 and so on. For Amsterdam, the formula was skewed slightly higher; the capital was expected to deliver 8,000 bikes.

Amsterdam was home to about 300,000 bicycles at the time, so—even after accounting for women's and children's bikes and bikes belonging to those exempt from the requisition—8,000 was but a small percentage of the eligible two-wheelers. Yet if the Nazis believed it would be simple to net 8,000 bikes, such logic overlooked one key element: the tenacity of the Amster-dammer to prevent losing his main mode of mobility to the Germans.

AT 11 P.M. on Saturday, July 18, Edward J. Voûte, the Nazi-installed Dutch mayor of Amsterdam, received a telegram from Secretary-General Frederiks demanding that 8,000 bikes be mustered and delivered to the German army by Tuesday evening. The following morning, Voûte consulted a group of city officials on how best to meet this command. Three types of raids were considered: on-the-street, house-to-house and cycle garages. The first idea was dismissed because, given that it was Sunday, few people would be commuting on their bikes. The second idea was dismissed because with much of Amsterdam's housing consist-ing of apartment buildings, going house-to-house was deemed both time consuming and unproductive. So the group settled on the third option.

Because the telegram had specified that bikes belonging to laborers shouldn't be impounded, the officials decided to exclude cycle garages on the city's west, east and north sides, home to many working-class neighborhoods. Sights were instead set on the more tony Amsterdam-South area (excluding the working-class De Pijp neighborhood).

Since city officials had no comprehensive record of the esti-mated 100 neighborhood cycle garages in the targeted areas of Amsterdam-South, motorcycle policemen were dispatched to ride through the area and compile a list. That afternoon, word drifted up from Amstelveen, a town bordering Amsterdam to the south, where bike confiscations had already begun. That news, coupled with the sightings of the police surveying the cycle garages, created a panic among bike owners. One eyewitness wrote:

> Word spread through the city like wildfire. In the evening, the public broke into the cycle garages—closed or not—and indiscriminately grabbed bikes and took them home. On that Sunday, in a cycle garage in my neighborhood, I stood and watched for a few minutes. I am not a cyclist myself, so I was able do this with ease. But I'll never forget the pushing and grappling and shouting that accompanied the hasty retrieval of bikes!

One diarist wrote:

> Some policemen warned the cycle garage owners that, in an hour, they'd have to stand guard. Then, as fast as possible, the garage owners warned their customers to take away their bikes. In a flash, there was a run on the garages. By the time the police took up their posts, practically all the bikes were gone.

Some garages were blockaded right away by officers who allowed only doctors or civil servants to remove their bikes. Soon many who hadn't yet rescued their two-wheelers began enlisting family, friends or acquaintances who were doctors or civil servants to display their credentials in order to retrieve bikes for them. Not all police officers carried out their orders as dutifully as the Germans would have liked. One cop who was remembered fondly on that night was "the kind-hearted Amsterdam policeman who, at 9:30 p.m., stepped into a cycle garage on Roerstraat, blew his nose and asked, 'Have all the bikes been removed, people? All right then, I'm going to guard this garage.'"

The rescued bikes were whisked into apartments, where many of them were disassembled. Bikes and bike parts were stashed in attic storage units of apartment buildings, hidden on rooftops and even buried in backyards. Within hours, the Germans unintentionally accomplished what the Amsterdam police had been trying (and failing) to achieve since the beginning of the occupation: Amsterdammers were safeguarding their bikes.

ON MONDAY MORNING, at seven o'clock, after guarding them through the night, when the police opened the garages to begin nabbing the bikes, few bikes were to be found. "The result was beautiful," wrote one diarist that day. "There was one garage where around 600 bicycles had been stored but when the 'guarded' garage was opened, only 12 bikes remained. And so it was everywhere." Judging from the sheet of instructions that Mayor Voûte had issued to policemen and civil servants involved with the confiscations, the mayor not only expected to reach the 8,000-bike target by five o'clock that afternoon, he'd even made contingency plans for what to do with the *extra* bikes if the target was exceeded that day. With the garages mostly empty, though, the mayor was later forced to sheepishly concede, "The element of surprise was completely lost."

"Today Amsterdam was a different city than it was the day before yesterday," observed a diarist. "Few, if any, bicycles were on the streets; it looked strange." Word of the hunt for men's bikes had spread citywide, making that morning's rush hour unlike any that had preceded it. In an internal Nazi report, a German official wrote: "This operation created a great excitement in the city. As a result, this morning only a few cyclists took to Amsterdam's bustling streets. Because they feared the seizure of their bicycles, workers walked to their job sites." Many other cyclists opted instead to ride the trams to work. "The trams were besieged," wrote an eyewitness. "There were even fights on them. The people rode crammed together like tightly packed sardines." The start of the workday at many large firms was delayed because so many employees arrived late.

"Toward noon," went another report, "it appeared that Leidsestraat—usually Amsterdam's cycling El Dorado—had the atmosphere of Queen's Day: everyone walked, no one cycled. Only now, the mood was by no means animated as on Queen's Day." It was also joked, "This measure . . . forced the *zwijntjes-jagers* to take a day off because they were no match for the massive competition from their German 'colleagues.'"*

Given that the cycle garage requisitions had proved ineffectual, the mayor decided to conduct street requisitions during the lunch rush hour. From 12:00 until 12:30 p.m., a group of forty policemen and city hall employees took up positions at four intersections along Herengracht. On a normal workday, so many cyclists raced home for lunch that the noon rush was even listed in a guidebook as a Dutch attraction not to be missed. But on this afternoon, any tourists present would have been sorely disappointed, as was the mayor: only 67 bikes were seized. Not only

---

*Other jokes that made the rounds in the city that day: "If they want to get to Germany, great, they can have my wife's bike, too!" and "One thing's for sure, they're *not* going to England!"

were there few cyclists on the streets, but those headed toward the traps were cautioned by strangers. "Everyone warned everyone," noted an eyewitness.

With the street requisitioning so unsuccessful, the mayor scrapped the idea of repeating it during the evening rush hour. Instead, that afternoon, the police pillaged the cycle garages at Central Station and at major bank buildings. A 31-year-old employee of Rijksverzekeringsbank, located in a large modern building on Apollolaan, wrote in her diary:

Civil servants were exempt. So on Monday morning, many of them who had gotten their bikes, rode them to the bank. The large majority, though, had left their bicycles at home. At around ten a.m., a report came in that the bank's cycle garage was being guarded. So then began the sport of stealing one's own bike. Quickly, the bikes were snuck from the cycle garage directly into the bank. At first I thought this was pointless because if the bank was searched, they would be found in no time. And such a racket was made that it couldn't possibly have gone unnoticed. During the working hours and the lunch hour, almost all the bikes were smuggled through a side door with the assistance of the police. Later, these policemen would go stand inside so that you could no longer remove any bikes from the garage. But even then, a few more were taken away. No, we can't say anything else except that [the police] had assisted us. In total, about sixteen bikes were left over.

Since the cycle garages at the train station and the bank buildings also yielded few bikes, the authorities then switched tactics yet again, this time to house-to-house requisitioning. Late that afternoon, in the Watergraafsmeer neighborhood, an area of many smaller residential buildings, 70 policemen and city hall employees searched door to door for men's bikes. And just as they had done at the neighborhood and bank building garages, the police weren't always terribly strict when enforcing their orders. "The police officers are lenient with this also, because if you say no, they look no further," wrote the bank employee in her diary. "If you don't open the door as if you aren't home, they just move on." That afternoon, house-to-house searches netted a grand total of 140 bikes. Thus the cops had worked three hours to rustle up, on average, two measly bikes each. At such a pathetic rate, reaching the 8,000-bike target within days was already proving to be a daunting challenge.

Not only was the paltry *quantity* of bikes apprehended displeasing to the Nazis, so, too, was their low *quality*. One internal Nazi report complained that the Dutch police accepted any "old ham with the most impossible tires" because "it doesn't matter to them whether they're handed an old bike or a new one, as long as it's a bike." Another Nazi whined in a report: "Found among the seized bicycles were a lot of old and useless ones, which is simply the result of the anti-German attitude among many of those doing the confiscating."

THE UNDERGROUND PRESS reacted swiftly to these events. Just three days after the launch of the campaign, the illegal newspaper *Vrij Nederland* criticized it as "a sudden, savage attack on the most basic, indispensable means of transport: the bicycle." Two days later, the illegal *Het Parool* newspaper reported that nothing else "the German *zwijntjesjagers*" had done had "caused such a wild fury, such a great embittering as had this mass bicycle theft. . . .

Whoever still has a decent bike is warned to ensure the safety of his possession, for it can be used in the struggle against our liberators."

A flyer printed by the Resistance was more blunt. It read:

BIKE THEFT BY THE NAZI HORDES

The *moffen* in the Netherlands are on a robbery spree for the umpteenth time. Now it's the bikes of the people that these vultures are stealing on a large scale.

Is there anything these thieves won't steal from the people? Robbing and plundering for the benefit of their war machine. Netherlanders, there is but one answer to give. Refuse en masse to surrender your bicycles.

Ensure that these tyrants don't get the chance to ride on our bicycles. Their fear for the coming invasion is a sign of the facts. They have waltzed into our country, now appear to be troubled and soon they must flee. Don't give them this opportunity! . . .

Now, show us your united will and fight against these sadists. Resist against the persecution of the Jews, against the massive bike theft! Refuse to hand over or to turn in your bikes. Rather: smash your bikes to bits; slice your tires to pieces. Throw them in the water. Destroy everything that could be useful to them. Sabotage and strikes in every area. Against any plundering by them.

Give these *moffen* hordes no chance whatsoever, so they can be destroyed sooner. Fight against these Nazi bandits, against the NSB and Mussert. . . .

Fight for your property. For your economic existence. For your wife and children. For a free Netherlands.

There were reports of some Dutchmen heeding these calls. Fearing that their own bikes could be used against them, they had slashed their own tires or chucked their bikes into canals.

INTERNAL NAZI REPORTS also acknowledged that the bike appropriations had created a fury among the Dutch. One German army officer wrote in an official report: "Probably no German measure has caused such bitterness in all ranks of society as has the confiscation of the bicycles."

Another German army official stated:

> The seizure of the bicycles has caused a tremendous excitement among the people. . . . The Dutchman—who is practically born on the bicycle—views the seizing of his bike as just about the worst thing that can happen. Therefore, he tries everything possible to prevent his bike from being taken away. . . . Another consequence of the bicycle campaign is the frequent occurrence of men riding women's bikes since it's well known that those are not seized.

In his report sent to the Foreign Office in Berlin, Otto Bene, Germany's Ministry of Foreign Affairs representative to Holland, wrote:

> The whole thing caused a large rift because, for the Dutchman, the bicycle is a part of his everyday clothes. . . . For several days, one no longer saw men on bicycles . . . . Many people have hidden their bikes or each other's bikes making

the search operations in the houses of the better residential areas almost entirely fruitless.

Curiously, among all of the Nazi's shenanigans in Holland up till then, the commandeering of bikes appeared to have struck the rawest of Dutch nerves. In fact, in Bene's report, the paragraph about the bike confiscation was sandwiched between a section about the relatively tame reaction to the Nazis taking 600 prominent Dutch citizens hostage (the arrests were reported as being merely "widely discussed") and a section about the relatively tame reaction to the most recent anti-Jewish measures and the deportation of 26,000 workers to Germany (only the church groups complained). Another German report addressed this directly: "If the bicycle seizure gave cause within the population for lively discussions and for embittered criticism, then the shooting of the five hostages was accepted with an almost eerie silence."

The Nazi reports also all agreed that this initial confiscation was poorly executed. The targeted number of bikes wasn't being reached. The bikes received were of poor quality. And—particularly disturbing for the Nazis—Dutch contempt for the Germans had been fueled. The Nazis blamed the bike fiasco on sabotage. The telegraph operators who had sent and received the initial orders to the mayors were suspected of sabotaging the plan by leaking the information. Secretary-General Frederiks, in turn, was suspected of sabotage for having elected to transmit the information via telegram. While the Nazis suspected the Dutch police of sabotage for their leniency when collecting bikes, at the same time, the Nazis also blamed the police (of Amsterdam, in particular) for being "inflammatory"—for purposefully being ruthless when nabbing bikes as a way of stirring up anti-German resentment among the populace.

THE SEIZURE OF bikes proceeded more smoothly elsewhere in the Netherlands. The officials in one town, not wanting to inconvenience its citizens, simply purchased secondhand bikes that were then handed over to the Germans. In The Hague, where one Nazi report said the campaign "was very versatile and quick," even Secretary-General Frederiks' bike had been snatched.

But in Amsterdam, the story was different. Amsterdammers, after all, had a national reputation for being difficult. One prewar commentator had noted: "In our capital city mentality lives a rather strong need to resist against any [rules]."

On the afternoon of Tuesday, July 21 (deadline day), more house-to-house searches were conducted in the city. This time, 120 officers requisitioned 220 bikes in the areas around Apollolaan and Willemsparkweg. That evening, after the German army's deadline passed, the occupiers were still far short of attaining the target number. So the following day, 100 policemen worked the same areas. Their take: 85 bikes. On Thursday and Friday, more house-to-house seizures in parts of Amsterdam-South, Watergraafsmeer and the Overtoom area netted decreasing returns.*

One of Mayor Voûte's excuses for the campaign's poor results was that about 80 police officers were too busy processing the

---

*These house-to-house searches for bicycles alarmed the Anne Frank group. Worried that such a search could expose their hiding place, a decoy bookcase was installed in order to better camouflage the secret passageway that led to their clandestine quarters.

flood of applications for exemptions from bike requisitioning. On Friday morning, an eyewitness reported seeing a thousand such applicants lined up outside city hall. That week alone, about 10,000 applications would be approved, while only around 50 were rejected. Almost immediately after the first exemption permits had been issued, Resistance counterfeiters in Amsterdam began creating falsified permits for its members.

On July 23, the director of the Rijksmuseum wrote to the mayor imploring immunity for his employees by stating:

> In cases of bomb attacks, the outbreak of fire and other such calamities, it is imperative for our institution that these people can get from their homes to the museum building as fast as possible in order to rescue the artworks that are still here. Moreover, bicycles are essential to members of the museum staff for their inspection trips to the various parts of our country where artworks . . . have been temporarily evacuated.

The director of the Artis zoo created for his personnel custom exemption permits that bore the zoo's stamped seal and read (in German): "The bearer of this permit . . . needs his bicycle to serve the 'Natura Artis Magistra' Zoological Society. To ensure the utmost care and safety of the Society's irreplaceable, exotic animals, all German departments and units are implored to not confiscate [the bearer's] bicycle."

WITH THE INITIAL deadline missed for the first 8,000 bikes— and with an additional 8,000 bikes expected to be delivered by August 8—Mayor Voûte found himself in a bind. On Monday,

July 27, he was one of eight mayors who received from Secretary-General Frederiks a scolding telegram, which read:

> In contrast to the vast majority of other municipalities, it appears that your municipality still has not reached the number of bicycles specified in the telegram of July 18, 1942. Under the direction of the German authorities, I strongly urge you to use all available means to provide the remaining number of bicycles to the German Army by Tuesday evening, July 28, at the latest.

Now desperate, Mayor Voûte made a frantic effort to fulfill the city's quota. Dispatching municipal employees to go and get the bikes from the people had failed; maybe forcing the people to bring their bikes to municipal employees would net better results. So the mayor's office immediately issued a flyer that was slipped through mail slots and reprinted in Tuesday morning's newspapers. It read: "By order of the German Army, all owners of MEN'S BICYCLES are instructed to turn in their bicycles TODAY, Tuesday, July 28, 1942, from 9 a.m. to 4 p.m." Three collection sites were noted, as was a long list of people exempted from this order (among them: policemen, firemen, those who worked for the German government, those who worked for the air raid services, factory workers, manual laborers, farm hands, artisans, "anyone who has been issued an exemption from the mayor" and, of course, the Germans themselves). The flyer ended: "Those who do not comply with this summons will be subject to serious punitive measures."

Despite the severe threat, the mayor's ultimatum went largely unheeded. The following day, a city hall official, who knew intimately how poorly the mayor's latest effort had fared, proudly wrote in his diary: "Good job, Amsterdam!" In an underground newspaper, another resident of the city stated:

> This is how it is: if you touch an Amsterdammer's bike, you
> touch his life. Therefore, punishment or no punishment, the
> great mass flatly refused to comply with the order. I don't
> know how many bikes were ultimately turned in, but it was
> both sad and amusing to note that only a small percentage
> *could have been* surrendered, even though there was hardly a
> bicycle on the streets of the capital to be seen.

One contemporary account reported the way some Amsterdammers handled the situation:

> Ingenious couples knew how to delightfully hoodwink the
> Germans! If they wanted to go for a ride, the guy took the
> gal's bike and she jumped on her beloved's bike! And that
> worked great! The [authorities] fell for it each time. With
> eagle eyes, they looked to see if any men were riding on
> men's bikes. They also paid attention to the ladies. However,
> usually they looked not at her bike, but at her pretty figure!
> That's how spouses and loving couples rode unhindered!*

---

*The female cyclists of Amsterdam were indeed a sight for the Germans, one
of whom, in 1942, noted:
> *The Amsterdam ladies who—as they return home from shopping or an ap-
> pointment, or home from the office or a weekend ride with a companion in the
> countryside—don't bother to hide their usually quite well-built legs. The wind
> from the sea—which blows continually through the city of many canals—lifts
> their skirts and reveals the presumed liberal approach of going stocking-less. Yet
> they ride calmly and they don't resist the playful wind. This goes unnoticed by
> the Dutchman, who is also so relaxed and easygoing and grounded that it takes
> more than a pair of female legs to bowl him over.*

The summons to turn in bicycles exacted a great toll from German sympathizers. While the city's anti-Nazi majority clung tightly to their two-wheelers, Dutch fascists (a tiny minority in Amsterdam) were largely the ones who voluntarily handed over their bikes. One internal Nazi report read: "The measure had a devastating effect on the mood within pro-German circles." On this occasion, in terms of bike ownership, collaborating with the enemy proved disadvantageous.

Despite Secretary-General Frederiks "strongly urging" Mayor Voûte to meet the new deadline, come the evening of July 28, Amsterdam failed to meet its quota. When August arrived, Amsterdam was *still* short. Then, on August 7, a letter written on Seyss-Inquart's behalf to Secretary-General Hirschfeld (and marked "Strictly Confidential") stated, "Due to the arrival of motorized units in the Netherlands, the other 50,000 bikes are not needed for now." Amassing the first 50,000 bikes had created such a headache for the Germans, apparently they dared not attempt another such operation.

While the news meant that Amsterdam was relieved of collecting an additional 8,000 bikes, the city was still on the hook for part of the first 8,000: as of August 8, Amsterdam had only delivered to the German army 3,500 bikes. So the confiscations continued, if only in dribs and drabs. For example, on September 17, the city handed over a grand total of three bikes. And on November 11, Amsterdam delivered to the German army another 800 bikes—a seemingly impressive number, yet 746 of them lacked tires!

Then, on November 27—more than four months after the Germans ostensibly needed bikes to combat a suspected Allied invasion (which had never transpired)—Mayor Voûte sent a letter to Secretary-General Frederiks. The German army's demand for 8,000 bikes had finally been fulfilled. It was 132 days after the initial edict, which had specified that the bikes be turned over *within three days*.

By then, citizens, both male and female, were once again cycling on the streets, if ever so cautiously. Amsterdammers—looking to reduce their risk of losing a bike to the Nazis—tried to spend as little time as possible on their bikes by speeding through the city. One evening in December 1942, when Anne Frank ventured from her hiding place in the annex to the adjacent, darkened front building, she snuck a peek through the window and noticed the decidedly "terrible hurry" of the passersby out on the street. "The cyclists whiz by so fast," she wrote, "I can't even tell what sort of person is on the bike."*

While the threat of large-scale confiscations of bikes had passed for the time being, Amsterdammers would soon face a new difficulty: keeping their bikes in good enough working condition in order to simply survive.

*These days, "whizzing by" the Anne Frank House on a bike is often challenging due to the ever-present tourists milling about the narrow roadway.

11
You No Longer Think, You Just Pedal: The Final Years of the Occupation

I n 1943, as the occupation of Amsterdam dragged on, the city's cyclists continued to defy the Nazi-imposed traffic laws. Despite all the efforts to change their riding habits, the cyclists were still riding in the middle of the roadway, still running red lights and still riding three or more abreast. By now, such behavior clearly couldn't be disregarded merely as ingrained arrogance of the cyclists—or even as ignorance of the Nazis' cycling restrictions. That Amsterdam's cyclists were so troublesome to the Nazis appeared to be nothing less than flat-out, full-on, widespread resistance to the occupiers.

"Resistance came in all forms," recounted one Amsterdammer who survived the occupation. "Demonstratively turning one's head when . . . troops marched loudly through the streets was resistance. . . . Jeering in the movie theater when the German newsreels of the war were shown was resistance. Avoiding cafés frequented by Germans and their sympathizers was resistance. Such resistance required no great stock of courage, to be sure. Yet it still ripened the soul."

According to one author on wartime Amsterdam: "There was doctors' resistance, artists' resistance, church resistance, school resistance, professors' resistance, tax resistance." To that list, there should be added: cyclists' resistance, which was probably practiced on a scale far more widespread than any other form of resistance.

These cyclists had known family, friends, neighbors, classmates and coworkers who had been rounded up and shipped off to prisons, labor camps and death camps. They'd seen their countrymen executed in the streets. Their civil liberties had been violated, their jobs taken from them. They suffered shortages of food, clothing and many other basic commodities. The cost of practically every product available for purchase had been greatly inflated. Through newspapers, books, films and radio (before their radios had been taken), they'd been expected to swallow a steady diet of propaganda about how the Germans were fighting in their interests. So many facets of their lives had been transformed . . . for the worse.

These Amsterdammers, in their hundreds of thousands, were outraged. They detested the Nazis. But how could they ever safely express their rage? If a lone Amsterdammer had approached a German soldier on the street and yelled, "Fuck the *moffen!*"—the act would have been suicidal. If he had openly distributed a pamphlet that declared: "Fuck the *moffen!*"—it would have been suicidal. If she had publicly painted on a wall: "Fuck the *moffen!*"—suicide. Yet on the streets of Amsterdam, on their bikes, in their clusters, with their workmates or classmates or lovers, they could lollygag in the middle of the lane while behind them an impatient German driver honked incessantly. Or they could run a red light while cutting off a Mercedes-Benz that had the green. By frustrating and hindering the military traffic, they were sabotaging the German war effort, with some small but sweet sense of satisfaction. In their hundreds of thousands, these cyclists were collectively—if silently—proclaiming to the German motorists: "Fuck the *moffen!*"

IN APRIL 1943, one Amsterdammer noted in her diary: "All over the city, the streets are wrecked, they're not being repaired. The heavy trucks of the Germans race over them and destroy the asphalt." While the deterioration of the streets added to the frustration of Amsterdam's cyclists, they were distressed by an even graver problem: the deterioration of their tires. "Just look on the streets," wrote one journalist, "and every ten yards you'll see a chunk [of bicycle tire]."

During the bike confiscations of the summer of 1942, one illegal newspaper had called for Hollanders to retaliate via sabotage. It had proclaimed: "Tacks and broken glass can be very useful!" By 1943 and 1944, sharp objects littered many streets of Amsterdam-South, particularly around Europaplein (where many German officials were quartered), around Olympiaplein (near the Gestapo's headquarters) and on De Lairessestraat (where Seyss-Inquart kept an apartment). At night, in the blacked-out darkness, Amsterdammers chucked nails, caltrops, bottles and other glassware from the rooftops down onto the streets. Though targeting the tires of the German vehicles, these attacks plagued Amsterdam's cyclists. "Their tires are now as precious as jewels," read one newspaper account, "and they pamper their possession with the greatest care. Glass is one of their most feared enemies."

Another article reported:

> Glass is the nightmare of every cyclist because his aged tire
> treads rarely survive an assault. The vicious stab made by
> a shard is—in most cases—fatal. With a bang that sounds
> like gunfire to passersby, the air escapes and what's left is a
> pathetic rubber skin, torn and battered.

By then, for many, new tires were but a distant memory. Cyclists who still rode on tires in decent condition were said to be regarded as exceptional (because it meant they pedaled too fast for the Germans to nab their bikes) or suspect (because it meant they "belonged to the other side"). When a tire completely fell apart or when an inner tube became so porous it could be patched no more, Amsterdammers became tremendously creative in order to keep their bikes functioning. Some people placed a second threadbare tire over the first. Many others replaced their front wheels with the small wheels from children's bikes or scooters, usually jerry-rigging a second set of forks to create a single, long chopper-style front fork. Some tires, in place of inflated inner tubes, were filled with strips of rolled-up rubber floor coverings or old linoleum. One Amsterdammer developed a cork inner tube; another invented a tire made of a metal spiral spring (a sort of Slinky tire). Some folks lined their rims with rope, garden hoses and even vacuum cleaner hoses. Many more lined their rims with rubber strips sliced from car or truck tires (known as "cushion tires," "anti-pop tires" and—most commonly—"solid tires"). One Amsterdammer who rode on a bike with a solid tire on the rear and a kid's bike wheel on the front boasted, "It wasn't pleasant cycling, but at least I didn't have to fear getting a flat tire!"

The most popular commercially produced wheel-covering surrogate, though, was the wooden tire. In 1941, when a business organization announced a contest seeking the best inventions for bike tire substitutes, it received more than 2,000 entries. Each of the three winning ideas was a variation on a wooden tire. The first design was a solid wooden hoop that fit around the rim. The second used small wooden blocks, each individually screwed directly into the rim. The third was a strip of small blocks linked together by spring coils, which lined the rim. Around 100,000 wooden tires of the third design were eventually manufactured. But in August 1943, their public sale and purchase was forbidden when the tire-rationing system began distributing coupons for these wooden tires in place of rubber ones.

While all the tire stand-ins looked strange, the noises many of them made were even stranger. Though the spiral metal tires were said to make "only a slight rattle," one woman wrote that her wooden tires made "an irritating tumult," while a witness claimed that such tires "skip over the cobblestones" with a "rattle and crunch."

If wooden tires were known for being clamorous, the tire solution of very last resort was even more notorious for making noise. When tires had disintegrated and no replacement was available, many cyclists simply rode on the wheels' metal rims. Tireless bikes became known as "tanks" because, when ridden, they sounded like the caterpillar tracks of armored vehicles. During the occupation, one Amsterdammer claimed, "These cyclists no longer need to ring their bells since they can be heard from afar, before they even turn the street corners." When two teenage girls biked on rims from the city's south side to the city's east side in order to bring homemade onion cookies to a hospitalized friend, their four tireless wheels made—one of the girls recalled—"what they call in Amsterdam 'a fucking racket.'" In addition, the cyclist said, "The trembling and shaking hurt our arms. Our hands turned crimson. We had to shout to hear each other. Windows flew open and curses rained down on us."

Tireless rims—especially if the roadway was wet or icy—easily slipped or slid or, as one teenaged boy put it at the time, made the bike "spin around like a top." On such a bike, engaging the coaster brakes to decelerate or stop often induced more slipping and sliding. Riding without a tire caused spokes to break and the rim to weaken until, eventually, the wheel collapsed. Therefore, one rode on rims with the utmost care. An observer noted that each time one biker crossed tram tracks on a tireless bike, he then subjected the wheels to "a meticulous inspection."

In the first months of the occupation, back when everyone still had access to adequate tires, one Dutchman had prophetically declared: "The bike? It belongs in Holland like cattle belong in the pasture. Even if we have to ride on iron tires like in the early days, the Dutch shall remain cycling!" And indeed, with tires or without, they continued doing just that.

AFTER LIVING FOR more than two years in hiding, on August 4, 1944, Anne Frank and her group were discovered and arrested. Within days, they would be shipped out of the city on their way east to the concentration camps.*

---

*One of the Frank family's helpers, Victor Kugler—"Mr. Kraler" in Anne's diary—was arrested and sent to a labor camp near Zwolle, sixty miles east of Amsterdam, where he was forced to salvage usable parts from broken-down, confiscated bikes in order to create roadworthy models for the Germans.

During the two years after the mass bike confiscations of 1942, the threat of losing one's bike to the Germans had diminished. While Germans or their collaborators (particularly those in the Landwacht, a Dutch military unit made up of Dutch fascists) continued commandeering a few bikes for themselves or for friends and relations, these were usually isolated incidents. The fear of large-scale bike thefts had dissipated, and Amsterdammers cycled with alertness but without a fear on the scale that had been present during the requisitions of the summer of '42.

Any relaxed, but cautious, attitude in Amsterdam about cycling changed in September 1944. Three months earlier, on June 6, 1944—D-Day—Allied troops had landed on the French coast and, after much fighting, had liberated Paris on August 25. The Allies, moving toward Holland, had freed Brussels on September 3 and Antwerp the following day. On September 5, word swept across Amsterdam that the Allies were on their way and would liberate the capital within hours. Hope and excitement cheered the Dutch (many lined the major approaches into the city from the west in anticipation of welcoming their liberators). At the same time, fear and anxiety gripped the Germans. Rumors ran rampant and everyone became a bit crazy. "A jittery tension drives everyone out into the streets," wrote one diarist that day who watched long columns of "motor coaches full of *moffen*" leaving the city. "No one is sleeping tonight. Tonight Amsterdam will be liberated from the swastika."

On that day (which quickly became known as Dolle Dinsdag—Mad Tuesday), crowds of Amsterdammers stood and watched the Germans and their collaborators scurry to Central Station, desperate to catch eastbound trains. Given that too few train cars were available to accommodate all those who wished to flee the city, according to one onlooker:

> Raids were launched on bicycles across the city. The Germans needed bikes for their exodus and they took them from everyone. In the street, a group of ten or, sometimes, twenty men appeared with a rifle at the ready, summoned each cyclist to step off and examined each bike. If its tires appeared sound and air-filled, then it was pinched. . . .
>
> The interest on the part of the public was great. But whoever stood watching was threatened with being shot. Of course, the public spread a large-scale warning. Approaching cyclists were intercepted so they had time to turn back. Or they were snuck into houses until the raid was over. Many riders tried to escape by quickly riding straight through. But this was dangerous, because if the summons to stop was not heeded, the Germans immediately fired.
>
> In front of the passage under the Rijksmuseum, an old man stood warning the cyclists. Hundreds turned back. The Germans, who were nabbing bikes behind the Rijksmuseum, eventually wised up because no cyclists were coming through. One of the soldiers walked through the Rijksmuseum. The old man was caught in the act and taken away.

The soldiers rejected any bike that had solid tires, lacked tires or had pneumatic tires that were bandaged from the outside to contain the air. When people realized this, they commenced wrapping their tires with decoy rags to ward off the Germans.

One young city resident—who fled by bike with his fascist boy scout unit—wrote in his diary: "We cycle slowly through

Amsterdam. The people look upon us with astonishment and derision and laughter."

Unfortunately for Amsterdammers—and contrary to the popular belief of both the elated Dutch and the panicked Germans—the Allies did not push northward to Amsterdam; they were not yet prepared to fully invade Holland. Unbeknownst to everyone, the city's liberation wasn't just hours away. Freedom actually wouldn't come for another eight long months.

Within days of Mad Tuesday, many of the Germans and NSB-ers who had fled town returned to their posts in Amsterdam. The sour mood that had already reigned during the occupation now grew even darker and grimmer. One eyewitness stated:

As the front came closer, the part of the country that was still occupied became smaller. There were, therefore, proportionally more Germans among us. They became nastier and nastier as their military position became less secure. They all wanted our bicycles now and would stop us in the street and take them.

Peter Lindeman, a resident of Cornelis Krusemanstraat in Amsterdam-South, saw from his apartment window Landwachters sealing off the street. "Bike confiscation," warned his wife. Lindeman later wrote:

I run downstairs, cross the street and go into the cycle garage. It's busy here as people rush to get their bikes out. Behind the garage is a narrow walkway and the bikes are quickly being handed to neighbors there. . . . By the time the Landwachters arrive, the garage will be empty.

With my bike in hand, I cross the street. In the middle
of the roadway, about forty yards from each other, there are
Landwachters with rifles slung over their shoulders. When
I reach my building, my wife opens the door and lets me
in. I go inside and my wife shuts the door. Right then, I
hear someone scream. Through the little window, I see a fat
Landwachter with a red face storming toward the door. He
bangs the door with the butt of his rifle and screams, "Open
this door!"

"There goes your bike," my wife says.

I open the door.

"What can I do for you?" I calmly ask him.

"Get out here with that bike!" he shouts.

"I live here and I have a permit for my bike. I need it for
my work."

"Doesn't matter!" screams the hysterical troublemaker.
"Get out here!" he shouts while pointing his rifle at me.

With trembling knees, I step outside.

Despite the terrorization, Lindeman's exemption permit ultimately enabled him to retain his bike. Many others weren't as
fortunate. After a performance at the Concertgebouw, audience
members and musicians alike discovered that their bikes had been
pilfered from the building's cycle garage. *De Vrije Kunstenaar* (The
Free Artist), an illegal newspaper devoted to the arts, reported,
"Neither the dismissal of the Jewish orchestra members nor all
the manhunts conducted up until now could have procured an
outcome like with this bicycle theft. Evidently, this attack on
property was regarded as the straw that broke the camel's back."
The musicians went on strike; the concert series was canceled.

Most, but not all, Amsterdammers whose bicycles were confiscated at least survived the theft. One deaf Amsterdammer who failed to hear a German's order that he stop and relinquish his bike was shot and killed. Another Amsterdammer, cycling with a child, was ordered to stop by a Landwachter. The cyclist failed to do so and the Landwachter opened fire. "A 'Dutchman' shoots at a fellow countryman and his child," lamented the illegal newspaper *Ons Volk*, "all for the sake of a bike. . . ."

Despite the horrors, some Hollanders were able to express a defiant humor about the situation. A piece in one underground newspaper parodied the sanctimonious manner in which the Nazi-controlled press praised every German act. It read:

> From the headquarters of the Führer, the supreme commander of the German army has let it be known: After a long and obstinate fight, five large units have successfully forced an enemy cyclist off his bike. The front wheel was smashed to the ground; the bell was silenced by the storm troopers, while the handlebars were captured. The frame and the generator fell into our hands. The tire valve and the bike pump were bombed by the air force. Sergeant Heinz has particularly distinguished himself in this battle by heroically puncturing a hole on the rear tire. The SS Death's Head Division had a major impact on this successful attack. Our own losses are small, only some missing uniform buttons. Furthermore, we have learned there is still heavy fighting for the tail light.

IN LATE 1944, the liberation of Amsterdam was not only still months away, but the period ahead would prove to be the most

difficult of the occupation. Amsterdammers would face a strenuous winter that would become known as the *Hongerwinter*—the
Starvation Winter. The Germans, fighting a losing war, became
increasingly obsessed with self-preservation. As a result, basic
necessities for civilians became even scarcer. On October 25, the
Nazis cut off the city's supply of gas—the fuel used for heating
and cooking in many Amsterdam apartments. Two weeks earlier, the Nazis had cut off the city's electricity supply. In many
apartments, Amsterdammers pedaled on propped-up bikes to
create small amounts of electricity via the bike's generator.[*]

Without electricity, the city's tram system no longer operated;
the tramcars themselves were hauled off to Germany. An effective strike by the nation's railroad engineers—aimed at impeding
the movements of the Nazis—halted train service throughout
the country; the trains themselves wound up in Germany. And
for those few autos and trucks that had not already been stolen
by the Nazis, gasoline was not available—and had not been since
the previous year. Due to this lack of motorized transport, hardly
any food managed to reach the city. As one Amsterdam diarist
recorded that winter:

> We live . . . without gas, light, electricity, without enough
> fuel, without enough food. There are no longer any films, no
> trams, no showers or baths, no clothing available, no luxury,
> no comfort. What we have to survive on: one kilogram of
> grain (1¼ loaves of bread) and one kilogram of potatoes per
> week. One by one, the other rations have been scratched

---

[*]Many of the Resistance's printing presses that produced underground
newspapers were run on electricity generated by the pedaling of stationary bikes.

from the calendar. Meat, milk, butter and sugar have become historical concepts. Cheese also ran out this week.

The lack of food in the city forced Amsterdammers to venture into the countryside on *hongertochten*—hunger treks—seeking foodstuffs at their sources. From farmers, they bought mostly potatoes, flour, bacon, butter and lard but also eggs, milk, cheese, cream, ham, sausage, rabbit, oats, barley, carrots, apples, pears, salt, peas, onions, beans, cabbage, Brussels sprouts, vegetable oil, sugar beets—any marginally edible item they could get their hands on, even flower bulbs. One Amsterdam office worker who regularly ate flower bulbs that winter noted in her diary, "At this moment, we're just dogs that will eat anything." Another Amsterdam diarist wrote that the amount of food available was "too little to live on and too much to die from."

At first, the trekkers paid for the food in cash. Then later, short of cash, they bartered whatever they had: gold, silverware, jewelry, watches, antiques, china, linen, furniture, paintings, sculptures, clothes, shoes, wooden clogs, rubber boots, bicycle parts, wool, towels, books, tools, labor, petroleum and coal (before fuel items themselves became scarce), baby supplies, bleaching powder, balls of string and even, it was said, pianos. When the trekkers ran out of goods, they offered the farmers their bicycles. And when they had absolutely nothing of material value left, they simply offered the only things they had: a gaunt look, a few tears and a hard-luck story that they hoped could be exchanged for sympathy in the form of something—*anything*—to eat.

After the farms nearest Amsterdam were depleted, the trekkers traveled increasingly farther from the city in search of food. Incredibly, those very same broken-down bikes that couldn't be trusted to survive a jaunt across the city were now expected not only to cross dozens of miles of countryside but to then return bearing hefty amounts of food. According to the sociologist Dr. G. J. Kruijer, who, after the war, extensively surveyed Amsterdammers who had undertaken such expeditions, more than half of all Amsterdam households conducted at least one such quest for food. So many trekkers from the city crowded the country roads, one Amsterdammer declared that a particular out-of-town stretch was "busier than Kalverstraat"—the city's main shopping street. Another hunger trekker claimed the roads north of Amsterdam were filled with "endless processions of atrophied people, old and young—often *too* old and *too* young for such traipsing through wind and rain."

Because the farmlands to the west, south and east of Amsterdam were targeted by trekkers from Dutch cities in those areas, many Amsterdammers headed north. From behind Central Station, they would ride the ferry on its short trip across the IJ waterway before venturing into the North Holland countryside. One food seeker wrote:

At four a.m., when it was still dark, the march started and the tail end of the melancholy hunger procession is still lost among the blocks of the capital. Everybody marches in one direction and we involuntarily think back to happier times. Back then, it was springtime and the merry stream from Amsterdam went westward to the bulb fields. Beaming sunshine. Glittering bicycles with top-notch tires. Take no risk: just put on a new tire before you leave home. . . . Just stop at the wayside inn for a glass of milk, a bar of chocolate, a ham sandwich. . . .

Back then: everyone on bikes to the bulb fields!

Nowadays: on a wobbly, rusty old bike to the farmers for spuds.

"General Hunger" has called the roll on the IJ Ferry and his emaciated followers have reported themselves present. Wretches with ramshackle vehicles, patched up cargo bikes without tires, rented handcarts or the chassis of a baby carriage laboriously dragged along by a rope.

"General Hunger" points toward the north. . . .

With a thousand other starvelings, we have pedaled on bare rims from Amsterdam to the extreme north of North Holland. . . . A thousand starving wretches, a thousand bicycles without tires, rattling and clattering like machine-guns, bumping and jolting over bricks, rubble and concrete. . . .

Who preached that hell would be a scorching furnace? This is hell: benumbed feet in sopping shoes, lashing rain, icy wind, a burden as heavy as lead and a gloomy darkness all around. A bicycle wheel that collapses, weariness that leads to a swoon, and—in all this chilly rain—a burning thirst and a gnawing sensation of hunger. . . .

Right in front of us, raucous curses are heard. And behind us an anxious voice whispers a heartrending prayer: "God, don't let that rim collapse now! I am thirsty, hungry. I can go no farther. How am I to get home?"

The fear of the collapse of one's wheels (which were likely already missing several spokes) was ever present. Kruijer calculated that the average haul of food by bike was an astounding *120 pounds.*[*] Unfortunately, so much weight on such weak wheels foreboded ruin. One trekker described an incident witnessed on the road back to Amsterdam: "An elderly man's front wheel has collapsed to the fork. He lies there. No, fortunately, he scrambles to his feet. What now? He stands there with a broken bike and a lot of bags, heavy bags of potatoes. You ride on, for what can you do? You can't carry any more yourself." Another trekker from Amsterdam wrote of seeing such distraught souls sitting alongside the road "staring at that broken wheel as if it would fix itself."

One hunger trekker, on the road back to Amsterdam, repaired the back tire of her bike, which was loaded with 77 pounds of potatoes. Her effort was all for naught; the tire soon went flat again. So the woman decided to ride home on the flat tire. Writing that winter, she described the trip back to Amsterdam:

> Dreary is the road. Dreary is the long line of people . . .
> cycling on rims, on solid rubber tires, even on pneumatic
> tires. But most people are walking with their bikes in hand.
> Flat tire, flat tire, flat tire. . . . Into the wind with that flat
> tire. But you're still going faster than those walking. . . . You
> think that you now can go no farther and yet you go farther.
> Swirling rain brings the cold with it. Drab is the day. Even
> more drab is the endless hunger march back to the city. You
> pedal on. You no longer think, you just pedal. Yet more
> walking people who push little carts, pull little wagons, drag

---

[*] One Amsterdammer who had made the treks noted: "What an immense amount a bicycle can transport and what a load a man can bear when it means fighting his and his family's hunger."

heavily laden bikes. All going to the city. The city where you'll soon be welcomed by a checkpoint. That menacing thought has been with you all day.

Indeed, if trying to survive a trek on a decrepit, untrustworthy bike wasn't distressing enough, there also loomed a constant threat of the seizure of the garnered food, the bike itself or any male aged 16 to 45 (who, by now, had all been ordered to labor in German work camps). Along the way, food could be stolen by random patrols of German troops or the Landwacht ("robbers of a different feather," as one trekker called them). More likely, because gathering food was branded as black market trading and thus illegal, agents of the Crisis Control Service, a national governmental agency, searched through the contraband and appropriated the most prized items—ham, bacon, eggs, sausage, etc. The seized articles were then, in theory, furnished to hospitals and soup kitchens. Because the routes from the farmlands north of Amsterdam funneled to the IJ Ferry, these authorities (under the watchful eye of German soldiers) would often establish a checkpoint at the ferry landing where the trekkers waited to board the boat. One young woman who had been forced repeatedly to surrender her food at the ferry, wrote: "You had thus made the trip for absolutely nothing and I can assure you that then, you really had to cry."

Even if one was fortunate enough to avoid an inspection, once back in the heart of the city, danger still lurked. Two women who embarked on a three-day trip on borrowed bikes ("our own completely shot to the hell, ramshackle frames, the spokes loose or missing, tires stolen") returned to Amsterdam with potatoes, lard, bacon and apples late on the afternoon of Christmas 1944.

One of the women recounted in her diary:

> On the IJ Ferry, a large crowd pressed together, all with bikes
> loaded down with crammed, bulging sacks and boxes, suit-
> cases and crates. It was striking how little was spoken by the
> emaciated crowd. Silent, silent, they went to shore, then away.
>
> When we went under the [Central Station] viaduct,
> suddenly there was no one left to be seen, the city looked
> deserted. We pedaled hard. Then suddenly we came upon
> those who, because of the darkness and their speed, we could
> not see. We heard them shout: "Bike-swiping on Martelaars-
> gracht!" Thanks a lot, guys! We quickly changed direction.
>
> A little later, shots rang out; and then again shots, from
> the still, desolate city. Gruesome. At exactly six o'clock, we
> dismounted, quickly ran inside with the bikes and the bag-
> gage, and then shut, gloriously shut, the door, with the locks
> and the bolts.

In order to feed his family of seven, the 50-year-old Amsterdammer Pieter Oostervink undertook numerous hunger treks on
bikes that had garden-hose tires, solid tires or no tires at all.
Toward spring, he was cycling back to the capital when an enormous wave of Allied bombers rumbled overhead en route to their
targets in Germany. In his diary, Oostervink wrote: "My rusted
chain squeaks: 'The *moffen* are going to be beaten to a pulp.' The
front and back wheels rattle: 'Beaten, beaten.' Pebbles bounce to
the side and whisper: 'Beaten.'"

Oostervink would survive to see the Germans beaten. The
same couldn't be said for many of his fellow citizens, tens of
thousands of whom were suffering from edema. Each week

during the Starvation Winter, Amsterdammers died by the hundreds. According to official city statistics, almost 2,500 citizens succumbed to "starvation" or "cold."

IN THE WAKE of Mad Tuesday and through the Starvation Winter, the bicycle became an even more important tool to everyday Netherlanders. The bicycle was increasingly significant to those active in the Resistance movement. The transport of messages, illegal newspapers, weapons and even shot-down Allied airmen relied heavily upon bikes. Even Audrey Hepburn, then a youngster living in Arnhem, was called to duty by the Resistance. "I stuffed [illegal leaflets] in my woolen socks in my wooden shoes, got on my bike and delivered them," she later recalled. Of course, though, these bikes used for anti-Nazi activities were difficult to hold onto. For example, among the staff of the underground newspaper *Vrij Nederland*, one member lost bikes to theft three times between October 1944 and February 1945, while another had two bikes confiscated and one stolen during roughly the same period. (Then again, in order for them to have transportation for carrying out their activities, members of the Resistance themselves sometimes stole bikes.)

In March 1945, during the dwindling weeks of the war, bike thieving at the hands of the Germans reached yet a higher level. This seemed to have been triggered by a particular event. At around midnight on the night of March 6, on a country road sixty miles southeast of Amsterdam, members of the Resistance ambushed a BMW car that happened to be conveying Rauter, the head of the SS and police forces in the Netherlands. Rauter's chauffeur and adjunct were both killed, but Rauter himself, despite being shot six times, managed to survive.

228 In the City of Bikes

The retaliation for this attack was swift. On March 8, at five different locations around the country, the Germans executed a total of 263 Dutch prisoners, most of whom were captured members of the Resistance or political prisoners. Among these were 53 men who were lined up in the early morning by the Amsteldijk in Amsterdam-South and gunned down by agents of the German "Green Police."* Passersby were forced at gunpoint to witness the murders; the bodies of the executed were left where they fell as a diabolical warning to the citizens of the capital.

Later that day, the Green Police—in, apparently, another reprisal for the attack on their leader—set a number of traps for cyclists in various parts of the city: Leidseplein, Overtoom, Amstelveenseweg and elsewhere. When confiscating bikes the year before, the Germans had simply collected the cycles on the spot, which limited each thief to riding away with a maximum of just two bikes. Now, though, they employed a new tactic. At each trap set during the late-afternoon rush hour, they snared upward of hundreds of unsuspecting cyclists (even children on kids' bikes). Then, under armed guard, these poor souls—pushing or riding their bikes—were led in long columns to the Colonial Institute (now the Tropics Museum), headquarters of the Green Police. There the bikes—thousands of them—were confiscated en masse.

One eyewitness wrote that day: "Once again, they're acting like wild beasts! Everything is being confiscated, even women's bikes and bikes with or without solid rubber tires. Some people think this is evidence that they're leaving here. If only that were

*The Green Police were noted for their green uniforms and known by Amsterdammers as the "green executioners," "green murderers," "green demons," "green bandits," "green thieves," "green *moffen*," etc.

true!" Unfortunately, it wasn't true. The Germans did not leave town on those bikes that day. Worse still, German policemen and soldiers continued to trap cyclists in the weeks that followed. Exemption permits became worthless; any Hollander's bike was fair game, even one belonging to a doctor.

While the Germans used the bikes mainly as a means of transport, the stolen bikes were also used as a means of extortion. For example, one Amsterdammer was threatened with his bike being confiscated—unless he produced a package of shag tobacco. Another man was told he could keep his bike in exchange for a civilian suit. Some bikes nabbed by the Germans were offered for sale or barter to other Amsterdammers.

The manner in which these confiscations were now occurring became even more ruthless than they'd been in previous years. On the morning of April 5, for example, a man who tried to escape a trap laid for cyclists on Tweede Constantijn Huygensstraat was shot dead. The week before, in the same area, a 60-year-old man who wasn't quick enough when handing over his bike was bludgeoned to death with the butt of a German's rifle.

The illegal newspaper *Het Parool* cautioned its clandestine readers:

> Don't help the enemy gain means of transportation! Leave your bike at home! The bike confiscations will continue occurring in the coming days. Don't think: I'll slip right past. When you lose your bike, it's not only a personal loss, it's a little advantage for the Germans. In the afternoons, when the confiscations tend to reach their peak, no bike should be seen on the streets.

ONE HOLLANDER WHO managed to protect her bike from thieves—be they common or uniformed—was Elsa Caspers, a highly active courier for the Resistance. Throughout the occupation, she had used her bike to shuttle escaped Allied prisoners of war. But then, on the afternoon of May 5, 1945, just hours after German commanders in Holland had signed the terms of surrender, SS troops, in the midst of looting the Dutch town of Leersum, nabbed Caspers' bike. Then, three days later, Caspers borrowed a bike and was cycling with another member of the Resistance to the town of Driebergen. She recalled:

> Near Doorn we were stopped by two SS men—were they never going to leave us in peace? This time they wanted our bikes. I said I was a nurse and had a permit for mine and he couldn't take it. His answer was to aim his rifle at me and say, "Choose between giving me your bicycle or being shot." I had, of course, no choice and I was livid. I had managed to hang on to my bicycle all through the war and now, in the first three days of freedom, I had lost two! It was maddening.

Unfortunately, just hours before Caspers lost her first bike, her fellow Resistance courier, Annick van Hardeveld, was given no choice between life and death. Annick was shot dead in cold blood.

AT THE MAY 4 Remembrance Day gathering, one of the bike couriers saw me standing alone and without a beer. He held out a Grolsch to me and asked if I was a courier.

"No," I told him as I accepted the beer. "I just like biking."

He pointed at the small monument for Annick van Hardeveld and said, "Yeah, she was killed on her bike while delivering newspapers."

"Actually," I said, "she was delivering a message."

The courier grimaced and shook his head. It was a familiar look, one I'd received often from other Dutch people while discussing historical events of their country. When speaking Dutch, the words fumble from my mouth in a way that only discredits whatever I'm saying. To ensure that my comment wasn't lost in translation, I said in English, "She wasn't delivering newspapers."

The courier shook his head again and then called over another courier standing nearby. The first asked the second, "Annick was killed while delivering newspapers, right?"

The second courier gulped his beer, then replied, "Yeah, that's right."

"*Ja*," a third one chimed in, "delivering illegal newspapers for the Resistance."

"See?" the first courier asked me.

"Yeah, but—" I began to explain before a demanding "SHHH!" spread through the small crowd. It was eight o'clock; the customary two minutes of silence were beginning. On the street beside us, two trams came to a standstill. Several taxis stopped and cut their engines. The sudden silence, here in the center of the city, was eerie. It was broken only by the murmur from an approaching group of four tourists. Noticing the silent gathering and the stock-still vehicles, one of the tourists wondered aloud in English, "What's happening?"

The two minutes of silence, observed annually, are intended for reflection on not just those who suffered in World War II but on those victims and veterans of all wars. And that's what I was doing. Well, actually I was thinking I needed to explain to the messengers that Annick *didn't* die delivering illegal newspapers. She'd been cycling to Amsterdam-North to verbally deliver a message to four members of the Dutch underground. German commanders had signed an unconditional surrender earlier that evening in which they agreed to end all hostilities in Holland, effective the next morning. But if, for some reason, the Nazi leaders quartered on Museumplein refused to surrender, the Resistance wanted to be ready for them. So Annick had been dispatched that night to inform these four fighters about a meeting scheduled for the following morning. During those late curfew hours, she wore a guise popular among Resistance couriers: a Red Cross nurse's uniform. (Nurses were exempt from the curfew prohibitions.) But while Annick was cycling northward to the IJ Ferry, Green Policemen in an attack vehicle opened fire on her. The following morning, when Annick and all four Resistance members she'd been dispatched to contact failed to arrive at the appointed meeting place, the other members of her unit realized something was amiss.

But why had the Germans fired on Annick? Could they not discern her nurse's uniform in the dark? Or were they simply submitting to bloodlust, claiming one final martyr before leaving town? No matter the reason, the result was the same: Annick was shot 21 times and died almost instantly at just about the very spot where we three dozen were now observing the silence, here at the foot of Martelaarsgracht—Martyr's Canal.*

---

*While Martyr's Canal received its moniker many centuries before Van Hardeveld's murder (and for reasons now unknown), in 1997 a new square in Amsterdam was christened Koerierstersplein—Couriers Square—in honor of the women who worked for the Resistance as couriers.

During the two minutes of silence, I was eager to explain all this to the courier. But when the two minutes expired, a couple of messengers used bike inner tubes to strap white roses to the sides of the monument. A white ribbon that accompanied the flowers read: "We shall never forget." This struck me as odd. How could the couriers forget when they hadn't known in the first place?

By now, the three misinformed guys I'd briefly talked with had fallen in with the rest of the crowd. I was left standing by myself, waiting to get their attention. Frustrated, I felt like climbing atop the small monument and screaming the truth about Annick. But then, I realized, maybe the truth didn't conform to their legend of their patron saint. To those engaged in the delivery of physical goods, it probably wouldn't be appealing to know Annick had been conveying a verbal message, not newspapers. In fact, she was explicitly expected to carry out her tasks *without* possessing any evidence of illegal activities. The myth of Annick distributing illegal newspapers, though, at least provided a tidy motive for her killing: she'd been caught in possession.

In the end, I kept my mouth shut. Having faithfully adopted Annick as their own, the couriers deserved whatever fable best fulfilled their fantasies.

Having paid my respects, I quickly finished my beer. Then I got on my bike and rode away.

12
Give My Father's Bike Back: The Occupation's Legacy

uring the final days of the war in Europe, Hitler—the "chief robber," as one Dutchman who'd lost his bike to German soldiers called him—committed suicide. An early death awaited other leaders who had tampered with the bicycles of the Dutch. Reich's Commissioner Seyss-Inquart was captured and taken to Nuremberg, Germany, where, along with other top Nazi officials, he was tried by the Allies. During the trial, a lawyer asked Seyss-Inquart if he'd "turned over the essential transportation means of the Netherlands to the Reich." Seyss-Inquart replied:

> I could not, in principle, dispose of the means of transportation; that was a matter for the Transport Command of the Armed Forces. Once I merely took part in requisitioning 50,000 bicycles—there were 4,000,000 bicycles in the Netherlands—for the mobilization of the troops within the Netherlands.

Seyss-Inquart was found guilty of committing war crimes, committing crimes against humanity and waging wars of aggression. It's unclear under which count, if any, his "merely" stealing 50,000 bikes fell. His sentence: death. On October 16, 1946, Seyss-Inquart, along with nine other Nazi leaders, was hanged in Nuremberg.

Hanns Albin Rauter, the head of both the SS and the police forces in Holland, was not tried at Nuremberg after the war but in a special Dutch court. Rauter—who had banned cyclist hand-holding, banned dinking, banned pedicabs and ordered the confiscation of the Jewish bikes—was charged with, among other things, persecuting the Jews, killing hostages, pillaging and appropriating Dutch property.

In his defense, Rauter argued: "The population of the occupied territory, in violation of the laws and customs of war, had refused to bear quietly the burden of the occupation and in every possible manner had rebelled against the German authorities." In other words, Rauter blatantly blamed his own atrocious acts on those Dutch who had resisted: the members of the underground, the people who had gone into hiding, *the cyclists*! *They* hadn't played fair, he whined, and therefore *he* hadn't been obligated to play fair. His argument fell flat with the judges. Rauter was found guilty on all counts. Though capital punishment hadn't been practiced in Holland since 1870, a special exception was made for war criminals like Rauter. He was executed by firing squad in Scheveningen on March 25, 1949.

Anton Mussert, the leader of the NSB, was also tried in a Dutch court. Mussert prided himself on his role in repealing the bicycle tax, but that accomplishment apparently didn't sway the Dutch judges; they found him guilty of, among other things, aiding the enemy. Mussert, too, met his end before a firing squad.

Edward Voûte, the wartime mayor of Amsterdam who had overseen the city's role in the 1942 bike confiscations, got off lighter. Convicted of treason, Voûte served three years in prison before being released in 1949. He died the following year.

Commissioner Claas Bakker—the longtime head of the traffic police who had enforced the Nazi-mandated crackdown on Amsterdam's cyclists—was investigated by a postwar Ministry of Justice panel that sought to purge wartime collaborators from public office. At the panel's behest, Bakker was fired from his position. Despite having served the city's police department for more than forty years, Bakker was denied his right to his pension. He died in 1949.

As for the 140,000 Jews of the Netherlands, some 75 percent perished in the Nazi death camps. The Jewish population in Amsterdam had stood at 80,000 when the Nazis invaded and was only 5,000 after the war. Among the eight members of the Anne Frank group, only Anne's father, Otto, survived.

DURING THEIR TIME in Holland, the Nazis had stolen everything that hadn't been nailed down. If it *had* been nailed down, they got a crowbar, pried it free and stole it—then they stole the crowbar. Factories were picked clean of both finished products and the machinery itself. Hospitals, museums, laboratories, libraries, etc. were looted. After the war, the Dutch Central Statistics Bureau estimated that, of the 100,000 cars that had been in the country before the German invasion, only 34,000 remained. Of the 53,000 trucks, only 14,200 remained. And of the 4 million bicycles, only 2 million remained, most of which were—as one observer at the time put it—in "extremely poor condition."

At military installations where German soldiers had been quartered during the occupation, enormous heaps of dilapidated bikes were discovered. The Germans (or, rather, their slave laborers) had picked over the bikes for useful parts; the bicycles' rusting carcasses now lay useless. Many other bikes were said to have been used by the Germans as ironwork when concrete was poured in constructing bunkers along the coastline. Still other bikes were taken to Germany, where some were used as means of transport while others were melted, their metal recycled. During the war, Allied planes had sunk a cargo ship in the south of the Netherlands, in Zeeland. Two decades later, the sunken vessel was recovered. The ship, which had been retreating from the advancing Allies in 1944, was discovered to be loaded with weapons and the "countless remains of requisitioned bikes."

The novelist and reporter Hans Koning—born and raised in Amsterdam—became attached to a French army unit during the war. Not long after VE-Day, Koning—stationed in occupied Germany—was ordered to accompany a German woman into a Polish displaced-persons camp to look for a bicycle she said a Pole had stolen from her. "When the bicycle was found, it turned out to be a Dutch one," Koning later wrote, "and I asked the Polish [displaced person] to keep it, of course. The German woman told me I'd be sorry."

One German officer, who had no intention of walking from Amsterdam to a prisoner-of-war camp, had a Dutch bike with him to make the trip. A Canadian soldier, who was escorting the captured Germans, took the bike from the officer and gave it to the first Dutchman who happened to pass by. It was, as one (no-longer-illegal) newspaper reported in those first days of freedom, "a symbolic deed that warmed the heart."

From the thousands of German POWs who were marched back toward Germany over the Afsluitdijk (the 20-mile-long dike separating the IJsselmeer from the North Sea), Canadian troops recovered 2,000 bikes. According to some reports issued within weeks after the end of the war, a total of 60,000 bikes had been taken from the 120,000 German soldiers who had been captured in the Netherlands and repatriated to Germany. Many repossessed bikes were sent to the Simplex bike factory in Amsterdam, where they were restored and redistributed. Returning recovered bikes—or any bike lost to any thief during the occupation—to their rightful owners was a virtually impossible task. As one Canadian staff officer at the time remarked about the situation, "A thousand and one problems cropped up for which there were no answers in the book—and no book." While a few miraculous tales were told of an owner being reunited with his or her bike, the overwhelming majority who'd had a bike stolen from them weren't so lucky.

Despite the disorder among the bicycles, foreigners in post-liberation Amsterdam were just as amazed by the bikes as pre-war visitors had been. Except now, it wasn't the sheer *quantity* of bikes that dazzled the visitors; it was the sorry *quality* of those bikes. One British observer, in Amsterdam less than two months after the city's liberation, wrote:

> When I stand at a street corner in Amsterdam and watch the hundreds of cyclists go by, I cannot help thinking that Nederland is, at the moment, a Crazyland of Wheels. . . .

How expert they have to be to ride some of those machines!

Some have tires—of sorts. Sometimes the inner tube is all but surrounded, though by no means protected, by an outer cover with huge, bandaged rents. Often such tires give up the struggle with a "ping" and a hiss, but the rider goes pedaling on. Some such tires have no bandages and flying ends of rubber go "flip-flapping" along the smooth roadway.

Many bicycles just have no tires at all and the riders rattle by on long suffering rims. One has known a solid tire on the front wheel and a more or less pneumatic one on the rear. . . .

There can be no arguing with Nederland cyclists; they are what we would call at Westminster, the "party in power."

And such expert riders too! To see them balancing the whole family on the handlebars, crossbar and carrier, to see them skillfully threading their way through dense traffic and doing "figure of eight" crossings at a cross-roads arouses the envy of the less expert Britisher. Far from performing such feats, the average British cyclist could not ride one of the tire-less machines without breaking his neck.

And so he stands at the street corner as I have done, gazing in wonderment at the host of flip-flapping, creaking, groaning machines.

A special Amsterdam guidebook issued to the Canadian occupying forces in Holland informed its readers: "You will hear people come rattling by on the naked rims of their bicycle-wheels, and you can be assured that at each jolt they curse the 'mof' who was the cause of their discomfort." Indeed, embitterment toward all the misdeeds of the Nazis would be expressed through comments about the bike confiscations for years to come.

Several other bike-related legacies emerged from the occupation. Among them:

- The annual bicycle tax, scrapped by the Nazis, was never reinstituted.
- Because the few operable bikes were in great demand, in order to make maximum use of them, dinking became prevalent.
- Due to the confiscation of so many men's bikes, after the war it wasn't unusual to see (as a writer put it in 1945) "the wondrous appearance of a gentleman on a lady's bike." Nowadays, a large percentage of male cyclists in Amsterdam still ride unabashedly on women's model bikes.
- The Nazi-imposed law mandating that cyclists yield to motorists at unrestricted intersections (even if the biker was approaching from the right) remained part of the vehicular code. This law did not revert to its pre–World War II status until 2001.
- In the immediate postliberation years, the rate of bike theft in the city dropped drastically in comparison to the years preceding the invasion. After all that Amsterdammers had endured with their bikes during the occupation, it was as if the bicycle had been elevated to the status of a sacred possession not to be tampered with. By the mid-1950s, though, any such sacred status had vanished; bike thievery became commonplace again.

But of all the bike-related legacies of the war, "cursing the *moffen*" about the bikes was easily the most notable. It would thrive for decades.

AFTER THE WAR, Holland suffered a great shortage of bicycles, bike tires and inner tubes. In 1946, it was estimated there were 160,000 bikes in Amsterdam, a little more than half the total the city had in 1940. It would take several years for Amsterdammers to own bikes at their prewar levels because the factories of many Dutch bike manufacturers had been decimated by Nazi looting and sabotage. For example, at the vast Gazelle bicycle plant in Dieren, in late 1944 a special unit of the German army hauled off to Germany a number of the factory's machines. Then, just before the liberation, the Demolition Squad—slash-and-burn specialists—sabotaged the remaining apparatus. The stolen machines were returned to the plant in January 1946, though, and the first postwar Gazelles rolled off the assembly line in August of that year.

Before the occupation, 90 percent of bicycle tires sold in the Netherlands had been manufactured domestically. Now, immediately after the war, the country was fortunate to quickly gain the necessary raw materials (from the United Kingdom) to once again produce tires. Nevertheless, despite possessing the rubber as well as the materials to produce the inner canvas linings of the tires, for a period far fewer bicycle tires were being fabricated than the factories were capable of producing. According to the country's then minister of economic affairs, this was due to the canvas factories lacking workers. Why? "Because [the workers] had no tires for their bikes to get them to the factory." The minister called this chicken-and-egg scenario "bizarre."

In the meantime, the Dutch relied heavily on the importation of bikes and bike tires from France and Britain (and, to a lesser extent, from Belgium, Sweden, Switzerland, Italy and Czechoslovakia). But since those nations were also trying to fulfill their own postwar needs, the volume of these imports fell far short of the Dutch demand. The need for bikes was so great that in 1946, when one hundred musicians from Amsterdam's Concertgebouw Orchestra performed in the United Kingdom, at the end of their weeklong tour it was reported that the musicians "decided their most important acquisition was a pedaled speedster." So they returned to Holland each "carrying his instrument and a brand-new bicycle."

IN THE 1950s, the postwar economies in both Holland and West Germany flourished. By now, Dutch factories were producing an unprecedented number of bikes, enough for both the Holland market and for export.* The improved economies also enabled—a decade after the Nazi invasion—a "second German invasion." Tourists from Germany flocked to the Netherlands. But upon arriving in Amsterdam, many suspicious locals pondered what the adult males among the tourists had done during the war. In 1954, when two Germans entered a small Amsterdam café and ordered (in German) "zwei Helles"—two light beers, the café owner replied: "Eerst mijn fiets terug"—First, return my bike. The two tourists, correctly sensing hostility, turned and departed.

*In 1951, Dutch bicycle manufacturers shipped bicycles to America in an attempt to establish a foothold in the U.S. market. Instead of the traditional Dutch black, these bikes were painted red and blue—"specially colored to suit American tastes."

Though the Germans had inflicted far worse atrocities upon the Dutch (such as murder, enslavement, imprisonment, terrorism, etc.), for a nation of cyclists—who had been forced to become ever more reliant on their ever less reliable bikes during the hardships of the occupation—the bicycle thefts came to symbolize the lingering animosity toward the Nazis for all of their misdeeds. Over the next few years, whenever a German tourist in the Dutch capital asked a local for directions, the Amsterdammer was apt to either give false directions or ask for his bike back. If a German requested service in an Amsterdam café or restaurant, oftentimes the response was: "First, return my bike."

IN JULY 1965, less than a week after the announcement of Crown Princess Beatrix's engagement to the German Claus van Amsberg, the two embarked on a day trip through Amsterdam. It was the princess's way of introducing Claus and the capital to each other. Unfortunately for Beatrix, many in the "red city" lacked passion for the royal family, which they exhibited by giving the royal couple's procession the cold shoulder.*

Among the Amsterdammers who did turn out to greet the royals were a pair of young writers, Joop van Tijn and Renate Rubinstein. The two, both Jewish, unfurled a banner with a message directed at Claus, who—as a teenager—had briefly

---

*At city hall (where less than half the city council bothered to put in an appearance on this occasion), when Mayor Gijs van Hall officially welcomed Claus, the mayor apologized for the sparse and unenthusiastic crowd by saying, "Amsterdam is known as a troublesome city and Amsterdammers are certainly troublesome people."

served in the German army in the closing months of the war. The protesters attached the banner to 20 children's helium balloons, intending to elevate the whole shebang to where it could be seen by the royal procession. But "after much injudicious fumbling with gravity and balloons" (as Van Tijn put it), the banner failed to ascend. Out of desperation, the banner was instead displayed along the railing of the bridge on Zwanenburgwal—without the princess or her fiancé ever seeing it. The banner read: MIJN FIETS TERUG (RETURN MY BIKE).

The phrase used by Amsterdammers who'd actually lost bikes was now being expressed by activists, some of whom hadn't been born by the time the Germans invaded Holland (Van Tijn was a toddler in 1940). A new generation of Dutch had inherited the postwar grudge against the Germans.

When, in March 1966, Beatrix and Claus wed in the city, some 2,000 antimonarchist/anti-German youths took to the streets, intent on spoiling the festivities. By then, Amsterdam's radical youth movement had mushroomed, due in large part to the activities of the Provos (see chapter 16). At the intersection of Raadhuisstraat and Spuistraat, just after the royal couple had passed in their golden carriage, protesters heaved bikes into the street. Two blocks farther on, homemade smoke bombs were tossed at the carriage. On Keizersgracht, across the canal from the Westerkerk—the church that served as the site of the wedding—police on horseback charged at rebellious youths, who responded by flinging dozens of bikes into the paths of the horses. Elsewhere in the city, one cop suffered injuries after being struck in the head by a hurled bike. While the most popular chant among the protesters was "Long live the republic!," along the wedding procession's route the newlyweds were met by placards that demanded, "Give me back my bike!" and walls painted with "I want my bike back."

IN THE EARLY 1970s, the anti-German phrase grew even more popular after Dutch soccer fans adopted it. When West Germany hosted the soccer World Cup in 1974, the Dutch team, with its dazzling "Total Football" style of play, knocked out the favored Brazilian side in the semifinals. The night before the final match—to be played against West Germany in Munich—Dutch revelers congregated in that city's center, where they sang, "Give me back my bike!" During the final game itself, in the stands banners read "First, return my bike." Despite the overwhelmingly popular sentiment in the Netherlands that theirs was the better team, the Dutch side lost to West Germany. This bitter defeat did nothing to alleviate the animosity toward the Germans.

The following year, the Dutch soccer club F.C. Amsterdam traveled to Cologne, Germany, to play F.C. Cologne. While the Amsterdam team bus drove through the city center, right back Frits Flinkevleugel—a noted jokester who was born and raised in Amsterdam—led the other players in singing, "I want my bicycle back." Then, upon seeing a parked bike, Flinkevleugel instructed the driver to stop the bus. As he hauled the bike aboard, Flinkevleugel reportedly quipped, "My grandpa asked me to retrieve his bike."

In 1988, at the European soccer championship held in West Germany, Holland met the host team in a semifinal match in Hamburg. After the Dutch won, 2–1, the nation exploded in delirium. As one jubilant Dutch player put it, "The

Germany-syndrome is off our backs." An overjoyed Dutch fan proclaimed, "The German soldiers stole my bicycle fifty years ago, but now it's okay." At the championship match in Munich, when Holland beat the Soviet Union, 2–0, thousands of Dutch fans in the stands joyously chanted, "Grandma, we've found your bike!"*

FINALLY BEATING THE Germans—and the passage of time— may have softened the Hollanders' lingering acrimony toward their neighbors, but by no means did the victory completely erase the bitterness or the resentment about the stolen bicycles.

In June 1997, when leaders of the European Union nations gathered in Amsterdam for meetings and the proceedings broke for lunch, Amsterdam's Mayor Schelto Patijn (known for regularly commuting between the mayor's official residence and city hall by bike) presented each head of state with a gift: a new Dutch bicycle. The men were then invited to use their two-wheelers to make the 300-yard trip across a bridge to the Amstel Hotel, site of the luncheon. The Dutch prime minister, Wim Kok (known for regularly commuting between the prime minister's official residence and parliament by bike), immediately hopped on the bike given to him. The leaders of Britain, France, Spain, Italy, Ireland, Belgium, Sweden,

---

*Wartime references are also a part of the fan banter at soccer matches between Ajax of Amsterdam and Feyenoord of Rotterdam—the fiercest rivalry within the Dutch domestic league. Perversely, Ajax supporters taunt fans of Feyenoord by gleefully singing about the Nazi bombing of Rotterdam. In turn, and equally perverse, Feyenoord supporters taunt fans of Ajax—a team with historic Jewish connections—by collectively hissing, an invocation of the Nazi gas chambers.

Austria, Denmark, Finland and Greece all playfully followed suit with the youthful, newly elected British prime minister, Tony Blair, quickly pedaling into the lead. As hundreds of reporters and cameramen looked on, one national leader was noticeably absent from the peloton. Declining to bike, opting instead to walk, was the portly German chancellor Helmut Kohl. "Understandable," cracked one Dutch magazine writer about Kohl's decision. "If he'd been hoisted upon the bike seat, he would've immediately heard that they wanted that bike back."

Such anti-German sentiment had become—according to Queen Beatrix's husband in 1998—cliché. Despite the rough treatment he had received decades before in Amsterdam at both his introduction and his wedding, many Dutch people now regarded Prince Claus to be a sympathetic figure. While reacting to an opinion poll that showed Dutch youth disliked Germany, Claus told a German television program, "When asked why they're opposed to Germany, the children say, 'They stole my grandfather's bicycle.' . . . The story about the bicycles has become something of a national epos that is passed on from generation to generation."

. . . To generation. My friend Florian moved from Germany to Amsterdam in 1981, when he was 26 years old. Days after arriving, he stepped inside a shop to buy a scooter. When the shopkeeper heard the German accent, he refused to serve Florian, saying only, "First, give my father's bike back." Despite the rude reception, Florian remained in Amsterdam. During his years as a music teacher, some of his nine- and ten-year-old students have said to him: "First, return my bike." These are children so young that it's possible even their *grandparents* weren't yet born during the war. (Or—in the case of children with immigrant backgrounds—at the time of the occupation, their families were still decades from even migrating to Holland.) Nevertheless, Florian laughs off the taunts for their irony. He once explained to me, "Since living in Amsterdam, I've had about twenty bikes stolen from me." If anyone deserves his bikes back, Florian's got a strong case.

AFTER MORE THAN a half century of goading, chanting, singing and teasing for the return of the bikes, in 2009, a former German soldier who had swiped a Dutch bike expressed personal regret. He now wanted to atone for his misdeed, 64 years after the fact. The thief—who requested anonymity—said he'd taken a bike that had stood in front of the Catholic church in the Dutch town of Nijkerk—35 miles east of Amsterdam—as his unit was fleeing from the advancing Allies just weeks before the war's end. After he contacted officials at the Dutch church, he gave them a sum equal to the value of a new bike. The church officials' call for that bike's owner to come forward and collect the money made national news in both the Netherlands and Germany. A special feature of the stolen bike—which would have been known only to the bike's owner and wasn't publicly announced—was that only the left crank turned. That the right crank had been specially fixed in a locked position probably meant the bike's owner didn't have use of his or her right leg. For months, church officials searched for the rightful claimant to the former soldier's offer. Yet despite several serious inquiries, in the end, no rightful claimant was ever found.

This wasn't the first documented case of a German soldier attempting to make good on a stolen bike long after the war had ended.* But with increasingly fewer German wartime bike thieves—and fewer of their victims—still living, this was quite likely the last opportunity for such a theft to be rectified. Nevertheless, to this day, some Dutch continue to demand the return of their (grandparents') bikes—as will, possibly, generations to come.

---

*For example, in 1984, after decades of remorse, a German soldier who'd seized a bike from a Dutchman during the Battle of Arnhem donated a sum equal to the value of a new bike to a nonprofit organization in Arnhem.

13
After You Passed: The Mystery Rider

In March 2004, after twice living in the Westerpark area and twice living in the city center on Spuistraat, Amy Joy and I moved into our fifth Amsterdam apartment in our twenty months in the city. Like all our previous dwellings, this one—in Amsterdam-East—was also a temporary living situation. We could sublet the apartment for one year while the two Dutch lease-holders cycled around Southeast Asia.

Having found an affordable place that enabled us to remain in Amsterdam for another year was a tremendous relief. It was also great that the apartment provided us with a view of Wibaut-straat, where, at all times, at least one cyclist—if not dozens—was always in view. The most exciting aspect of our new place, though, was the basement storage unit. At all our previous apartments, we had to leave our bikes out on the streets overnight, where they faced the perils of the city on their own. In fact, by then, AJJ II had been stolen, as had her successor, AJJ III, while each had been locked outside overnight.

Now that we had access to indoor bike parking, Amy Joy determined it was safe enough for me to upgrade my bike. She took Brownie with her to work one day and traded him in for another old, used bike. Of course, I was reluctant to part with Brownie, the dear bike who had introduced me to Amsterdam. Nevertheless, I was thrilled to receive his replacement; it had hand brakes and three gears, all of which actually worked. Ever since I was eight years old, I'd almost always only rode bikes that had a lone gear. (Though some of those bikes were multigeared, broken shifters left them stuck in one gear.) While living at any of our four previous Amsterdam addresses, I never would have dared to own such a fancy, enticing bike.

For decades, back in America, I'd ridden up and down the hills of San Francisco, Portland, Pittsburgh, etc. always using just one gear. But now, in flat Amsterdam, riding with three whole speeds, I became a shifting maniac. Any change in elevation—no matter how slight—demanded gear adjustment. Up and over a little canal bridge? I'd slam it into first gear for the ascent and then shift back down again for the descent. I even shifted when ascending toward a street that—having once been a dike centuries earlier—was only three or four feet higher than that of the surrounding streets. Sure, it might have seemed pointless to have shifted gears for such a "climb," but not only did I routinely do so on my new bike, I also enjoyed—while riding in a pack with other commuters—hearing the *click-click-click* as some of those around me also shifted.

Not long after Amy Joy had presented me with my three-speed, the city's public transportation workers conducted a one-day strike. For an entire day, all buses, trams and metro trains remained idled. Because no ferries sailed, either, one of the two tubes of the IJ Tunnel—the tunnel for motorized traffic that runs underneath the waterway separating the city center from

Amsterdam-North—was opened to cyclists and pedestrians.

That afternoon, I rode back and forth through the tunnel, climbing and descending and climbing and descending like a skateboarder on an almost mile-long ramp. Down beneath the city, I was in heaven. Whenever I'd been asked what I missed about my hometown of San Francisco, I'd always answered: my family, burritos and *hills*. The two ends of the tunnel weren't exactly hills, but they fit the bill, if only for an afternoon.

After several rounds, I stopped at the northern end of the tunnel and watched the cyclists. Of the 1,000 that I noted exiting, 342 of them—one in three!—were *walking* their bikes. A great many of the remaining two-thirds were panting heavily as they wobbled back and forth, struggling up the incline as if they were nearing a peak in the French Alps. Surely some of those flatlanders had spent their whole lives only ever cycling in level, smooth Holland. And now this was the first day they'd ever ridden up a hill—or, at least, had attempted to do so.

ON THE MORNING of November 2, 2004 (the day of the presidential election between George W. Bush and John Kerry), I didn't have to work at the dust factory. That morning, I cycled from our new apartment and arrived at my other janitoring job a few minutes before 8:30. I quickly swabbed the locker room floor just in time for the legion of street sweepers and garbagemen to return for their morning break and muck it up again. I emptied some garbage cans and then dashed upstairs to the cafeteria to grab an assortment of newspapers that the garbagemen had brought in from their rounds.

As I was gathering the papers, Marta, the cafeteria lady,

rushed over to me and said, "I just heard on the radio that Theo van Gogh has been killed."

Theo van Gogh—the great-grandnephew of Vincent—was a Dutch filmmaker. I'd seen several of his films in my ongoing marathon of Dutch movie viewing. Aside from filmmaking, Van Gogh was best known as an outspoken critic of Islamic immigrants in the Netherlands. As a well-known provocateur, many found Van Gogh to be rude or boorish. Regardless, he declared, "I'll say what I think." Never one to mince words, Van Gogh was known for often referring to Muslim immigrants as "goat fuckers." He also wrote a weekly newspaper column that I read in my broom closet every week. In one such column—that I'd read a few months prior and that had stuck with me—Van Gogh stated, "My God is a pig . . . I call my pig Allah." Indeed, he didn't mince his words.

Six months earlier, at a heated public debate held in a sold-out Stadsschouwburg, Dyab Abou Jahjah—the leader of the radical Arab European League—became livid when Van Gogh called him "the pimp of the prophet." Jahjah walked off stage; discord reigned. Outside the theater, pushing and shoving ensued; verbal threats flew at Van Gogh. The organizers of the event, fearing for Van Gogh's safety, wanted to send him home in a taxi. Van Gogh refused the offer. Instead, he cheerfully lit a cigarette—and rode away on his bike.

Because Van Gogh had received threats on so many occasions, he could have asked for police protection. Friends had recommended he hire a bodyguard. With his pudgy build, customary suspenders and mop of curly hair, Van Gogh was easily recognizable from his countless television appearances. "He rode on his bike through Amsterdam," said a friend of his, "and everyone could pick him out of the crowd with that prominent head and those steel blue eyes." The fact that he routinely traveled alone on his bike, had his home address listed in the telephone directory and kept a nameplate posted on his front door made Van Gogh an easy target for any offended or disturbed militant. Nevertheless, he stated, "I will not be intimidated." Van Gogh wished to retain the normalcy of his life, the epitome of which seemed to be commuting to work on a bike, just like anyone else.

In the cafeteria, Marta explained that the details of Van Gogh's murder were still sketchy, but she'd heard that it had occurred outdoors, on Linnaeusstraat.

"I just rode by there an hour ago!" I said. "I didn't see anything."

"It must've happened just after you passed," Marta said.

On Linnaeusstraat, Van Gogh had been riding his old, black bike; a wicker basket hung from its handlebars. He'd been heading to his office, where he'd been working on a film about—coincidentally—the 2002 assassination of Pim Fortuyn, the Dutch politician who was also outspoken about the issues surrounding Muslim immigrants in the Netherlands.* At the same time, where Linnaeusstraat passed under the train trestle, Mohammed Bouyeri—a 26-year-old fundamentalist Muslim born in Amsterdam to Moroccan parents—was sitting on a woman's-style bike, ready to pedal at a given moment. Witnesses reported seeing Bouyeri stationed there as early as 8:18 a.m., around the

---

*Though Fortuyn stood far to the right politically, he was a homosexual who spoke openly about his joy of frequenting "dark rooms"—the areas of certain gay bars where anonymous sex occurred. Fortuyn feared that an unchecked rise of radical Islamism in the Netherlands could one day put an end to many freedoms, such as those he enjoyed as a homosexual in a secular society.

very time I passed the same spot (though I didn't recall seeing him).

When Van Gogh rode under the train trestle, Bouyeri set off after him. After about a hundred yards, Bouyeri pulled up alongside the filmmaker and clapped him on the shoulder. When Van Gogh turned to react, Bouyeri fired at least four shots from a handgun. Struck by at least one bullet, Van Gogh fell off his bike. He got up and ran across the street, shouting, "Have mercy!" Bouyeri dumped his bike and gave chase. On the other side of the street, Bouyeri continued firing. Van Gogh fell in the southbound bike path. As Van Gogh lay on his back, his attacker shot him several more times, then slashed his throat with a machete and stabbed him repeatedly.

After the attack, Bouyeri then calmly walked to Oosterpark. Minutes later, he exchanged gunfire with policemen. The killer's intended martyrdom was foiled when police officers, after shooting him in the leg, managed to capture him alive.

FOR THE NEXT few days, on my way to and from work, I stopped at the scene of the crime. A massive impromptu memorial had sprouted in the parking spaces alongside the bike path. Two bullet holes were visible in the bike path's asphalt where Van Gogh had died. Hundreds of bouquets, wreaths, candles and inscribed cards filled the area. A similar memorial sprang up a few blocks away, in front of Van Gogh's house, where one card read: "And you always cycled so peacefully on our street."

As was my custom, I left flowers here at a spot where an Amsterdam cyclist had died. It felt odd, though, to add a bouquet to the hundreds of others. Van Gogh's end hadn't come due to the recklessness of a drunk driver or because a trucker had accidentally right-turned into him; he'd been gunned down by a madman. But it had been Van Gogh's steadfast refusal to not relinquish his cycling habits—a basic right taken for granted by hundreds of thousands of Amsterdammers (myself included)—that had made him so vulnerable.

In light of Van Gogh's murder, the nation's minister of justice, Piet Hein Donner, was asked how—as a high-profile official himself who regularly commuted by bike—he regarded his own personal safety. Donner stated he wouldn't cease cycling to work. "On a bike, you take certain precautions," he said. "You make sure that the route doesn't become predictable. There are many ways to get from my house to the Ministry and back." In Van Gogh's case, it seemed he *didn't* vary his route.

While hanging around the memorial site, I overheard numerous discussions about the right to the freedom of expression without fear of reprisals of violence, about the need for immigrant assimilation and the need for understanding. Foremost on my mind, though, was Van Gogh's insistence to live his life unencumbered by threats.

A WEEK AFTER Van Gogh's murder a large wake was held in his memory; next to the simple pine coffin stood his bike. The following day, leaders of a Moroccan-Dutch organization wished to express their abhorrence of Bouyeri's heinous crime. In what they termed a "symbolic bike trip," they cycled from the city's west side (where Bouyeri happened to have lived) to the east, ending in a park a block from the memorialized site of Van Gogh's death.

I happened to encounter this group as they crossed a bridge over the Amstel River. The procession was particularly noteworthy because the participants were using the most Dutch means of transport to express themselves. But watching about three dozen riders pass by, one thing stood out: almost all of them were riding on identical bright red rental bikes—normally the glaring sign of a tourist. In their attempt to stem the backlash toward their community by showing that Moroccans in the city are integrated enough to cycle as well, the attempt seemed to backfire: the perception they gave was that actually they didn't even own their own bikes.

One negative prognosis that cycling advocates and professionals have made about the future of the bicycle in Amsterdam is that the city's cycling levels could likely drop due to many immigrants and their offspring biking far less frequently than the native Dutch population does.* In some minority communities, bike riding holds a stigma not unlike the stigma Americans of the early 20th century held toward cycling.

This stigma was noted a few months before Van Gogh's murder by Merdan Yagmur, a Turkish-Dutch politician who regularly cycled: "When I step into a Turkish coffeehouse and people see my bike, almost everyone laughs at me. They ask, 'If you're a councilman, then where's your chauffeur-driven car?' A bike shows no status; a Mercedes or a BMW does." Yagmur further explained, "Especially Turks, Surinamers and Hindustanis think

---

*While the native (white) Dutch population of Amsterdam cycles more frequently than members of the major immigrant communities (Moroccan, Turkish, Surinamese, Antillean), according to the city's statistics bureau, the members of one populace are actually even more fervent cyclists than the native Dutch: residents with origins from other "Western" countries—that is, immigrants from other European nations and the United States.

that cycling shows no status. But in their homelands, there is no prevalent bike culture like there is here."

Actually, in Amsterdam, according to the city's statistics bureau, those who cycle the least are the Moroccans. In Morocco, cycling is viewed as transport for the lower social classes. One Moroccan-Dutch student in Amsterdam explained this view:

If you have a good job, then you need to show it. You need to wear a sharp suit, have an expensive telephone and drive an expensive car. With a nice car you can show others that you have it made, that you're doing well financially. When he's seen by others, a man on a bike should be embarrassed.

When asked how a government minister who commuted by bike would be regarded in Morocco, another Moroccan-Dutch student responded, "In Morocco, a minister is a man who must command respect within the community. You don't get that by riding a bike."

In order to try to combat the low cycling rates among some immigrant communities, over the years Amsterdam politicians have made various proposals. One was to encourage the newcomers to become cyclists by giving all recent immigrants a new bicycle. Another proposal was to give each Amsterdammer a bicycle upon their twelfth birthday, which would also help in general to combat the trend of teenagers of all ethnic backgrounds so quickly becoming scooter riders.

One idea that *has* taken hold, though, is the provision of bike-riding lessons to women with immigrant backgrounds. Since the 1980s, various community centers and nonprofit groups in

260 In the City of Bikes

Amsterdam have offered such lessons.* In safe, sequestered envi-
ronments (oftentimes, men are not allowed to be present) such as
municipal gyms or community center halls, these women receive,
typically, twelve weeks of basic bike-riding training. Eventually
the groups move on to cycling in parks or on streets. Ultimately,
the students take a cycling exam, which enables them to earn
diplomas as independent riders.

These bike riding classes have their detractors, though. Some
in the Moroccan community despise the thought of a woman
riding a bike in her djellaba—the traditional Moroccan ankle-
length robe. One bike-riding teacher described the quandary
faced by some Muslim women:

> If she sits on a bike, then you can easily see the shape of her
> buttocks and that's not proper for a Muslim woman. They
> find it troublesome that the men on the street see them
> cycling. They encounter these men also when they are walk-
> ing or riding the tram, but as a woman on a bike, you're even
> more vulnerable.

On this subject, one strictly religious 23-year-old Moroccan-
Dutch Muslim male living in Amsterdam (an almost identical demographical match to Van Gogh's killer) stated: "As a
Muslim woman, you must propagate piety. If a Muslim woman
rides a bike, her clothes can cling to her and that's an immoral
display."

*While courses have been known to be offered to male immigrants, these
have been rare due to a lack of interest. Some bike-riding instructors have attributed this to a prevailing macho attitude that would make it shameful for
a man to be caught learning how to ride a bicycle.

What exactly Bouyeri himself thought about Muslim women riding bicycles is unknown. Since Bouyeri never spoke to investigators or his court-appointed lawyers about his actions, even his relationship to the bike he rode on that fateful morning is unclear. When he attacked Van Gogh, the police figured Bouyeri didn't own the bike he was riding. Because the lock fixed to the frame had been cut, it was thought he'd been riding a bike that had been stolen specifically to carry out the murder. The police also suspected Bouyeri hadn't even ridden the bike from his home five miles away in Amsterdam-West to the location of the attack. They theorized that either he'd ridden the tram that morning or his neighbor (who drove a delivery van and worked near Van Gogh's home) had given a lift to both Bouyeri and the stolen bike.

At his trial, Bouyeri was convicted of murder and sentenced to life in prison without the possibility of parole.

ONE MORNING, A few weeks after Van Gogh's death, I left for work at the dust factory at 5:54 a.m. Because the hour was so early and the commute so routine, I rode with my eyes barely open. By then I was so familiar with each pothole and every speed bump along the way, I knew instinctively where to swerve and when to brake. With so few trams, pedestrians, autos or even other cyclists on the streets at that hour, it felt like I could do the 16-minute ride with my eyes *fully* closed, like I could just sleep-ride all the way to work.

On this particular morning, though, the fog was unusually thick. I didn't have the luxury of half-asleep cycling; actually I had to be more alert than ever. Unable to see what else was out on the streets, I was not only concerned that I might slam into something or someone but was even more worried that something or someone might slam into me. Yet if I pedaled any slower, I'd certainly be late for work. (While I could be completely lax while on the job, my employers at both job sites were fanatical about my arriving at and departing from work precisely on time.)

As I cautiously cruised east along Populierenweg, a street that ran parallel to the elevated railroad tracks, the fog grew thicker. My vision decreased from 20 feet to ten. Then I watched my own front wheel gradually fade from view. Eventually my headlight shone on nothing but the mist just inches in front of it.

Spooky.

Even eerier: the stillness. I not only saw nothing; I heard nothing. I had no choice. I slowed down.

Suddenly, just as I was about to cross Linnaeusstraat— *Dring!*—a bike bell rang out.

Where it came from, I had no idea. Even more worrisome, I didn't know where the bike attached to that bell was heading. For all I knew, it could have been bearing down on me. I tightened my grip on the handlebars and braced for the worst.

Then the bell rang again.

Dring!

This time I determined the bike was about 30 feet in front of me. But was the cyclist heading toward me or cutting across my path? In blind desperation, I frantically rang my bell.

Drringg drringg!

A casual reply came from off to my left.

Dring!

I rang again: *Drringg drringg!*

Like ships passing in the night, we were now keeping each other abreast of our positions.

Because the next reply—*Dring!*—came from farther off to my left, I gauged the other cyclist was heading up Linnaeusstraat, toward Oosterpark. In fact, he or she was following the very same path Van Gogh had been riding during the last seconds of his life.

When, from the distance, I heard a faint, final *dring*, I realized the mystery cyclist was just feet from—if not exactly upon—the very spot where Theo van Gogh had been gunned down on his bike.

Suddenly I had an image of Van Gogh making his final ride once again. A shiver ran down my spine.

Fog be damned, I sped up.

14
It's Chaos with the Bicycles: The 1950s

After World War II, with the economic upturn that began in the late 1940s, bicycles again filled the streets of Amsterdam in large numbers. The addition of each new bike helped return street life to its pre-occupation status. Once again, willy-nilly-parked bikes that clogged the sidewalks became a civic issue. Once again, taxi drivers blamed lackadaisical cycling for causing traffic jams. And lovey-dovey cycling—so loathed by the Nazis—once again blossomed and thrived.*

The great postwar influx of bikes into Amsterdam led the cyclists to, once again, ride with an indifferent attitude toward traffic laws. For example, in 1949, after the first fixed stop signs (meaning, not operated by traffic cops) had been installed on the side streets leading into De Lairessestraat and Cornelis Krusemanstraat, cyclists flew right past the new traffic signs with, according to one observer, a "metropolitan flourish." Amsterdam's

---

*The baby boom that accompanied the economic boom provided a new twist to lovey-dovey cycling. One American tourist in Amsterdam at the time reported seeing "a young couple, each on a bike, with a baby buggy between them—each with a hand on the handle of the buggy. They were riding nonchalantly pushing their baby through the traffic."

traffic police attempted to combat such cycling misconduct. But the traffic cops, no longer under Nazi authority, didn't employ the austere measures the Germans had prescribed during the occupation. Instead, the Amsterdam police commenced a far more Dutch-like campaign: they stood along the streets and distributed flyers to passing cyclists. On the flyers, a polite message requested cyclists obey the traffic laws.

This good-natured approach, though, seemed to have had as much effect on the cyclists as the heavy-handed approach favored by the Germans. One reporter watched the cops hand out flyers; then, for fifteen minutes, he eyeballed those on bikes. "Not a single cyclist stuck out his hand to signal before turning right or left," he wrote. "And entire troops of cyclists rode in the middle of the street." According to the reporter, the motto of these "horrid" bikers appeared to be "The street is our domain!" After their riding demeanor had been subjected to—and survived—Nazi persecution, the cyclists of Amsterdam now seemed to ride more empowered than ever.

AS IN HOLLAND, the 1950s was an economically prosperous time in the United States. During this period, America embarked on the construction of the massive Interstate Highway System. These new freeways not only aided cross-country travel; they also enabled the white-collar, briefcase-toting professionals who dwelled in the new suburbs to commute to their downtown offices. From the new outer residential districts of Amsterdam, white-collar professionals also commuted to city center offices. A major difference between these two groups was, of course, their means of transportation. While America's Ward Cleavers traveled to work by car, their Amsterdam counterparts went by bike.

The morning routine of these Dutch commuters was described by the Amsterdam author Albert Alberts in 1955:

They strut to the cycle garage with the self-assuredness of a cowboy approaching a wild bull. Rather routinely, they pull their bike from the rack. Outside, without haste, they strap their briefcase onto the back rack. . . . They get on their bikes and immediately become one with them. However, they don't move fast because there is not yet a queue; there is not yet a squadron. They are, at most, four or five men, exiting the garage. Every couple of seconds, four or five men exit a cycle garage in Amsterdam-West, Amsterdam-South or Amsterdam-East. The show begins. . . .

They come from everywhere and join together and become even more numerous. At the end of Overtoom, they are a cavalcade; and by Jan Pieter Heijestraat, an army. They glide forth, faster and faster. The ones up front see that the traffic light yonder is still green and they bend lower over the handlebars. Then, with just five or ten yards to go, the light turns yellow. Without so much as a moment's thought, they brake. The back tire skids across the asphalt and, just before the crosswalk, they come to a standstill. The ones in front never fear that the men behind will collide into them. That never happens. They know themselves to be artists and like good artists, they are exceptionally well disciplined during the performance.

THE MOST FRANTIC rush-hour traffic of the year during the 1950s came not in the morning but in the afternoon, whenever

the fifth of December—the day before St. Nicholas' feast day—
fell on a weekday. Following Dutch custom, early on the evening
of the fifth, families gathered to await St. Nicholas to deliver
presents to the homes of well-behaved children. Yet despite December 5 being one of the most cherished Dutch holidays, it
remained a workday. On a typical workday, offices, factories and
shops generally closed at either 5, 5:30 or 6 p.m. These staggered
quitting times helped keep Amsterdam's hectic afternoon rush
hour from becoming complete gridlock. But on December 5, a
great many employers all cut their employees loose early, at 4
p.m. At the same time, legions of last-minute gift shoppers also
happened to be returning home. The result was an instant stam-
pede of frenzied commuters. Cyclists rode in "tight jams" as they
charged home for the family festivities. The commute became
known as the "December 5th chaos."*

After the celebrants had reached home, the outdoor scene
in Amsterdam couldn't have changed more dramatically. The
streets became, as one columnist observed, "ghostly quiet." This
columnist spent the early evening of December 5, 1957, wheeling through the deserted city, speeding (!) through a desolate
Leidsestraat and watching vacant tramcars roll past unpopulated
tram stops. At the intersection of Eerste Constantijn Huygensstraat and Overtoom, he pulled up at a red light beside a student
dressed as St. Nicholas who was sitting on a bike, his Black Pete
helper perched on the rear rack. Over his shoulder, St. Nicholas
said to Pete: "It's completely superfluous to leave the traffic lights
on for St. Nicholas Evening!"

---

*As we'll see, "chaos" was easily the most popular word used in the 1950s
when describing various aspects of Amsterdam cycling.

In the 1950s, another annual Amsterdam event wasn't as widely beloved. Every year on Luilak—the Saturday before Pentecost Sunday—the city's youths wreaked havoc at the crack of dawn. Many kids would hit the streets at about 4 a.m., though early birds got started even earlier; the first calls regarding disorderly behavior usually reached the police by 2 a.m. Celebrants of Luilak (which means "lazybones") would ring doorbells, beat drums, blow horns, crash pot lids together, scream "Luilak!," sing a Luilak song, drag strings of empty tin cans behind their bikes, overturn garbage cans, bang windows, break windows, light bonfires, ignite fireworks, drink bottles of milk left out by the milkman, set buckets of water over doorways and trigger false fire alarms. They did anything and everything to annoy sleeping adults. This yearly debauchery—particular to Amsterdam and a few surrounding towns and with unknown origins—was centuries old.* While Luilak was commemorated by boys and girls aged anywhere from six to 18 years old, its most ardent practitioners were boys around eight to 12 years old.

Each year, the city government, the police department and the local newspapers warned adult Amsterdammers to take precautions. Before going to bed the night before Luilak, adults were advised to: disconnect their doorbells, bring garbage cans indoors, close all windows, avoid sleeping in street-facing rooms and wear earplugs. Since the intention was to try to wake the neighborhood, one policeman counseled: "The dumbest thing people can do is react. Those children like

---

*In 1578, one diarist in Amsterdam noted on the Saturday before Pentecost: "I saw . . . many children who, early in the morning, had made a great racket and had sung a very inappropriate song about the Pentecost flower. They ranted and raved as if anything went."

nothing better than when a man or a woman in nightclothes yells out a window. Then it *really* kicks off. Of course, the pinnacle of their pleasure is reached when a gentleman in pajamas and slippers runs out of his house to chase after the kids." As one lad explained: "Because those are exactly the people who provide the best laughs."

The most universal advice, though, was: *do not leave bicycles outside*—even if it meant carrying one up to a fifth-floor apartment. The city's hundreds of thousands of bikes parked on the sidewalks stood as alluring targets for the delinquents. The kids would remove the valves from bike tires, deflating the inner tubes. They would throw bikes in the canals. They would hang bikes in trees or on shop awnings or—far more commonly—from lampposts. They would stack bikes in the entryways of buildings, creating obnoxious barriers to any residents trying to exit.

The most popular bike-related exploit, though, was to scatter cycles across roadways—especially on streets lined with tram tracks—to create roadblocks. Any tram driver who stopped to untangle and remove such a barricade often found that by the time he returned to his seat in the tram, the barricade had already been rebuilt. Immobilized motorists were subjected to taunts and mockery. If police officers dismantled a bike blockade, its builders might scatter and lie low. But as soon as the cops departed to attend to mischief elsewhere, the kids would immediately resurface and rebuild the roadblock.

In general, the police tended to overlook the delinquents' activities, since if they tried to arrest every offender, they'd have to round up tens of thousands of children. Some junior transgressors *were* detained, though, while others who were picked up by the police were driven out to Kalfjeslaan or Nieuwe

Utrechtseweg—spots on the edge of the city—where they were dumped off and left to hike back to their homes.

On Luilak in the late 1950s, leaders from some community centers and playgrounds organized events for the children, such as 4 a.m. neighborhood bicycle races. The idea was to channel the mischievous energy away from petty criminal acts. In 1959, the city government further attempted to curb the annual delinquency spree by paying to have 40 movie theaters throw open their doors at 5 a.m. and provide the kids with free entertainment, such as Abbott and Costello movies.

While more than 20,000 children did succumb to the lure of free films in 1959, thousands of other youngsters remained resolutely faithful Luilak practitioners. As kids lined up outside the Capitol theater on Rozengracht, one boy, with a drum in hand, stood across the street and shouted, "Filthy traitors!" Another loyalist was a girl who was spotted—with her unused movie ticket defiantly pinned to her jacket—riding her bike while towing a huge, clanging washtub. Some youthful scofflaws who had been collared by cops were lugged inside movie theaters, where they were then set loose.

Though free movies and organized activities did help decrease delinquent behavior on Luilak in 1959 and 1960, by no means did the organized fun kill the centuries-old Luilak spirit. By 1961, the willful kids had resumed cavorting as rowdily as ever. Of the Luilak celebrations that year, one newspaper reported:

> Especially the bicycles were hit hard. In various places, usually after the valves had been removed from their tires, bikes were thrown across the roadways in huge heaps. Sometimes they were thrown in front of moving trams.

The damage to the trams and the bicycles is immense. The beefed-up police presence did what it could. Yet, as for the three hundred calls received by the police between four and nine o'clock Saturday morning regarding exasperating rowdiness, there was no remedy.

By the middle of the 1960s, in the days leading up to Luilak, Amsterdam's police—hoping to disarm the youth—would clear the sidewalks of obviously abandoned bikes. Yet despite the best efforts of the cops, the kids still managed to successfully fulfill their mischievousness by acting out on the city's bikes.

IN THE MID- to late-1950s, Amsterdam's 900,000 residents owned an estimated 500,000 to 600,000 bikes—about double the number of bikes owned just before the war. In the city center, an estimated 400 cycle garages operated, each with an average capacity for 175 bikes. Despite dedicated off-street parking for around 70,000 bicycles, this capacity fell far short of the demand created by the hundreds of thousands of cyclists who descended upon the city center each workday.

Even when off-street parking *was* available, cyclists didn't always use the facilities. For example, outside De Bijenkorf (The Beehive)—the distinguished department store situated on Dam Square—a huge sign read CYCLE GARAGE with an arrow pointing toward the side of the building. Many cyclists, who scoffed at the notion of paying to park one's bike while shopping, ignored the sign. "Don't ever believe that that garage will ever fill up," a municipal worker stated in 1958. "People prefer to set their bikes—in vast numbers—on Dam Square." Indeed, on the square in front of the doors to De Bijenkorf, a mob of haphazardly placed bikes invariably stood.

Haphazardly parked bikes wasn't an issue confined to Dam Square. "In the already cramped city center, wherever a pole or a tree is planted, wherever a wall rises up or a fence is placed, there are bikes. Sometimes they stand six or seven deep," read one news account of the time. "The city center has become a bicycle warehouse."

In response to randomly parked bikes, a new phenomenon spread across the city. In the windows of storefronts and ground-floor apartments, and on the façades of buildings, signs began materializing that conveyed the commands of many residents and business owners toward the deluge of parked bikes. Such signs read: NO BICYCLE PARKING, NO BIKES AGAINST THE WINDOW, BICYCLE PARKING FOR CUSTOMERS ONLY, BICYCLES WILL BE REMOVED and so on. In 1955, one sign—on the façade of a secondhand bookshop on Oudezijds Achterburgwal—read: BICYCLES PARKED HERE WILL BE DESTROYED. While it may have seemed that frustrated citizens had taken matters into their own hands, their signs actually carried no legal weight. "Now I've seen everything," laughed one police inspector when asked about this outbreak of signage. "It may sound crazy, but we prefer bikes to be parked against residential buildings. That's where they're most out of the way."

Nevertheless, in 1955, Amsterdam's police began systematically clearing carelessly parked bikes from "forbidden places." This campaign's first phase involved a sweep of the bridges. On the hundreds of small bridges that spanned Amsterdam's canals, thousands of bikes stood parked against the railings. These bikes often blocked the bridges' narrow walkways, forcing pedestrians to walk among the moving vehicles on the bridge roadways. These bikes actually violated an ordinance that prohibited bike parking on bridges. "Indeed, people know that it's forbidden," said one policeman about the issue, "but they don't bother in the least with the ordinance." Officers were especially troubled by the bikes on one particular bridge: the little Grimburgwal bridge, where, a half century later, I would sit and monitor junkie bike thieves. "On some days, on the bridge in front of the Binnengasthuis [Hospital], Amsterdam's cyclists go much too far," reported the newspaper *Trouw*. "The ambulance drivers often pull their hair out because they can't come or go due to the barricade of bicycles on and along the bridge."

"Warnings don't appear to have helped," announced the police, "and that's why every offender, without mercy, will be cited!" Police began impounding the bikes parked on bridges; in a half hour's time, they could load a truck with 20 bikes. The bikes were then held for a day ("on bread and water") before their owners could pay a fine to reclaim them.

After the bridge campaign, in 1956 the police turned their attention to narrow walkways and alleyways, particularly those around the Muntplein and Rokin area. Then, in 1957, the police refocused their sights yet again. This time they took aim at the recklessly parked bikes at Central Station—"the scene of the chaos." As the *Vrije Volk* newspaper reported that year: "For years on end, no other police ban in Amsterdam has been violated so massively and with so much pig-headedness as the ban against parking bicycles against the railings along the Open Harbor in front of Central Station." As the greatest bike magnet in Amsterdam (if not the entire Netherlands), this was hardly a new issue. As early as 1898, back when bicycles were still pricey novelties of the leisured class, abandoned bikes were discovered at Central Station to the astonishment of some. "How is it possible that someone . . . leaves his bike standing forever *unclaimed*?" pondered the editors of *De Kampioen* magazine that year. "We find it inexplicable, but it's true! We've seen it with our own eyes!"

Given that the police who were rounding up bikes at Central Station were—as one account put it in the 1950s—"fighting a losing battle," a new tactic was attempted in 1957. To alleviate the bike-parking problem, hundreds of special paving stones—each with a groove cut in it to accommodate the tire of a parked bike—were installed outside Central Station. In the years immediately before and after the occupation, thousands of such paving stones had been placed throughout the city. Slotted paving stones were all the city had to offer to assist sidewalk bike parking, as sidewalk bike racks wouldn't become the norm in Amsterdam until decades later. Though cyclists complained that the grooves—too often filled with leaves, dirt, mud and/or trash—were useless, the slotted paving stones were considered a partial solution, albeit a small one, toward alleviating the bike-parking problem. "Maybe we'll never be able to completely end the bicycle chaos at the station," commented one insightful policeman, "but those grooves are a step in the right direction." While bikes would continue to swamp Central Station for the following half century, how to tidily store all those bikes would remain a constant conundrum.

AFTER THE IMPOUNDMENT of bikes parked illegally on bridges, in alleyways and at Central Station, in the fall of 1958 the police launched a new and far more widespread crusade.

They focused on a problem that would have been unimaginable just a decade and a half earlier. Back then, during the last years of the occupation, an orphaned bike on an Amsterdam street was as common a sight as a unicorn. Yet by the late 1950s, the city had become completely overrun with unwanted bikes. The capital was becoming—as one newspaper reporter at the time put it—a "bicycle graveyard" filled with an estimated 50,000 "bike cadavers." Another reporter described these wrecks:

> There they stand, crumpled and half-rusted, leaning against fences and walls and trees in the center of Amsterdam by the dozen—no, by the hundreds. No one cares about them. They slouch there—for who knows how long—in the wind and rain, drooping and forgotten.

Forgotten by everyone, that is, except by the city's youths who used these bikes to indulge both their inherent mechanical skills and their penchant for vandalism. Under their guidance such bikes followed a familiar pattern of decay: "First, the bell disappears. Then the light and back rack. Finally, the seat, the tires and, sometimes, even entire wheels. But the frame remains standing—for hours, days, months, years. . . ."

In calling for the removal of these eyesores and obstacles, the *Vrije Volk* newspaper pleaded: "Amsterdam is already so often compared to a museum. Let's not also turn it into a bicycle museum." So in October 1958 the Amsterdam police set out to "make a clean sweep" of the wrecks. The police's motto: "Wherever a wreck is removed, space is created for a bike that's operable." In addition to freeing up room on the sidewalks, another goal of the campaign was to recover stolen bikes and return them to their rightful owners. During the previous seven years, bike thefts had risen markedly due, in large part, to the increase in joyriding.

Bikes that stood obviously abandoned were loaded onto trucks and taken to a gigantic space on Overamstelstraat where their notable features (serial number, color, brand name, location taken from, etc.) were recorded in the hope that they could be retrieved by bike theft victims. During the first three days of this campaign, the police seized a thousand bikes. But with so many more orphaned bikes still on the streets, storage space quickly became an issue. One police inspector complained: "It's chaos with the bicycles. I could easily collect ten thousand abandoned bikes from the streets of Amsterdam. They're just standing there. No one knows who owns them. But where would we put them? To store them all, we'd have to construct ten exhibition centers."

While the police beseeched the public to combat joyriding by locking their bikes, 22-year-old University of Amsterdam student Hugo Brandt Corstius (who would later become one of the Netherlands' most celebrated writers) thought it would be more effective to do just the opposite: *stop* locking bikes. In 1958, in the university newspaper *Propria Cures*, Brandt Corstius wrote:

In view of people's borrowing habits and the considerable interest in bicycle ownership, I propose the following: Why not nationalize bicycle ownership for the common good? This could be accomplished with one little law: "It is forbidden to have a bicycle in one's possession or to make a bicycle inaccessible to others." Anyone who needs a bike simply takes one, rides it to his destination, then leaves it there.

The cyclist need not worry about returning, theft, storage, repairs, etc. The state will attend to the repairs and the periodic supplementation of the fleet. The police force can then be halved. Once the bike is as much public property as the road itself, all the world's troubles will come to an end.

While Brandt Corstius' plea for public-use bicycles fell on deaf ears, the police department continued its campaign against orphaned wrecks. Within a year of its start, almost 8,000 bikes had been removed from the streets. One cyclist who visited the storage facility described it as "a very large space with a dreary overhead light, and there stood thousands of bicycles. There were people walking around inconsolably, past those endless rows, searching for their little beast." Many little beasts were indeed reunited with their rightful owners. And due to the campaign, awareness of the joyriding situation was heightened. This led to cyclists being more vigilant when parking their bikes. As a result, while bike thefts continued to rise in other large Dutch cities, in Amsterdam the number of bike thefts dropped.

WHILE JOYRIDERS AND *zwijntjesjagers* caused many Amsterdam bikes to be left abandoned in the late 1950s, possibly an even greater cause was the rise in ownership of mopeds, scooters and cars. With the postwar Dutch economy continuing to prosper, the price of a motorized vehicle—especially a moped—was now within easy reach of many Amsterdammers. And what did these new former cyclists do with their old bikes? "They leave it be wherever they last plunked it down. Because what's its value?

In boom times like we're now experiencing, who buys a second-hand bike?" asked *De Spiegel*. "[T]hose hundreds and hundreds of bikes . . . stand rusting and languishing as if they had never cost a penny."

In 1958, not only was Holland's rate of car ownership still drastically lower than America's, but Amsterdam's rate paled in comparison to that of other European capitals. In Paris, for example, there was one car for every 7.5 people. In Stockholm and Brussels, the rate was one car for every 10 people. London: one for every 11.5 people. Even bike-friendly Copenhagen had one car for every 15 people. But the story was different in Amsterdam, where there was just one car for every 23 inhabitants.

Despite the relatively low rate of car ownership in Amsterdam, the number of cars was multiplying. With this increase, the writer Jen Vlietstra predicted at the time that cycling in Amsterdam would follow the same path cycling in America had taken during the car's initial ascendancy there.

Maybe—if we look to the distant future—the bicycle here will also largely disappear from urban traffic. Not so much because it must be shoved aside by the automobile, but because the cyclist has been given the opportunity to ride in a car. Because, let's be honest, cycling is fun and healthy, as people say, but driving a car is a tad more pleasant. And societal development will undoubtedly continue to push toward a higher standard of living for everyone. Whoever is still riding a bike will, by tomorrow, probably already have a scooter and, in a couple of years, a car—even if it's just a little secondhand one.

The era of mass car ownership was finally dawning on Amsterdam—and it didn't bode well for the cyclists.

IN THE MID-1950s, another era came to an end. In 1948, Queen Wilhelmina had abdicated the throne in favor of her daughter Juliana. Afterward, Wilhelmina retired to Het Loo Palace, where, for the next few years, she often cycled on the palace grounds or through the adjacent woods. Once, when an international conference on the future of Europe convened at the palace, Wilhelmina's distinguished guests arrived in a fleet of black Cadillacs. As they gathered at a lakeside pavilion, Wilhelmina shocked the VIPs by simply riding up on her bike, stepping off and leaning it against a tree.

In her retirement years, the former queen would also cycle into town on errands. One time, while she was cycling to a dentist's appointment in Apeldoorn, a motorist behind her barked: "Hey lady, ride on the right side of the road!"

"Please excuse me," Wilhelmina responded politely, if not regally.

"Yeah, yeah," the driver said, "just keep to the right."

According to a member of her staff, Wilhelmina considered such "nutty incidents"—like being scolded as any common cyclist—to be "splendid."

Unfortunately, Wilhelmina's retirement-era cycling also had its setbacks. She suffered several bad falls from her bike, including one she described in a letter to Juliana that had left her with "two severe lumps on my colorful pallet." Finally, in early 1956, at the age of 75, Wilhelmina, who some 60 years earlier had vehemently fought for her right to cycle, had to give up cycling.

Though no longer riding, during Wilhelmina's remaining years, at the rear entrance to Het Loo Palace, her bike stood—"ready to be ridden." In 1962, on the day Wilhelmina died, when her corpse was taken from the palace, it was carried right past her trusty bike.

Though Wilhelmina had retired from cycling in the mid-1950s, her daughter pedaled onward. Queen Juliana, who, as a young woman, had frequently accompanied her mother on bike rides, was now herself becoming known internationally as the "Queen on a bicycle." She cycled to church or to a neighbor's house for tea, sometimes with her youngest daughter, Princess Marijke (later Christina), riding as a passenger. All four of Juliana's daughters would commute to high school on bikes, even Marijke who, despite having been born with a visual impairment, overcame her condition in part, it was said, by learning to cycle.

WHEN DID AMSTERDAM'S pendulum swing from being a solid bike town to it becoming more car-centric? It was probably October 3, 1960. Throughout the month prior to that day, Leidsestraat—that renowned cycling thoroughfare—had been inaccessible to all vehicles. The street had been dug up and new sewer pipes, telephone cables and tram rails had been laid. While Leidsestraat had been closed to traffic, Mayor Gijs van Hall and the city's *wethouders* made a drastic, unexpected move: they imposed a three-month trial ban on cycling on the street that would take effect as soon as the street reopened.

When Leidsestraat reopened at daybreak on October 3, thousands of cyclists—whose commutes had been rerouted for weeks—tried to do what the trams, autos and pedestrians were doing that morning: use Leidsestraat. But while the other road users were allowed through, the cyclists were met by signs that read: NO CYCLING. A small army of policemen, posted at intersections along the entire length of the street, directed cyclists instead toward Leidsegracht or Spiegelstraat, the parallel routes flanking Leidsestraat. Those cyclists who, "cool as a cucumber," attempted to slip past the police and onto the forbidden street were immediately halted. Hundreds of cyclists ignored the suggested detours and instead walked their bikes along Leidsestraat's newly paved sidewalks. The cyclists gazed longingly at the street's fresh asphalt.*

This abrupt switch angered many bikers. If one form of transportation had to be prohibited from Leidsestraat, they felt it should have been the automobile. A ban on cars would have adversely affected far fewer commuters, since far fewer motorists used Leidsestraat than cyclists. In addition, cars consumed more street space and posed more dangers to pedestrians. Amsterdam's traffic police claimed bicycles were banned and not cars—instead of the other way around—because cyclists had more options for alternative routes than motorists. Such logic was lost on cyclists who felt unjustly punished. "The policemen didn't have it easy," reported *De Volkskrant*. Irate cyclists grumbled comments at the

---

*At the time, the cyclists were already being denied access to a nearby bike path a few hundred yards from Leidsestraat. In 1959, the Rijksmuseum passageway was closed to cyclists while the building underwent renovation. This closure was scheduled to last for just one year, but the construction work dragged on and on; various reopening dates came and went with the gates still locked tight. In the meantime, the Rijksmuseum leadership grumbled a familiar line about wanting to permanently ban cyclists from beneath the building. Ultimately, when the passageway finally reopened in 1963—after four full years of being dormant—the cyclists once again enjoyed complete access to that most incredible of bike paths.

officers, like "Big money wins out again" and "The common man must make the detour." One overly optimistic cyclist shouted, "In three months, the cars will be banned!"

While the Leidsestraat cycling ban was viewed as a victory by some of the street's remaining posh stores, the oft-cited maxim that cyclists weren't "buyers" proved a fallacy for keepers of other Leidsestraat shops. A bookstore owner said the bike ban had caused his business "severe damage." The owner of an art reproduction shop told a reporter, "My steady customers keep complaining about the fact that we're so difficult to access now." The owner of an automat griped, "During the day, it's become considerably quieter. We particularly miss the rushing multitudes of cyclists, among whom a couple always could find the time for a croquette or a chow mein ball. One can only hope for their speedy return."

In a 1953 booklet published in Amsterdam and titled *The Selfish Private Car*, author W. Valderpoort, a Dutch civil engineer, outlined the grave situation that faced "unorganized" traffic users like pedestrians and cyclists. Motorists, though consituting a small minority of road users at the time, almost universally belonged to politically active motorist organizations. More important, virtually anyone who had influence over traffic policy (elected officials, high-ranking civil servants, etc.) either owned a car or, as a job perk, had one at his or her disposal. While these well-placed, well-organized motorists "beat the drum to promote their own interests," the individual pedestrian or cyclist had little recourse for advancing their cause beyond penning a letter to the editor; and as Valderpoort pointed out, "even the possibility of that nowadays is very limited."

One example of the type of planning done by car-centric government officials without the cyclists in mind was the IJ Tunnel.

In previous decades, the port towns of Rotterdam and Antwerp had built tunnels under their busy waterways that included facilities for bike traffic. In early 1940, Amsterdam had gotten so far in the planning stage of a similar tunnel system that it had conducted studies (using unemployed workers on bikes) to test the cycling capacity for such a tunnel. During the Nazi occupation, though, these plans were shelved. By the time the idea of an IJ Tunnel had returned to the forefront of civic planning in the 1950s, government authorities decided the tunnel would be limited to motorized traffic; bikes and pedestrians would remain restricted to the ferry boats. While cyclists grumbled about this decision (in letters to the editors, just as Valderpoort had predicted), they were unable to state their case more vigorously since they weren't organized.

Though cyclists were not united in an association that fought for their interests, organized protests on bicycles occasionally transpired in Amsterdam. Some notable examples:

- In 1923, after the Dutch government raised the tax on *jenever*, the beloved Dutch gin, about 200 young men and women cycled through the streets with placards demanding the workers' right to their alcohol.
- In 1933, more than a thousand unemployed communists rode through the streets demanding employment opportunities. When they ignored a traffic cop's stop sign at the Keizersgracht/Leidsestraat intersection, the cop brought the whole procession to a standstill by drawing his revolver.
- In June 1940 (during the occupation), the male employees of one restaurant, dressed in their work garb and armed with placards, cycled through the city to protest the res-

taurant's recent hiring of female workers. Eventually the police broke up their demonstration on Leidseplein and issued citations to the protest's leaders.

None of these or other two-wheeled protests, though, actually concerned bicycles or biking. But then, three weeks after the inauguration of the Leidsestraat cycling ban, cyclist discontent led to what was most likely a first in Amsterdam history: a protest conducted on bikes that concerned a cycling issue. On the afternoon of October 28, 1960, 40 or so university students from a debating club—armed with banners, flyers and a bullhorn—civilly disobeyed the new ordinance by cycling onto Leidsestraat. The students, who asserted that the ban violated the rights of the cyclists, chanted the slogan emblazoned on one of their banners: "No need to fuss, we're just cycling here!" But fuss is exactly what the police did; they broke up the demonstration and arrested several protesters. Though the students' protest was short-lived and ultimately ineffective, their tactic—direct action in the streets on their bikes—presaged how cyclists could fight for their right to the city's roadways.

Despite the demonstration of the students and the concerns of some Leidsestraat shopkeepers, in December 1960 the mayor and *wethouders* extended the Leidsestraat cycling ban for another six months. Then, in June 1961, they made the ban permanent.

In March 1961, city officials stated, "A special route for cyclists and moped riders is being considered." No such special route (for example, a bicycle bridge from Leidsegracht to Nassaukade) ever materialized, though. The loss of access to Leidsestraat in 1960 was but an indication of the fate that awaited the cyclists in the decade to come.

15
A Bike Is Coming: The New Additions

After training for ten months at De Fietsenmaker, Amy Joy repaired bikes for five months at a rental shop. Then she landed a job at a tiny bike shop in De Pijp neighborhood, in what had been until recently a ground-floor apartment; the wheels and tires were stored in the old kitchen. The workspace was so cramped, only one bike at a time could be worked on. The secondhand bikes for sale stood open to the elements on the dirt in the narrow backyard.

Amy Joy's two new coworkers were both young Dutch guys with Mohawks who lived in squatted buildings. One of them, on Amy Joy's first day, expressed surprise that she wanted to be a bike mechanic. "All bike mechanics are good at drinking," he warned her, "and bad at relationships." It was a warning that Amy Joy jokingly repeated when she arrived home that evening—as well as in the years that followed.

With Amy Joy now gainfully employed, we decided I could quit my janitoring jobs and start training at Jos' bike shop myself.

The day after working my final shift as a janitor, I started my training with Jos at De Fietsenmaker. When I walked in, a row of three bikes with flat tires awaited me. The following day I began researching Amsterdam's cycling history. Then, just five days after I had scrubbed my last toilet, we learned Amy Joy was pregnant.

In the months that followed, as my wife's belly grew, she continued riding her bike and continued fixing other people's bikes. I was excited to be learning how to repair bikes myself and to be poking around in various archives unearthing Amsterdam's biking history.

In the midst of the pregnancy, our one-year sublet ended and we had to find a new apartment. When we called about a place we saw advertised online and asked about the cost of the rent, the guy said not to worry. When asked if we could legally register ourselves at the address, again, the answer was: don't worry. We went and looked at the place in Amsterdam-North. Though something seemed fishy about the situation and the guy (he said he would technically remain living there and as proof to any nosy authorities, he would keep his own [smoke-drenched] clothes in the row house's smaller bedroom), the fact was: we could afford the place, we could legally register there and—most important—we could have it. So we took it, happy and relieved to still be living in Amsterdam.

Unlike previous moves within Amsterdam, where I had moved all our belongings on Brownie, this time I transported all our stuff on a huge cargo bike borrowed from Amy Joy's employer on a snowy February day. A few months after we had settled into our new digs, it was time for the baby to appear. When its due date arrived, though, the kid was still nowhere to be seen.

To try to coax the kid out, Amy Joy employed every old wives' tale remedy said to induce labor, including eating pineapple cores, drinking a raspberry leaf infusion, doing breathing/push-ing exercises, eating spicy food, drinking tonic water, receiving foot reflexology, eating parsley, stimulating her nipples, sniffing tropical flowers, drinking a small glass of red wine before bed, eating ginger, receiving acupressure above her heels and in the crevice of her thumbs, having intercourse, drinking castor oil, eating dark chocolate, ingesting a blue cohosh tincture, orgas-ming daily and eating eggplant parmesan. Eighteen different remedies in all. Nothing worked; the kid didn't budge.

Two weeks after the baby's due date, we went to the hospital to have the labor induced. To get to the hospital, we could have taken the bus or a taxi. But since she'd been cycling pretty much every day since the baby's conception—this day seemed no different—Amy Joy rode her bike to the hospital to give birth.

Eventually, at the hospital, with the help of a scalpel, out came a baby boy. We called him Ferris. When it came time to go home, Amy Joy and Ferris took a taxi; I rode my bike while I ghost-rode Amy Joy's.

WHEN OUR BABY was only nine months old, the status of our living situation was made clear to us when two housing officials knocked at the door and clued us in. Technically, we were living illegally in someone else's social housing unit. We were evicted and given only weeks to find a new place. Once again, we were stressed about finding another home.

By this point, I'd been keeping my eye on an apartment di-rectly behind our place, the one above the bike shop where Amy Joy had bought her "mama bike." In that apartment, a single lightbulb had burned round the clock for months until, finally, it appeared to have burned out. In the months afterward, the place remained dark. Since the apartment appeared vacant, I suggested to Amy Joy that she ask the bike shop owner about it.

With our baby in her arms, Amy Joy stepped into the shop and spoke to Jaap, the shop's old-timer owner and lone worker. Jaap explained that, months earlier, his most recent tenants had skipped out on him in the middle of the night, and since then he hadn't bothered to find new tenants. To a family in desperate need of housing in a city with such a tight housing market, it was inconceivable that Jaap was just sitting on a vacant apartment. Even more remarkable: before Amy Joy had even looked at the unit or without Jaap even inquiring about us or our finances, he told her we could have the place, which was technically a shopkeepers' apartment (the residence was accessed via the storefront).

Of course we took the place and we soon moved. Since Jaap hadn't bothered to ask us about ourselves, we didn't bother to tell him that Amy Joy was working as a bike mechanic or that I had any interest in biking.

Jaap's shop dated to 1928. As a 15-year-old growing up a couple of blocks away, he had begun working in the shop in 1958 and eventually took it over from his uncle in 1982. It appeared that not much had changed since his uncle's days. Everything—the bikes, the tools, the vibe—looked and felt timeworn and antiquated. In the glass display case beside the front door, its contents—cans of spray paint ringed with dried foam, bottles of sewing machine oil, a hand-scribbled sign advertising a no-longer-present WINTER SET (whatever that might have been)—were all covered in layers of dust and priced in guilders, a currency that the euro had replaced four years prior. The display case mainly served as a bug mausoleum; its dust-covered shelves were littered with the corpses of flies, gnats, moths, mosquitoes, spiders. . . . By my count, they numbered 337.

After we had lived in the apartment for a few months, the greengrocer next door informed us that Jaap planned to retire soon. Not long after, I mentioned to Jaap that Amy Joy was a bike mechanic.

"You're a bike mechanic?" he asked her. "Then you should take over my shop."

And there it was. Amy Joy's exact fantasy—owning a bike shop in Amsterdam and living in an apartment above it—was presented on a silver platter.

For more than a year after that, Amy Joy worked 15 hours a week for Jaap in exchange for our rent and utilities. Then, just before the takeover was complete, Jaap suggested—not for the first time—that we move. He said he spoke from experience that living above a bike shop that one owned and operated was a recipe for divorce.

AT MIDNIGHT ON January 1, 2008, Amy Joy became the official owner of the bike shop. After she and I exchanged much hurrahing and congratulatory kissing in the living room, Amy Joy invited me downstairs to the shop.

"You need a safer bike for riding Ferris on," she said as she turned on the lights. "So pick out a new bike."

I was dazed. I hadn't owned a new bike since buying the Dill Pickle when I was eight years old. Together we examined the stock and settled on a seven-speed Gazelle. I immediately took it for a quick spin and found myself riding beneath and among the celebratory fireworks that our neighbors were shooting off almost as if they were lauding my new bike.

WHEN FERRIS WAS old enough to hold his head up on his own, we added an infant/toddler seat to one of our bikes. Ferris now could sit right behind the handlebars and right in front of the cycling parent. The new seating arrangement afforded our son a front-row seat on Amsterdam's streets, buildings and canals. I played tour guide to him, pointing out all I found interesting.

"Toot toot!" he routinely yelled at motorists who were waiting patiently at cross streets. "A bike is coming!" He also went through a long phase in which every time he saw a bike lying on the ground, he'd point and scream: "Uh oh!" One could never guess how great a number of bikes are lying down in Amsterdam until a two-year-old eagerly attempts to point out each one.

By the time he was three years old, Ferris and I had begun playing a game called "Which Way?" We'd come to an intersection and I'd ask "Which way?" Ferris would look left, right and straight ahead and then decide which way we should proceed. He led me all over the city, directing us to wherever interested him. Eventually, as he learned his way around, Ferris was leading me to places he knew he wanted to go—to Vondelpark, to the library and back home.

16
A Bike Is Something, Yet Almost Nothing!: The 1960s

The 1960s was not a kind period for Amsterdam's cyclists. The sort of mass motorization that had swept the United States four decades earlier now overwhelmed Holland's capital; from 1960 to 1970, the number of automobiles in the city quadrupled. This inundation of cars greatly affected those on bikes, of course. In 1963, a newspaper article titled "Safety of Cyclist Exists Only in His Dreams" examined just how dire the conditions had become for the city's bikers. A 56-year-old office worker told the reporter, "Mister, when I'm riding my bike, I'm never sure of my life." Each morning, the man rode for half an hour from his home in a newly built neighborhood in Amsterdam-West to his workplace in the city center. "Every day when I get there," he said, "I heave a sigh of relief."

A 38-year-old deputy manager told the reporter, "If you don't experience this yourself daily, then you don't know how terrible it is. . . . [O]n the bike, it's slowly becoming crazy." This same cyclist pointed to the recent massive rise in the number of scooters. "Those moped riders always scare the living daylights out of me.

The young guys that ride them have no decency. They pass you on the left and on the right. They cut you off and don't give turn signals. In short, there's no traffic regulation they don't continually violate."

Another dangerous nuisance was the bus drivers who maneuvered their vehicles through traffic with little regard for those on bikes. In response, according to the reporter, the cyclists directed much of their cursing at the bus drivers. At the time, the favored expletives used by cyclists were "*Sufferd!*" ("Dope!") and "*Boerenhengst!*" ("Country bumpkin!").

Those who most vexed the cyclists were, of course, the car drivers. "Even sticking one's hand out to indicate turning is a problem," a cycling office worker from Amsterdam-West testified. "It's already happened to me several times that a car has struck my arm. The motorist then looked back at me with a smirk."

Not only did the great many cars in transit pose hazards for the cyclists (collisions and traffic deaths rose dramatically); so, too, did the increased number of *immobile* cars. With few off-street parking options, parked cars were strewn everywhere much the way parked bikes had cluttered the city in previous decades. A key difference, though, was that a single parked car occupied as much space as ten parked bikes. Many of the city's squares—Leidseplein, Rembrandtplein, Nieuwmarkt, for example—sites that for centuries had served as places for public gatherings and/or outdoor markets, had become ad hoc parking lots. The epidemic of sidewalk parking, bridge parking and double-parking hindered cyclists while riding their bikes and when looking to park their bikes.

The concerns of the cyclists, though, mattered little to those who ran the city. In 1964, Mayor van Hall vented his disdain for the bicycle when he boasted that in the previous seventeen years, he'd succumbed to cycling just one time: on a Sunday when his wife had taken the family car. Local leaders from across the political spectrum saw the explosion in the number of cars only as progress: right-leaning pro-business city fathers viewed it as a triumph of capitalism while left-leaning pols in the city's powerful Labor and Communist parties—who felt working stiffs deserved cars as much as bosses did—viewed it as a triumph of the working class. In 1967, Labor Party member Joop den Uyl—who had been an Amsterdam *wethouder* a few years earlier and who would become the nation's prime minister a few years later—was asked if everyone should have a car. Den Uyl famously replied: "Yes, I've had a car since 1953. I find it delightful. I've always defended the car from cultural pessimists. I think it's hypocritical to have something against cars. . . . Everyone has the right to own a car."

For those auto owners who thought the city's politicians weren't disposed toward liking cars, a new, single-issue political party—the Safer Traffic Party—was established. In the 1962 municipal elections, the platform of this pro-car party called for more curbside parking spaces, more parking garages, the replacement of the electric-powered trams with diesel-fueled buses and—its chief campaign issue—the filling in of the city's canals to create more space for autos. When the party's head—Ton Hamers—was asked about Bloemgracht, the picturesque canal where he was born, he replied, "It should be filled in." When asked about Lauriergracht, the picturesque canal where his place of business stood, Hamers responded: fill it in. "Then, at least, I'll have a place to park my car." His party received more than 13,000 votes, enough to earn it a seat on the city council.

In the 1960s, several specialists noted how the change in Amsterdam cycling was impacting the well-being of the cyclists. For example, Dr. A. J. Dunning, a distinguished Amsterdam cardiologist, observed, "[I]n terms of public health, the disappearance of the bicycle from some sectors of Dutch society should be regarded as a great loss." Likewise, Dr. William Noordenbos, chief neurosurgeon at an Amsterdam hospital, stated, "The number of deaths and severe injuries due to traffic accidents—which we read about in the newspaper every day—hardly makes an impression anymore." In turn, H. Tielrooy, chief inspector of Amsterdam's traffic police, said, "The busyness is becoming greater and greater. More and more people are driving cars. Consequently, public transportation becomes less attractive because the trams are always stuck in traffic. As a result, even more people buy cars." Under such conditions, Tielrooy claimed, there was no longer room in Amsterdam for pedestrians or cyclists. "Cycling nowadays is tantamount to attempting suicide."

The city's downtrodden cyclists were being pushed to the margins, but one tiny group of Amsterdammers in the 1960s would step forward to extol the virtues of urban cycling.

ON THE EVENING of Tuesday, July 27, 1965, two young men were arrested in Amsterdam for wheat-pasting copies of a flyer to a wall. The handwritten flyer was titled "Provo's Bicycles Plan." It read:

Amsterdammers!
The asphalt terror of the motorized bourgeoisie has
lasted long enough. Every day, human sacrifice is made to

the newest authority that the bourgeoisie themselves are at the mercy of: the Auto-Authority. The smothering carbon monoxide is their incense; their likeness poisons thousands of canals and streets.

Provo's Bicycles Plan presents liberation from the car-monster. Provo introduces the White Bicycle for public ownership.

The first White Bicycle will be bestowed upon the public and the press on Wednesday, July 28, at 3 p.m. at the Amsterdam *Lieverdje*—the Addicted Consumer—on Spui Square.

The White Bicycle is never locked. The White Bicycle is the first free, collectivized means of transport. The White Bicycle is a provocation of capitalistic private property because the White Bicycle is anarchistic.

The White Bicycle can be used by whoever needs it and afterward must be left unlocked. More White Bicycles will follow until everyone can make use of the white transport and the automobile danger is eliminated. The White Bicycle symbolizes simplicity and cleanliness in contrast to the gaudiness and filthiness of the authoritarian auto.

After all, a bike is something, yet almost nothing!

Despite the grandiose language of the flyer, the event it advertised proved to be a decidedly low-key affair. On the stated afternoon, on Spui Square, about two dozen people assembled around *Het Amsterdams Lieverdje*—The Amsterdam Rascal—a four-foot-tall bronze statue of a mischievous-looking boy standing with his arms akimbo. Thom Jaspers—the "Traffic Safety Magician"—distributed flyers he'd created titled "Do You Drive?

I Don't" that accused all motorists of murder. Then it was the turn of 33-year-old Robert Jasper Grootveld, the "Anti-Smoking Magus" and a central figure for the recently formed anarchist group called the Provos.* Grootveld shook a rattle as he ranted to the small crowd about this plan for public-use bicycles.

That day, Grootveld explained to a reporter:

[The bicycle] is a national symbol, known everywhere abroad. For years, the bikes have drawn thousands of American tourists to the Netherlands. That shouldn't be shoved aside by the auto. . . . The city government must be provoked until a [White Bicycle] service is implemented. The police now thin out the bikes by rounding them up and selling them for scrap metal. Those bicycles should be repaired and released into free circulation—with an eye-catching color. The bicycles must be placed in the city center, where they should be widely propagated.

When asked why the bikes were white and not the traditional anarchist colors red and black, Grootveld replied, "It's an inversion: a bike is usually black, so just to give it a new look, a new color."

A variation of such a bike scheme was already in operation at Amsterdam-North's sprawling NDSM shipyards (where Grootveld and fellow Provo Luud Schimmelpennink had each briefly worked years before). There, employees and visitors traversed the grounds on a fleet of red bicycles. Public-use bicycles, of course,

*"We're called Provos because we want to provoke the masses," one of them told a reporter that week.

had been proposed in 1958 by Hugo Brandt Corstius. A few weeks after the Provo bike launch, Brandt Corstius joked that the Provos' plan was "a beautiful idea, but it can be even more beautiful. The Provos should bestow just one bike upon the community, but this time a black one. Then, if you see a black bike somewhere"—in a city full of black bicycles—"don't hesitate to make use of this gift from the Provos. And when you get where you wanted to go, just leave it for the next user."

Grootveld—who had long been intrigued by bikes (a decade earlier he'd ridden a cargo bike from Amsterdam to Paris)—said in an interview (in English) the following year that he'd conceived public-use bikes as a kid during the occupation.

> I got this idea from during the war—'44–'45—the Hunger Winter, when there was hunger in Amsterdam. I was playing with kids outside Amsterdam and I would like to have a bike. But bikes weren't there anymore; they were all stolen by the Germans. I got the idea of lots of people having these bikes free, from this time already.

No matter the initial conception of the idea, among the Provos the one who would articulate the plan, vigorously promote it and quickly become known as its "father" was 30-year-old Luud Schimmelpennink. Unlike most other Provos, who were college-aged and/or bohemians, Schimmelpennink had been, in his own words, "a very respectable man" in his pre-Provo days. He was married, had two children and worked as a plastics engineer. Living around the corner from the *Lieverdje*, Schimmelpennink was lured to the Provos upon hearing of their progressive ideas about traffic issues.

ON THE AFTERNOON of the launch of the White Bicycles Plan, while Grootveld addressed the crowd, a couple of Provos slathered white paint on the event's main attraction: three old bicycles. One of the painters—22-year-old philosophy student Roel van Duijn—was a founder of the Provos and the author of the flyer that announced this affair. Van Duijn and the others intended to deploy the bikes for public usage after the ceremony. But when that anticipated moment arrived, the three bikes couldn't perform their celebrated function; the paint was still wet. So, instead of releasing them to the public, the Provos themselves departed with the bikes, riding them up Spuistraat, against the flow of traffic. Then, that evening, after the paint had dried, the three White Bicycles were placed out on the streets (with at least one being set on Leidseplein). There they were left available to be ridden by anyone who cared to ride them.

Van Duijn, a few days later, would explain to a reporter:

We're seeking something in between violence and nonviolence. With violence you achieve just as little as with nonviolence. We propose Provocation instead of Revolution. You can compare us to the earlier Dadaists, who likewise provoked society. In the Provos' White Bicycles Plan, you'll recognize the Dadaist humor.

The birth of the White Bicycles Plan couldn't have been less auspicious: a few young eccentrics and anarchists ranted about cars and painted some bikes in front of a handful of onlookers—many of whom were their own cohorts. It would have been easy to disregard that day's activities as a harmless prank. Grootveld felt otherwise. That afternoon he proclaimed to a reporter, "You have to imagine that this is world news. Amsterdam—that old city sitting below sea level—takes bikes that had fallen into disuse and makes them available as White Bicycles. I swear that's publicity fit for *Time* and *Life* magazines."

World news? The event barely registered as local news: fewer than half of the nine daily newspapers published in Amsterdam at the time gave the event any ink; even the above-quoted interview with Grootveld went unpublished. Quite likely, the whole scheme would have remained marginal local news if it wasn't for one of the few spectators who had been there: Police Commissioner Pieter Landman. Landman, head of the nearby Singel police station, had listened to Grootveld's ravings and watched the Provos' bike painting. Then he told a reporter, "I'll leave them be. They want us to intervene. But as long as the traffic isn't hindered, it appears best not to get involved."

If Landman had only followed his own council, the White Bicycles Plan might have been quickly forgotten. Without police involvement, those first three White Bikes very likely would have been ridden around by various people for a few days. Then someone in need or someone with greed might have slapped a lock on one of the bikes and claimed it as his or her own. More likely, delinquents would have simply chucked those three White Bikes into a canal; any subsequent White Bikes would inevitably have suffered similar inconspicuous fates.

But Landman didn't take his own advice. The police *did* get involved; they confiscated the three original White Bikes on the grounds of the statute dating back to 1928 that required bicycles parked in public spaces to be locked. According to the rationale behind that law, unlocked bikes provided easy prey for thieves, which only created more police work. One Amsterdam cop who dealt with the Provos would later remark: "The mere idea that a bike stood unlocked and could be used by everyone subverted the normal ownership customs and encouraged theft."

"The police have told us that such bikes would quickly be stolen. Well, they were stolen," Van Duijn said several months after creating the first White Bikes. "Or rather, the police took them away and never gave them back."

The confiscation of these three bikes set off what proved to be a series of events that eventually led to the White Bikes becoming, as Grootveld had predicted, world news. The following year, *Life* magazine's international edition published a four-page spread and the *New York Times Sunday Magazine* ran a seven-page spread, both pieces profiling the Provos and their various antics and schemes, the most prominent being the White Bicycles Plan.

ON THE DAY the White Bikes were introduced, when asked how he expected the program to get off the ground, Grootveld replied, "That's the problem. We don't have any money, so we need to rely on spontaneous donations. We should have a regular depot where bikes can be donated. The desire to give is in us all. So bestow your bike upon the community. It'll be painted white and will be at everyone's disposal."

Donated bikes would be accepted and painted white at the Provos' weekly "happenings," which occurred on Saturdays at midnight on Spui Square, the site where the first three bikes had been painted. On the night of July 31, three days after the White Bike launch, hundreds of people gathered around the *Lieverdje* statue to witness the Provo happening. Grootveld, who had been conducting such street theater happenings at this site for more than a year already, was the main attraction at these events. While waiting for Grootveld to arrive and begin the proceedings, Van Duijn stood on the bumper of a parked car and tried to enlighten the crowd about the White Bicycles Plan. "It doesn't work," he later recalled. "I'm not demagogical enough to really scream into the hearts of these people the necessity for a collectivized means of transport." Then, much to Van Duijn's surprise, a guy stepped forward from the crowd and proffered his bike for the cause.

Van Duijn grabbed the bike and, standing in the street in front of Café Hoppe, began whitewashing it. Suddenly a Volkswagen Bug squad car drove up and screeched to a halt. Four cops jumped out and ordered the crowd to disperse. One of the policemen shouted at Van Duijn, "Sir, get out of here!"

"Why?" Van Duijn asked.

The cop replied by walloping Van Duijn with a baton. The can of white paint fell from his hand and splattered in the street.

Until that point, the police had more or less turned a blind eye to the Provos' happenings. But the moment the cops began swinging their batons, things changed; the innocence of both the Provos and the cops vanished. At the same time, the police also established themselves as both a foil for the Provos and as the Provos' greatest, though unwitting, publicists.

AT THE FOLLOWING Saturday's midnight happening, 200 people attended as more bikes were painted white, firecrackers were lit, a newspaper bonfire was ignited around the pedestal of the statue and a can of white paint was dumped over the

Lieverdje's head. When one Provo tried to bring a White Bicycle to the statue, a cop confiscated it and, in the ensuing tumult with the crowd, proceeded to use it as both a weapon and a shield. Seven people were arrested.*

On August 9, the Provos issued a communiqué to the press, which read:

> Recently, the anarchistic movement Provo proposed the dis-
> tribution of White Bicycles to the Amsterdam public. As is
> already known, the White Bicycles are public property; after
> they've been used, they're left unlocked. For various rea-
> sons, we are convinced the police have abused this collective
> aspect by confiscating the White Bicycles and are withhold-
> ing them from Amsterdam's cyclists. Apparently, the police
> refuse to recognize that traffic in Amsterdam has become a
> bloody, air-polluted chaos due to the auto-terror and that the
> White Bicycles are a constructive step on the road to safer
> and healthier traffic.
>
> We therefore demand that the police not disturb the
> White Bicycles and that the White Bikes already seized be
> given back to Amsterdam.

For their part, the police issued a press release of their own, which warned the public to steer clear of Spui Square the following Saturday night—August 14. Of course, just as when

---

*Days later, the sculptor of the *Lieverdje*, 49-year-old Amsterdammer Carel Kneulman, said that though he had "warm sympathies" for the White Bi-
cycles Plan, he was angered that someone would dump paint on his creation. "The defiling of such a simple little statue is downright terror. . . . I'm terribly sorry, but I just don't see the point of it. Why doesn't a guy like that do something constructive? Why doesn't he write a book?"

Amsterdam's cops first directed street traffic, when they set the first cycling speed traps, when they held the first stop signs, when they conducted the first stoplights and when they cited cyclists without tax plates, Amsterdam's cops drew a ready audience. So an official warning to stay away was received by many as an explicit invitation to attend. Two thousand people filled the square to witness whatever might transpire between the Provos and the police. A survey of some of the spectators in attendance that night included "shopkeepers, accountants, traveling salesmen and their wives."

The Provos in attendance chanted, "Coppers! Where's my white bike?" and when they attempted to lay flowers at the feet of the Lieverdje, police officers prevented them from doing so. Confrontations ensued and the police began trying to disperse the crowd by swinging their batons at impeccably dressed onlookers—men in coats and ties, women in heels and dresses, clutching their handbags. (One cop even almost whacked the police chief, who was watching the proceedings in his civvies.) This time, though, when the police attacked, they were showered with a rain of bicycle bells.[*]

The next day, when Police Commissioner Landman was asked why the Provos conducted these weekly Saturday night happenings, he replied, "I don't know. If you're normal, you can't understand a crazy person. No sir, this is actually not a job for the police; it's a job for the psychiatrist."

---

[*]The top half of a typical Dutch bicycle bell could easily be unscrewed from its base fixed to the handlebars. From the late 1950s to the mid-1970s, during various confrontations between young people and the Amsterdam police, it was standard practice to remove the metal dome from a parked bike's bell and fling it at the cops.

While the clamor was occurring on Spui Square on the night of August 14, Van Duijn and a few other Provos snuck off to Nassauplein, where they laid flowers at the Ferdinand Domela Nieuwenhuis statue and painted a bike white. These actions were carried out to inveigh against the police violence on Spui Square and to honor the anarchist Domela Nieuwenhuis. "We continue to protest against the police confiscation of various White Bicycles," the Provos announced in a press release. "Once again, we demand that these bicycles be given back to the community."

DAYS LATER, ON August 17, the second issue of *PROVO* magazine hit the streets. It contained Schimmelpennink's White Bicycles manifesto, which read, in part:

It is absolutely essential that the center of Amsterdam (inside the ring of old canals) be closed to all motorized traffic (cars, motorbikes, etc.). . . .

To supplement public transportation, we propose that every year the municipality buy 20,000 White Bicycles (cost: one million guilders). These White Bicycles would belong to everyone and to no one. This will solve the traffic problem within a few years. As the first step toward the annual 20,000 White Bicycles, Provo offers volunteers the opportunity to have their bikes painted white every Saturday night at midnight by the Lieverdje on Spui Square. . . .

A car is acceptable as a means of transport only within thinly populated areas or from a thinly populated area to the city. Cars are a dangerous and totally unsuitable means of transport within the city. There are better ways of moving from one city to another. For these purposes, the automobile is an outdated solution. . . .

Political indecisiveness and bogged-down, inane confor-mations must NOW be breached by a radical solution:

NO MOTOR TRAFFIC,

JUST WHITE BIKES!

OVER THE NEXT few months, Provos continued whitewashing bikes and leaving them on the street—all to no avail. "The plan isn't working," Van Duijn claimed in October, "because the po-lice have confiscated the fifty bicycles we had set out in the city center."

In addition to their initial plan, the Provos introduced a num-ber of other "White Plans." Among them were the White Chim-neys Plan (calling for the reduction of air pollution in the city), the White Women Plan (calling for women's lib) and the White Homes Plan (calling for vacant apartments to be thrown open to those in need of housing). The White Chickens Plan ("chicken" being an old Amsterdam term equivalent to the American pig in regard to the police) called for policemen to be transformed into social workers who would carry with them for dispensing to the public: matches, bandages, contraceptives, candies, oranges and chicken drumsticks. These police would also be responsible for bringing in broken White Bicycles for repairs. The Provos' most lively plan was executed on March 10, 1966, when they helped create the disturbances on the day of Crown Princess Beatrix's royal wedding (see chapter 12).

Shortly after that wedding, the group established Provo as a political party and set its sights on the June 1966 municipal elections. Weeks before the election, Provo member Duco van Weerlee published a small book titled *What the Provos Want*, which concluded with 17 "concrete political objectives." Among these: more playing space on the streets, broader sex education, equal rights for homosexuals, more nighttime public transportation, later open hours for museums (for the workingman), increased oversight of the city council, an end to depopulation of the city center, the return of the Royal Palace to its original function as city hall and for Mayor van Hall ("the good soul") to take a permanent vacation. Named first and foremost on this list, though, was the White Bicycles Plan—for "the communal possession of all Amsterdammers who want the tin-canned status symbols [that is, cars] out of the city center."

Placed at the top of the Provo party ticket (due to his public speaking abilities) was Bernhard de Vries, a 25-year-old student who had been involved with the Provos for only a few months. In the election, the party received 13,105 votes, which earned it one seat on the city council. (The pro-car party, victorious four years earlier, received fewer than 4,000 votes and lost its lone seat.) Responding to the news of the electoral triumph of those who had relentlessly attacked him, Mayor van Hall said, "The Provos will soon see what it means to govern a city. Painting everything white is no solution." (As far as Van Hall was concerned, the Provos would get the last laugh. Due to the brutality exercised by the police toward the Provos, Police Chief H. J. van der Molen would be fired and Van Hall forced to resign within a year.)

Once in office, though, De Vries did little agitating for the

White Plans. In fact, he didn't even get around to introducing a bill calling for the city to implement the White Bicycles Plan until March 3, 1967—two weeks after he'd already announced he'd soon be leaving office.*

De Vries' bill called for the "purchase of 3,000 white bicycles; said bicycles shall belong to everyone and to no one." His speech in favor of the bill consisted almost entirely of his reading, nearly verbatim, the 1,400-word manifesto Schimmelpennink had published 18 months earlier in *PROVO* #2 (the major exception: the initial number of White Bicycles was reduced from 20,000 to 3,000). Reading from the text, De Vries argued

> that, in a space where almost one million people live, tons of poisonous gasses are produced and spread; that the streets and sidewalks are disappearing underneath the automobiles; that hundreds of deaths and thousands of casualties are being offered up to the laziness of a minority of motorists; and that a unique city is suffering irreparable damage inflicted by the auto-holic part of the population.

While some of the incendiary language from Schimmelpennink's original text was muted, De Vries still read some of the more fiery lines attacking the automobile-based culture: "Exhaust fumes were also, in Nazi Germany, a much-used and effective means for the gassing of the Jews."

---

*De Vries announced this to the council as a major reason why he would be leaving office: the voluminous amount of mail he was receiving daily from the city in regard to his function was overwhelming the 85-square-foot attic apartment he shared with his girlfriend.

The bill had just one cosponsor: 27-year-old Jeanne Baank-Meijer.* Labor Party councilman—and future Amsterdam mayor—Ed van Thijn said that though he wouldn't vote for the bill, he did believe the mayor and *wethouders* should study the idea. Gustav Hamm, *wethouder* for traffic affairs, said he opposed De Vries' "swan song," arguing that tram passengers had to pay for public transport, so why shouldn't the riders of White Bicycles?

Just before the White Bicycles Plan was to be voted on, De Vries—expressing concern that the council was about to "torpedo" his bill—immediately withdrew it from consideration and announced that his successor in the Provo seat would reintroduce the bill at a later date.† Three days later, at the close of De Vries' final city council meeting, he attempted his true swan song: the lighting of a homemade smoke bomb. But just before De Vries ignited his farewell gift, a neighboring councilman managed to snatch it from him.

The Provos replaced the ineffectual De Vries with someone far more passionate about implementing the White Bicycles Plan: Luud Schimmelpennink. At the time, one Provo explained: "Bernhard de Vries doesn't believe in a lot of the Provo plans. Luud does. The White Bicycles Plan is Luud's and he's the right person to stand up for it." A few weeks before assuming his position on the city council, Schimmelpennink spoke out about the city's traffic issues:

*Baank-Meijer made for a curious ally, as she'd been elected as a member of the right-wing Farmer's Party and would, three years later, campaign *against* banning cars from the city center.

†Unlike in the United States—where, if an elected representative steps down, the vacated post is usually filled via an election by the populace or by an appointment from a governing official—in the Dutch electoral system the party retains the seat and fills it with another member of the party.

The car is antisocial. The car is the enemy of a mirthful city center. That thought must ripen. That can happen with the White Bicycles Plan. It's a question of mentality improvement.

Five years ago, someone who spoke out against the car was an enemy of progress. The view that the auto is an antisocial object is beginning to take hold. Many more people will realize this soon if they can again walk in the city center. People will also be able to communicate on the street again. Now they have to worm their way between the parked cars or they have to jump out of the way so they don't get hit.

Two months after Schimmelpennink joined the city council, the Provos concluded that as onetime thorn-in-the-eye outsiders who now had an office, phone number, post office box and regular newspaper—they'd become too official. So, on May 13, 1967, a raucous crowd (smoke bombs galore) of almost 500 people gathered in Vondelpark. There, the decision was made to disband Provo. When the question arose about what should be done with Provo's council seat, Schimmelpennink told the crowd that despite the demise of Provo, he would retain the seat, because the White Bicycles Plan still needed to be formally proposed.

AT THE OCTOBER 4, 1967, meeting of the city council, two bills written by Schimmelpennink were presented—concurrently—to the council for consideration. The first bill called for the city to provide more "social/cultural" centers for Amsterdam's youth and for the planned centers (the future Paradiso among them) to be run by the youths themselves. The second bill—the White Bicycles Plan—proposed three things:

1) banning cars from the city center, 2) increasing the frequency of public transit and 3) the "purchase and maintenance of 2,000 white-painted bicycles of a distinct model that will be made available for general usage in the city center . . . , particularly as supplementary transport for users of tram, bus, taxi and train."

In the official minutes of the meeting, the text of the ensuing discourse runs for more than 20 pages. Yet almost every word uttered concerned the heated and emotional debate over Schimmelpennink's first proposal and his attacks on the city's youth affairs policy. Several times, Mayor Ivo Samkalden stopped the proceedings and threatened the boisterous Provo supporters with clearing the gallery if they didn't settle down and extinguish their burning incense. Amid the commotion, the proposed White Bicycles Plan was almost completely overlooked; the only mentions of it were made merely in passing as party heads simply stated that their parties would not support it.

When, after 90 minutes of talk, Mayor Samkalden announced an end to the debate, Schimmelpennink—eager to expound the not-yet-discussed White Bicycles Plan—said he still had more to say. Samkalden curtly replied, "That's not possible because the discussion is closed." The mayor then put the two bills to a vote. The first was defeated by a vote of 36–1. The second—Schimmelpennink's proposal for the city to create a system of public-use bicycles—fared only slightly better; it lost 35–2. Baank-Meijer was, once again, the lone council member to lend support.*

---

*Less than three years later, in early 1970, Baank-Meijer would clash with Roel van Duijn (then occupying the Provo seat on the council), whom she considered a megalomaniac. Baank-Meijer's husband—Joop Baank, a right-wing radical who feared the rise of countercultural Amsterdam—then kidnapped Van Duijn in Amsterdam before freeing him hours later in Belgium.

The press cared little that the White Bicycles Plan had been formally presented to the council. In their lengthy reports of the council proceedings, some newspapers gave only the briefest of mentions to the vote on the White Bicycles Plan; other newspaper reports contained no mention at all. The Provos had managed to bring a plan they'd initiated on the streets all the way to a city council vote. They had promoted a much-heralded idea that had garnered international attention in the previous two years. Despite all that, the White Bicycles Plan had now died an inglorious death. "The bicycle was viewed as passé," Schimmelpennink would later explain. "In the eyes of the politicians of the time, the bike was out-of-date. They said flat out: it belongs back with the Starvation Winter; we've taken up with the magnificent future of the car."

Schimmelpennink would soon begin working on another idea for ridding the city center of the private auto glut: the *Witkar*. As public-use cars, the White Cars, a fleet of space-age, bulbous, golf-cart-like electric cars would operate under a premise similar to the White Bikes. The three-wheeled, two-seated cars would be available to be driven by Witkar program members for short trips across the center of Amsterdam. Once a trip was completed, the car would be returned to a street-side docking station where the electric battery would recharge and the car be made available for the next user. This innovation—which predated, by decades, the rise in popularity of both electric cars and urban car-share programs—was eventually realized in 1974. At its peak, 38 cars and five docking stations operated in the city center for roughly a decade, until the program was disbanded in the mid-1980s.

17
A Big Success: The Urban Myths of the White Bicycles

Aside from the few dozen old White Bikes that the Provos had distributed in 1965—and the odd bike that an individual had—the Provos' White Bicycles Plan never came close to fruition. Even so, White Bikes would live on as a key symbol of Amsterdam as a countercultural center.

For example, when Arthur Miller spoke to University of Amsterdam theater students, a group of them presented him with a White Bike. A couple of years later, in March 1969, just after marrying in Paris, John Lennon and Yoko Ono drove their Rolls-Royce to Amsterdam, where they spent a honeymoon week holed up in the Hilton hotel. During their "Bed In" for world peace, the couple received a number of reporters, well-wishers and gifts. One such gift, placed on the bed where Lennon and Ono lay in their white robes, was a typical Dutch bike—enclosed chain guard, fenders, generator light and U-shaped handlebars—that had been sloppily brushed with white paint.

An American that I know spent—as a young man—a few months in Amsterdam in the late 1960s. When I asked him if he had any recollections of the White Bikes, he told me he'd seen hundreds of them in the city at the time. "*Hundreds* of them?" I asked, both surprised and skeptical.

"Well," he said, "I saw *a lot* of them."

When I mentioned to him that no actual White Bicycle program ever existed and that only a handful of bikes were ever on the streets (and, even then, only briefly), he thought for a moment. Then he asked, "I must have seen at least *one* White Bike, right?" He wasn't sure. In a matter of just seconds, he'd gone from proclaiming he'd recalled hundreds of White Bikes to questioning whether or not he'd ever seen any.

When I relayed this anecdote to Luud Schimmelpennink, the old Provo laughed and admitted he was well aware of the phenomenon. "Hundreds of people," he said, "have told me that they recall spending years riding White Bikes."

Though the overwhelming defeat by the Amsterdam city council in 1967 had put an official end to the Provos' White Bicycles Plan, by no means did the defeat dampen the White Bikes' legacy. The myths had taken root and, over decades, those myths spread far and wide. Outside of Holland, one popular legend was that the plan had been fully operational but that, ultimately, it proved to be a spectacular fiasco. Among the purported reasons for the program's failure and demise:

- "[T]he experiment fizzled out after too few bikes were made available." (newspaper, 1972)
- "[T]he police started arresting the Provos for using bicycles they did not own." (book, 1979)
- "The plan worked for a while, until the bikes suffered from selfish vandalism." (book, 1995)

- "[P]eople just took the white bikes and painted them some other color." (book, 2004)
- "In the end, the bikes . . . became too beat-up to ride." (newspaper, 2007)

Embellishing and spreading urban myths of the White Bicycles Plan wasn't a job reserved for clueless foreigners. In 2000, in a paper presented at an international meeting of urban cycling advocates and professionals, the bike coordinator within Amsterdam's transportation agency, Joep Huffener (whose position existed, in part, because of the pro-cycling advocacy the Provos had begun more than three decades earlier), also spoke of the failure of the plan due to those who broke the "rules" by stealing the bikes and making them their own. He went on to say, "Some people failed to take proper care of the bicycles, so that they quickly became unusable. There were no fixed collection or assembly points, whereby little or no control was possible. No one could state with any certainty how the bicycles were being used."

Indeed, there *had been no* collection points, there *had been no* control and there *had been no* certainty because there simply *had been no* operating White Bicycles Plan.

ANOTHER VARIATION ON the White Bike urban myth: that the plan had been operational in the 1960s—and it had been an ongoing success. For example, *New York* magazine reported in 1970 that the plan was in operation. Two years later, in *The Clear Creek Bike Book*, an author who purported to have been to Amsterdam declared: "The city provides a free bike for anyone caught short. You will see them anywhere and they stand out

318 In the City of Bikes

because they are painted white. Sometimes sloppily so, as if some city painter had lined them up and did a hit-and-miss job with a whitewash brush."

For a long time, much of this mythologizing remained innocuous banter. But then, in 1994, the White Bikes myth made for profound consequences. In mid-August of that year, Tom O'Keefe, a man living in Portland, Oregon, lost his bike to theft, which got him thinking about public trust. "I had read about the bike program in Amsterdam and how successful it was at promoting trust within the community," O'Keefe would later state. A couple of weeks later, O'Keefe and his friend Joe Keating—both organizers at a nonprofit community organization—saw a film that would enjoy an extended theatrical run in Portland: Jonathan Blank's 1994 documentary about life in progressive Holland, titled *Sex, Drugs and Democracy*. Midway through the film, a brief segment is devoted to the Provo movement. While archival footage is shown of a Provo happening on Spui Square and of Bernhard de Vries riding a White Bike, Robert Jasper Grootveld, in his broken English, recalls the White Bicycles Plan:

> We started telling there should be a bike free. Cities should
> pay for it. Hundreds, thousands of bikes standing in the
> streets. Anyone who needs a bike, he just takes the bike and
> then he goes. He just leave them and then another take it.
> Okay! White Bike Plan was born. White Bikes became a big
> success of the Provo movement.

Though the film focused on the White Bicycles for under thirty seconds, the imagery coupled with the testimony from Grootveld (who never shied from using hyperbole) gave the

impression that the White Bicycles Plan had not only been enacted, but had actually been "a big success." When O'Keefe and
Keating saw this part of the film, they were spurred to action. As
Keating put it a couple of months later, "There was this wonderful scene about the free community bikes in Amsterdam. We
looked at each other and said, 'Okay, let's do it.'"

Over the next few days, Keating and O'Keefe collected from
friends ten "somewhat damaged" bicycles, repaired them and
spray-painted them, not white but yellow. Keating and O'Keefe
attached a small sign to the rear of each bicycle's seat that read:
FREE COMMUNITY BIKE. PLEASE RETURN TO A MAJOR STREET
FOR OTHERS TO USE. USE AT YOUR OWN RISK. A listed phone
number could be called if a bike was in need of repair. Then the
bikes were set on the streets of Portland.

"Our aim is to promote a little honesty, sharing, caring and
non-polluting commuting," stated O'Keefe. But what if that
honesty wasn't respected? What if these bikes were stolen? Keating (in answers taken from various interviews) replied:

> I'm sure a few bikes disappear, but we're not concerned
> about it. . . . You'd have to be pretty hard up to steal these
> bikes. They're fixed up and safe to ride, but they're basically
> clunkers. . . . You can't steal these bikes. They're free. That's
> the beauty of it. . . . We would rather have someone take our
> bikes, rather than yours.

Within a couple of months, the new Yellow Bike Project refurbished and released more than a hundred bikes. This garnered attention from dozens of media outlets; *Good Morning America*, *Inside
Edition* and the *New York Times* all did features on the Yellow Bike

Project.* Much of this media coverage served to further mytholo-
gize Amsterdam's White Bicycles Plan. For example, just days after
the launch of the first Yellow Bikes, Portland's daily newspaper, the
Oregonian, reported: "The program is modeled after a project based
in Amsterdam. In that Dutch city, though, the bikes are white and
the city manages the program, including the necessary funding."
The following month, in a *Seattle Times* article about the Yellow
Bike Project, the reporter wrote: "[I]n Holland . . . free community bicycles are used by everyone, from the down and out to daily
commuters." Keating himself continued to spread the myth of the
White Bikes when, half a year after the release of the first Yellow
Bikes, he told *Bicycling* magazine: "Amsterdam has a state-run free
bike program. But it's really causing sparks here in the U.S."

The idea was indeed catching on. Throughout 1995 and 1996,
in dozens of North American cities, individuals, nonprofit organizations and even some municipal government agencies followed the lead of the Portlanders. Otherwise unused bicycles
were gathered, fixed up and spray-painted a uniform color. They
were painted purple in Spokane, Washington; red in Madison,
Wisconsin; blue in Victoria, British Columbia; green in Boul-
der, Colorado; orange in Tampa, Florida; and pink in Olympia,
Washington. Many of the coordinators of these projects cited
as their influence not only Portland's Yellow Bikes but also the
"success" of the White Bicycles of Amsterdam.†

---

*So broad was the appeal of this story that even the trashiest of supermarket
tabloids—the *Weekly World News*—ran a piece on the Yellow Bikes (in an issue that also bore the front-page headline SPACE ALIEN CAPTURED BY U.S.
NAVY).

†Curiously, among the many public-use bicycle projects that materialized
throughout North America during this period, apparently none used bikes
painted white.

With the introduction of each new public-use bicycle program, when the question of theft arose, these new coordinators mimicked the Portlanders by stating: 1) thefts were to be anticipated, but the number would be small, 2) anyone desperate to steal an old clunker was welcome to it and 3) a critical mass of available bikes on the streets would eventually be achieved, rendering bike theft pointless. After many of these programs were up and running, though, the inevitable thefts proved overwhelming.

For example, in Minneapolis, of the 30 yellow bicycles issued in 1995 only two remained by the end of the year. The following year, another 150 bikes were distributed, but within months, only 60 remained. "Things were getting better," said the program's director, "but that was still terrible." In January 1996, the Rotary Club began placing the first of 450 yellow bicycles on the streets of Fresno, California; by October 1997, few, if any, of those bikes could be found. "We put about one hundred bikes out and they all disappeared," said a coordinator of Tucson's program in September 1996. "The truth is it didn't work. It's terrible to see them all disappear."

Even in Portland, epicenter of the public-use bicycle movement, theft and vandalism had devastating effects. Within 14 months of the launch of the program, more than 450 Yellow Bikes had been publicly distributed. Yet in November 1995, when a newspaper reporter searched the streets of Portland, he was only able to locate a single one, and it was locked to a tree. By September 1997, the total number of Yellow Bikes issued exceeded 1,000, the magic number that had often been cited by Keating as the tipping point for ensuring the program's success. Nevertheless, sightings of the bikes remained a rarity.

During this period, I frequently passed through Portland.

Once, I happened to be in town when a hundred more Yellow Bicycles were released to the public. That evening, I saw dozens of cyclists parading the Yellow Bikes up NW Glisan Street. Since I was staying in an office space downtown and had no bike of my own, I immediately envisioned making full use of the program. The following day, though, I saw only two Yellow Bikes; both were already in use. I didn't spot another Yellow Bike until a week later, when I found one standing on a downtown sidewalk. I hopped on it and started to ride. The bent front sprocket made pedaling difficult. Fortunately, I couldn't pick up much speed, having quickly realized that neither set of handbrakes was operable. I pulled over, slowed to a stop and left the bike leaning against a parking meter and continued walking. Of the other 100 Yellow Bikes I'd seen parading through the streets the week before, I never saw another one of them again.

The thefts of Portland's Yellow Bikes eventually took their toll. Citing the high rate of burnout incurred by the project's volunteers, who had tirelessly refurbished and distributed bikes only to have them immediately disappear, Portland's original Yellow Bike Project formally disbanded in October 1997. "A lot of folks took the bikes," Keating announced. "They have, at this point, lost their communal nature." A Portland cop put it another way: "It didn't take people long to figure out that a free bike is just a free bike."

The fantasy of Amsterdam's White Bicycles Plan had inspired a generation of public-use bike programs. Yet given that the Provo plan had never become a reality, it's not surprising that these public-use bicycle schemes failed.

WHILE THE PUBLIC-USE bike programs were sweeping North America, Luud Schimmelpennink was busy working on a new version of the White Bicycles Plan in Amsterdam. In the new scheme, the bikes would require a coin deposit while they were in use. He had already tried revisiting the White Bicycles idea in 1981 (without success) and had now been busy with his new idea—the Depo bike—since 1991.

Nine months after Portland's first Yellow Bikes hit the streets, the city of Copenhagen, Denmark, launched its own public-use bike program, for which Schimmelpennink had served as a consultant. The Danish program differed from the many unsuccessful programs tried in North America. Copenhagen's White Bicycles weren't simply left willy-nilly around town; they were stalled in special bike racks where a coin deposit (worth around three dollars) unlocked the bike. After use, the bike was to be returned to a rack where the deposit would be refunded.

In Amsterdam, after a decade of planning and false starts, the Depo system was finally launched in 2001 with an initial stock of 250 white bicycles and a dozen or so docking stations. The plan was for the system to eventually expand to 750 bikes and 45 docking stations.

One city official claimed that, thanks to the Depo system, "there are likely to be around 15,000 fewer bicycle thefts in the Amsterdam city center each year." Presumably, a drop in thefts would occur because joyriders would use the system instead of nicking bikes. Thefts of the Depo bikes themselves would be negligible, it was thought, because of the customized, "asshole-proof" bike racks and the peculiar appearance of the bikes (one person described the Depo bike as looking like "a cross between a folding bike and a home trainer"). The bike had spokeless wheels and solid rubber tires. "Who would buy a stolen White Bicycle?" Schimmelpennink wondered. "Everyone will recognize those things. It would be very conspicuous."

Though the bikes' unique look gave them little resale value and a redesigned rack system was touted as being impervious to thieves, the city's *zwijntjesjagers* seemed to treat these security measures as if they were a dare. "Despite the [improved] racks," Schimmelpennink was forced to admit, "this system couldn't withstand the bike thieves either." Of the 250 bikes placed in the program, about 70 were reported stolen. The Depo scheme suffered other problems, too, particularly technical issues with the computer system and the payment method.

Long-standing doubts prevailed about the viability of a public-use bikes scheme in Amsterdam. After all, the problem wasn't the need for more *bikes* but rather the need for more *accommodation* for the great many existing bikes. "I think Schimmelpennink is a brilliant man," said Green Party city councilwoman Vera Dalm in 2002, "but I just don't think his plan will ever work in Amsterdam."

The Depo system hobbled along for a year or so and was no longer even functioning when the city finally pulled the plug on the program's government subsidy.

"It's a shame that it was met with so much difficulty," Schimmelpennink would later say. "But, on the other hand, it's nice that in other cities it appears to work." Since the demise of the Depo system, a great many bike-share programs in hundreds of cities worldwide—Paris, Montreal, Taipei, Barcelona, Melbourne, Buenos Aires, London, Washington, D.C., Munich, for example—have, indeed, succeeded.

IN 2010—42 YEARS after having stepped down from office and just days shy of his 75th birthday—Schimmelpennink again won a seat on the city council, this time as a member of the Labor Party. As a councilman once more, Schimmelpennink immediately announced he would be unveiling yet another new version of the White Bicycles Plan for Amsterdam. "It's going to happen now," he promised. Ever the inventor, Schimmelpennink revealed that the new bikes would be chainless, would store and use electricity generated from the pedaling and would have seats that automatically adjusted to a rider's preferred height. To Amsterdammers with decades of experience of hearing about the promise of the White Bicycles Plan, the announcement was met mostly with indifference. Schimmelpennink was criticized for the obvious conflict of interest between his roles of entrepreneur and councilman (if he was to pursue legislation to create such a program). Ultimately, though, this plan also came to nothing.

After 1965, for many years, public-use bicycles appeared to be but a pipe dream. Now, though, such schemes are flourishing in an increasing number of cities around the world. But unlike Amsterdam, those other cities don't have an enormous rate of bike ownership (it's now presumed that Amsterdam has more bikes than residents), a great number of existing bike rental establishments (the number of which has quadrupled over the past decade) or a historic problem with bike theft. Thus, in the city where the idea of public-use bikes was born, a half-century later, it looks unlikely that such a scheme will ever take hold . . . no matter how convincing urban myths may be.

18

A Typical Amsterdam Characteristic: The Bike Fishermen

Seeing the photo of 1950s cyclists on Leidseplein in Lawrence Halprin's book had been the major influence in my move to Amsterdam. But after settling in and becoming engrossed with all things concerning Amsterdam cycling, I began to realize how serendipitous my migration across the world had been. If I'd never seen that photo, I probably would never have moved to Amsterdam. And if Halprin's book had instead featured such a photo from some other city, I might have moved there instead. What if the photo had been from, say, Copenhagen—Europe's other biking metropolis? Would I have emigrated to Denmark instead? Would I have spent years trying to understand Danish culture while fumbling over the Danish language on a daily basis?

This led me to wonder: *Had* I migrated to the right city? After all, maybe Copenhagen was the *true* cycling capital and I'd unknowingly settled for second best simply because of a single photo. Maybe my interest in and affection for Amsterdam was actually minuscule compared to what it could be for Copenhagen—a place where I knew a public-use bicycles program actually worked. I harbored all these thoughts, yet I'd never been to Copenhagen. So, in order to compare the two contenders for the title "cycling capital," Amy Joy and I planned a little trip to Denmark. Once and for all, I could see if I'd moved to the right city.

Upon our arrival in the Danish capital, one difference between the two cities immediately became clear. Outside Copenhagen's Central Station, hundreds of bikes were fastened by locks that looked—to someone from Amsterdam—shockingly vulnerable. They were so skinny and flimsy, they seemed like they could be snipped open using little more than fingernail clippers. Many bikes—even racing bikes, fixed-gear bikes, cargo bikes—were secured by nothing but a single toy-like lock. And, curiously, only the front wheels of many bikes were locked, which left the rest of the bike ripe for the taking. By my count, only one in 30 bikes was secured by two locks.

When I found not one but two bikes whose locks still had their keys in them, I was baffled. Was this some sort of Danish courtesy to thieves? Or were there simply *no* thieves to fear? I went and reported my findings to Amy Joy, who, in the meantime, had retreated with our son to a sidewalk café. "Really? Keys in the locks?" she asked dubiously. I dragged my family from the café and showed them first the keys and then all the chintzy locks. Amy Joy's eyes went from bike to bike; she was speechless.

Our stunned reaction was hardly original. In 1919, when a Dutchman visiting Copenhagen noticed that the city's many bikes stood unlocked and unbothered, he was shocked. "It's unbelievable, but true," he remarked. "In the Danish capital Copenhagen, one can calmly leave his bike, even in the busiest of streets. In front of banks, the post office, hotels, etc., you see entire jumbles of bikes leaning upon one another. . . . The Danes appear to be the most honest people on earth."

During our four days in Copenhagen, after further investigation, I was only able to find a single bike that was secured by three locks. Coming from Amsterdam—where using two locks is the norm and three locks not unheard of—it should have come as no surprise that this lone thrice-locked bike was a Gazelle, a Dutch brand. The sticker on its rear fender was that of a bike shop in the town of Zaltbommel, 50 miles south of Amsterdam. Apparently you can take a Dutch cyclist out of the Netherlands, but you can't take the apprehension toward bike thieves out of a Dutch cyclist.

THE TRIP YIELDED some other observations. Copenhageners are less likely than Amsterdammers to: smoke while cycling, adorn their bikes with plastic flowers, transport dogs on their bikes, ride with an umbrella in the rain or dink each other. (Though most of the bikes had rear racks [as in Amsterdam], I didn't see a single one used as a passenger seat.) The Danes are also far less likely to talk on cell phones while cycling, because, apparently, it's illegal to do so (unlike in Amsterdam, where at times it feels like it's illegal *not* to use a cell phone while on a bike).

On the other hand, Copenhageners were *more likely* than Amsterdammers to: use pronounced hand signals, stop for red lights (having many wider, busier streets and more complex intersections than Amsterdam, this was understandable) and wear helmets. One morning on Hans Christian Andersen Boulevard, of 1,000 cyclists that passed, I counted 178 wearing helmets. This was an enormous difference from Amsterdam, where, if one was to watch a thousand cyclists ride by, she'd find it challenging to spot a single helmet. (Aside from the four types of people who are apt to don helmets in Amsterdam—children, couriers, tourists and those on racing bikes heading to or from a long countryside ride—I'd estimate that about one in 5,000 Amsterdam cyclists wear helmets, or, statistically speaking, 0.02 percent.)

It appeared that Amsterdam and Copenhagen shared equally only one aspect of urban cycling: countless gorgeous women on bikes.

AS AMY JOY and I were walking around a canal-lined Copenhagen neighborhood named—of all things—Little Amsterdam, she said, "Look!" She pointed down at the water where, about ten feet below the surface, a bike lay on its side. A moment passed before I could register what I was seeing.

"The water is so clear here," Amy Joy said, "you can actually see the bottom of the canals."

This was in stark contrast to Amsterdam, where the mud-bottomed canals are obscured by dark, murky waters. As we stood at the edge of the rock-bottomed canal in Copenhagen, staring down at this lone bike, my mind reeled. What if the water in Amsterdam suddenly turned this clear? Not only would the watery grave sites of thousands of bikes suddenly be revealed, but the task of Amsterdam's bike fishermen—those employees of the sanitation department responsible for removing junk from the canals—would be made far easier.

I FIRST CAME upon Amsterdam's bike fishermen a few weeks after my arrival in the city. I was cycling along Keizersgracht when I spotted a small crowd lining the quay; they were drawn by something happening on the canal. I pulled over, joined the crowd and took a look. On the water were two boats: one was equipped with a small hydraulic crane, and the other was a barge filled with wet, decrepit bikes. A man, reclining in a padded lounge chair, was operating the crane with a five-pronged grappling hook at its end. He plunged this claw into the water and it grasped at whatever lay on the canal bottom, about ten feet below the surface. It resurfaced with nothing in its clutches but sludge and water. The claw dropped again. Again it came up empty-handed. On the third attempt, though, the claw reemerged clenching a muddied, gnarled bike. The crane operator swung his catch over to the barge and dropped it atop the tangled pyramid of other muddied, gnarled bikes. Not only had this bike been hooked, but now, so was I.

For almost an hour and a half, I followed the bike fishermen. While the claw operator did the actual fishing, the other crew member piloted the boat at a speed slower than a walking pace (so slow, in fact, he was able to tend to other tasks, like preparing the tea). Along the way, the number of onlookers rhythmically swelled and contracted. Whenever the fishermen had a dry spell, the crowd grew as people lingered and expectations increased. Then, when a bike was finally nabbed, the seemingly satisfied crowd would disperse. Though the claw hoisted up other junk—three car tires, two scooters, a no-parking sign, a long metal pipe, a chair—the vast majority of the time, when a catch was made, it was a bicycle. In less than 90 minutes, I watched the fishermen land 47 bikes.

TOSSING ANY AND every type of refuse into the canals was "a typical Amsterdam characteristic" that dated back to the Middle Ages. A Frenchman visiting Amsterdam in 1922 was astonished by the "rubbish and garbage" floating in the city's canals. "You see there old mattresses, repulsive rags and bags filled with one knows not what," the tourist wrote. "As to the odor, I prefer to pass that by without description."

When, in 1954, the city's police chief proposed filling in several canals to create more space for roadways and car parking, his plan was widely criticized. One magazine writer stated: "The Amsterdammer does not, in the least, go easy on his canals. It's true, he'll become highly indignant if someone attacks 'his' canals with talk of filling them in. But there are Amsterdammers who, in a haze of slovenliness and laziness, have already begun filling them in."

A couple of years later, the *Trouw* newspaper called Amsterdam's canals "those traditional garbage cans where we take our visitors on boat trips." During the 1950s, among the discarded items that were noted for ending up in the canals were potbellied stoves, wooden crates, old shoes, tin cans, car tires, phone books, bed frames, Christmas trees, baby carriages, cardboard boxes, rotting wood, washtubs, chairs, rags, pillows, furniture, house pet cadavers and—naturally—bicycles and bicycle parts.

Of mattresses dumped in the canals, one eyewitness wrote:

They float there like little melancholy islands, usually among discarded teakettles and tarnished orange crates. The entirety would make a rewarding still life for an enthusiastic painter if only the old doormats garnished with fish offal weren't muddling the picture.

In the mid-1950s, about once a week, on average, a car went into the canals. Almost all of them were then lifted back out by a brigade of the Amsterdam fire department that specialized in recovering people and cars (and, in earlier days, horses) from the canals. At the time, it was joked that Amsterdam's fire department spent more time hoisting cars out of the canals than putting out fires. When, in 1958, the captain of a dredging boat was asked if his five-man crew ever brought up anything "peculiar," the man with 25 years of experience in canal dredging replied: "No, nothing peculiar is ever dredged up. Sure, a car comes up, a motorcycle comes up. Handcarts and cargo bikes come up; bed frames and regular bikes come up. But anything peculiar? Never."

BIKE FISHING HAD already become a common sight by the 1930s, as both professional and amateur hunters of scrap metal plied the waters sitting in scows; the scavengers used long, hook-ended poles to prod the canal bottoms in search of hidden treasure, a prized find being a bike. As one newspaper account put it in 1937, "After a laborious life, bicycles—that had enjoyed a peaceful existence for years in the sludge on the bottom of our canals—saw their peace cruelly disturbed and their existence end in the glowing jaws of the blast furnaces."

As long as bike fishermen have existed, so, too, have bike-fishing spectators. In 1935, a reporter who watched a man in a scow using a hooked pole to bring up bicycles, baby carriages, chairs, etc., joked, "No bodies, though I suspect the crowd[s] of onlookers were waiting for relatives."* In 1958, one Amsterdammer professed, "It's a captivating sight to watch such a man haul in his catch." The following year, another city resident admitted: "As true Amsterdammers, we've all stood and watched this 'fishing' for hours."

In 1977, Hannes Köhler—a bike fisherman who had been working for the municipal sanitation department for more than 30 years—explained that both the drawbacks and the perks of his position usually involved the spectators. "With this job, all day long we draw a lot of attention. They hang around on the bridge and yell that you're a pig." (To such detractors, Köhler's standard reply was "Shouldn't you be looking for a job, brother?") Other onlookers would see the workers sitting and drinking coffee and call the head office to complain, "The dredging crew is already taking another coffee break."

On the plus side, though, Köhler said his job on the canals allowed him to sit back and appreciate the city's beauty. "There's an awful lot to see in Amsterdam," Köhler told a reporter. When asked if this included the "pretty girls" on the bridges, Köhler replied, "Yes, of course. It wouldn't be healthy if we didn't take a look." Then he added, "You know, I'm one of those Amsterdammers who's really got it made in this city."

IN THE 1980s (by which time two more staples would be added to the list of typical items fished out of the canals: shopping carts and

---

*Turning up bodies when looking for bikes? It could also happen the other way around. Through the years, whenever Amsterdam police divers have dragged canals in search of a corpse, usually they've turn up countless bikes.

parking meters), the city embarked on a civic campaign to reduce the amount of junk tossed into the canals. By then, the barges of the sanitation department were lined with signs that read: THE CITY'S BEAUTIFUL CANALS AREN'T GARBAGE CANS. After centuries of dumping trash in the canals, the antipollution message began to sink in. "If somebody threw something in, somebody else would come over and say something," said Gerrit Huijgen, head of the canal cleaners. "It happened. It's social control."

With greater awareness of the environment in general, Amsterdammers tossed less and less everyday garbage and refuse in the canals. But while the canal-polluting habits had largely changed, one habit hadn't: bikes—lots of them—still ended up in the water.

FOR DECADES, THE hooked poles and the dredging machines were the standard tools for clearing Amsterdam's 75 miles of waterways. The pole method, though, was slow and plodding. For example, in 1958, a bike fisherman working the waters in front of Central Station—one of the city's richest bike-fishing grounds—typically hauled in 12 to 15 "from almost new to completely wrecked" bikes per hour. While the other fishing method of the era—dredging—could haul the junk from the water more quickly, dredging was bulky and invasive, and required a large crew.

Then, in 1965, a new age dawned on the bike fishing world: the sanitation department added to its fleet a customized scow. Built onto the boat was a hydraulic crane with a fingered grappling hook. This vessel would eventually replace both the hooked-pole and dredging operations. The grappling hook could drop into the water and yank up hefty treasures with much more agility than the dredging method and much faster than the hooked-pole approach. In 1982, for example, from the waters of the Singel, around Koningsplein, in about an hour's time, according to one eyewitness, a bike fisherman used the mechanized claw to reel in 250 bikes. "Every stab by the crane," claimed the spectator, "was a bull's eye."

ONE WARM SATURDAY afternoon, I was cycling along the Singel with my five-year-old son on my bike. Suddenly I shouted, "Check it out! Bike fishermen!" I pointed to the two men on a boat; one steered while the other sat in the easy chair operating the grappling hook. The adjoined barge already contained two dozen wet, wrecked bikes. "They're fishing for bikes with that claw," I said.

In Ferris' lifetime, I'd only ever seen the bike fishermen when I was alone or when we were rushing somewhere on the bike and didn't have time to stop and properly pay attention. Today, though, we were just meandering on two wheels; we had plenty of time.

I stopped the bike and Ferris climbed off. He squeezed through the crowd and took up a front-row vantage point along the railing that overlooked the canal. This was a momentous occasion. Some papas long for that day when they take their son to his first ball game. Me? I was excited that my boy would get to witness his first bike-fishing expedition.

With rapt attention, Ferris watched the grappling hook drop into the water, root around and then resurface. Only sludge and water were in its grasp. When the claw plunged again, Ferris asked, "Why are there bikes in the water?"

It was a good question and my mind raced to form a succinct

answer. For decades, anyone who's ever caught sight of bike fishing has, at some point, pondered this very riddle. Bikes under water? It defies logic. And it's not just a few bikes; it's *heaps* of bikes. Though the sanitation department has never kept official tabs on how many bikes they remove from the canals, from the 1970s until the turn of the century, estimates routinely ranged from 5,000 to 20,000 bikes per year. By any estimate, the grand total for all the bikes ever lugged out would number in the hundreds of thousands.

So just how *did* all those bikes end up in the canals? I myself had never seen one go into the drink, nor had any of the dozens of Amsterdammers that I'd asked. The novelist John Irving once mused about this very quandary.

Each wreck has a story. . . . Was it someone in crisis who threw his bike into the water out of pure frustration? Was it a thief who had arrived at his destination and wanted to rid himself of the evidence? Was it a case of vandalism? Or was the bike just broken beyond repair?

The stories behind some of the wrecks *are* known. Among them:

- In the 1920s and '30s, when parked cars didn't yet line many of the canals (creating barriers between the roadways and the canals), it wasn't uncommon for cyclists to ride straight off the street and into the water. (Many such cyclists then drowned.) This hazard became even riskier during the Nazi occupation, when cyclists were forced to navigate the city in blacked-out darkness (especially during the months when rush hours occurred before dawn and/or after dusk).

- In 1932, when a group of fascists held a gathering at a meeting hall on Prinsengracht, a group of communists— armed with knives—tried to force their way inside to fight their political enemies. Failing to gain entry, the communists set their sights on a different target: they grabbed the fascists' bikes parked in front of the meeting hall and chucked them into the canal.

- When the Nazis began confiscating bikes in 1942, to prevent them from falling into the hands of the enemy, some Amsterdammers heeded the call from the Resistance and flung their bikes into the canals.

- Also during the occupation period, there were several different reports of bike thieves using canal waters as clandestine, temporary spots to stash stolen bikes or as places to dump frames after bikes had been stripped of their valuable parts (that is, tires in good condition).

- In the 1950s and '60s, as many Amsterdammers were purchasing their first scooters and cars, it was said that oftentimes they took their now-unused bikes and tossed them into the canals.

- As described in chapter 14, on Luilak—especially in the 1950s and '60s—the city's boisterous youth got their jollies by throwing bikes in the canals.

- In January 1990, when an intense storm swept across the Netherlands (95 mph winds, 23 deaths), in Amsterdam, bicycles and even some cyclists were blown into canals (including one man who, with his bike, was blown into the Lijnbaansgracht and was rescued by a bus driver).

- In October 2005, a late-night street fight on Prinsen-gracht resulted in a 24-year-old Polish man being shoved into the water. One assailant threw a bike down on the Pole, who then drowned.
- Throughout the years, there have been numerous accounts of motorists who, while parking their cars alongside a canal, have—sometimes intentionally, sometimes not—bumped a bike from the parking space into the water.

While all of the above reasons account for *some* of the bikes, by no means do the scenarios account for *all* of the cycles. The most popular theory—for many years—has been that the bikes in the canals had been stolen, joyridden and then, upon reaching a destination, dumped in the water. During the peak era of joyriding (1950s–'90s), this could have been a plausible explanation. Yet this theory raises a couple of nagging questions: Why would a thief need to give a watery burial to a stolen bike? Wouldn't just parking and walking away from a bike create far less suspicion than tossing it—however sneakily—into a canal? And, second, if the bikes in the canals *were* dumped there by joyriders or thieves, then why are a great many of the fished-out bikes still locked?

If anyone knows the answers, you'd think it would be the bike fishermen themselves. Over the years, though, they have routinely stated they have no definitive answer for how bikes end up in the canals. In fact, their purported ignorance makes me only more suspicious. It's possible, I believe, they know more than they let on.

A clue to this puzzle might lie in the 1963 film and novel *Fietsen naar de maan* (*Cycling to the Moon*), by Jef van der Heyden. In one scene, a drunken bike fisherman saunters along a dark, quiet Amsterdam canal at 1:30 a.m., until he comes upon a bike leaning against a lamppost. Then, according to the book:

> With a supple hand grip, he places the bike on the edge of the canal. He leans against it with a look of indifference, giving an impression like he's just standing and waiting for his gal. But then, all at once, it happens. He kicks back with his right foot. The bike disappears from the quay and into the water. A splash and then nothing more. Only the increasingly larger ripples of reflecting rings of water indicate the bicycle's grave. The man lights another cigarette, marks a little white *x* on the lamppost and continues on his way.

The bike fisherman returns the following day with his boat and—with a hook-ended pole—publicly excavates the bikes he'd deposited the previous night. As is his routine, he eventually sells these bikes to a fence on Waterlooplein.

Could *that* be the major cause? Like firebug firefighters who secretly ignite blazes that they're then employed to extinguish, do the bike fishermen covertly dump bikes in the canals so they can then be employed to hoist them out? If this was indeed the case, then I couldn't blame the fishermen for taking such extreme measures. An occupation where one guy lounges in a chair performing carnival-game-like tasks while the other pilots a boat so casually he could easily read a book? If it was me, I'd want to hold tight to a plush gig like that, even if it meant having to stock the pond every now and then.

I TRIED TO formulate an appropriate answer to Ferris' question. Not wanting to burden my son with long historical explanations or hysterical conspiracy theories, I simply replied, "People throw bikes in the canals."

He accepted this answer without question, then we both resumed watching. Again and again the claw plunged. Each time that it resurfaced sans treasure, the collective anticipation of the growing crowd intensified. The heyday of yore, when a crane operator would catch a bike each time he cast his hook, was, obviously, no longer upon us.

Finally, on the fisherman's 15th attempt, he had a bite. Out from the water the claw lifted a woman's red Gazelle; a cable lock secured the front wheel, a ring lock secured the rear one. The appreciative crowd erupted with cheers and applause. The crane operator threw up his arms in glory as if he'd just scored for the Dutch in the World Cup final. Then he dumped his catch on the stack of other wet bikes.

I watched a smile of wonderment fill Ferris' face.

"Just think," I told him, "when you grow up, *you* could do this job. Would'ya like that?"

Without hesitation, Ferris replied, "No." Then he turned away from the canal and walked straight back to our bike. I was confounded. I didn't know if I should feel sad—that maybe bike-fishing didn't (*gasp!*) interest him, or if I should feel glad—that maybe he had other, grander aspirations for his life.

AS TO THE question of Copenhagen versus Amsterdam: After Amy Joy, Ferris and I had spent a few days in Copenhagen, I began wondering what it would be like to live in a major biking

342 In the City of Bikes

city where I didn't need to fear bike theft. A place where, if some nutcase (a visiting Amsterdammer?) chucked my bike into a canal, it would be clearly visible and easily retrievable. While it was certainly appealing to ponder such scenarios, I also kept in mind that Copenhagen's major biking artery in the city center contained *ten lanes* of noisy, polluting vehicular traffic, something completely unheard-of in Amsterdam. So, in the end, my vote remained cast for the narrower streets of Amsterdam, even if it had more thieves and murkier canals. Actually, the debate in my head was pointless, since, when it came down to it, I simply couldn't emigrate again. After years of trying to grasp the Dutch language and learning Dutch history and culture, my Dutchified brain couldn't possibly handle doing it all over again, this time in Danish.

19
Death to the Car!: The 1970s

The Provos had helped popularize Amsterdam in the late 1960s; by the beginning of the 1970s, the city had become renowned worldwide as a countercultural hot spot. Thousands of "freaks, nomads, beatniks, hippies, exiles, riffraff, travelers, students, an International Circus of Youth" (as one American eyewitness described them at the time) flocked to the city that became known as "Swinging Amsterdam," "Magic Amsterdam," "Freak City," "the Youth Capital of the Western World" and "Paradise."*

Many of these young visitors were attracted by the city's growing reputation for tolerance: its liberal attitude toward soft drugs (marijuana and hashish could be smoked openly without hassle) and "divergent sexual practices" (in 1969, an American reporter called the city "a new Sodom, the world's Mecca for homosexuals"). Amsterdam's "shrine for kids" (as one young American put

---

*Robert Jasper Grootveld, the Provo who had correctly predicted the worldwide attention the White Bikes would garner, also foresaw this new status for the city when he wrote in 1966: "Amsterdam is the magic center of our western asphalt jungle. I'm certain hundreds, thousands, millions of Americans will come here to be brainwashed."

it) were the large, government-subsidized youth centers like the hip Paradiso, housed in an old church. In 1972, even the normally stuffy *New York Times* had to admit that "the free atmosphere found within these clubs often blows the minds of young tourists from uptight America." Many of these foreign youths found it easy to get by in Amsterdam during the summer months as hundreds slept overnight in the open air on Dam Square. After sleeping in Dam Square was banned in August 1970, the next few summers saw Vondelpark transformed into a de facto giant campground for young visitors. The fact that the city council initially refused to ban sleeping in the park only helped enhance the city's reputation for tolerance.

A great many of the young people who made the pilgrimage to Amsterdam came from the United States. Pan American airlines even ran special weekly "hippie flights" from New York to the Dutch capital with reduced fares for travelers under the age of 26. On board the jumbo jet, the airline employed a 22-year-old bearded, long-haired guitar player who serenaded the hundreds of young passengers with Bob Dylan and Cat Stevens tunes. Organic meals were served, and stewardesses didn't bat an eye when joints were rolled.

When one long-haired young man from Houston—a recent college graduate making his second trip to Amsterdam—was asked about his fondness for the Dutch capital, he replied: "What really draws me to this city is the relaxed atmosphere. There's more freedom." To eager and impressionable young foreigners, this period in Amsterdam represented freedom, relaxation and tolerance. To the cyclists of Amsterdam during this same period, the city exuded no such groovy vibes. In fact, the peak of Amsterdam hippiedom came during a nadir for Amsterdam cycling.

In May 1971, Pieter Niehorster—an Amsterdam journalist who normally traversed the town by car—was assigned by the newspaper *Het Parool* to cycle the streets for an afternoon and assess the conditions of those on bikes. After completing his task, Niehorster concluded, "The cyclist is the stepchild of the big city." Though he was surprised to find that it was easier to navigate or park a bike in Amsterdam than it was to navigate or park a car, Niehorster argued that when it came to road construction, detours, traffic lights, tunnels, etc., conditions greatly favored the motorist. "Motorized transport is pampered," wrote Niehorster. "The cyclists must suffer at every turn. Therefore, cycling in Amsterdam means riding in a city that is consciously pumping more and more carbon monoxide into its air. It's no picnic."

Niehorster's revelations would hardly have shocked Amsterdam's cyclists, or at least those few who remained at the beginning of the 1970s. As conditions for cycling deteriorated, unsurprisingly the number of cyclists decreased. Between 1965 and 1970, between the hours of 7 a.m. and 7 p.m., the daily number of cyclists entering the city center dropped by 60,000. At the same time, the number of cars entering the same area rose by 74,000. In turn, the number of traffic deaths in Amsterdam reached ever higher levels.

AROUND THIS TIME, a number of different protest movements emerged in the city. For example, students at the University of Amsterdam, unhappy with the way the school was run, occupied the administration building for several days. Young women took to the streets to demand equal rights for females. And as early as May 1966, antiwar demonstrators cycled to the heavily secured American consulate on Museumplein, where they remained outside, ringing their bike bells in protest against the U.S. war in Vietnam.

During this period of demonstrations, protests in favor of cyclists' rights began. Early on the morning of February 17, 1970, two dozen bundled-up youths (many of them medical students) pedaled 25 rented three-wheeled cargo bikes—*bakfietsen*—through the snow on Utrechtsestraat to Dam Square. For a period, the cyclists tied up the morning car commute by riding at a deliberately unhurried pace around Dam Square (which, at the time, was still a large traffic center). During their ride, the cyclists handed out hundreds of copies of a flyer that, in part, read:

> On a *bakfiets*, we're taking up as much room as a small car, but we aren't spewing exhaust; we aren't honking; we aren't mowing down children; and we aren't rumbling like thunder. So now who's the crazy one? If it's commonplace for a single person to go to work in an otherwise empty car, then, by the same token, we should be able to ride on an empty *bakfiets*.

"Of course it would be lunacy to ride a *bakfiets* to work," spokesman Marten Bierman told a news reporter. "Commuting to work by car is just as ridiculous."

The protest was organized by members of an activist group called De Lastige Amsterdammer (The Troublesome Amsterdammer).* The group had been founded in 1968 by several young activists, chief among them the 30-year-old architect and graphic designer Bierman and the 28-year-old sociologist

*The group took its name from the phrase Mayor van Hall had used in 1965 to describe Amsterdam and its inhabitants to Prince Claus.

Henk Bakker. After several years of penning articles, pamphlets and a book decrying how the car adversely impacted Amsterdam and other cities, the two decided that only writing about the problem wasn't enough. A new tactic was needed: direct action. So they'd taken to the streets on *bakfietsen*.

After the protest ride, Bakker announced, "This was actually the practice run. We'll continue on." Sure enough, two weeks later, on a Monday morning, a greater number of Lastige Amsterdammers took to the rush hour again. Departing from five outlying neighborhoods, cyclists on sixty *bakfietsen* converged on the city center. Along the way—on Utrechtsestraat, on Muntplein, on Spui Square—they hindered the motorized traffic via their slow and purposeful pedaling. On the otherwise empty beds of their *bakfietsen*, some rode with signs like: RATHER LIVE THAN DRIVE or CARS HAVE BEEN A NUISANCE TO US FOR YEARS. On one cyclist's back hung a circular traffic sign: a black car surrounded by a red circle—the symbol for NO CARS ALLOWED.

Thwarted motorists honked incessantly and verbally abused the cyclists, a favored slur being "Dam Square sleepers!" At least two hysterical drivers intentionally struck *bakfietsen* with their cars. Other drivers pulled cyclists off their bikes. Two fights broke out. To contain the conflict, riot police arrived in armored vans, and regular police arrived on motorcycles with sidecars. The demonstrators actually welcomed the presence of the police, since the additional vehicles helped to ensnarl traffic. On Dam Square, the police arrested a 21-year-old office worker for illegally passing out flyers. The police also confiscated a *bakfiets* that lacked a legally mandated bell.

Afterward, when asked why the protesters hadn't applied for a permit for their demonstration, Bierman replied, "We had no fixed routes mapped out and we also didn't ride in a procession. . . . Incidentally, why don't motorists who drive behind one another need a permit? In practice, is that not also a procession?"

A couple of weeks later, in the pages of a magazine, Henk Bakker debated the appropriateness of the *bakfiets* protests with J. Leonard Lang, a 67-year-old automobile importer. Bakker stressed that car exhaust was pollution and smelly, and that the cars themselves were noisy and consumed too much space in the city.

> Lang: But don't you think it's antisocial to occupy more space in the city than necessary? You could just as well have ridden a regular bike if you wanted to cycle so badly.
>
> Bakker: It was a demonstration to make it very clear to the public just how crazy it is [for everyone to ride alone in a car].
>
> Lang: But you stopped traffic with your *bakfietsen*. And you incensed a few high-strung people.
>
> Bakker: We, ourselves, were traffic.

Lang tried to bolster his argument by lamely stating, "The *bakfiets* is out of style."

A few weeks later, in an interview, Bakker proclaimed:

> Death to the holy cow, away with it! There's but one solution for the parking problem: shove those cars out of the city. An end must be put to the terror of the so-called experts who believe the city can't be closed off [to cars]. Nonsense. It's not me but they who are radical. What's more radical than

continually tearing down chunks of the city to appease the traffic?

In yet another interview, Bakker declared, "Capitalism has become so dependent on the automobile that if you battle the car, you're also fighting the system."

AT ALMOST THE exact same time that members of De Lastige Amsterdammer were fighting the system via bikes, another group began doing the same. Two days after the first *bakfiets* protest ride, members of De Kabouters (The Gnomes) established the "Car-Elimination Service." The Kabouters themselves had been formed just two weeks earlier by Provo founder Roel van Duijn. This new activist movement, in which Van Duijn called for "an ecological transformation of society," established the Orange Free State, an independent, borderless nation. Van Duijn assumed the role of the Orange Free State's ambassador to the Netherlands. Various cabinet departments were formed within the Orange Free State, such as the Ministry of Gratification and the Ministry for the Sabotage of Power and Violence. The Car-Elimination Service fell within the jurisdiction of the Ministry of Environment and Hygiene.

A week after the first *bakfiets* demonstration, the Kabouters conducted their own bike demo. During the morning rush hour, several dozen Kabouters cycled in a pack from Museumplein to Dam Square in an attempt to draw attention to the chaos created by the automobile traffic. A week later, a second "bike rally" attracted fewer riders. (One news report mused that too many of the Kabouters had overslept that morning.) On Vijzelstraat, this rally was brought to a premature end when the dozen or so cyclists were stopped by motorcycle cops who had been lying in wait.

After concluding that the bike rallies were ineffective, the Car-Elimination Service then turned its attention to Leidsestraat, the street that, by then, had been off-limits to cyclists for a decade but was still accessible to motorists. On April 7, 1970, the group blockaded entrances to the street, allowing through pedestrians and trams while denying admittance to cars. On cars that were unable to enter the street, Kabouters stuck stickers that read: I AM AN AIR POLLUTER. After blocking Leidsestraat on four different days in the month of April, the Kabouters were somewhat shocked when the mayor and *wethouders* announced that, as an experiment, cars would temporarily be banned from driving on Leidsestraat. The head of the Car-Elimination Service, the man responsible for coordinating the Leidsestraat blockades—Maarten Manson—reacted to this news by joking, "But then I'll be out of a job!"

In the June 3, 1970, municipal election, the Kabouters—as a political party—recorded a stunning victory by receiving almost 38,000 votes; five of their candidates (including Roel van Duijn) won seats on the city council. That evening, on Spui Square, jubilant Kabouters spontaneously invited passing motorists to cut their engines and instead let their cars be pushed down the street by Kabouters.*

Soon after the election, at a Kabouter general meeting, Maarten Manson announced that he no longer wanted to coordinate the Car-Elimination Service or have his name associated

---

*At their first city council meeting, several of the newly elected Kabouters openly smoked hashish during the proceedings.

with it in any way because he suspected the cops had been keeping tabs on him. Manson's fears weren't unfounded. Among the many, varied (and often illicit) activities of the Kabouters, the police were taking a particular interest in the Car-Elimination Service. In fact, one Kabouter who declared a desire to succeed Manson was Henri Brookman. Brookman had ridden in a Kabouter bike rally and had participated in the blockades of Leidsestraat. He was also, though, one of two undercover cops who had successfully infiltrated the Kabouters.

AFTER THE ELECTORAL victory of the Kabouters, the group became less of a force on the streets. Other activists, though, continued with guerrilla-style campaigns. In May 1971, for example, on Herengracht, a half-dozen Lastige Amsterdammers used sledgehammers to smash the windows and body of a small, abandoned four-door Renault while they chanted "Death to the car!" (The police then arrived and confiscated the sledgehammers and impounded the car.)

That same month, 15 cyclists protested against the anticyclist design of the IJ Tunnel by pedaling with the motorized traffic through the tunnel. Two cars followed behind the group to shield the cyclists from any possible aggressive motorists—a wise move, given that at least one enraged motorist tried, without success, to plow his way through. Two weeks later, a larger group—40 cyclists—attempted a repeat of the tunnel ride. Before they could enter the tunnel's northern end, though, the activists were intercepted by awaiting police, who'd apparently been tipped off by an informant. Unable to enter the tunnel, the protesters instead crossed the IJ by ferry and rode to Leidsestraat, where they blocked the car traffic. (A month later, cars were finally permanently banned from that street.)

In 1972, a tiny new radical weekly newspaper—the *Amsterdams Weekblad*—took a very pro-bike stance that was reflected in a regular column titled "Bike Guerilla." The column's introduction usually read: "The reports from the bicycle front gradually make one despondent. City Hall fails to do anything when it comes to the most perfect form of transportation of all time." Bike Guerilla's anonymous author urged cyclists to take action and offered "methods you can use in your own private war with the car." Among these "practical tips": on narrow streets, don't give way to an oncoming car ("See who has the most patience"); on wider streets, ride in the middle of the roadway ("If someone starts honking, then stop, turn around and act surprised"); and whenever possible, inflict scratches and dents upon new cars. One "Bike Guerilla" column ended: "WARNING: These methods are not without risks. Many stink-car users quickly become aggressive. So always remain calm. And if the situation becomes too dangerous, vanish quickly on your trusty two-wheeler."

Guerrilla action against the overwhelming influx of cars became rife in Amsterdam. Residents came together in various neighborhoods—on Rozengracht, on Frederiksplein, on Wittenburgergracht, on Spui Square—and painted their own crosswalks across busy streets (which led to some arrests). On Johannes Verhulststraat, in some curbside parking spaces for cars, residents illegally installed bike racks. On Reguliersgracht, where illegally parked cars were known to be scratched with keys, residents painted their own pedestrian walkway. And all around town, activists used super-strength glue to fill the keyholes of double-parked cars and cars parked on sidewalks.

IN LATE 1973, cycling in Amsterdam received an unexpected boost from an unlikely source: major oil producers. In October of that year, during the 1973 Arab-Israeli War, the Netherlands had sent weapons to aid Israel. In retaliation, the oil-producing Arab states named the Netherlands as the second country (after the United States) to be slapped with an oil embargo. With a diminished oil supply, an energy crisis struck Holland. The Dutch national government decided the best way for the nation to survive on less oil would be to limit Sunday driving. Of the 3 million cars in the country, all would be restricted from Sunday usage except for those with foreign or diplomatic license plates and roughly 16,000 cars belonging to "essential professionals" (doctors, for example).

Driving bans were actually nothing new to the Dutch. Just before and just after World War II, the Dutch government had imposed Sunday driving bans in order to conserve fuel in times of scarcity. And in the winter of 1956–57, during the Suez Crisis, another weekly Sunday ban had been instituted.* But since those previous Sunday driving bans had occurred during periods when the Dutch still owned relatively few automobiles, the bans' effects were hardly crippling. In 1973, though, Netherlanders owned *ten times more* cars than in 1956. This created great uncertainty about the effect the driving ban would have on public life.

Many in the business community feared the driving ban would hamper their car-dependent customers' shopping, creating an economic disaster.

It was two days before the first carless Sunday of 1973.

---

*On the first Sunday of the 1956–57 ban, a significant number of the permitless drivers stopped by Dutch police were Americans.

Hoping to assuage such fears while modeling a carless lifestyle, a grinning Prime Minister den Uyl rode a bicycle around on the grounds of his official residence in front of news cameras. Den Uyl, the man who just six years earlier had proudly proclaimed that everyone should own a car, now said that due to the oil embargo, the Dutch would need to rethink "constantly buying cars and driving faster and faster."

One sector of Dutch business didn't fear the looming car ban. "The telephone won't stop ringing," said Nico Koenders—owner of a shop on Utrechtsedwarsstraat that rented bikes—about the many people looking to secure bicycles for the coming Sunday. Many car owners—and business owners—sought to survive the car ban with the help of bikes. At the Hotel Americain, in an effort to accommodate those who'd be cycling instead of driving, a number of bike racks were placed in front of the building, and the hotel stationed a security guard to monitor them.

On the big day, November 4, 1973, Amsterdam was transformed. While 19 drivers were busted in the city for ignoring the ban, the cyclists had, according to one news account, "recaptured the cityscape for the first time in years." One couple who took a stroll in the south of Amsterdam noticed the change: "What especially caught our eye was the number of cyclists. Kalfjeslaan was swarming with them. On streets where cars would otherwise usurp all the asphalt, we now saw a couple peacefully cycling beside each other; he, like a picture of nonchalance, a curved pipe in his mouth."

Despite the police authorities having publicly forbidden cyclists from riding on the freeways during the driving ban, many bikers did just that. Elsewhere in the country, kids held roller-skating races on a freeway. Just outside Amsterdam, on the freeway leading to the airport, a group of 40 youths laid out a picnic across two lanes. When three squad cars eventually arrived to move the picnickers along, the youths initially resisted (with one boy shouting: "Wait, we're not ready. We haven't cooked our French fries!"). Within Amsterdam, the "natural target of the cyclists" (as *De Volkskrant* newspaper put it) was the IJ Tunnel. When a group of 300 to 400 cyclists arrived at the car tunnel with the goal of riding through it, their plan was stymied by a barricade of cop cars at the entrance.

On that Sunday, at Koenders' bike shop, it was a madhouse. "We rented out everything, including the three-person tandems," Koenders reported. "I have never seen so many Hollanders before; usually it's just foreigners here." The restaurant at Hotel Americain was full, as was the Rijksmuseum. The Stadsschouwburg reported a very good turnout for a performance of *King Lear*, while business that afternoon at the movie theater on Rembrandtplein was busier than usual. Though far fewer patrons reached the Artis zoo by car than usual, a zoo employee noted, "[T]hat was counterbalanced by the fact that even more people came by bike."

Amsterdammers had, for a day, taken a break from the cars they'd grown so dependent upon in the previous decade and a half—and found they could survive without them. Panic about how the ban would affect business or individuals quickly faded; after the first couple of Sundays, the ban barely remained newsworthy.

Within a couple of months, the Sunday ban was replaced by a system of gasoline rationing. A report in early January 1974 noted: "Thanks to the oil crisis, hearty Amsterdammers are walking and cycling more than they've done since the automobile took over Amsterdam in the last decade—and they're enjoying it."

During the oil embargo, bike sales shot up. Less than a month after the driving ban had begun, at Gazelle—one of the country's largest producers of bicycles—the director reported, "Six thousand bikes come off the line each week but orders are running at 10,000 weekly." Batavus, another leading manufacturer of Dutch bikes, saw sales in the last three months of 1973 increase 70 percent over that of the same period in 1972. "At least a sixty percent increase could be attributed to the oil embargo alone," said a Batavus spokesman. In 1974, a record number of new bikes would be sold in the country: 1.2 million. It was more than twice the number sold just seven years earlier—and the first time the million mark had ever been breached.

One of the buyers of these new bikes was an Amsterdam businessman who, in 1974, said that, since the oil embargo had begun, he'd purchased three bicycles: one each for himself, his wife and his son. "Bicycling adds a new dimension to life, and I like the exercise," he proclaimed. "But I guess I wouldn't have bought the bicycles if it hadn't been for the energy crisis and the fear that I wouldn't be able to use the car on occasions."

Where attitudes about cars and bikes were concerned, a corner was definitely being turned.

THE 1973 OIL embargo and resulting energy crisis caused a great many people to reconsider the role of the automobile in Amsterdam. In this context of expanding environmental and ecological awareness, in early 1974, several neighborhood and activist groups joined to form Amsterdam Autovrij (Car-Free Amsterdam)—an umbrella group with the mission to reduce the number of cars in the capital. In May 1974, Amsterdam Autovrij organized the city's first large-scale pro-bike/anti-car protest. One thousand cyclists assembled on Dam Square and then, for two hours, they cycled as a pack through the streets. Among those participating was the former Provo and Kabouter leader Roel van Duijn who, with many others, wore a surgical mask as a protest against car pollution. After the trek around the city ended back on Dam Square, protesters distributed flowers to the police.

The following month, in June 1974, Amsterdam Autovrij organized another bike demo. In the weeks prior, volunteers passed out thousands of pamphlets that publicized the ride. The activists wheat-pasted hundreds of posters around the city that read: KICK THE CAR OUT OF THE CITY. The publicity was apparently effective: this time, twice as many people—2,000—participated. During the ride, a German motorist on the Weteringcircuit tried to drive through the parade of cyclists and was, according to the *NRC Handelsblad* newspaper, "molested" by the pack. After the official procession ended, a hundred demonstrators cycled in circles around Dam Square, which blocked traffic. Small fights broke out between protesters and motorists.

That same year, Roel van Duijn was again elected to the city council, this time as a member of yet another political party, the PPR (the Radicals Political Party). Van Duijn's party joined the ruling coalition, and the city council elected him as one of the eight *wethouders* on Amsterdam's executive council. That the nation's most infamous antiauthoritarian was becoming the *wethouder* overseeing the city's various municipal companies made front-page news around the Netherlands.

Van Duijn's new esteemed position came with a perk: while

he was conducting official city business, a chauffeur-driven black Mercedes would be at his disposal. Getting around town by luxury car, though, was deemed both preposterous and impractical by the avowed cycling proponent. "We wanted a city with fewer cars and more bikes," recalled Van Duijn, "so I couldn't go driving around in a car, and especially not in a big car." Van Duijn immediately announced he would spurn the "environment-polluting Mercedes." Instead, to execute his official duties, he'd go by bike.

On the day Van Duijn was inaugurated as *wethouder*, Mayor Samkalden dropped by his office and tried to convince him to accept the car by arguing a bike would be "really too slow for a *wethouder*." No problem, Van Duijn replied; his bike would have ten gears. The mayor then insisted that Van Duijn would need the Mercedes if he had to meet with national government officials in The Hague. Van Duijn retorted that if he had to go to The Hague, he'd take the train. The mayor was displeased, as were Van Duijn's fellow *wethouders* from the Labor and Communist parties, who felt his rejection of the amenity showed them up as pampered and greedy. Nevertheless, Van Duijn remained steadfast.

That same day, Van Duijn visited his neighborhood bike shop on Leliegracht and selected a new Gazelle Champion Mondial that cost 500 guilders (which, far cheaper than a Mercedes, city officials agreed to pay for). Though it was a racing bike, Van Duijn had it outfitted like a typical Amsterdam bike, complete with fenders, bell, rear rack and generator light. And the bike's color? White, of course.

Once in office, the mayor and Van Duijn's fellow *wethouders* soured on some of his initial ideas. For example, his calls for organic food to be offered in the city hall cafeteria and for wind turbines to generate electricity for the city's power company were both regarded as wacky. A few weeks into his term, when Amsterdam Autovrij announced that a third bike demo would occur in October, Van Duijn declared he'd participate on his new city-issued bike. Since the planned demonstration would be, in essence, a protest against the traffic policies of the mayor and *wethouders*, Van Duijn's announcement inflamed Mayor Samkalden. The mayor prohibited Van Duijn from cycling in the demo. If he *did* participate, Samkalden threatened that he would resign as mayor. The threat didn't deter Van Duijn, who told a reporter, "I am a free *wethouder*."

The route of the October 1974 demonstration led specifically through 17 perilous intersections to raise awareness of their dangers and the need for their transformation. At the Weteringplantsoen, the demonstrators planted 101 black wooden crosses to commemorate the 101 traffic fatalities suffered in Amsterdam the previous year. This was followed by a minute of silence to honor the dead. At one point along the way, the cyclists chanted, "Phew! It stinks here! Away with the cars!"

Van Duijn not only pedaled his ten-speed in the bike-demo, he also addressed the cyclists at the ride's conclusion on Amstelveld, where he told the crowd, "A bike is just about nothing, that's why it's so good." In addition, Van Duijn called for the city center to be free of car traffic for a full week in 1975. Afterward, despite his earlier pledge, Mayor Samkalden did not resign. Instead, he called the planting of crosses tasteless and jettisoned the idea of a car-free week.

Van Duijn's antics led to further disdain from his fellow *wethouders*. Two weeks after the October 1974 bike demo, Labor

Party *wethouder* for economic affairs Cees de Cloe snapped at Van Duijn: "You're working against me. How am I supposed to carry out an economic policy if you're riding a bike and babbling about windmills?" Van Duijn also recalled De Cloe griping to him: "Imagine I'm showing around some Americans who are considering opening a factory in Amsterdam, and they see a *wethouder* on a bike. They'll think: We can't invest here because these people are too primitive."

Then, one evening in January 1975, Van Duijn stepped into the city hall courtyard that served as the parking lot for the *wethouders*' official vehicles (a half dozen or so Mercedes and one bike). There he discovered that the front wheel of his work bike was missing. When Van Duijn inquired around city hall, Labor Party councilman Pelle Mug admitted to him that members of his party had enjoyed a few after-work drinks that evening. Later (according to Mug), a drunken *Wethouder* de Cloe had unscrewed Van Duijn's front wheel, removed it from the bike and—"in a fit of craziness"—chucked it into the waters of the Oudezijds Voorburgwal, the canal in front of city hall.

After enduring more than a year of harassment and name-calling from the other *wethouders*, Van Duijn eventually resigned his position in January 1976. Upon leaving office, Van Duijn kept the white Gazelle; he purchased the bike from the city and brought it with him when he took a break from Amsterdam to live and work on an organic farm in Groningen.

IN 1975, MEMBERS from various activist groups from around the Netherlands met in Utrecht to create a new, nationwide pressure group to advocate for the rights of cyclists. The new group would call itself the ENWB—an abbreviation for the "One and Only Dutch Cyclists Union." This name was a direct jab at the ANWB—whose initials had once stood for the "General Dutch Cyclists Union." The ANWB had formed in the 1880s as a cyclists group. By the early 1900s, though, it had largely abandoned urban cycling interests to become the nation's preeminent lobbyist for car owners.*

"Our aim is to stimulate people to take back possession of their streets," said the new group's chairman, Jan Wittenberg. One of the organization's very first members was Maria C. J. Snethlage, who, at 80 years of age, was so old that she'd learned to cycle as a young lady at the long-gone Fongers bike-riding school. Though Snethlage still cycled regularly through the heart of Amsterdam, it wasn't her advanced age that affected her cycling but rather the parked cars that cluttered the streets and the motorists that cut off cyclists (she'd been run down twice in the mid-1970s). "My heart has never gone out to the car. I'm a bit of a car hater. Just give me my bike!" stated Snethlage. "Still, as a cyclist in Amsterdam, I feel a bit like the king of the road because by bike, you can worm your way through anywhere."

AFTER AMSTERDAM'S THREE large-scale bike demonstrations in 1974, in the summers of 1975 and 1976 bike demos became annual events that drew ever bigger crowds—3,000 participants in 1975, 4,000 in 1976. Then in June 1977, an even larger bike demo took place. Nine thousand Amsterdammers—including a

---

*The ANWB eventually successfully sued the ENWB, forcing the cycling advocacy group to change its name. These days it goes by the name De Fietsersbond (The Cyclists' Union).

great many senior citizens and families with children—rode on a route that originated on Beursplein and ended in Vondelpark. The dense procession of cyclists stretched for two-thirds of a mile.

A flyer was distributed to the cyclists at the outset of the 1977 ride. The flyer outlined the planned route and also advised how to handle anyone irritated by the demonstration: "Avoid getting into a wrangle with motorists. You don't need to come to blows with loudmouths. There are already enough (traffic) casualties. Maybe, due to your dignified demeanor, they'll join us next time—on a bike." A number of obstructed motorists did indeed bombard the cyclists with abuse. "Bastards!" shouted one motorist. "Tonight you'll be asking me for a ride again!"

A feature of the 1977 demo was a carefully coordinated stop on Museumplein, where thousands of the cyclists lay down with their bikes on the streets to commemorate the 3,000 traffic fatalities suffered annually in Holland. After a moment of silence and a short eulogy, the cyclists then arose and rang their thousands of bike bells. Then they "cycled for their lives" to the closing festivities in Vondelpark.

In 1978, Luud Schimmelpennink, the former Provo leader, mastermind of the White Bicycles Plan and a main organizer of these annual demonstrations, declared that 1978's bike demonstration—the seventh large-scale demo in four years—would be the last. "We're ending the pattern of annual demonstrations. This demonstration is the last for us. We now want something to show for the time, money and energy we've expended. Amsterdam is not yet ruined. It won't cost a lot to make the city again what she ought to be: a healthy body."

The timing of this protest ride was planned to effect maximum change at city hall; the ride was held just four days before Amsterdam's city council elections. Organizers correctly anticipated a record crowd: 15,000 cyclists participated. To accommodate this great mass, the riders were split into three smaller groups. Each group departed from Dam Square in a different direction and followed a different route before converging again in Vondelpark, where various cabaret and musical acts performed and Schimmelpennink addressed the crowd.

Four days later, the energy and effort put into the bike demo apparently paid off. The newly elected city council appeared to be far more sympathetic toward the plight of the cyclists. Many of the new council members felt that the Traffic Circulation Plan (TCP)—the city's principal traffic policy— unfairly promoted car usage over other forms of transport. So in November 1978, the council considered the adoption of a new TCP that called for the reduction of car traffic and parking spaces in the city center, the stimulation of public transportation, and more attention devoted to the needs of pedestrians and cyclists.

Nevertheless, the proposed altering of traffic policy had its opponents, or, as one councilman called them during the debate, a "club of car crazies." "TCP? Traffic Circulation Plan? More like Traffic Chaos Plan," said one such "crazy," the leader of the faction of the VVD party, who feared the plan would negatively impact drivers. The dissenters were actually few, though; the plan passed by a 38–7 vote. (Of the seven parties represented on the council, only members of the VVD voted nay.)

In the previous thirteen years, Amsterdam had seen everything from guerrilla-style street protests to national pro-cycling advocacy. Now, change at the bureaucratic level in Amsterdam was finally within reach. "In the coming years," the new plan read, "the policy must strongly focus on elevating the bicycle climate." For the cyclists, victory seemed to be at hand.

20

It's a Joy to Be on a Bike Again!: The 1980s Onward

After many months of enjoying his perch on the front of my bike, Ferris was growing so fast, he'd soon be too big to safely ride there. "We have to put a kid's seat on the back of your bike," Amy Joy said.

A *rear* seat? But then my back would be just inches in front of my son's nose; his view would be almost completely obstructed. He'd be so far away. I wouldn't be able to sing into his ear or show him the sights. He'd be unable to show me the route he wanted us to follow. Wasn't there some other solution? Couldn't he remain up front if we somehow slowed his growth? Maybe he could skip some meals. Or maybe he could burn off some pounds by racing around the playground on his tricycle.

Despite my ambivalence, Ferris grew taller and heavier. A switch to a rear seat became inevitable. On the day Amy Joy replaced the front kid's seat on my bike with a rear one, Ferris and I went for a ride. Only a few blocks from home, I heard the faint sound of his voice.

"What did you say?" I asked.

" . . . brown . . ."

"What?!"

" . . . KITTY! . . ."

Argh! I pulled over and turned to him. "Sorry, but I didn't hear you. Could you say it again?"

"I asked if you saw that brown kitty cat back there."

"Oh." I looked back . . . and saw no cat. "No, I didn't see it."

My heart broke. Stupid rear seat, I thought. Miles and months of biking together while chatting and singing and giving each other tours of Amsterdam had come to an abrupt end. During the next few weeks, what had long been one of our most entertaining activities was now a drag.

Amy Joy responded to our frustration with a solution: a *bakfiets*—a two-wheeled model with a box up front where a kid could sit. She purchased a new one (at a wholesale price), and when she and Ferris arrived home with it, our son was sitting up front like a little prince in his chariot, a satisfied smile stretched from ear to ear.

The following day, Ferris and I took the *bakfiets* for our inaugural ride. Once again, he was riding with an unobstructed view. Once again, we were singing together. And once again, he was leading the way, this time directing me to Vondelpark.

After we entered the park, a jogger in shorts ran past us.

"Pete," Ferris said, calling me by my first name like the world's shortest-ever roommate, "what's that guy doing?"

"He forgot to put on his pants," I replied, repeating one of my dad's lamest jokes, "and now he's running home to get them."

"Oh," Ferris said, absorbing the joke. "He *forgot* his pants."

Then he laughed.

And I laughed, too.

The *bakfiets* was a hit.

THOUGH RIDING AS a passenger had its pleasures and advantages, when Ferris was three years old he began demanding to be taught how to ride his own bike. So we took him to the Twiske recreational area just north of the city, where we coached him in his debut attempt at bike-riding. At first, the kid wobbled hopelessly and fell over. But then, much to our surprise, he quickly got the hang of it. It should have been no surprise. From within hours (if not minutes) of his conception, Ferris had spent hundreds of hours on bikes. Now, within days, he was whizzing around the pedestrianized square in front of our apartment as I chased after him, unable to keep up.

A few weeks later, Ferris was again riding his two-wheeler around the square. At one point he zipped past me wearing a sly, suspicious grin on his face. Then he tentatively lifted his hands off the handlebars. Just three years old—and already trying to ride no hands. His stunt lasted for just a couple of seconds before the bike teetered, and then it and the boy crumpled in a tangled heap on the brick pavement. I ran to him and was amazed to find him only stunned and showing no signs of being in pain.

"You see that?!" he asked. "I rode no hands!"

"Yeah, I saw it," I said, my heart thumping. "But please promise you won't do that again till you're *much* older."

He smiled up at me and said, "I promise."

Then I untangled Amsterdam's newest stunt cyclist from his bike.

IN THE LATE 1970s, a major restructuring of the city's traffic circulation took place. It involved orienting the so-called Outer Ring (Stadhouderskade/Nassaukade) to car traffic and the parallel so-called Inner Ring (Sarphatistraat, Weteringschans and the southern part of Marnixstraat) to bike traffic. By 1980, after some parts of the Inner Ring were made one-way for motorists and on other parts vehicular through traffic was restricted, the change was perceptible. Between 1975 and 1980, bicycle usage on that stretch increased by 56 percent, while auto usage dropped by that same percentage.

The results of the municipal election that occurred days after the 1978 bike protest had given much hope to the city's bike activists. That year, not only had the city council adopted a pro-cyclist traffic policy, but a pro-cyclist city councilman—Michiel van der Vlis—had been named as the *wethouder* for traffic affairs. (While in office, Van der Vlis expressed solidarity with the cyclists by proclaiming, "I, too, cycle through red lights.") In reality, though, bike activists were left deeply disappointed by the lack of attention the municipal government paid to the cyclists' point of view. Aside from the establishment of the Bicycle Work Group—which consisted of members of the Fietsersbond and civil servants from various city agencies who met monthly to examine biking-related issues—little was done to directly address the many needs of the cyclists.

For example, a major item on the bikers' agenda, increasing the bike-friendliness of Spiegelgracht—the direct route between the Rijksmuseum passageway and the city center—proved frustrating. Despite street protests on Spiegelgracht (which included blocking the street to cars), that issue dragged on unresolved and would become, in the words of the Fietsersbond, "a never-ending story."

Another important issue the cyclists needed the city to tackle: more sidewalk bike-parking spaces. At the time, many neighborhood bike-parking garages were disappearing, as the valuable real estate they consumed was converted to other commercial or residential uses. Of the 234 neighborhood garages in 1975, only 155 of them remained in 1981. By 1988, the number was down to 116. As more and more people were forced to park their bikes on the sidewalks in front of their apartment buildings, the city had very few public bike racks to accommodate them.

Frustrated by the city government's inaction, and with the May 1982 municipal elections approaching, bike activists began organizing their first cycling protest since 1978. When announcing the protest ride, the Fietsersbond stated that the city government had "proven to have little more to offer than its predecessors. The bicycle policy of *Wethouder* van der Vlis has been nothing more than a flop." The delay in implementing a pro-bike policy was blamed on governmental apathy and municipal bureaucracy. Of the unsatisfied cyclists who would soon be taking to the streets again, one journalist remarked, "He's the Indian who refuses to be forced onto a reservation."

After the bike demo and the election in 1982, the city government's attitude toward biking finally changed significantly for the better. Across the city, municipal workers began installing sidewalk bike racks. New bike bridges spanning canals increased bikers' accessibility to and within various neighborhoods. There was, for example, a new bridge at Minervalaan near the Amsterdam-South train station, and the new bridges over the Nieuwe Vaart and the Entrepotdok on the city center's east side. Many new separated bike paths were installed, enabling cyclists to travel with far less exposure to the dangers posed by cars and trucks. Other streets were redesigned to favor cyclists over motorists (such as the conversion of the roadway through the Amsterdams Lyceum building into bike paths). In 1986, the city even began subsidizing the local Fietsersbond office, recognizing the benefits of the advocacy group's growing expertise in influencing positive changes for those cycling in the city.

When the 1980s began, the city had been allocating virtually no money to specifically address the needs of the cyclists. By the end of the decade, though, the city of Amsterdam had spent an estimated 30 to 40 million guilders on (as one person at the time put it) "executing hundreds of projects—large and small—in all parts of Amsterdam. Much has been improved."

The improvements of the 1980s were readily apparent to one Amsterdammer: Marnix Bruggeman. Around 1980, after his 26th bike had been stolen, Bruggeman abandoned cycling and took to getting around town on foot and by public transit. But in 1989, after friends had convinced him to give cycling another shot, Bruggeman was amazed. "Oh, oh, oh, it's a joy to be on a bike again for the first time in ten years!" he wrote.

> Riding a bike in Amsterdam is pleasant, especially when you know exactly what the Fietsersbond in Amsterdam has achieved for cyclists. Then, suddenly, at every intersection you notice: Ha, the Fietsersbond has tackled this problem spot here. Actually, as far as cycling through Amsterdam goes, there's just one thing that's still really bothersome: all those cars.

More improvements to the city's bike infrastructure were implemented in the 1990s, which made the city an even more inviting place to cycle. By one measure, between 1980 and 1995, the number of people cycling in the city center had increased by more than 29 percent, while the number of those driving had dropped by 24 percent. "It's unbelievable how many people you see on bikes these days," reported one bike shop owner in 1999. "I see entire streams of cyclists in the city center, especially during rush hour. There's been an enormous increase in recent years, even when it's raining."

Way back in 1971—when cars were on the rise, bikes on the decline and before a mass pro-cycling consciousness had taken hold—the head of Amsterdam's traffic police, Commissioner H. Vos (who commuted to work by bike), predicted the future of traffic in the city:

> You can't turn back the clock. Naturally, the automobile traffic in the city will decrease; that's the future. But the waves of bikes like there were before the war or after it up till about 1955: I don't see that ever returning. Indeed, it's obvious that soon more and more people will ride a bike again. But that won't be the masses, like we had before.

A quarter century later, Vos' premonition proved to be dead on. The number of cars in the city center was dropping while the number of cyclists, though not as high as in the 1950s, continued to rise.

CONDITIONS FOR CYCLISTS in Amsterdam were clearly changing. But one thing that apparently *hadn't* changed was the cyclists' disorderly behavior. "It appears as if people think that in Amsterdam anything goes," commented Police Commissioner

Eric Nordholt in October 1992, when characterizing the city's road users. To combat this mentality, that same month the police launched a "crusade against the massive disorderliness of Amsterdam's cyclists." Checkpoints would be established on major cycling routes. Bike riders who ran stoplights were to be issued citations. And those caught riding without lights would be given a choice: pay a $36 fine or pay $18 to have the generator lights on their bikes repaired (or installed) on the spot by a municipal employee. For those who chose the latter—while the lights on their bikes were being readied—there was an additional option: sit in a police command vehicle and watch a "gripping" 10-minute educational video about "bike accidents with deadly consequences."

"I don't need to see that film; I know what can happen to me," said one young man on the first evening of the campaign. He had elected to stand in the cold, pouring rain rather than sit in the warm, dry police vehicle while his lights were being repaired. He wasn't alone; that night, of the 30 apprehended cyclists who chose to have their lights repaired, only two stepped forward to watch the film.

Many cyclists called the crackdown repressive. When the Fietsersbond announced that it actually supported the police action, several disgruntled members quit the organization in protest. One apprehended cyclist grumbled, "Why should I repair my bike when it's just going to get stolen anyway?" Another lightless cyclist, when given the choice of paying the fine or paying for the repair of his lights, handed his bike to the cops and walked away. The $18 for the repair, he said, was more than the total value of the bike. One cyclist who had opted to have his lights repaired then rode off into the night . . . with his lights *off.* A cop watching this shook his head and said, "Old habits die hard."

Despite the cyclists' discontent, three weeks into the crusade, the press hailed it as a "success." Of course, this wasn't the first time the city's police had targeted disobedient cyclists—nor would it be the last. In fact, such crackdowns throughout the past century occurred with such regularity that a pattern could be discerned:

- Police authorities declare cyclists to be out of control.
- Police officers issue citations to biking scofflaws.
- Cyclists initially voice shock and dissent.
- Cyclists ultimately acquiesce and become more law-abiding.
- A few months or a year after the start of the campaign, police declare victory and terminate the crackdown.
- Cyclists—slowly but surely—resume their disorderly riding habits.
- Eventually, police authorities declare cyclists to be out of control.
- The cycle repeats.

For example, three years after the 1992 crackdown, cyclists were ignoring the decades-old ban on bike riding on Leidsestraat so routinely that one newspaper wrote: "It's a joke! Nothing scares off a cyclist in Amsterdam." The following year, a man and his wife who lived on the Witte de Withstraat spent two evenings noting all the cyclists who rode past. Their findings: "We saw 220 cyclists. Two hundred of them had no lights and four had just a front light or just a rear light. Only 16 bikes had proper lighting."

In 1997, after the police had launched yet another new campaign against cycling misconduct, a 24-year-old medical student was asked why he cycled through red lights. "I don't do it just because everyone else does it," he replied. "I just think that the rules here in Amsterdam are so evolved that it's actually permitted."

After the 1997 crackdown ended, the cycle reset itself in the fall of 2000, when the police launched a new offensive against "antisocial cyclists." By the time I arrived in Amsterdam in the summer of 2002, though, there was little evidence of previous crackdowns; red-light-running and cycling without lights was rampant. The following year, the police launched yet another crackdown. During this one, I repeatedly stopped and observed the traps the police had placed in various parts of the city. Once, at the Hugo de Grootplein intersection, I noticed the cops on the far side nabbing bikers who had run a red. I pulled over and began warning approaching cyclists about the trap that loomed ahead. After I had cautioned more than 50 (usually grateful) fellow cyclists, a finger tapped my shoulder. I turned to find a none-too-pleased cop standing beside me. "Scram!" he said.*

The following year, Police Chief Jelle Kuiper expressed satisfaction with the results of the latest crackdown. "It used to be that the cyclist who remained waiting at a red light was the exception," he said. "Now it's the other way around."

---

*Four years later, this same intersection was converted into a signal-free roundabout that gave cyclists the right-of-way over motorists. Instead of worrying about red lights or the possibility of receiving a citation, cyclists barely need to slow down when passing through the intersection.

IN MANY WAYS, conditions for Amsterdam cycling had improved greatly during the 1980s and '90s. But conditions deteriorated in one regard: bike theft (as described in chapter 3). As one Fietsersbond official in Amsterdam said at the time: "A bicycle policy doesn't just mean constructing bicycle paths, it also means taking measures to fight bicycle thievery." In 2002, Jos Louwman, owner of the MacBike rental shops, commented, "Over the past twenty years, bike thievery has gotten worse. People are dispirited by it and that feeling seeps into all aspects of life. The whole world would be better off if we did something about this." That year, the Amsterdam municipal government, the city's police department and the justice system announced they were indeed going to do something about it.

Among the broad, multipronged attack launched against bike thievery, one new measure banned the on-street selling and buying of bicycles. One reason why *zwijntjesjagers* had been able to publicly operate with impunity was the difficultly the police had in proving a bike had been stolen (especially since so few bike thefts were reported to the police). Banning *all* on-street sales starved the *zwijntjesjagers* of a major outlet for selling their product.

Another standard outlet for *zwijntjesjager* bike sales was stymied by a second new measure: anyone who wanted to sell a secondhand bike to a bike shop was now required to present photo identification. Shopkeepers were to maintain records of the provenance of their inventory (which were subject to police inspection). With the implementation of this new regulation, one shopkeeper said he witnessed an immediate effect: "When people offer to sell me a bike and I ask to see their ID and they say they'll go get it, they never come back." Another shopkeeper said he noticed that these two measures had an added effect: in one year, his annual sales dropped by 600 bikes. He claimed this was proof that fewer bikes were being stolen since fewer people had needed to purchase replacement bikes from him.

In 2002, in the city center, teams of municipal workers began confiscating bikes that were either parked illegally (for example, parked longer than 28 days straight at Central Station) or were determined to be abandoned. This helped to both thin out targets of bike thefts as well as to return to owners bikes that had been reported stolen. The following year, in the western harbor area, the Amsterdam Bicycle Processing Center (later renamed the Bike Depot) opened its doors to receive such confiscated bikes. Bikes still unclaimed by their owners after 90 days were then either sold in bulk to bike shops or sent to the scrap heap. By 2006, about 23,500 bikes a year were being processed by the depot. By 2011, this figure more than doubled as municipal workers hauled 55,000 impounded bikes (or about 150 per day) to the depot.

One more component in the fight against bike thievery was an attempt to change the "societal acceptance" of the crime among the bike thieves, the purchasers of hot bikes (particularly students) and the general public. Of the first group, a police spokesperson said, "We arrested a man who every day—*every day*—stole ten bikes from in front of Central Station. 'That's my job,' he said. If we can provide such people with a normal existence, we can solve a lot." To deter thefts, punishments for stealing and fencing bikes were increased.

To help wean students from the habit of purchasing cheap stolen bikes, a student organization began routinely purchasing secondhand bikes by the hundreds from the Bike Depot and then refurbishing and selling them to students at an affordable price (billing them as "the cheapest legal bikes in Amsterdam").

If cheap, legal bikes were the carrot used to lure the students away from buying hot bikes, then the sticks were the annual warnings from city officials. In 2005, Amsterdam's head police commissioner, Bernard Welten, spoke in an auditorium to a standing-room crowd of freshman university students in the Dutch capital. Welten attempted to scare straight these potential purchasers of stolen bikes by warning them:

> The average Amsterdammer loses no sleep when an organized crime member is murdered, but he's pissed when his bike is stolen. . . . If you get caught buying a stolen bike, you'll have a record. You can then forget about your career. And don't fool yourself that you can buy a bike for twenty dollars. If you think you can, then you haven't enough sense to be attending school here.

Three years later, in 2008, Mayor Job Cohen spoke in similar terms to incoming freshman students who filled the Carré Theater. "If you buy a bike for thirty dollars, you can be sure that it's stolen," he warned them. "And buying stolen property is, according to the criminal code . . . a crime."

In order to prevent thefts in the first place, a publicity campaign titled "Don't Give Thieves a Chance!" was launched. Amsterdammers were urged to better secure their bikes. Advertisements showed citizens in everyday situations—sitting in a dentist's chair, walking through a museum, standing in the shower at a swimming pool—all the while clutching their bikes.

By 2005, a city official commented, "Collectively, these measures form a closing net within which it's increasingly difficult for bicycle thieves to operate." Indeed, the measures had an effect: between 2001 and 2008, the bike theft rate in Amsterdam dropped by half. While all the various measures seemed to contribute to this, a factor that also helped was an unintentional one: the number of the city's heroin addicts—all potential bike thieves—had dropped dramatically.

That's not to say bike thievery wasn't still a problem. In June 2012, for example, city officials admitted that more than a hundred bikes—particularly pricier ones—that were parked at sidewalk bike racks had had their locks cut by circular saws in broad daylight by men wearing municipal worker garb. The bikes were then loaded onto trucks and hauled away—not to the Bike Depot, though, but to parts unknown. The men were not municipal workers but were in fact cleverly disguised thieves.

QUEEN WILHELMINA HAD earned the Dutch royal family a reputation as a cycling monarchy. Wilhelmina's legacy was carried on by her daughter Queen Juliana and, to a far lesser degree, by Juliana's daughter Queen Beatrix, who assumed the throne in 1980. Though Beatrix sent her three sons to public school on bikes, she didn't share quite the same enthusiasm for cycling as her grandmother Wilhelmina. The biking monarchy, under Beatrix's reign, became more of a cliché than a reality. Still, the idea of a cycling monarchy reinforced a view of the royal family as everyday folks just like their subjects.

In 1999, the nation learned that Beatrix's eldest son—Crown Prince Willem-Alexander—was wooing an Argentinian woman. At a time when the girlfriend—Máxima Zorreguieta—had yet to be spotted in public, *De Telegraaf* published huge, front-page photos of the prince biking with a woman purported to be his new love interest.

"With some awkwardness, Máxima mounted a heavy granny bike," reported the newspaper about the woman who, hailing from a country indifferent to biking, presumably did not know how to cycle. "Máxima appeared to be a fast learner because, before long, she was sailing right along." The following day, though, the newspaper was forced to retract this account; the woman in question was actually a platonic friend of the prince.

Two years later, the real Máxima had been spotted plenty of times. After the announcement of Willem-Alexander and Máxima's engagement, the nation took an even greater interest in the woman who would be marrying the heir to the throne. And still, the question persisted: Could this foreigner cycle? When a reporter asked Máxima if she knew how to ride a bike, the soon-to-be princess shot back, "Yes, what do you think? I'm not from another planet. Of course I can ride a bike." When Willem-Alexander and Máxima biked together through a Dutch town, one witness reported back to the rest of the nation: "Máxima has a good, confident style. She doesn't look like a hesitating refugee who has mounted a Dutch bike for the first time as part of the integration process. One hand on the handlebars, the other one waving. Easy peasy." The nation was apparently encouraged by this bit of news: after the royal wedding, Máxima quickly became one of the most popular members of the Dutch royal family.*

---

*In the days leading up to the 2002 royal wedding in Amsterdam, city workers cleared the procession route of 412 parked bicycles. Among the owners of those bikes, only 85 endeavored to retrieve their property from the city.

IN 1998, THE Rijksmuseum passageway was closed to cyclists for more than a year while the building was renovated. After it reopened, the question remained whether cyclists should be excluded from the passageway. "There's a fear in this country about saying that cyclists should no longer be allowed through the Rijksmuseum," complained the museum's head director, Ronald de Leeuw, in 1999. "Here, it's a huge ordeal; in France, no one would give it a second thought. That's typical of the way things are discussed in this nation." That same year, it was announced the museum would undergo massive renovations and that the overall plan would involve the age-old idea to transform the passageway into the building's main entrance.

Seven architectural firms submitted plans of their visions for the "New Rijksmuseum" (as it was being billed at the time). While the proposed designs generally called for the museum entrance to be relocated to the passageway, De Leeuw reported, "None of the architects regarded the bicycle traffic through the passageway as a problem." A commission selected the entry from a pair of Spanish architects as the winning design. "Regarding the discussion about the cyclists . . . we'll keep a safe distance," said one of the Spaniards. "That's a matter for the Dutch."

De Leeuw said that with the renovations, the windows from the interior courtyards would—for the first time in more than a half century—be uncovered in order to transform the passageway into a cathedral of light. "In that cathedral, there's room for the bike," the *NRC Handelsblad* newspaper assured its readers. "Deservedly so because, just as the queen of our country belongs on a bike, the cycling Dutchman belongs in the heart of the National Treasury. The architects have expressly made room for the cyclists."

This space for the cyclists, however, was much narrower than the space they had enjoyed since the 19th century. The passageway's two middle portals would be devoted to a grand new entrance to the museum, while the cyclists would be shunted to the narrower side portals. This change angered many cyclists. And in January 2004 a new umbrella organization—the Committee to Save the Passageway—formed to oppose the museum's plans, which it claimed threatened "one of the wonders of Amsterdam." One of these dissenters compared the old bike path width and the new proposed width to open-mouth breathing and breathing through a straw. "You can . . . breathe through a straw," she said, "but such breathing isn't very pleasant."

In reaction to the cyclists' complaints, in early 2004 spokespeople for the museum said: "Many people fear that the museum wants to ban cyclists, but that won't happen. Nowhere else in the world is there a museum that you can cycle through; the Rijksmuseum's directors want to keep it that way."

IT WAS MARCH 2004, late in the evening of the last day that the passageway was open to the general public before renovations were to begin. I cycled through the building while on my way home. Several other cyclists and pedestrians happened to be passing through silently as well. No street musicians were on hand that night to perform an encore. In fact, the atmosphere was decidedly subdued; nothing marked the significance of the moment. When I exited, I turned and read the sign posted at the entrance: RIJKSMUSEUM PASSAGEWAY CLOSED UNTIL AT LEAST JANUARY 2008.

Geez, I thought, *Two thousand and eight?* That's *four years* off. Yikes!

I turned my bike around, rode back into the passageway and made several farewell round-trips.

The following year, in 2005, a subcommittee of the local neighborhood council unanimously voted against approving the Rijksmuseum's plan for the new entrance to be placed in the middle of what had been the passage's roadway. While disappointed, the Spanish architects drew up new plans in which the cyclists retained the middle portals, while pedestrians entered the museum via the passageway's smaller outer portals.

The issue seemed to be settled. But then in 2008 it flared up again. Within weeks of the appointment of a new head director of the museum—Wim Pijbes—and with the renovations nowhere close to finished, Pijbes stated that his "ideal image" of the passageway included a complete ban of cyclists during daytime hours.

In the months and years that followed, Pijbes' public declarations indicated that his major concern was certainly not the cyclists of the municipality of Amsterdam (the entity that owned the passage's roadway). Rather, he was preoccupied by how people outside the country regarded the situation he called a "chronic parochial commotion." "Abroad, they laugh about it," Pijbes complained. "A reporter for the *New York Times* recently asked me if I was still dealing with the cyclists. He had a grin on his face." On another occasion, when speaking of his foreign colleagues in the art world, Pijbes grumbled, "When I'm abroad, they speak not about the museum's collection, but of the cyclists."

In 2011, with the renovations still two years from being completed, Pijbes amped up the rhetoric by launching a new attack on the cyclists' right to the passageway—a place he called a prime location where soon millions of people will walk and where events can be held. In no way is this still the bicycle tunnel of the past. Bike traffic doesn't belong here anymore. We've invested [$500 million] in this building; we didn't do that to accommodate a covered bike path. . . . For too long the discussion has been dominated by—not to say, held hostage by—the cyclists.

Pijbes then called for cyclists to be completely banned from the passageway when the museum reopened in 2013. This idea picked up steam when, in May 2012, the local district council voted to restrict the cyclists' access to the passageway. While it appeared likely that bicyclists would indeed be banned, any such change required the approval of the city council.

In June 2012, the city's executive board advised the city council to vote to keep the passageway accessible to the cyclists. Pijbes reacted with fury. A century of museum directors' dreams of banning two-wheelers from the passageway had come closest to becoming a reality. Now, though, the dream was on the verge of vanishing because of what Pijbes called a "pig-headed, fundamentalist bicycle lobby" that was only interested in a "bike path—a bike path and nothing else."

Apparently realizing that the Rijksmuseum was on the brink of losing another battle in its fight against the cyclists, Pijbes sent an uncharacteristically conciliatory letter to the city's *wethouder* of traffic affairs. "The museum is indeed sensitive to the demand of the Amsterdammer to be able to again cycle through the passageway," wrote Pijbes. "We also realize that the ordinary Amsterdammer will again have a place in his heart for the Rijksmuseum if he can cycle through it." Pijbes proposed a compromise: instead

of an outright ban, the cyclists would have access to the passageway—outside of the museum's open hours.

On the eve of the city council's vote in July 2012, it seemed
possible that the vote would go in favor of the cyclists—and
against the Rijksmuseum. A desperate-sounding Pijbes stood in
the passageway and insisted to a reporter, "It's *not* a bike path."
The city council felt otherwise. A majority supported the cyclists
retaining the rights they had enjoyed since the 19th century: access to the central portals of the passageway.

21
Let's Ride: Looking Back and Looking Forward

Several times over the years I've been asked if my interest in Amsterdam would ever wane. Before my move to Holland, I'd spent a decade bouncing around, constantly feeling restless after spending just days or weeks in one place. Despite my initial excitement about Amsterdam, I didn't know if the city's luster would wear off in a week or a month or a year—or ever. But now, after having lived in Amsterdam for more than a decade, I'm still just as enthusiastic, still just as fascinated by the place, as when I stepped off the plane at Schiphol Airport.

I still enjoy sitting—on a park bench, at an outdoor café, on the rear rack of my bike—and watching Amsterdam's cyclists in action.

I still snap photos of bike repair shops and bike rental shops (and remain astounded at how often new ones emerge).

I still claim—while leading enraptured foreigners on bike tours—to be able to point out three pregnant cyclists in an hour. (More often than not, the quota is met.)

I still ride often on the Spuistraat bike path, where, on my first day in town, I'd unknowingly walked until the cyclist who slammed into me helped to set me straight. (Personally, I go easy on the tourists walking on that bike path; I merely ring my bell and avoid slamming into them.)

I still stop and watch the bike fishermen reel in their catch from the canals (and still have yet to see a bike on its way *into* the canals).

I still sometimes hang out on the top level of the three-story Central Station bike garage to eat my lunch or to read to my son while we enjoy the view.

I still ride down Linnaeusstraat occasionally and look down at the bullet holes in the bike path where Theo van Gogh was murdered.

I still can be amazed by the improvements and solutions that are made to the city's cycling infrastructure (new separated bike paths and new bridges, for example).

I still am captivated by the history of Amsterdam and its cyclists (and it's still hard to believe I'd known next to nothing about the Dutch or the Netherlands before my arrival).

I still glance at the rear fenders of bikes parked in long rows. The hope is that I'll see one with "AJJ," "AJJ II" or "AJJ III" written on it. (Though the Sharpie ink has certainly long since faded, the search goes on.)

I still attend the annual May Fourth Remembrance Day services at the Annick van Hardeveld monument (and seem to remain the only person in attendance with a bike that's not a fixed-gear).

I still swing by the Grimburgwal bridge where I try to show my son the *zwijntjesjagers* selling stolen bikes. (The bridge's heyday has clearly passed, though; I've yet to point out a single *zwijntjesjager* to Ferris.)

I still am extremely vigilant when securing my bike, always double-locking it even when I'm just running into a newsstand for a newspaper or a candy bar. (After losing AJJ, the one time I let my guard down and absentmindedly walked away from a bike without locking it, I returned for the bike a couple of hours later to find it gone. An experienced Amsterdam *zwijntjesjager* once claimed you can't call taking someone's unlocked bike theft. "A guy like that is just asking for it.")

I still ride all over the city with Ferris on my bike (though these days, instead of singing or indicating which way we should go, he's just as interested in reading a book, either quietly to himself or aloud to me if I'm lucky).

I still watch Dutch films, but nowadays my repertoire is mostly limited to the kids' movies I watch with my son. (One such flick— *Foeksia de miniheks* [*Fuchsia the Mini-Witch*]—garnered interest from an American distributor who considered screening the film in the States. He ultimately begged off because, according to the film's director, the movie contained scenes deemed unacceptable for American viewers: the sight of a boy cycling—sans helmet.)

I still have never worn a helmet in Amsterdam—well, at least not while riding a bike. The last sighting of my helmet came during a fit of spring cleaning, while I was cleaning out my closet. I held it up for Ferris to see.

"You know what this is?" I asked him.

My son looked up from his *Donald Duck* comic book. "A bike helmet?"

"Yeah," I said. "But not just *any* bike helmet. *My* bike helmet."

"Why don't you ever wear it?"

"I *used* to wear it every day, back in America."

"Put it on," he said.

I blew and shook the helmet free of several dust bunnies, then plopped it on my noggin and clasped the strap. Apparently my head size hadn't changed; the helmet still fit perfectly. I removed it and shoved it to the back of my closet, vowing to revisit it again next spring, if only to remove another year's worth of dust bunnies.

IN NEWS ACCOUNTS and opinion pieces about Amsterdam's cyclists, the words "chaos" and "anarchy/anarchists" are still as liberally used now as they were in news accounts and opinion pieces during every decade of the past century. For example, in a recent piece titled "Chaos," a columnist for *De Telegraaf* wrote:

> Of all antisocial beings who inhabit the capital, the cyclist is the most prominent. In the anarchic city called Amsterdam, he's the biggest anarchist. For him, there is no God nor commandment. He flouts traffic regulations; rudeness is his main feature.

The adjunct head editor of *Het Parool* recently wrote about the existence on the city's streets of an

> obvious desire for freedom [that] is a recipe for chaos and danger. The traffic in the city is becoming rougher and more brazen. The law of the jungle trumps the commonly recognized traffic regulations. Within that anarchy, cyclists take the cake; they do whatever they want.

The topic of the "chaotic/anarchistic" cyclist was touched on at a symposium that I attended about the state of Amsterdam cycling, hosted by a municipal agency. A member of the city's traffic department screened a new short film that provided an aerial view of the Mr. Visserplein intersection. It was presented as a five-minute glimpse into the misbehavior of the city's cyclists. The time-lapsed film slowed down several times in order to highlight cycling rule-breakers (that is, those running a red light or riding in the pedestrian crosswalk or riding outside the bike path). During these moments, the presenter and the audience of hundreds laughed. The message was clear: *Ah, those anarchistic, chaotic cyclists of Amsterdam!*

At first, I chuckled as well. After all, I have a keen interest in the long history of bicyclists behaving badly. But then—mid-film—I stopped laughing when I noticed something. The film drew the audience's attention to each renegade cyclist, leading us to overlook the obvious: the vast majority of the cyclists were actually *obeying* the traffic rules. Later I watched the film again. The number of cyclists highlighted as lawbreakers? Nine. The number of cyclists in the film who broke no laws (that is, stopped for the traffic signal, rode within the bike lanes)? One hundred and seventy-four. By featuring the 5 percent of the cyclists in view who were scofflaws, the film helped to embellish the image of the Amsterdam cyclist as out of control. Yet if the film had highlighted the law-abiders, the message could just as easily have been this: 95 percent of Amsterdam's cyclists obey traffic laws. Maybe we aren't such a bad lot after all.

ONE THING I *don't* still do is search for cycling nuns. One day, as I was riding on Overtoom, two women in nun habits were pedaling a hundred feet ahead of me. At first I figured they were a pair of sorority girls dressed up as part of a hazing ritual, the kind often seen on bikes at the beginning of the school year. Then again, I thought they might be members of some bachelorette party, also common sights in town. I sped up.

When the two women stopped at the red light at Nassaukade, I pulled up behind them. Now I could see these two were *not* hazed students; they were middle-aged. And they didn't behave like members of a drunken bachelorette party; they acted quite sober and serious—neither had a plastic penis strapped to her habit.

Then it struck me; I couldn't believe it. These two women appeared to be *actual* nuns. After so many years of searching, I was finally seeing nuns on bikes! I was so excited.

After the light turned green, I tried to pass them on their left. And they moved left. So I tried to go right; they moved right. Eventually, no longer excited about nuns, I rode up onto the sidewalk and zipped around them.

AMY JOY STILL runs her bike shop. The last time I worked on my bike there (an evening of trying—without success—to fix whatever was causing the *ker-chunk-chunk* coming from my rear wheel's hub), I went to wipe some grease off my hands. When I reached into the rag box, I was surprised to pull out a swatch of flowery green material. I immediately recognized the remnant. It was a piece of the dress that, ten years earlier, Amy Joy had worn on her very first day of cycling in Amsterdam. I could still picture her on that afternoon as she blissfully rode AJJ II down Haarlemmerdijk. Now, apparently, she had consigned the dress to scrap; torn pieces of it filled the box of assorted rags.

I held the swatch for a moment and felt reluctant to smudge the gunk from my hands on such an icon of our past. But, as it's said, all good things must come to an end. I admired the flowery pattern one last time, then I wiped my hands clean.

FERRIS STILL SPENDS time on a bike almost every day. He has routinely crossed Amsterdam on bikes as an embryo, fetus, baby, toddler, boy and young man. I often wonder what it will be like for him as a teenager to bike on his own across the city to high school. Or how it will be for him to cycle through these same streets as an adult. I sometimes even wonder—if Amsterdam and parenthood are in his future—how it will be for him to cycle with his own kids. Will he ride with his offspring through the Rijksmuseum? Will he stop and watch the bike fishermen with them? Will he wonder about his own children's futures as cyclists? If the cycling rates in the city continue to grow, could he witness an era when being stuck in a bicycle traffic jam in Amsterdam is viewed not as quaint, but as a frustrating component of bike congestion—just as annoying to cyclists as freeway congestion is to motorists?

I STILL GO back to the States on occasion. During my last visit to Portland, Oregon, one afternoon Ferris and I were sitting on a downtown curb as we watched four lanes of one-way traffic pass by. Ferris—then three years old—eagerly pointed out each cyclist who rode past. It was odd to see that every bike was a fancy road racing bike, a fancy mountain bike, a fancy fixed-gear bike, etc. Not a single (Amsterdam-style) clunker was to be seen among them.

In Portland, as in many other cities that I'd visited since moving to Amsterdam (New York, Pittsburgh, Chicago, San Francisco, for example), friends had enthusiastically asked if I had noticed the surge in cycling since I'd last been to their city. Indeed, I had noticed an increase in cyclists, bike lanes, bike racks, etc. I had to laugh when telling Ferris about having once been ecstatic to spot 19 Portland cyclists in 30 minutes. But still, even in America's biking capital, seeing those cyclists riding among the great many cars reminded me that America remained very much "the land of the automobile."

On that same trip, a few days later, in my hometown of San Francisco, I found myself as a reluctant driver at the wheel of my mom's car. With my mom in the passenger seat and Ferris in the rear, we sat in stalled traffic on the I-280 freeway. Having rarely found myself ever sitting in a car—let alone ever being stuck in freeway traffic jams—for the last few years, I was unused to being immobilized this way. As an Amsterdam cyclist, I was far more used to being almost constantly in motion.

"Pete," Ferris said, "are you sick of driving?"

I didn't know what had tipped him off. The anguished look on my face? My silence? The air of general frustration?

"Yeah," I answered.

"If we were on bikes," Ferris said, "we could ride fast over there in the bike lane." He pointed to his right, to the freeway's breakdown lane.

"We can't ride bikes on the freeway," I told the boy who had so little experience with riding in cars, much less the workings of a freeway.

"Why not?"

"It's too dangerous," I said.

"Oh," Ferris said, sounding disappointed. He looked confused by this logic as he continued to stare over at the vacant breakdown lane.

A few days later, we flew back to Amsterdam. As the plane approached Schiphol Airport, we descended out of the clouds. Through the window, beneath us I saw a bike path that cut across the Haarlemmermeer countryside. A pair of cyclists were riding in the rain. As I watched them, a warmth overcame me.

As soon as we got back to the apartment, I dropped off the luggage and then said to Ferris, "Hey, let's go for a ride."

"Yeah," he said, nodding eagerly, "let's ride."

I lifted Ferris onto the backseat of my bike. Then, as I mounted, he added, "Let's ride *real fast*!"

So we took off, into the rain, happy to be home again in the city of bikes.

Acknowledgments

I would like to express a deep gratitude to the staff members of the Amsterdam Municipal Archives, the Dutch Institute for War Documentation, the International Institute for Social History, the many libraries of the University of Amsterdam (particularly the P. C. Hoofthuis Library and the IWO Book Depot), the Dutch Royal Library, the Dutch National Archives, the North Holland Archives, the Rijksmuseum Research Library, the Aletta Institute, the Vrije Universiteit Library, the Fietsersbond Amsterdam and the Amsterdam Public Library. Without the thousands of hours I spent prospecting, rummaging and napping in the fine reading rooms of these wonderful institutions, I could never have written this book.

I am also particularly thankful to Jos Dal at De Fietsenmaker for all his patience while trying to teach me how to repair bikes; Gerrit, Jona, Marushka and Patricia for their companionship at De Fietsenmaker; Robbie for the attic "office" that allowed me—when lost in thought—to gaze at 114 Amsterdam rooftops; Malia and Hyland Mather for the studio "office" that allowed me—when lost in thought—to gaze at a canal where at least one cyclist was always in sight; Chris and Vanessa Christman for their research assistance; Pete Menchetti for his helping hand; Linda Pluimers for the hospitality at her bike shop café; Amy

Abdou and Daniel Versteegh for their ceaseless hospitality; Robert Helms for the passwords; Lisa Friedman for teaching me so much and for repeatedly going above and beyond the definition of a mentor/writer relationship; Ronny de Klerk for proofreading and correcting all of my translations of quoted texts from their original Dutch, German, Spanish, Italian and French; Johan Kerstens for editing and translating my articles and column in *Oek*; Steve Krover for editing my column in the *Amsterdam Weekly*; David McCormick, my agent, for all his terrific work on my behalf; Michael Signorelli, my editor, for all his help and guidance; Amy Baker at HarperCollins for her endless patience; Cheryl Wagner for her years of support, encouragement and editorial feedback; everyone with whom I've ever discussed Amsterdam cycling (particularly Roel van Duijn, Luud Schimmelpennink, Martin Bierman and André Guit); my mom—Sarah Jordan—and my sisters and brothers—Cathie, Johnny, Joe and Sheila—for their continued support; AJ; and especially to Ferris for all the many hours we've spent together on the bikes.

Also, thanks to all of the bicycle advocates in Amsterdam (especially those at De Fietsersbond) and to the city's hundreds of bike mechanics, bike shop owners, bike renters, bike garage attendants and bike policy makers.

Finally, I'd like to express a hearty, special thanks to the hundreds of thousands of Amsterdammers who cycle as part of their daily routines. Observing them and riding among them has enabled me to go about my own daily routine with warmth in my heart. And every day, for more than a decade, they have inspired me greatly!

Notes

During the research for this book, I sifted through countless newspapers, magazines, books, films, songs, documents, diaries, records, etc. in search of "flavor and incident, anecdote and eyewitness" (to borrow a phrase from Luc Sante) that could help voice the story of the Amsterdam cyclist. My appreciation goes out to everyone whose words were quoted in these pages. All such material is referenced below.

1: Even a Man from America Can See a Few Things

4   "[T]he odd gaps": Hendrik Willem van Loon, *An Indiscreet Itinerary* (New York: Harcourt, Brace, 1933).

8   "The visitor must": *Nagel Travel Guide Series: Holland* (New York: Nagel, 1964).

8   "You'll think": Sydney Clark, *All the Best in Holland* (New York: Dodd, Mead, 1950).

8   "Don't be frightened": Jan Heyn Jr., *Holland Hails You* (Wormerveer, Holland: Flower Garden Press, 1945).

8   "You will need": P. J. Mijksenaar, *Amsterdam at Best* (Amsterdam: De Bezige Bij, 1955).

9   "If you feel like cursing": *Amsterdam: The Gateway to Europe* (Amsterdam: World's Window, 1949).

9   "Taxi drivers seem": Clark, *All the Best in Holland*.

9   "It is the daring 'foreigner'": Leavitt F. Morris, "Travel Editor's Diary," *Christian Science Monitor*, May 29, 1959.

11   "The Amsterdammer": Wilfred B. Millbank, "Amsterdam in vreemde ogen," *Het Parool*, October 2, 1954.

11 "Perhaps it will be thought": William Yoast Morgan, *A Jayhawker in Europe* (Topeka, KS: Crane, 1911).

11 "There seem to be as many": John Henry Cowles, "Journeyings of the Grand Commander," *New Age*, February 1929.

12 "Nowhere else in the world": "De fiets heeft weer toekomst," *De Spiegel*, April 3, 1965.

12 "At first you cannot refrain": Félix Martí-Ibáñez, *The Mirror of Souls, and Other Essays* (New York: Potter, 1972).

12 "The foreigner . . . may have": Walter H. Waggoner, "Eisenhower's Enthusiasm for Bicycling Meets Warm Response in the Netherlands," *New York Times*, January 3, 1957.

2: Lucky Few: The 1890s

22 "The pneumatic tire": Henri Polak, "Onze wegen en hun verkeer," *Haagsche Maandblad*, February 1924.

23 "In Amsterdam . . . the 'Wilhelmina'": Albert de Leur, "Free Trade in Europe," *Los Angeles Times*, December 22, 1897.

23 "[T]he Streets so exactly straite": John Evelyn, *The Diary of John Evelyn*, ed. E. S. De Beer (London: Oxford University Press, 1959).

23 "Certainly Amsterdam": William Carr, *An Accurate Description of the United Netherlands* (London: Timothy Childe, 1691).

23 "the lumpy heads": "Het automobilisme te Amsterdam," *De Kampioen*, November 2, 1900.

23 "nothing less than a mountainous": "Wielrijden door Amsterdam," *Het Algemeen Handelsblad*, May 1, 1898.

24 "Really, when I sit": "Dames-Brieven," *De Sumatra Post*, June 12, 1902.

24 "Even the sturdiest": "De rijwiel-oekase van B. & W.," *Het Algemeen Handelsblad*, July 17, 1906.

24 "Wherever you look": G. & E., "Een Zondagochtend in het Vondelpark," *Het Nieuws van de Dag*, May 10, 1897.

24 "But you'd look sweet": Harry Dacre, "Daisy Bell" (1892).

25 "In the streets and on the squares": A. J. M. Rövekamp, "Van Hogesluis naar Overtoom," *Ons Amsterdam*, April 1979.

25 "And then just run alongside": Leendert Harmsen, "Kost verdienen met en op de fiets," *Ons Amsterdam*, May 1978.

26 "'Cyclist School'": "Velox," *Het Nieuws van de Dag*, July 29, 1898.

26 "extremely practical and pleasant": "Velox," *De Groene Amsterdammer*, July 31, 1898.

27 "figure cycling": "Velox," *Het Nieuws van de Dag*, July 29, 1898.

27   "a school for beginners": Ibid.

27   "We practiced for weeks": "Fietsbespiegeling," *Het Algemeen Handelsblad*, April 18, 1936.

27   "lucky few": "Elk jaar een half miljoen nieuwe fietsen in omloop," *Het Parool*, August 6, 1964.

28   purchased an "excellent" bike: "Onze Koninginnen en de Wielersport!," *Nieuwe Amersfoortsche Courant*, November 24, 1897.

28   "The precedents cited": "A Queen Cyclist," *West Australian*, December 25, 1897.

29   "many a tear": Duchesse De Belimere, "Doings of the Young Queen of the Dutch," *The State*, September 9, 1898.

29   "She sighed like a biker": "A Queen Cyclist," *West Australian*, December 25, 1897.

29   "savage persecution": "The Cycle or the Throne?," *New York Tribune*, November 29, 1897.

30   "Back then, it wasn't": L. A. A. Cohen, "Gerrit Brinkman," *Ons Amsterdam*, February 1951.

30   "the principal traffic hindrance": "Het verkeer in de hoofdstad," *Het Algemeen Handelsblad*, December 3, 1912.

30   "If there is one category": Zadi, "Amsterdamsche Brieven," *Het Nieuws van den Dag voor Nederlandsch-Indië*, August 28, 1906.

30   "that peculiarity": "Wielrijden door Amsterdam," *Het Algemeen Handelsblad*, May 1, 1898.

31   "so funny": "De veiligheid in onze straten," *Het Algemeen Handelsblad*, May 17, 1905.

31   "Wonderful!": Zadi, "Amsterdamsche Brieven."

31   "ridiculous": "Den nieuwe Amsterdamsche Chinoisorie," *Het Nieuws van den Dag*, July 18, 1906.

31   "repressive": "Ingezonden," *Het Nieuws van den Dag*, July 25, 1906.

31   "terrorism": "Rijwielvordening," *Het Algemeen Handelsblad*, July 19, 1906.

32   "The Amsterdammer enjoys": Cohen, "Gerrit Brinkman."

32   "In less than no time": Ibid.

33   "Maybe the people": Ibid.

33   "his absolute independence truncated": "Verkeersregeling," *Het Nieuws van de Dag*, September 17, 1913.

33   "Where the authorities": "Het verkeer in de hoofdstad," *Het Nieuws van de Dag*, August 17, 1918.

3: Piggy Hunters: The Bike Thievery

37   "The bicycle has": "Fietsen," *De Groene Amsterdammer*, June 8, 1940.

39   "To me it would": "Onveilig Den Haag," *Het Nieuws van de Dag voor Nederlandsch-Indië*, March 23, 1923.

39   "choice selection of bicycles": "Herinneringen van een oud-commissaris van politie," *Leeuwarder Courant*, April 1, 1932.

40   "It is forbidden": "Sloten op de rijwielen!," *Het Algemeen Handelsblad*, March 21, 1928.

40   denounced as "immoral": "Fietsen, fietsenstalling en fietsendieven," *De Telegraaf*, September 2, 1934.

41   "There is no other city": "Probleem No. 1: de onbeheerde fiets," *Het Volk*, August 8, 1940.

41   "a criminal epidemic": "Rijwieldiefstallen," *De Telegraaf*, May 9, 1942.

42   "code of honor": "Twee minuten zijn voor een fietsendief genoeg," *Het Parool*, July 26, 1958.

42   "Could he honestly": Ibid.

42   "Regardless of the day": Ibid.

42   "where Amsterdammers": "Amsterdam, geliefde," *De Waarheid*, April 16, 1955.

42   "nonchalants": "De politie houdt grote schoonmaak," *De Spiegel*, November 15, 1958.

42   "weep and wail": Ibid.

43   "Bicycle thieves": Ben Kroon, "De fietser als anarchist," *De Tijd*, August 15, 1980.

43   "The entire northern part": "Waar blijven al die gestolen fietsen?," *De Waarheid*, July 22, 1977.

43   "But when you lose": Gerben Hellinga, "Ons Dorp," *Avenue*, June 1972.

44   "devote any attention": Maurice Punch, *Fout is fout!* (Meppel, Netherlands: Boom, 1976).

44   "Whoever lives": "Waar blijven al die gestolen fietsen?," *De Waarheid*, July 22, 1977.

45   "foreign freaks": Janette Grainger, ed., *Living Guide to Amsterdam* (Amsterdam: Grabjack Press, 1972).

45   "In Amsterdam there is": Ibid.

45   "Often I'll nick": Henny de Vos, "'Ik denk dat ik zo'n 10.000 fietsen heb gejat,'" *IJmuider Courant*, September 5, 1987.

46   "There's only one way": Chiel van Zelst, *100.000 Fietsventielen* (Amsterdam: Nijgh & Van Ditmar, 1999).

48   "A minimum price": "Helen voor beginners," *Folia*, August 26, 1994.

48   "there are too many": Truska Bast, "Geheeld voor een geeltje," *Het Parool*, June 7, 1997.

48   "It used to be enough": Paula Kesteren and Ger Homburg, *Fietsdiefstal* (The Hague: Stafafdeling Informatievoorziening, Directie Criminaliteitspreventie, Ministerie van Justitie, 1995).

49   "But even if it's": Bast, "Geheeld voor een geeltje."

49   "The market here": Bast, "Geheeld voor een geeltje."

49   "[He] seldom casually": Anna Visser, "Oprecht verbaasd," *NRC Handelsblad*, November 11, 1999.

49   "On weekends": Roelien Wiestra, "'Gestolen tang, gestolen fiets,'" *Vogelvrije Fietser*, July/August 2001.

50   "No, not anymore": Bast, "Geheeld voor een geeltje."

50   "It's logical that people": Ibid.

50   "It used to be only students": Ibid.

50   "How they know about it": Joris Luyendijk, "'Studenten zijn nog op het rechte pad terug te brengen,'" *Folia*, August 26, 1994.

51   "disposable object": Bast, "Geheeld voor een geeltje."

51   "If a repair costs": Gerda de Bruijn, "Jaap Molenaar over heling," *Oek*, no. 55 (November 2001).

51   "It's a real market": "Gestolen die fiets? Niet aan gedacht," *Het Parool*, September 1, 1999.

51   "Let me be clear": Martin de Jong, "'Amsterdam is gemaakt voor fietsers,'" *Vogelvrije Fietser*, May/June 2000.

51   "The mentality of the Amsterdammer": "Amsterdams offensief tegen fietsendiefstallen," *Leidsch Dagblad*, February 7, 2002.

4: King of the Street: The 1920s

53   "That endless, unbroken": "Het verkeer in Amsterdam," *De Telegraaf*, April 15, 1922.

54   "belong to the people": Ernst Polak, "Straat-tanks," *Het Algemeen Handelsblad*, October 20, 1921.

55   "In the past couple": Sicco de Jong, *Geschiedenis eener Nederlandsche Vereeniging: RAI 1893–1968* (Bussum, Netherlands: Van Dishoeck, 1968).

56   "the abnormal increase": *Gemeenteblad van Amsterdam*, deel II.2 (1922).

56   "But on the bike": "The town of the million bicycles," *De Sumatra Post*, November 13, 1923.

56   "The time that a bicycle": W. J. L., "De zwarte bal geheschen," *De Kampioen*, September 28, 1923.

57 "One now goes everywhere": Xavier de Montrecourt, *Een heer: Regelen voor den modernen Gentleman* (Amsterdam: Cohen Zonen, ca. 1925).

57 "The bicycle no longer demands": Marguerite de Viroflay, *Een dame: Wat zij moet doen en nalaten* (Amsterdam: Cohen Zonen, ca. 1925).

57 "Presently, one bicycles": De Montrecourt, *Een heer.*

58 "Why is that so?": "Een praatje over het rijwiel," *De Kampioen*, May 23, 1924.

58 "The Netherlands is preeminently": "Het rijwiel," *Het Vaderland*, February 18, 1928.

58 "The Amsterdam cyclist": Gozewijn, "Onder de Keizerskroon," *Het Algemeen Handelsblad*, August 22, 1926.

59 "On the brick-paved streets": Francesco Sapori, *Pellegrinaggi Olandesi* (Livorno, Italy: Belforte, 1922).

59 "While the traveler in Holland": "About Holland," *Punch*, September 14, 1927.

59 "the city of a million": "Amsterdamsche Brieven," *De Sumatra Post*, January 6, 1922.

59 the "misery" caused: *Gemeenteblad van Amsterdam*, deel II (1923).

59 "public entertainments": Ibid.

59 "traffic anarchism": "Peddelend Amsterdam," *Het Algemeen Handelsblad*, August 16, 1927.

60 "often ride very carelessly": Ibid.

60 "It happens repeatedly": "Verkeersproblemen," *Het Algemeen Handelsblad*, October 30, 1921.

60 "as if it counted": "Dagboek van een Amsterdammer," *De Telegraaf*, May 23, 1922.

61 "a ridiculous enterprise": Ibid.

61 called this "scandal": "De verkeerspolitie in aktie," *Het Volk*, May 16, 1922.

61 "Every cyclist on Utrechtestraat": "Verkeers-varia," *Het Algemeen Handelsblad*, August 17, 1922.

61 "respectable establishments": Kitty de Leeuw, *Kleding in Nederland, 1813–1920* (Hilversum, Netherlands: Verloren, 1993).

62 "Leidsestraat is for cyclists": "Amsterdam op straat," *De Sumatra Post*, February 16, 1928.

62 "What is more dangerous": "Tweede Kamer," *Het Volk*, December 4, 1920.

62 "red with rage": W. v. L., "Amsterdams verkeer in veiliger banan," *De Telegraaf*, August 13, 1926.

62   "The Leidsestraat issue": "In en om de Hoofdstad," *Leeuwarder Courant*, October 22, 1927.

63   "cyclist has become a nightmare": "Fietsers-invasie in de Leidschestraat," *De Telegraaf*, November 9, 1927.

63   "fly-by-night stores": *Gemeenteblad van Amsterdam*, deel II.3 (1927).

63   "Bicycle riders are generally": N. T., "Het verkeersvraagstuk," *Het Algemeen Handelsblad*, December 20, 1927.

63   "most ladies go shopping": "De Leidschestraat," *Het Algemeen Handelsblad*, October 26, 1927.

63   "I have but one bit": "Fietsers, vereenigt U!," *De Telegraaf*, November 13, 1927.

65   "Whoever takes a look": "Verkeersproblemen," *Het Algemeen Handelsblad*, April 5, 1922.

65   "*the* great event": Cohen, "Gerrit Brinkman," *Ons Amsterdam*, February 1951.

66   "On Weteringschans": "Stop!," *Het Algemeen Handelsblad*, October 2, 1925.

66   "the crowds that constantly": "Verkeers-offensief," *Het Algemeen Handelsblad*, October 26, 1925.

66   "Naturally, these are": Van Walgcheren, "De eerste semaphore in Nederland," *Wereldkroniek*, October 10, 1925.

66   "A bicycle tax": W. J. L., "De zwarte bal geheschen," *De Kampioen*, September 28, 1923.

67   "the market for stolen": "Met de stillen op stap," *Het Algemeen Handelsblad*, July 4, 1934.

67   "no more, no less": Ibid.

67   "eagle-eyed" officials: Sini Sana, "In en om de hoofdstad," *Leidsch Dagblad*, July 17, 1926.

68   "many an Amsterdammer": Ibid.

68   "clearly an utmost": Ibid.

68   "In Amsterdam, it's not": Van Siegen, "Brieven uit de Hoofdstad," *Leeuwarder Courant*, September 17, 1932.

68   "crept slowly past us": "Jacht rijwielplaatjes," *Het Algemeen Handelsblad*, April 13, 1926.

68   "bit of fun": Sana, "In en om de hoofdstad."

69   "a bicycle auction": Ibid.

69   "Seldom did the police": Cohen, "Gerrit Brinkman."

5: *It Made My Head Swim: The Elephants, Centaurs, Punks and Nuns*

73   "If you're going to hunt down": "Aangehouden op fiets na vijf bier," *Spits*, May 6, 2008.

74   "the cyclist who stops": Peter Brusse, "De fietser die voor rood stopt," *De Volkskrant*, May 13, 1995.

74   was called an "idiot": Ibid.

74   "Often, I stand": Willem Breedveld and Gonny ten Haaf, "De toestand in Amsterdam," *Trouw*, July 11, 1998.

74   "age-old anarchy": Kurt van Es and Jos Verlaan, "Goedgekeurd door Patijn," *Het Parool*, April 27, 1996.

74   "the insane fact": Schelto Patijn, "Amsterdam is nog lang niet af, er is nog heel veel te doen," *Het Parool*, January 3, 2xs.

75   "Cyclists behave like anarchists": Paul Vugts, "De rare alinea gaat dit jaar over de F-side," *Het Parool*, January 4, 2000.

75   "It's not just the youth": Monique Snoeijen, "Nieuwe gedoogcategorie," *NRC Handelsblad*, February 29, 2000.

75   "Because I realize": Jan Hoedeman and Frank Poorthuis, "'Een overheid kan niet functioneren zonder gezag,'" *De Volkskrant*, September 17, 2002.

75   "I do everything": Maaike Schoon, "Hier heerste anarchie," *Het Parool*, June 10, 2011.

75   "no pure, innocent angel": "Wielrijders als weggebruikers," *De Telegraaf*, October 29, 1932.

75   "An almost universal": Maurice Punch, *Policing the Inner City* (London: Macmillan, 1979).

76   "A real Amsterdammer likes": Maurice Punch, *De Warmoesstraat* (Deventer, Holland: Van Loghum Slaterus, 1983).

76   "minor criminality": Monique Snoeijen and Herman Staal, "Nieuwe Amsterdamse korpschef Jelle Kuiper stapt uit schaduw van voorganger," *NRC Handelsblad*, September 11, 1997.

76   "He wants to go down": Monique Snoeijen and Herman Staal, "Geen man voor feesten en partijen," *NRC Handelsblad*, November 16, 1998.

76   "I call them anarchists": Frits Abraham, "Anarchisten," *NRC Handelsblad*, October 7, 2003.

76   "just like elephants": Ibid.

77   "in droves like buffalo": Don Herold, *Doing Europe—And Vice Versa* (Boston: Little, Brown, 1932).

77   "a splendid army": Presto, "Fietsend Amsterdam Sluit de Gelderen," *De Groene Amsterdammer*, November 3, 1934.

77 "like salmon": Anthony Bailey, *The Light in Holland* (New York: Knopf, 1970).

77 "the cyclists go in flocks": Virginia Woolf, *The Diary of Virginia Woolf*, vol. 4, *1931–1935* (New York: Harcourt, Brace, 1983).

77 "And then those bicycles": Karel Čapek, *Letters from Holland* (London: Faber & Faber, 1933).

78 "shoots through the bustle": Johan Luger and Jo Spier, *De Amsterdammer: Zwart op Wit* (Amsterdam: Andries Blitz, 1938).

78 "They used to swarm": Geoffrey Cottrell, *Amsterdam: The Life of a City* (Boston: Little, Brown, 1972).

78 "The Dutchman is a modern centaur": Martí-Ibáñez, *The Mirror of Souls*.

78 "bacteria of the street": René Didde, *Blik op oneindig* (Amsterdam: Ravijn, 1992).

78 "They don't belong": Buning, "Over auto's en fietsen," *De Tijd*, July 8, 1935.

78 "No, the black sheep": "De Amsterdammer leert trappen en sturen, maar niet . . . FIETSEN!," *Wierings Weekrevue*, January 12, 1956.

79 "Like lurking hyenas": Ben Speet, *Als de Dag van Gisteren* (Zwolle, Netherlands: Waanders, 1990).

79 "It is quite possible": William W. Yates, "Cyclists Make Visitors Jump in Amsterdam," *Chicago Tribune*, October 28, 1956.

79 "street fleas": Presto, "Fietsend Amsterdam Sluit de Gelderen."

79 "as overgrown vermin": Evert Werkman, *'n Grote stad op palen* (Amsterdam: C. De Boer Jr., 1958).

79 "In the jungle of Amsterdam": "Veiligheid van fietser bestaat slechts in zijn dromen," *Het Nieuws van de Dag*, July 10, 1963.

79 "a dream of gold and smoke": Albert Camus, *La Chute* (Paris: Gallimard, 1956).

83 "Many a young Dutchman": "Uncle Ray's Corner," *Big Spring Herald*, October 20, 1954.

83 "Girls, in theater dress": Leavitt F. Morris, "Travel Editor's Diary," *Christian Science Monitor*, May 29, 1959.

83 "typical Dutch courtesy": "Een jonge Brit over Nederland," *Leeuwarder Courant*, January 25, 1958.

84 "We were astonished": Elsa Caspers, *To Save a Life* (London: Deirdre McDonald Books, 1995).

84 "A Dutchman would never": Ibid.

84 "Those American guys": "Jonge Amerika is thuis in Amsterdam," *Trouw*, September 13, 1952.

86   "Whoever is not used to it": J. Rentes de Carvalho, *Waar die andere God woont* (Utrecht: Meulenhoff, 1972).

88   "and just about everyone else": Rich Landers, "Do as the Dutch Do and Ride a Bicycle," *Spokesman Review*, July 28, 2002.

88   "their briefcases dangling": E. E. Bennett, "The Charm That Is Holland," *Christian Science Monitor*, October 15, 1952.

88   "in pressed white": Cynthia Gorney, "Holland on Wheels," *Washington Post*, September 27, 1998.

88   "plumed hats": Norma Jost and Ruth Carper, "All Aboard," *Mennonite Life*, July 1952.

88   "woolen berets": Sapori, *Pellegrinaggi Olandesi*.

88   "long full skirts": Laura M. Budden, "First Visit to Holland," *The Motor Cycle*, March 26, 1931.

88   "Fodor's guidebook": Charles J. Rolo, "Tourist in Holland," *Atlantic*, May 1957.

89   "frumpy dresses": "Bicycles Are Second Nature in Netherlands," *Miami Herald*, October 22, 1989.

89   "a chic dress": Murray J. Brown, "In Holland, They Bike, Hike Dike," *St. Petersburg Times*, December 1, 1963.

89   "low-cut cocktail dresses": Dick West, "To Live Long, Ride a Bike," *Dallas Morning News*, September 21, 1959.

89   "miniskirts": Gorney, "Holland on Wheels."

89   "pedal like mad": West, "To Live Long, Ride a Bike."

89   "race along": Bennett, "The Charm That Is Holland."

89   "with long-stemmed gladiolas": Gorney, "Holland on Wheels."

89   "with the sensible purse": Mark Jenkins, "The Way It Should Be Is the Way It Is," *Bicycling*, June 2008.

89   "with their wool trousers": Gorney, "Holland on Wheels."

89   "in a Prince Albert coat": Jean Henri Nicolas, *A Rose Odyssey* (Garden City, NY: Doubleday, Doran, 1937).

89   "straddles his bike": Harley M. Leete, ed., *The Best of Bicycling!* (New York: Trident, 1970).

89   "black veil": Sapori, *Pellegrinaggi Olandesi*.

89   "aged nuns": Rolo, "Tourist in Holland."

89   "nuns with flowing habits": "Bicycles Are Second Nature in Netherlands," *Miami Herald*, October 22, 1989.

89   "pedal[ing] to her hospital": Kees van Hoek, "Modern Holland," *Canadian Geographical Journal*, September 1940.

89   "troupes of nuns": John Hillaby, *Journey Through Europe* (St. Albans, UK: Paladin, 1974).

90   "This is the best": Erik van den Berg, "Oermuziek in de passage," *De Volkskrant*, January 8, 2004.

91   "it seems impossible to count": "Uncle Ray's Corner," *Big Spring Herald*, October 20, 1954.

91   "I counted a hundred": Louis A. Weil and Blanche G. Weil, *Grandparents Go Abroad* (Port Huron, MI: Times Herald, 1949).

6: A Matter of Individual Expression: The Land of the Automobile vs. the Land of the Bicycle

95   "nation of cyclists": Ruth Broek Heineck, "Holland: A Nation of Cyclists," *Travel*, June 1934.

95   "the land of the automobile": "Amerika," *Het Vaderland*, February 18, 1920.

95   "If a referendum": Adriaan J. Barnouw, *Holland Under Queen Wilhelmina* (New York: Charles Scribner's Sons, 1923).

96   "The bicycle fantasy": "Raising Wages," *Railway and Locomotive Engineering*, December 1902.

96   "In all places where": Henri Meijer, "De concurrentie van Amerika," *De Kampieon*, November 2, 1906.

97   "every businessman": "Een stad van 'cars,'" *De Nieuwe Rotterdamsche Courant*, February 2, 1929.

97   "Often you can see children": Herbert J. Brinks, ed., *Dutch American Voices* (Ithaca, NY: Cornell University Press, 1995).

97   "Just as easily": "Een stad van 'cars,'" *De Nieuwe Rotterdamsche Courant*.

97   "Every ordinary person": "Automobilisme," *Het Algemeen Handelsblad*, September 7, 1921.

98   "with pride": Jo van Ammers-Küller, *Mijn Amerikaansche reis* (The Hague: Leopold, 1926).

98   "unbelievably filthy": Ibid.

98   "Ripe and unripe": N. A. de Vries, *De Nieuwe Wereld* (Groningen: Wolters, 1924).

98   "drove his plucky little Ford": Ibid.

98   "Almost nobody walks here": "Een stad van 'cars,'" *De Nieuwe Rotterdamsche Courant*.

98   "Whatever else an American": "Uit het verre Westen," *Leeuwarder Courant*, November 6, 1920.

98   "almost every motorist": Mary Pos, *Ik zag Amerika* (Amsterdam: De Lange, 1940).

99   "A bicycle here is as rare": "Amerikaansche Verkeersmaatregelen," *Het Vaderland*, October 14, 1927.

99   "In America, the bicycle": J. E. van der Wielen, *America en de oorlog* (Amsterdam: C. L. van Langenhuysen, 1918).

99   "without treacherous": Van Ammers-Küller, *Mijn Amerikaansche reis*.

99   "very common and permitted": "Amerikaansche notities," *Leidsch Dagblad*, January 16, 1931.

99   "When I read in a European magazine": "Naar Washington," *Het Volk*, November 25, 1919.

99   "Good heavens": Van Ammers-Küller, *Mijn Amerikaansche reis*.

100   "are so ridiculously cheap": Brinks, ed., *Dutch American Voices*.

101   "purchase of a little Ford": Marius G. Levenbach, *Arbeid in Amerika* (Amsterdam: Elsevier, 1926).

101   "The sale of secondhand autos": "Amerikaansche Brief," *De Indisch Courant*, November 27, 1930.

101   "The American is fickle": André Siegfried, *Les États-Unis d'aujourd'hui* (Paris: A. Colin, 1927).

102   "While there is already complaining": "Benzine en brandstoffen, die haar kunnen vervangen," *De Kampioen*, May 8, 1914.

102   "young lady, when she goes": "Automobilisme," *Het Algemeen Handelsblad*, September 7, 1921.

103   found it "striking": "Indrukken van Amerika," *Het Algemeen Handelsblad*, August 25, 1910.

103   "innumerable" cars parked: "Naar de Nieuwe Wereld," *Leeuwarder Courant*, April 15, 1916.

104   "those who can afford the luxury": "Automobilisme," *Het Algemeen Handelsblad*, September 7, 1921.

105   "An American thinks": Van Ammers-Küller, *Mijn Amerikaansche reis*.

105   "rather far away": Pos, *Ik zag Amerika*.

105   "Nobody finds this": "Terug naar de natuur," *Het Vaderland*, September 14, 1930.

105   "everything is cozily": Ibid.

106   "Almost without stopping": Pos, *Ik zag Amerika*.

107   "The Dutch life is beautifully": Heineck, "Holland: A Nation of Cyclists."

108   "To a Dutchman": Arthur Lionberger, "Holland: The Most Peaceful Country in Europe," *Independent*, February 25, 1928.

108   "Speed, rush, impatience": Barnouw, *Holland Under Queen Wilhelmina*.

108   "Everything, quick, quick!": Brinks, ed., *Dutch American Voices*.

109   "In many parts of America": William James Rolfe and William Day Crockett, *A Satchel Guide to Europe* (Boston: Houghton Mifflin, 1930).

109   "When our brothers, sisters and children": "Wielrijden door Amster-
      dam," *Het Algemeen Handelsblad*, May 1, 1898.

109   "[M]otor cars are not yet": John Howard Whitehouse, *Creative Educa-
      tion at an English School* (Cambridge, UK: [Printed by Walter Lewis] at
      the University Press, 1928).

109   "The motorists here respect": "Fietsende Amerikanen te Amsterdam,"
      De Telegraaf, July 29, 1936.

109   "America got so new-rich": Lee Shippey, "The Lee Side o' L. A.," *Los
      Angeles Times*, April 11, 1933.

110   "telegraph messengers, schoolboys": "Bike, Nearly 100 Years Old, Gets
      Its Second Wind," *Chicago Tribune*, November 6, 1938.

110   "The average American feels": "De triomf van den automobiel," *De Su-
      matra Post*, July 31, 1923.

110   "It seems so funny": John Falcon and Morris Pollock, "Junior Olympic
      Champs Send Open Letter to Friends Here," *Los Angeles Times*, Au-
      gust 22, 1928.

110   "People strongly advised against it": "Vereenigde Staten," *Het Algemeen
      Handelsblad*, December 4, 1912.

111   "Anyone here who does not have an auto": Brinks, ed., *Dutch American
      Voices*.

111   "quick, covert glance": "Amerika," *Het Vaderland*, February 18, 1920.

111   "He must look prosperous": William Ashdown, "Confessions of an
      Automobilist," *Atlantic*, June 1925.

112   "the abundance of bicycles": José Ortega y Gasset, "Precauciones que
      toma el viajero antes de hablar," *La Nación* (Buenos Aires), July 1936.

112   "is stupidly dangerous": José Ortega y Gasset, "Lo que el viajero per-
      cibe en las bicicletas de Holanda," *La Nación* (Buenos Aires), July
      1936.

113   "It's a question of uniformity": "Vereenigde Staten," *Het Algemeen
      Handelsblad*, December 4, 1912.

113   "Let us not be intimidated": "Het fietsen in Nederland," *Het Vaderland*,
      November 26, 1936.

114   "I am careful and I am thrifty": Ashdown, "Confessions of an Auto-
      mobilist."

7: Problem Children: The 1930s

116   Amsterdam's "cyclomania": Barbarossa, "Stadsschoon, Rokinwater en
      Fietsomanie," *De Groene Amsterdammer*, February 1, 1930.

117   "The bicycle rage": Presto, "Fietsend Amsterdam Sluit de Gelderen."

118   "How many people used to put": "Het publiek over het verkeer," *De Telegraaf*, October 28, 1932.

118   "If there really is anything": Van Loon, *An Indiscreet Itinerary*.

118   "As soon as they dare": Heineck, "Holland: A Nation of Cyclists."

118   "somewhat backward": Presto, "Fietsend Amsterdam Sluit de Gelderen."

119   "Considering it psychologically": "Tramperikelen in de hoofdstad," *Het Liberale Weekblad*, June 27, 1934.

119   "The cyclists of Amsterdam are the Masters": "Brieven uit de Hoofd-stad," *Leeuwarder Courant*, December 27, 1930.

119   "snail's pace": Ibid.

119   "Meanwhile," a reporter wrote, "the cheery": Ibid.

119   "pesky competititor": Ibid.

120   "a sign of her sincere desire": Thijs Booy, *De levensavond van Koningin Wilhelmina* (Amsterdam: W. ten Have, 1965).

120   "Wearing a gray sweater": Anne O'Hare McCormick, "Europe: The Tale of Three Cities Vivid with Contrast," *New York Times*, September 12, 1938.

120   "lady on the bicycle": Frederick Sondnern Jr., "King Wilhelmina," *Scribner's Commentary*, April 1940.

120   "Sitting very straight": Ibid.

122   "parked busses, cars with chicken coops": "Verkeersgevaar te Amster-dam," *Het Algemeen Handelsblad*, February 19, 1937.

122   "a more modern and worldly appearance": Paul Spies, *Het Grachtenboek II* (The Hague: Sdu Uitgevers, 1992).

122   "attempt to Americanize": *Gemeenteblad van Amsterdam*, Tweede Af-deeling 1936.

123   "Cheeky chattering is useless and idle": Margot Dijkgraaf, "Neuswijze kakeling," *NRC Handelsblad*, June 8, 2001.

124   "helter-skelter-driven cars": "De doorgang onder het Rijksmuseum," *Het Algemeen Handelsblad*, November 23, 1920.

124   "Seated on a bike": Wijsneus, "De 1001ste nacht," *Het Algemeen Handelsblad*, May 5, 1925.

125   "met by great opposition": Letter from Rijksmuseum Head Director Frederik Schmidt-Degener to M. A. M. Waszink, Minister of Educa-tion, Art and Science, February 22, 1928, Dutch National Archives.

125   "the cyclists jauntily chose": "De Rijksmuseum-doorgang gesloten," *Het Algemeen Handelsblad*, November 3, 1931.

126   "years-long abuse": Frederik Schmidt-Degener, *Rijksmuseum te Am-*

sterdam: Verslag van den hoofddirecteur over het jaar 1931 (Amsterdam: Rijksmuseum, 1932).

126   "soft music": "Receptie onder museumpoort," *Het Algemeen Handelsblad*, July 4, 1936.

126   "architectually exceptional, lovely space": Frederik Schmidt-Degener, *Rijksmuseum te Amsterdam: Verslag van den hoofddirecteur over het jaar 1936* (Amsterdam: Rijksmuseum, 1937).

126   "If only this could be incorporated": "Receptie onder museumpoort," *Het Algemeen Handelsblad*, July 4, 1936.

126   "charming architecture isn't getting its due": Schmidt-Degener, *Rijksmuseum te Amsterdam: Verslag van den hoofddirecteur over het jaar 1936*.

127   "strike now while the iron is hot": Letter from Rijksmuseum Head Director Frederik Schmidt-Degener to Jan Rudolph Slotemaker de Bruïne, Minister of Education, Art and Science, July 16, 1936, Dutch National Archives.

127   "Clumps of cycles": "Amsterdam Finds Problem Parking 250,000 Bicycles," *Christian Science Monitor*, July 3, 1935.

127   "Glittering bikes and gloomy bikes": "Fietsen, fietsenstalling en fietsendieven," *De Telegraaf*, September 2, 1934.

128   "threatening ghost": *Jaarboek der Universiteit van Amsterdam 1932–1933* (Amsterdam: Universiteit van Amsterdam, 1933).

128   "We are the nation of cyclists": "In Holland staat een huis!," *Het Vaderland*, July 29, 1932.

129   "Without bike thieves": "Fietsen, fietsenstalling en fietsendieven," *De Telegraaf*, September 2, 1934.

130   "ceremonious floral pieces": "Andere gevaren," *Het Algemeen Handelsblad*, July 25, 1925.

130   "baskets full of fruit and canned preserves": Ibid.

130   "the cannibals of the roadway": "In en om de Hoofdstad," *Leeuwarder Courant*, November 7, 1925.

130   "very powerful kings": J. C. E. Sand and P. Bakker, *Amsterdam: Zooals het leeft en werkt* (Amsterdam: Scheltens & Giltay, 1933).

130   "the young man [cycling]": "Andere gevaren," *Het Algemeen Handelsblad*, July 25, 1925.

130   "a shop servant with a divan": Ibid.

130   "four, five, six cake boxes": Ibid.

130   "flower pots, hat boxes": "Amsterdam op straat," *De Sumatra Post*, February 16, 1928.

130 "much-maligned, fast-riding butcher boy": "Het publiek over het verkeer," *De Telegraaf*, October 28, 1932.

131 "Messenger boys think nothing": Aldous Huxley, *Along the Road* (New York: George H. Doran, 1925).

131 "You people do everything": Barbarossa, "Stadsschoon, Rokinwater en Fietsomanie."

131 "The cyclist who is black with soot": Murray J. Brown, "Holland Is Nation of Pedalers Where Bike Is King of Road," *Hartford Courant*, January 5, 1964.

132 "Naturally," remarked one: Josef van Schaik, "Wijziging van de Motor- en Rijwielwet," *Handelingen Tweede Kamer 1923–1924* (The Hague: Algemeene Landsdrukkerij, 1924).

132 "courting couples": Capek, *Letters from Holland*.

132 "a pretty young girl": U. M. Unicume, "With the S.S. Vienna to Amsterdam and The Hague," *London & North Eastern Railway Magazine*, 1934.

132 "lovers": William S. Hall, "Salesman in Scandinavia," *Saturday Review*, May 11, 1935.

132 "couples holding hands": "Light from the Dark Continent," *Gopher Peavey*, 1936.

132 "the male party riding": "De Nederlandsche voetganger sterft uit," *Rotterdamsche Nieuwsblad*, January 2, 1937.

132 "a maid and a youth": Hendrik de Leeuw, *Crossroads of the Zuider Zee* (Philadelphia: Lippincott, 1938).

132 "frock coat": Frank Schoonmaker, *Come with Me Through Belgium and Holland* (New York: R. M. McBride, 1928).

133 "The life's motto of Dutch men": "De man en zijn fiets," *De Groene Amsterdammer*, July 15, 1939.

133 "As soon as a boy asks": Anne Frank, *Het Achterhuis* (Amsterdam: Contact, 1947).

133 "courting cyclists who ride hand in hand": "Parkeren en rechtshouden," *Het Algemeen Handelsblad*, March 17, 1933.

134 "put an end to this evil": *Gemeenteblad van Amsterdam*, deel I (1933).

134 "Let the sun shine in the water!": "Parkeren en rechtshouden," *Het Algemeen Handelsblad*, March 17, 1933.

135 "In fashionable quarters": "Bulb Sunday in Tulip Land," *Christian Science Monitor*, April 4, 1931.

135 "courting couples cycling": "Een Duitscher in de bollenvelden," *De Leidsche Courant*, April 28, 1933.

136 "flags on the handlebars": "De hoogtijdag der bollenvelden," *Het Vaderland*, April 23, 1934.

136 "many with bare legs": "De eerste bollen-zondag," *Het Vaderland*, April 16, 1934.

136 "to make it easier": "De hoogtijdag der bollenvelden," *Het Vaderland*, April 23, 1934.

136 "Everyone is gay": Marguerite Vance, *Capitals of the World* (New York: Thomas Y. Crowell, 1938).

136 "battlefield of human hordes": "De eerste bollen-zondag," *Het Vaderland*, April 16, 1934.

136 "And whenever a bicycle": "Bollen-Zondagavond," *Het Algemeen Handelsblad*, April 28, 1930.

136 "wanted nothing from the first ten": Ibid.

137 "bombarded with more beauty": Lawton Mackall, "Springtime in Tulip Land," *Atlanta Constitution*, April 8, 1928.

137 "soft-red": "Bollenzondag," *Het Vaderland*, April 28, 1930.

137 "wine-red": Ibid.

137 "glowing-red": Ibid.

137 "bright-red": "Bollen-Zondagavond," *Het Algemeen Handelsblad*, April 28, 1930.

137 "burning-red": "Duizenden trokken naar de bloeiende bollenvelden," *Rotterdamsche Nieuwsblad*, April 29, 1940.

137 "blood-red": Mackall, "Springtime in Tulip Land."

137 "a pasture overflowing": "Bollen-Zondagavond," *Het Algemeen Handelsblad*, April 28, 1930.

137 "The intoxicating fumes": "Bolletjes-dag," *De Nieuwe Rotterdamsche Courant*, May 10, 1929.

137 "orgy of color and scent": "De uittocht naar bloemenland!," *De Leidsche Courant*, May 10, 1929.

137 "dusty, hot, and happy": "In Tulip Land," *Times of London*, April 11, 1916.

137 "literally festooned": Mackall, "Springtime in Tulip Land."

137 "But the most beautiful": "Bolletjes-dag," *De Nieuwe Rotterdamsche Courant*, May 10, 1929.

138 "It's just like Leidseplein": Otto van Tussenbroek, "Bollenzondag," *De Groene Amsterdammer*, April 8, 1933.

138 "Good Lord": "Wij tellen . . . ," *Het Volk*, October 2, 1930.

138 "a secretive green switchboard box": "Verkeers-nieuwigheden in weking," *Het Algemeen Handelsblad*, October 17, 1932.

139   "This morning was the first": "Waar lichten wenken," *De Telegraaf,*
       October 17, 1932.

139   "think back to my first day": Cohen, "Gerrit Brinkman," *Ons Amster-
       dam,* February 1951.

139   "Amsterdammers who had taken": Van Siegen, "Brieven uit de Hoofd-
       stad," *Leeuwarder Courant,* October 22, 1932.

139   "unsuspecting cyclists": Ibid.

139   "First they lure you": "Dat is propaganda," *Het Volk,* October 17, 1932.

139   "a slight improvement": "Z. M. de fietser: Koning der straat," *De
       Telegraaf,* June 5, 1934.

140   "It's a recognized fact": "Een waarschuwing voor wielrijders," *Het Alge-
       meen Handelsblad,* November 17, 1936.

140   "hard to imagine there's a city": C. A. Castrikum, "'Ik zeg, dat de fiets-
       ers de oorzaak zijn,'" *Het Volk,* December 7, 1937.

140   "has done more for the spreading": Luger and Spier, *De Amsterdammer.*

140   "dangerous and equally ridiculous situation": "Achterlichtmisère," *De
       Telegraaf,* July 21, 1938.

141   "when high schools or factories or workplaces": "Het euvel der fietsers,"
       Het Algemeen Handelsblad, January 8, 1929.

141   "Proper traffic discipline": "Het loopen in een grote stad," *Het Algemeen
       Handelsblad,* August 12, 1930.

141   "has, among the cities of the world": "Commissaris Bakker jubileert 25
       jaar verkeersdictator," *De Telegraaf,* December 2, 1937.

141   "A story goes that a foreign tourist": "Het land der velocipedisten," *De
       Groene Amsterdammer,* July 13, 1940.

141   "unexpected complications": "Van behoorlijke fietsers en van onbe-
       hoorlijke," *Het Vaderland,* November 21, 1940.

141   "the nightmare of the motorists": "Een Franschman over ons land," *Het
       Vaderland,* May 23, 1928.

142   "Dreadful": "Met de Zwitsersche Post door onze Haagse omstreken,"
       Het Vaderland, January 23, 1929.

142   "The bicycle rules the road": Edward William Beattie, *Freely to Pass*
       (New York: Thomas Y. Crowell, 1942).

142   "[T]raffic in Holland": "One Land Keeps the Bicycle," *New York Times,*
       July 2, 1928.

143   "It took us two days": John Henry Cowles, "Journeyings of the Grand
       Commander," *New Age,* September 1936.

143   "Most vivid recollection": "Europe in a Day," *Christian Science Monitor,*
       September 30, 1937.

143   "In America I had my own car": Sarah Williams Bosman, "Life in
Holland," *New York Times*, October 10, 1937.

8: Which One's the Wrench?: The Settling Down
152   "The bike was in a pretty good condition": "Dutch Woman Reunited
With Stolen Bike After 24 Years," *San Diego Union-Tribune*, September 30, 2003.

9: We Were True Libertines: The First Two Years of the Occupation
159   "Swift and Nimble—Composed and Dignified": L. J. P. Knoops,
De Militaire Wielrijders (Son, Netherlands: Stichting Militaire Wielrijders, 1995).
159   "[T]he surprising spectacle": "Legerdag met Defilé Begonnen," *Het
Nieuws van de Dag*, July 30, 1938.
160   "We bike sometimes for ten hours": Knoops, *De Militaire Wielrijders*.
160   "sparked off laughter": P. J. Jager, "Het fietsen in Nederland," *Het Vaderland*, December 4, 1936.
161   "Our queen rides a bike": "Mijn Vriend de Thuiszitter," *De Groene Amsterdammer*, March 11, 1939.
161   "the declared objective": *Die Reichsstraßenverkehrsordnung vom 28. Mai
1934* (1934).
161   "Ultimately, we want": "Hitler kondigt de volksauto aan," *Het Vaderland*, December 18, 1937.
161   "Germany will be teeming with cars": "De Duitsche volksauto," *Het
Vaderland*, May 31, 1938.
162   "The great amusement": "De zonnige Hemelvaartsdag," *Het Nieuws
van de Dag*, May 3, 1940.
162   "Cyclists have a dangerous job": Knoops, *De Militaire Wielrijders*.
162   "The Cyclists put up a tough resistance": "De miskende kracht van de
Wielrijders," *Algemeen Dagblad*, July 28, 1992.
163   "while not translatable": Harry P. van Walt, *The Night Is Far Spent*
(Philadelphia: Dorrance, 1945).
164   "The Netherland people bicycle": "Dutch People Try to Find New
Life," *New York Times*, May 22, 1940.
164   "We are now in Amsterdam": Edward Tangye Lean, *Voices in the Darkness* (London: Secker & Warburg, 1943).
164   "fantastically high": "Heel Nederland op de fiets," *Het Algemeen
Handelsblad*, May 20, 1940.

165   "And now, due to the circumstances": "Leger der Amsterdamsche fiets-
        ers groiet," *De Gooi- en Eemlander*, July 16, 1940.

165   "The city is populated with swarms": "Fietsen," *De Groene Amsterdam-
        mer*, June 8, 1940.

165   "For 32 years": "Het land der velocipedisten," *De Groene Amsterdammer*,
        July 13, 1940.

166   "The 'people murderers'": "Allemaal op de fiets, ook de post!," *Het Volk*,
        September 4, 1940.

166   "Drivers worked diligently": Louis de Jong and Joseph W. F. Stoppel-
        man, *The Lion Rampant* (New York: Querido, 1943).

167   "The motorist, who always": "Berlijnsche vervoermiddelen," *De Nieuwe
        Rotterdamsche Courant*, April 10, 1926.

167   "with great doggedness": "Een Duitscher in de bollenvelden," *De
        Leidsche Courant*, April 28, 1933.

168   "the general public of Amsterdam": "Men houdt zich strict aan ver-
        keersregels," *Het Algemeen Handelsblad*, May 20, 1940.

168   "important position": "De maximumsnelheid om drie redenen vast-
        gesteld," *Het Vaderland*, August 6, 1940.

168   "six, seven or eight cyclists": Ibid.

169   "It is fully understandable": "Van behoorlijke fietsers en van onbehoor-
        lijke," *Het Vaderland*, November 21, 1940.

170   "We were true libertines": "Van fietsers en trammers," *Leeuwarder Cou-
        rant*, December 9, 1940.

170   "like an ordinary person": Frits Boersma, *Dagboek van Nederland* (Am-
        sterdam: Elsevier, 1984).

170   "If the conditions there": M. H. Brave-Maks, *De Koningin in Londen*
        (Zutphen, Netherlands: Walburg Pers, 1980).

171   "Ten pounds, Madam": Ibid.

171   "You see!": Ibid.

171   "blackout paper": "Lezers vragen," *Het Vaderland*, July 10, 1940.

172   "If a pedestrian does not fall": "In Holland," *Washington Post*, March 9, 1941.

172   "It seems as though": "Overstelpende fietsersstroom en . . . geen ver-
        keerslantaarns," *Het Volk*, November 14, 1940.

174   "undisciplined behavior of the cyclists": "Strenger optreden tegen fiets-
        ers," *Het Algemeen Handelsblad*, November 15, 1940.

174   "according to their own free will": Letter from SS and Police Leader
        Hanns Rauter to Secretary-General K. J. Frederiks, October 16, 1940.

174   "the shameless louts": "Van behoorlijke fietsers en van onbehoorlijke,"
        Het Vaderland, November 21, 1940.

174 "There are now so many bikes": "Overstelpende fietsersstroom en . . . geen verkeerslantaarns," *Het Volk*, November 14, 1940.

174 "Cyclists may not hold on to each other": "Waaraan de fietser zich houden moet," *De Telegraaf*, November 18, 1940.

175 "It would be bad": H. U. Wiesselmann, "Die Tandem-Taxe," *Deutsche Illustrierte Zeitung*, September 12, 1942.

175 "We have now yanked out": "Overstelpende fietsersstroom en . . . geen verkeerslantaarns," *Het Volk*, November 14, 1940.

175 "We will have to act even more stringently": "Het kostte ruim tweeduizen ventielen," *De Maasbode*, December 6, 1940.

175 "added surprise": Ibid.

176 "This measure was only very recently": Ibid.

176 "awfully nineteenth-century-ish": "Van fietsers en trammers," *Leeuwarder Courant*, December 9, 1940.

176 "reduce the premature wear and tear": Letter from SS and Police Leader Hanns Rauter to Secretary-General K. J. Frederiks, December 1940.

176 "How are your bike tires?": "Sanatorium voor banden," *Het Vaderland*, March 21, 1941.

177 "To get a new tire": De Jong and Stoppelman, *The Lion Rampant*.

177 "We must go easy": "Wie moeten zuinig zijn met onze fietsbanden," *Rotterdamsch Nieuwsblad*, April 17, 1941.

178 "People repeatedly ride their bikes": "Verscherpte distributie fietsbanden," *Rotterdamsch Nieuwsblad*, July 1, 1941.

178 "began to rise in value": De Jong and Stoppelman, *The Lion Rampant*.

178 "The bicycle is currently a very costly": "Rijwielstallingen doen goed zaken," *Het Algemeen Handelsblad*, October 9, 1941.

179 "There used to be many people": "Leger der Amsterdamsche fietsers groiet," *De Gooi- en Eemlander*, July 16, 1940.

179 "It is hereby forbidden": "Parkeren rijwielen's nachts verboden," *Het Algemeen Handelsblad*, June 5, 1941.

179 "Within the first hours": "Doe uw fiets op slot!," *Het Algemeen Handelsblad*, August 18, 1941.

180 "The custom has shown": "Uw fiets bij donker niet op straat!," *De Telegraaf*, November 19, 1941.

180 "proof that the occupying government": "Van 1 Mei af geen rijwielbelasting meer," *Het Vaderland*, April 24, 1941.

181 "an antisocial measure": Letter from Anton Mussert to Reich's Commissioner Arthur Seyss-Inquart, February 10, 1944, NIOD collection 123, inventory 924.

181   "fought against in vain": Ferdinand H. M. Grapperhaus, *Over de loden last van het koperen fietsplaatje* (Deventer, Netherlands: Kluwer, 2005).

181   "All of Holland is happy": "Opheffing rijwielbelasting," *Noordbrabantsch Dagblad Het Huisgezin*, April 21, 1941.

182   "Dutch rickshaw": "Moderne rickshaw," *Het Algemeen Handelsblad*, June 12, 1940.

182   "Chinese of Europe": [untitled], *Het Algemeen Handelsblad*, June 24, 1940.

182   "There are races and peoples": "Modern slavendom: Den Germaanschen mensch onwaardig," *Volk en Vaderland*, May 16, 1941.

183   "The Germans argued for the enactment": "Rijwieltaxi's zijn verboden," *Het Algemeen Handelsblad*, May 19, 1941.

184   "delicate souls": "Onze beschermers miskend?," *Vrij Nederland*, June 15, 1941.

184   "[The pedicab drivers] would": Ibid.

185   "The chauffeur does the pedaling": "Holland Has Bike Chauffeurs," *Christian Science Monitor*, July 13, 1940.

185   "if so desired, the passenger": M. J. Adriani Engels and G. H. Wallach, *Nacht over Nederland* ([Utrecht]: Ons Vrije Nederland, 1945).

185   "When the train arrived": Wiesselmann, "Die Tandem-Taxe."

186   "snake pattern": "Fietsers rechts van de weg!," *De Telegraaf*, November 29, 1941.

186   "The occasional disorderly conduct": Ibid.

187   "During the occupation": "Veiliger verkeer voor stad en land," *De Rotterdammer*, November 4, 1946.

10: Smash Your Bike to Bits, Slice Your Tires to Pieces: The Mass Bike Confiscation

189   "enormous success": "Theater van de Lach," *Het Joodsche Weekblad*, January 2, 1942.

189   "ode to the bicycle": "Revue Willy Rosen," *Het Joodsche Weekblad*, December 26, 1941.

190   "If you spend a beautiful Sunday": "Men neme hun fietsen!," *De Misthoorn*, May 23, 1942.

190   "Today we have entered": Etty Hillesum, *Het verstoorde leven*, ed. J. G. Gaarlandt (Haarlem: De Haan, 1981).

191   "Last Wednesday we all had to": Edith Velmans-van Hessen, *Het verhaal van Edith* (Amsterdam: Podium, 1997).

191   "Father gave Mother's": Frank, *Het Achterhuis*.

191   "It does not appear": "Calmeyer gibt folgenden Zwischenbericht zur Fahrradaktion," July 20, 1942, NIOD collection 20, inventory 1688.

191   "The condition of the delivered bikes": Letter from Rüstungsinspekteur to Generalkommissar Hans Fischböck, July 18, 1942, NIOD collection 20, inventory 1688.

191   "forbidden from making use": "Tweede Beschikking," *Het Nieuws van de Dag*, July 1, 1942.

192   "This week, they've stolen": Niek van der Oord, *Jodenkampen* (Kampen, Netherlands: Kok, 2003).

192   "It's sweltering": Frank, *Het Achterhuis*.

193   "as soon as possible": "Beschlagnahme von Fahrrädern," July 9, 1942, NIOD collection 20, inventory 1688.

195   "Word spread through the city": "Het Verhaal van een Vluchteling," *De Varende Hollander*, December 1, 1942.

195   "Some policemen warned": T. M. Sjenitzer–van Leening, ed., *Dagboekfragmenten 1940–1945* (The Hague: Nijhoff, 1954).

196   "the kind-hearted Amsterdam policeman": Engels and Wallach, *Nacht over Nederland*.

196   "The result was beautiful": Jan Cornelis van den Berg, diary entry, July 20, 1942, NIOD collection 244, inventory 1264.

196   "The element of surprise": Letter from Mayor Edward J. Voûte to Reich's Commissioner Attorney Hans Calmeyer, July 23, 1942, NIOD collection 20, inventory 1688.

196   "Today Amsterdam was a different": C. J. van Buuren, diary entry, July 20, 1942, NIOD collection 244, inventory 1230.

197   "This operation created a great excitement": "Stimmungsmässige Auswirken durch die Beschlagnahme der Fahrräder," July 20, 1942, NIOD collection 20, inventory 323.

197   "The trams were besieged": "Het Verhaal van een Vluchteling," *De Varende Hollander*, December 1, 1942.

197   "Toward noon": Engels and Wallach, *Nacht over Nederland*.

197   "This measure . . . forced": Ibid.

197   "If they want to get to Germany": Van den Berg, diary entry, July 21, 1942.

197   "One thing's for sure": Ibid.

198   "Everyone warned everyone": Van den Berg, diary entry, July 20, 1942.

198   "Civil servants were exempt": Sjenitzer–van Leening, ed., *Dagboekfragmenten 1940–1945*.

199   "The police officers are lenient": Ibid.

199   "old ham with the most impossible tires": Wehrmachtbefehlshaber Nederland, "Feldkommandantur 724: 'Lage- und Stimmungsbericht Nr. 25,'" July 31, 1942.

199 "Found among the seized bicycles": Wehrmachtbefehlshaber Nederland, "Feldkommandantur 724: 'Lage- und Stimmungsbericht Nr.
26,'" August 29, 1942.

199 "a sudden, savage attack": "Moderne struikrooverij," *Vrij Nederland*,
July 23, 1942.

199 "the German *zwijntjesjagers*": "Zwijntjesjagers! De massale rijwieldief-
stal door de Duitsche bezetters," *Het Parool*, July 25, 1942.

200 "BIKE THEFT": "Fietsen diefstal door de nazi horden," ca. July/Au-
gust 1942, NIOD signature IP30.23.

201 "Probably no German measure": Wehrmachtbefehlshaber Nederland,
"Feldkommandantur 724: 'Lage- und Stimmungsbericht Nr. 26.'"

201 "The seizure of the bicycles": Wehrmachtbefehlshaber Nederland,
"Feldkommandantur 724: 'Lage- und Stimmungsbericht Nr. 25.'"

201 "The whole thing caused a large rift": Report from Otto Bene to the
German Ministry of Foreign Affairs, August 1, 1942, NIOD collection 266, inventory BBT 4852.

202 "widely discussed": Ibid.

202 "If the bicycle seizure": Wehrmachtbefehlshaber Nederland, "Feldkommandantur 724: 'Lage- und Stimmungsbericht Nr. 26.'"

202 "inflamatory": "Stimmungsmässige Auswirken durch die Beschlagnahme der Fahrräder."

203 "was very versatile and quick": "Calmeyer gibt folgenden Zwischenbericht zur Fahrradaktion."

203 "In our capital city mentality": Sand and Bakker, *Amsterdam: Zooals het
leeft en werkt.*

204 "In cases of bomb attacks": Jetje Baruch and Liesbeth van der Horst,
Het Rijksmuseum in oorlogstijd (Amsterdam: Rijksmuseum, 1985).

204 "The bearer of this permit": Pieter Smit, *Artis: een Amsterdamse Tuin*
(Amsterdam: Rodopi, 1988).

205 "In contrast to the vast majority": Letter from Secretary-General K. J.
Frederiks to Mayor Edward J. Voûte, July 27, 1942, NIOD collection
20, inventory 1688.

205 "By order of the German Army": Mayor Edward J. Voûte, "Gemeente
Amsterdam," leaflet, July 28, 1942.

205 "Good job, Amsterdam!": Van den Berg, diary entry, July 29, 1942.

206 "This is how it is": "Het Verhaal van een Vluchteling," *De Varende Hollander*, December 1, 1942.

206 "Ingenious couples knew how": J. H. D. Kammeijer, *5 jaar onder
Duitschen druk* (Laren, Netherlands: Schoonderbeek, 1946).

206   "The Amsterdam ladies": Wiesselmann, "Die Tandem-Taxe."

207   "The measure had a devastating": "Fahrräder-Beschlagnahme," July 21, 1942, NIOD collection 77, inventory 992.

207   "Due to the arrival of motorized units": Letter to Secretary-General K. J. Frederiks, August 7, 1942, NIOD collection 212a, inventory 2a.

208   "terrible hurry": Frank, *Het Achterhuis*.

11: You No Longer Think, You Just Pedal: The Final Years of the Occupation

209   "Resistance came in all forms": Werkman, *'nn Grote stad op palen*.

210   "There was doctors' resistance": Bianca Stigter, *De Bezette Stad* (Amsterdam: Athenaeum-Polak & Van Gennep, 2005).

211   "All over the city": Mirjam Bolle, *Ik zal je beschrijven hoe een dag er hier uitziet* (Amsterdam: Contact, 2003).

211   "Just look on the streets": "Gevonden," *Dagblad voor Leiden en Omstreken*, November 22, 1944.

211   "Tacks and broken glass": "Moderne struikrooverij," *Vrij Nederland*, July 23, 1942.

211   "Their tires are now as precious": "Scherven die geen geluk brengen," *De Telegraaf*, May 25, 1943.

212   "Glass is the nightmare of every cyclist": "Glas op den weg," *De Telegraaf*, April 24, 1944.

212   "belonged to the other side": "De politie houdt grote schoonmaak," *De Spiegel*, November 15, 1958.

212   "cushion tires": Rudi Boltendal, "Dr. L. de Jongs steeds omvangrijker wordende boeken leiden voor de lezer tot slijtageslag," *Leeuwarder Courant*, October 30, 1976.

212   "anti-pop tires": "Voor fietsend Amsterdam," *De Waarheid*, October 21, 1946.

212   "solid tires": van Ribbentel-Magerbuick [pseud. for John C. Kennis], *O, dat Winterje '45* (Amsterdam: Tulpebol, Pulpeknol & Groot-Smullenburg, 1945).

212   "It wasn't pleasant cycling": J. G. Raatgever Jr., *Van dollen dinsdag tot de bevrijding* (Amsterdam: De Telg, 1945).

213   "only a slight rattle": "Geen lekke banden meer," *Hilversum Courant*, August 19, 1941.

213   "an irritating tumult": Leo Molenaar, *Marcel Minnaert, astrofysicus, 1893–1970* (Amsterdam: Balans, 2003).

213   "skip over the cobblestones": "Stadslawaai in andere toonaarden," *De Courant*, May 31, 1944.

213   Tireless bikes became known as "tanks": Ewoud Sanders, *Fiets! De ge-schiedenis van een vulgair jongenswoord* (The Hague: Sdu Uitgevers, 1997).

213   "These cyclists no longer need": "Stadslawaai in andere toonaarden," *De Courant*, May 31, 1944.

214   "what they call in Amsterdam": Gera van Schouwenburg, *Als je bent een grootmama . . . : Herinneringen aan bezet Amsterdam* (Amsterdam: [n.p.], 1994).

214   "spin around like a top": *Nederland in oorlogstijd* (Amsterdam: Stichting tot Uigave van Publicaties van het Rijksinstitut voor Oorlogsdocumentatie, 1946).

214   "a meticulous inspection": Engels and Wallach, *Nacht over Nederland*.

214   "The bike?": "Het land der velocipedisten," *De Groene Amsterdammer*, July 13, 1940.

215   "A jittery tension drives everyone": Bert Voeten, *Doortocht: Een oorlogs-dagboek, 1940–1945* (Amsterdam: Contact, 1946).

216   "Raids were launched on bicycles": Guustaaf de Clerq, *Amsterdam tijdens de hongerperiode* (Amsterdam: Van Soest, 1945).

216   "We cycle slowly through Amsterdam": Anonymous, diary entry, ca. September 5, 1944, NIOD collection 244, inventory 1164.

217   "As the front came closer": Caspers, *To Save a Life*.

217   "Bike confiscation": Peter Lindeman, *Herinneringen van een Amster-dammer* (Amsterdam: [n.p.], 1971).

218   "Neither the dismissal": "Concerten, ondanks alles," *De Vrije Kunste-naar*, December 1, 1944.

219   "A 'Dutchman' shoots": "Hard tegen hard," *Ons Volk*, September 15, 1944.

219   "From the headquarters of the Führer": Engels and Wallach, *Nacht over Nederland*.

220   "We live . . . without gas, light, electricity": Maria Takkenberg, diary entry, January 13, 1945, NIOD collection 244, inventory 1520.

221   "At this moment, we're just dogs": Takkenberg, diary entry, January 24, 1945.

221   "too little to live on": Nico Buijten, diary entry, November 12, 1944, NIOD collection 244, inventory 1694.

222   "busier than Kalverstraat": G. J. Kruijer, *Hongertochten: Amsterdam tijdens de hongerwinter* (Meppel, Netherlands: Boom, 1951).

222   "endless processions": Louis van Gasteren, "De Gysbrecht redde mij . . . ," *Dagblad voor Amersfoort*, April 7, 1948.

222   "At four a.m.": P. A. Donker, *Winter '44–'45* (Bilthoven, Netherlands: Donker, 1945).

224 "An elderly man's front wheel": "Aardappelen Halen!," *De Waarheid*, January 12, 1945.

224 "staring at that broken wheel": *Lettergieterij Amsterdam gedenkboek 1939–1945* (Amsterdam: Lettergieterij "Amsterdam" voorheen N. Tetterode, 1947).

224 "Dreary is the road": "Aardappelen Halen!," *De Waarheid*, January 12, 1945.

224 "What an immense amount": Van Gasteren, "De Gysbrecht redde mij . . ."

225 "robbers of a different feather": Pieter Oostervink, *De Weg: Oorlogsdagboek* (Rotterdam: Peter Oostervink, 1992).

225 "You had thus made the trip": Jan Huiberts and Peter Gramberg, *Zeven verhalen* (Amsterdam: Gemeente Amsterdam, Stadsdeel De Baarsjes, 2 225).

225 "our own completely shot to the hell": Henriëtte Mooy, *Het Duitse schrikbewind* (Utrecht: Ons Huis, 1970).

226 "On the IJ Ferry": Ibid.

226 "My rusted chain squeaks": Oostervink, *De Weg*.

227 "I stuffed [illegal leaflets]": J. D. Podolsky, "Life with Audrey," *People*, October 31, 1994.

228 "Once again, they're acting": Takkenberg, diary entry, March 8, 1945.

228 "green executioners": "Binnenland nieuws," *De Nieuwsbode*, April 7, 1945.

228 "green murderers": "Groene moordenaars voor Amsterdam," *Veritas*, October 11, 1944.

228 "green demons": Oostervink, *De Weg*.

228 "green bandits": "De Duitsche fietsendieven aan het werk," *Het Parool*, March 9, 1945.

228 "green thieves": "Razzia's in Amsterdam," *Het Parool*, February 19, 1945.

228 "green *moffen*": "Jodenvervolgingen zonder einde," *De Vonk*, September 29, 1942.

229 "Don't help the enemy gain means": "Fietsenrazzia's in Amsterdam," *Het Parool*, March 31, 1945.

230 "Near Doorn we were stopped": Caspers, *To Save a Life*.

12: Give My Father's Bike Back: The Occupation's Legacy

235 "chief robber": L. Pieters, "Gestolen fietsen," *Nieuwe Leidsche Courant*, May 30, 1973.

235 "turned over the essential transportation means": *Der Prozeß gegen die Hauptkriegsverbrecher vor dem Internationalen Militärgerichtshof Nürnberg*, vol. 16 (Nuremberg: Internat. Militärgerichtshof, 1946).

236   "The population of the occupied territory": *Het proces Rauter* (The Hague: Nijhoff, 1952).

238   "extremely poor condition": "De vooruitzichten zijn somber," *De Waarheid*, November 21, 1946.

238   "countless remains": "Geroofd fietsen na 20 jaar 'boven water,'" *De Telegraaf*, August 4, 1962.

238   "When the bicycle was found": Hans Koning, "A Life Colored by War," *Harper's*, May 1990.

239   "a symbolic deed": "Binnenland nieuws," *De Nieuwsbode*, May 15, 1945.

239   "A thousand and one problems": C. P. Stacey, "The German Surrender, May 1945," *Historical Section, Report No. 56*, U.S. Army Headquarters (1958).

239   "When I stand at a street corner": W. A. C., "Crazyland of Wheels," *Liberator*, July 4, 1945.

240   "You will hear people come rattling by": Johan Luger and G. H. Wallach, *All About Amsterdam* ([Amsterdam]: Salm, 1945).

241   "the wondrous appearance": Engels and Wallach, *Nacht over Nederland*.

242   "Because [the workers] had no tires": *Enquêtecommissie regeringsbeleid 1940–1945* (The Hague: Staatsdrukkerij- en Uitgeverijbedrijf, 1949).

242   "bizarre": Ibid.

243   "decided their most": "A Musician and His Bicycle," *New York Times*, March 16, 1946.

243   "second German invasion": "Op de tweede germansche invasive," *De Groene Amsterdammer*, April 24, 1954.

243   "zwei Helles": "Eerst m'n fiets terug," *De Groene Amsterdammer*, May 8, 1954.

243   "specially colored": "Dutch Send Sample Bikes to Test American Market," *Christian Science Monitor*, April 14, 1951.

244   "Amsterdam is known as a troublesome": "Verloofd paar ingehaald," *Het Parool*, July 3, 1965.

245   "after much injudicious fumbling": Joop van Tijn, "Amsterdam een republiek? Welnee!," *Vrij Nederland*, July 10, 1965.

245   "Long live the Republic!": "Smoke Bombs Mar Dutch Royal Wedding," *Edmonton Journal*, March 10, 1966.

246   "Give me back my bike!": Cottrell, *Amsterdam: The Life of a City*.

246   "I want my bike back": Konrad Boehmer and Ton Regtien, *Van Provo naar Oranje Vrijstaat* (Amsterdam: Socialistische Uitgeverij, 1970).

246   "I want my bicycle back": Matty Verkamman, "'Burenhaat' is zwaar overtrokken," *Trouw*, September 10, 1996.

246 "My grandpa asked me": Jaap Roelants, "Duitsers hebben niet veel fietsen terug te geven," *Algemeen Dagblad*, January 13, 1998.

247 "Germany-syndrome is off our backs": Arnold Mühren, *Nederland-Duitsland: Voetbalpoëzie*, ed. Theun de Winter (Amsterdam: Gerard Timmer, 1989).

247 "The German soldiers stole": "Soccer Fever in the Air," *New York Times*, July 17, 1988.

247 "Grandma, we've found": "Buitenlandse pers vol lof over Oranje," *Leidsch Dagblad*, June 27, 1988.

248 "Understandable": Henri Beunders, "Iedereen zichzelf," *Elsevier*, July 5, 1997.

248 "When asked why": "Prins Claus relativeert anti-Duitse houding jeugd," *De Volkskrant*, January 12, 1998.

13: After You Passed: The Mystery Rider

254 "I'll say what I think": "Theo van Gogh noemt Abou Jahjah pooier," *De Volkskrant*, May 10, 2004.

254 "goat fuckers": Theo van Gogh, "Ebru zonder schroom," *De Gezonde Roker*, March 24, 2004.

254 "My God is a pig": Theo van Gogh, "Het roze gevaarte," *Metro*, June 18, 2004.

254 "the pimp of the prophet": "Rel na schelden Van Gogh op leider AEL," *NRC Handelsblad*, May 10, 2004.

254 "He rode on his bike": *De Telegraaf*, "'Theo, pas je wel op?,'" November 4, 2004.

255 "I will not be intimidated": Ibid.

255 "dark rooms": Ivo Niehe, *TROS TV Show*, January 15, 2002.

256 "Have mercy!": [untitled], *De Volkskrant*, November 2, 2005.

256 "And you always cycled": Frenk der Nederlanden, "Frenk neemt afscheid van een buurtbewoner," *Het Parool*, November 3, 2004.

257 "On a bike, you take certain": René Moerland and Frank Vermeulen, "'Fundamentalisme is eigen aan ieder mens,'" *NRC Handelsblad*, December 28, 2004.

257 "symbolic bike trip": Samenwerkende Nederlands-Marokkaanse Organisaties Amsterdam, "Fietsen voor verbondenheid," November 8, 2004.

258 "When I step into a Turkish": Annelies Smit, "Allochtoon zit liever in auto dan op fiets," *Algemeen Dagblad*, May 19, 2004.

258 "Especially Turks, Surinamers and Hindustanis": Noor Tonkens, "Iedereen moet op de fiets," *Het Parool*, May 21, 2004.

259   "If you have a good job": Aafke Verbeek, "Met een djellaba aan kan je niet fietsen . . ." (dissertation, 2007).

259   "In Morocco": Ibid.

260   "If she sits on a bike": Ibid.

260   "As a Muslim woman": Ibid.

14: It's Chaos with the Bicycles: The 1950s

265   "metropolitan flourish": "'STOP' geldt ook voor wielrijders," *Trouw*, November 22, 1949.

265   "a young couple": Weil and Weil, *Grandparents Go Abroad*.

266   "Not a single cyclist": "Langzaam verkeer, pas op uw tellen," *De Tijd*, March 6, 1948.

267   "They strut to the cycle garage": Albert Alberts, "Van Spitsuur naar Pampus," *De Groene Amsterdammer*, November 12, 1955.

268   "tight jams": "Binnenstad overvol tijdens 'vervroegd spitsuur,'" *Het Nieuws van de Dag*, December 6, 1955.

268   "December 5th chaos": "Binnenstad was om half zes leeg," *Het Vrije Volk*, December 6, 1967.

268   "ghostly quiet": Adam, "Langs de wallekant," *Het Vrije Volk*, December 6, 1957.

268   "It's competely superfluous": Ibid.

269   "The dumbest thing": Henri Knap, "Wees Luilak te slim af!," *Het Parool*, June 3, 1960.

269   "I saw . . . many children": Wouter Jacobsz, *Dagboek van Broeder Wouter Jacobsz*, ed. I. H. van Eeghen (Groningen: Wolters, 1960).

270   "Because those are exactly": "Veel luilak-rumoer met weinig schade," *Het Parool*, June 4, 1960.

271   "Filthy traitors!": "Bioscoopstunt ging erin!," *Het Vrije Volk*, May 24, 1958.

271   "Especially the bicycles": "Luilak ontaardt in enorm vandalisme," *Het Vrije Volk*, May 20, 1961.

272   "Don't ever believe": "Fietsers negeren parkeertegels," *Het Nieuws van de Dag*, November 7, 1958.

273   "In the already cramped city center": "Amsterdam weet met fietsen geen weg meer," *Het Vrije Volk*, May 17, 1956.

273   "Bicycles Parked Here": Henri Knap, "Amsterdams Dagboek," *Het Parool*, June 22, 1955.

273   "Now I've seen everything": "Fietsers negeren parkeertegels," *Het Nieuws van de Dag*, November 7, 1958.

273 "forbidden places": "Politie zuivert straat van honderden fietsen," *Het Nieuws van de Dag*, August 8, 1956.

274 "Indeed, people know": "'Geen fietsen op die brug!,'" *Trouw*, October 15, 1955.

274 "On some days": Ibid.

274 "Warnings don't appear": Ibid.

274 "on bread and water": Ibid.

274 "the scene of the chaos": "In het gelid," *Het Vrije Volk*, October 30, 1957.

274 "For years on end": Ibid.

275 "How is it possible": "Ongelooflijk, maar toch waar!," *De Kampioen*, [unknown month] 1898.

275 "fighting a losing battle": "In het gelid," *Het Vrije Volk*, October 30, 1957.

275 "Maybe we'll never": Ibid.

276 "bicycle graveyard": "Hoofdstad bindt strijd aan met fietsenplaag," *De Gelderlander*, October 22, 1958.

276 "There they stand": "De politie houdt grote schoonmaak," *De Spiegel*, November 15, 1958.

276 "First, the bell disappears": Ibid.

276 "Amsterdam is already": "Amsterdam weet met fietsen geen weg meer," *Het Vrije Volk*, May 17, 1956.

276 "make a clean sweep": "De politie houdt grote schoonmaak," *De Spiegel*, November 15, 1958.

276 "Wherever a wreck is removed": "Fietsers negeren parkeertegels," *Het Nieuws van de Dag*, November 7, 1958.

277 "It's chaos with the bicycles": Flex, "Uw gestolen fiets staat op straat," *Trouw*, March 1, 1958.

277 "In view of people's borrowing habits": Hugo Brandt Corstius, "Fietsen," *Propria Cures*, June 14, 1958.

278 "a very large space": Unpublished interview, July 28, 1965, IISG, Provo archive, box 50, folder 8.

278 "They leave it be": "De politie houdt grote schoonmaak," *De Spiegel*, November 15, 1958.

279 "Maybe—if we look": Jen Vlietstra, "Bescherm die grillige fietsers!," *Het Vrije Volk*, October 8, 1955.

280 "Hey lady": J. F. Loois, *Koningin Wilhelmina*, ed. C. A. Tamse (Alphen aan den Rijn, Netherlands: Sijthoff, 1981).

280 "nutty incidents": Ibid.

280 "two severe lumps": Cees Fasseur, *Wilhelmina: Krijgshaftig in een vormeloze jas* ([Amsterdam]: Balans, 2001).

281 "ready to be ridden": Booy, *De levensavond van Koningin Wilhelmina.*

281 "Queen on a bicycle": Daniel L. Schorr, "A Dutch Woman Who Happens to Be Queen," *New York Times*, March 30, 1952.

282 "cool as a cucumber": "Leidsestraat weer open, maar niet voor fietsers," *Trouw*, October 3, 1960.

282 "The policemen": "Parkeerverbod voor grachten," *De Volkskrant*, October 4, 1960.

283 "Big money wins out again": Ibid.

283 "The common man": Ibid.

283 "In three months": "Velen nog via oude route," *Het Nieuws van de Dag*, October 3, 1960.

283 "severe damage": "Winkeliers prefereren een fietsloze Leidsestraat," *Het Nieuws van de Dag*, November 22, 1960.

283 "My steady customers": Ibid.

283 "During the day": Ibid.

283 "unorganized": W. Valderpoort, *Het zelfzuchtige personenauto* (Amsterdam: G. van Saane "Lectura Architectonica," 1953).

285 "No need to fuss": "Fietsers in Leidsestraat," *Het Parool*, October 29, 1960.

285 "A special route": "Fietsroute in overweging," *De Tijd*, March 8, 1961.

16: A Bike Is Something, Yet Almost Nothing!: The 1960s
293 "Mister, when I'm riding": "Veiligheid van fietser bestaat slechts in zijn dromen," *Het Nieuws van de Dag*, July 10, 1963.

295 "Yes, I've had a car": Aad van der Mijn, "'Politiek is 'n spel en ik probeert 't goed te spelen,'" *Het Parool*, January 14, 1967.

295 "It should be filled in": "Raadslid Hamers: 'Tegen politiek,'" *De Telegraaf*, June 1, 1962.

295 "Then, at least": Herman Hofhuizen, "De kleine partij," *De Tijd*, March 25, 1963.

296 "[I]n terms of public health": Dr. A. J. Dunning, *Het hartinfarct* (Amsterdam: Querido, 1966).

296 "The number of deaths and severe injuries": Henri Knap, *Twintig manieren om uw rijbewijs kwijt te raken* (Amsterdam: De Bezije Bij, 1968).

296 "The busyness": "Binnenstad was om half zes leeg," *Het Vrije Volk*, December 6, 1967.

296 "Amsterdammers!": "Provo's Fietsenplan," *Provokatie Nr. 5*, July 1965.

298   "[The bicycle] is a national symbol": Unpublished interview, July 28, 1965.

298   "It's an inversion": Ibid.

298   "We're called Provos": J. Van den Berg, "Het anarchism geprovoceerd," *Vrij Nederland*, July 24, 1965.

299   "a beautiful idea": Hugo Brandt Corstius, "Nieuwe Provoplannen," *Vrij Nederland*, August 28, 1965.

299   "I got this idea": Michael Apted, producer, *It's a Happening*, Granada Television, November 18, 1966.

299   known as its "father": Rozemarie Ruyter, "Luud Schimmelpennink," *Friese Koerier*, March 18, 1967.

299   "a very respectable man": Frans Bosman, "Een bevolgen idealist in harde kunststoffen," *Het Parool*, December 17, 1988.

300   "We're seeking something in between": Erik Olof, "Roel van Duijn: de zachtmoedige anarchist," *Haagse Courant*, August 5, 1965.

301   "have to imagine": Unpublished interview, July 28, 1965.

301   "I'll leave them be": "Provo-cerend cadeau voor hoofdstad," *Het Parool*, July 29, 1965.

302   "The mere idea": Hans Smits, "Het late gelijk van Provo," *Vrij Nederland*, September 29, 1990.

302   "The police have told us": "Roel van Duijn, de full-time provo," *Zutphens Dagblad*, March 23, 1966.

302   "That's the problem": Unpublished interview, July 28, 1965.

303   "It doesn't work": Roel van Duijn, *De Witte Gevaar* (Amsterdam: Meulenhoff, 1967).

304   "Recently, the anarchistic": Roel van Duijn, Luud Schimmelpennink and Rob Stolk, "Provo communiqué," August 9, 1965.

304   "warm sympathies": Martin van Amerongen, "De schepper van het Lieverdje," *Vrij Nederland*, August 21, 1965.

305   "shopkeepers, accountants": Henk J. Meier, "De vierde generatie," *Ratio*, August 1965.

305   "Coppers!": Van Duijn, *De Witte Gevaar*.

305   "I don't know": "Nachtmerrie rond het Lieverdje," *Wereldkroniek*, August 21, 1965.

306   "We continue to protest": Roel van Duijn, Luud Schimmelpennink et al., "Provo verklaring aan de pers," August 15, 1965.

306   "It is absolutely essential": Luud Schimmelpennink, "Provo's Fietsenplan," *PROVO*, no. 2 (August 17, 1965).

307   "The plan isn't working": Brigitte, "Intro's contra provo's," *De Telegraaf*, October 16, 1965.

308   "concrete political objectives": Duco van Weerlee, *Wat de provo's willen* (Amsterdam: De Bezije Bij, 1966).

308   "The Provos will soon see": "'Alles wit schilderen geen oplossing,'" *Trouw*, June 2, 1966.

309   "purchase of 3,000 white bicycles": *Gemeenteblad van Amsterdam*, Eerste Afdeling 1967.

309   "that, in a space where almost one million": Ibid.

309   "Exhaust fumes": Ibid.

310   "swan song": *Gemeenteblad van Amsterdam*, Tweede Afdeling (1967).

310   "torpedo": "'Witte-Fietsenplan' ter tafel," *De Telegraaf*, March 8, 1967.

310   "Bernhard de Vries doesn't believe": Martin Deelen, "Tijd van loop-gravenoorlog is voorbij," *De Telegraaf*, February 25, 1967.

311   "The car is antisocial": Aad van der Mijn, "Van Luud kunnen we wat leren," *Het Parool*, March 4, 1967.

312   "purchase and maintenance of 2,000": *Gemeenteblad van Amsterdam*, Eerste Afdeling 1967.

312   "That's not possible": *Gemeenteblad van Amsterdam*, Tweede Afdeling (1967).

313   "The bicycle was viewed as passé": Interview with the author, August 22, 2011.

313   "In the eyes of the politicians": Jaap Stam, "'Tijd is rijp voor wit vervoer,'" *De Volkskrant*, May 27, 2010.

17: A Big Success: The Urban Myths of the White Bicycles

316   "Hundreds of people": Interview with the author, November 5, 2002.

316   "[T]he experiment fizzled": Joyce van Meer, "Dutch Lead All Countries in Ownership of Bicycles," *Nashua Telegraph*, April 15, 1972.

316   "[T]he police started": Fazal Inayat-Khan, *Old Thinking, New Thinking* (San Francisco: Harper & Row, 1979).

316   "The plan worked": David P. Perry, *Bike Cult* (New York: Four Walls Eight Windows, 1995).

317   "[P]eople just took": *Let's Go Amsterdam: City Guide* (New York: St. Martin's Press, 2004).

317   "In the end, the bikes": John Ward Anderson, "Paris Embraces Plan to Become City of Bikes," *Washington Post*, March 24, 2007.

317   "Some people failed": Joep Huffener, "Bikes on Dikes: A Dutch Plan for (Almost) Free Wheeling," Amsterdam Department of Infrastructure, Traffic and Transport, June 2000.

317   "The city provides a free bike": Peter Lawlor, "Meditation," in *The Clear Creek Bike Book* (Bergenfield, NJ: New American Library, 1972).

318   "I had read about the bike program": Christopher R. Edginton, *Leisure and Life Satisfaction* (Boston: WCB/McGraw-Hill, 1998).

318   "We started telling": Jonathan Blank, producer/director, *Sex, Drugs and Democracy* (1994).

319   "There was this wonderful scene": "Portland Journal: Where Trust Rides a Yellow Bicycle," *New York Times*, December 9, 1994.

319   "somewhat damaged": Ibid.

319   "Our aim is to promote": Edward Epstein, "Free Bike Fleet Proposed for S. F.," *San Francisco Chronicle*, July 31, 1997.

319   "I'm sure a few bikes disappear": "Free Wheels," *Bicycling*, May 1995.

319   "You'd have to be pretty hard up": Bryan Smith, "Bicycle Built for You," *Oregonian*, November 20, 1994.

319   "You can't steal these bikes": "Take This Bike, Please," *New York Times*, December 18, 1994.

319   "We would rather": Epstein, "Free Bike Fleet Proposed for S. F."

320   "The program is modeled": Bryan Smith, "How the Idea Got Rolling," *Oregonian*, November 20, 1994.

320   "[I]n Holland": Marla Williams, "Bikes Give Portlanders Free Ride," *Seattle Times*, December 28, 1994.

320   "Amsterdam has a state-run": "Free Wheels," *Bicycling*, May 1995.

321   "Things were getting better": Mark Brunswick, "Here's a Free-Wheelin' Idea," *Star Tribune*, March 22, 1998.

321   "We put about one hundred bikes": Diego Bunel, "City Officials Lobby for Free Bike Program," *San Francisco Examiner*, September 25, 1996.

322   "A lot of folks took the bikes": Wade Nkrumah, "Failed Yellow Bikes Project Will Get Another Go-Round," *Oregonian*, October 20, 1997.

322   "It didn't take people long": Landon Hall, "Free bikes a nice idea, but . . . ," *San Francisco Examiner*, September 26, 1997.

323   "there are likely to be around 15,000 fewer": Huffener, "Bikes on Dikes."

323   "asshole-proof": Marcel van Engelen, "Witfiets gaat nu echt de straat op," *Het Parool*, January 8, 2000.

323   "a cross between": Monique Snoeijen, "Witte fiets (bis)," *NRC Handelsblad*, April 27, 1998.

324   "Who would buy a stolen": "Nog even en iedereen laat de auto staan," *Het Parool*, February 26, 2001.

324   "Despite the [improved] racks": Marieke van den Ende, "Witte fiets en Witkar nog steeds actueel," *Product*, July 2008.

324   "I think Schimmelpennink": Interview with the author, November 20, 2002.

324 "It's a shame": Van den Ende, "Witte fiets en Witkar nog steeds actueel."

325 "It's going to happen now": Stam, "'Tijd is rijp voor wit vervoer.'"

18: A Typical Amsterdam Characteristic: The Bike Fishermen

328 "It's unbelievable, but true": [untitled], *Schuitemakers Purmerender Courant*, October 15, 1919.

332 "a typical Amsterdam characteristic": "Exodus van het vuil uit Amsterdamse binnenwateren," *Het Nieuws van de Dag*, March 14, 1963.

332 "rubbish and garbage": Fernand Caussy, "Glimpses of Holland," *Living Age*, January 6, 1923.

332 "The Amsterdammer does not": "Stop ermee—vandaag nog!," *Wierings Weekrevue*, July 28, 1955.

332 "those traditional garbage cans": "De gracht als vuilnisbelt," *Trouw*, September 19, 1958.

332 "They float there": "Stop ermee—vandaag nog!," *Wierings Weekrevue*, July 28, 1955.

333 "No, nothing peculiar": "De gracht als vuilnisbelt," *Trouw*, September 19, 1958.

333 "After a laborious life": "Oudroest-hausse in ons land," *Leeuwarder Courant*, March 24, 1937.

334 "No bodies": William S. Hall, "Salesman in Scandinavia," *Saturday Review*, May 11, 1935.

334 "It's a captivating sight": Werkman, *'n Grote stad op palen*.

334 "As true Amsterdammers": "Amsterdam vervuilt door grote nonchalance van zijn bewoners," *Wierings Weekblad*, November 12, 1959.

334 "With this job, all day long": "Chronisch gebrek aan domme mensen," *De Volkskrant*, September 12, 1977.

335 "The city's beautiful canals": Henk Koetzier, "Vuilvergaren 'is niet smerig,'" *Het Parool*, August 1, 1977.

335 "If somebody threw something in": Barry Newman, "Amsterdam Bicycle Fisherman Wonders How They Got There," *Wall Street Journal*, July 25, 1996.

335 "from almost new to completely wrecked": "Amsterdam heeft rijwielstallingen onder water," *De Leidse Courant*, January 20, 1958.

336 "Every stab by the crane": "Fietsen vissen," *De Telegraaf*, February 24, 1982.

337 "Each wreck has a story": Hans Bouman, "Elk fietswrak heeft een verhaal," *De Volkskrant*, October 10, 1995.

340   "With a supple hand grip": Jef van der Heyden, *Fietsen naar de maan* (Blaricum, Netherlands: Bigot & Van Rossum, 1963).

19: Death to the Car!: The 1970s

343   "freaks, nomads": Izak Haber, "Tips from London & Amsterdam," *Rolling Stone*, June 8, 1972.

343   "Swinging Amsterdam": Jac. Vroemen, "Samkalden ziet liever Floriade dan het Vondelpark," *De Nieuwe Linie*, March 29, 1972.

343   "Magic Amsterdam": Jan Roelfs, "Gastvrouwen en gastheren international jeugdtoeristen," *Trouw*, July 1, 1972.

343   "Freak City": "Een freak-city op de Mookerij," *De Tijd*, June 3, 1972.

343   "the Youth Capital": Jules B. Farber, "Exploring the Hidden Soul of Europe's Hip Youth Capital," *New York Times*, March 19, 1972.

343   "Paradise": "Jeugd ziet Amsterdam als een paradijs," *De Stem*, March 28, 1972.

343   "divergent sexual practices": Haber, "Tips from London & Amsterdam."

343   "a new Sodom": John L. Hess, "Avant-Garde Right at Home in Amsterdam," *New York Times*, January 11, 1969.

343   "shrine for kids": Bernard Weinraub, "Dutch Club Is a Mecca for U.S. Youths," *New York Times*, July 2, 1971.

343   "Amsterdam is the magic center": Henk J. Meier, *Dit hap-hap-happens in Amsterdam* (Amsterdam: De Arbeiderspers, 1966).

344   "the free atmosphere": Farber, "Exploring the Hidden Soul of Europe's Hip Youth Capital."

344   "hippie flights": " 'Open de poort van Vondelpark, here we come,' " *Het Parool*, June 28, 1972.

344   "What really draws me": Wiecher Hulst, "Waarom naar Amsterdam?," *Het Parool*, July 1, 1972.

345   "The cyclist is the stepchild": Pieter Niehorster, "Fietser het stiefkind van de grote stad," *Het Parool*, May 10, 1971.

346   "On a *bakfiets*": "Protest-tocht met bakfietsen door het centrum," *Het Parool*, February 17, 1970.

346   "Of course it would be lunacy": Ibid.

347   "This was actually the practice run": "Bakfiets: hèt wapen tegen verkeers-escalatie," *Het Vrije Volk*, February 17, 1970.

347   "Dam Square sleepers!": Ibid.

348   "had no fixed routes": "Bakfietsen ontwrichten spitsverkeer in Amsterdam," *Het Algemeen Handelsblad*, March 2, 1970.

348   "But don't you think it's antisocial": Bert Vuijsje, "'Het verkeer rijdt zichzelf in de soep,'" *Haagse Post*, April 1, 1970.

348   "Death to the holy cow": Pieter Niehorster, "'Dood aan de heilige koe, weg ermee!,'" *Het Parool*, May 7, 1970.

349   "Capitalism has become so dependent": "'Particulier autoverkeer weren uit binnenstad,'" *Trouw*, June 12, 1970.

349   "an ecological transformation of society": Marina Groen, "Actievoeren en van binnenuit het systeem veranderen," *Ravage*, August 3, 2001.

350   "I am an air polluter": Coen Tasman, *Als een paddestoel op een rottende boomstronk* (Amsterdam: C. Tasman, 1996).

350   "But then I'll be out of a job!": Coen Tasman, *Louter Kabouter* (Amsterdam: Bablyon/De Geus, 1996).

351   "Death to the car!": "'Geen afbraak van huizen voor auto,'" *Het Parool*, May 17, 1971.

352   "The reports from the bicycle front": "Fietsguerilla," *Amsterdams Weekblad*, no. 10 (August 1972).

352   "methods you can use": "Fietsguerilla," *Amsterdams Weekblad*, no. 22 (November 1972).

352   "practical tips": Ibid.

353   "essential professionals": Nan Robertson, "The Netherlands Takes a Car-less Sunday in Stride," *New York Times*, November 5, 1973.

354   "constantly buying": "Den Uyl: liever één wèrkdag per week autoloos," *Het Parool*, November 20, 1973.

354   "The telephone won't stop ringing": "Zondag kan best gezellig worden," *Het Parool*, November 3, 1973.

354   "recaptured the cityscape": "Straat domein van kind, fietser en ruiter," *De Volkskrant*, November 5, 1973.

354   "What especially caught our eye": "Belevenis van de geluiden," *NRC Handelsblad*, November 5, 1973.

355   "Wait, we're not ready": Robertson, "The Netherlands Takes a Car-less Sunday in Stride."

355   "natural target of the cyclists": "Straat domein van kind, fietser en ruiter," *De Volkskrant*, November 5, 1973.

355   "We rented out everything": Frank Zijp, "Politie pakt 19 zwartrijders in Amsterdam," *Het Parool*, November 5, 1973.

355   "[T]hat was counterbalanced": Ibid.

355   "Thanks to the oil crisis": Jules B. Farber, "What's Doing in Amsterdam," *New York Times*, January 6, 1974.

356   "Six thousand bikes": Nan Robertson, "The Lights of Rotterdam Blaze

Defiance of the Arabs' Embargo," *New York Times*, November 26, 1973.

356   "At least a sixty percent increase": "Bike Sales Skyrocket Over Western Europe," *Los Angeles Times*, July 7, 1974.

356   "Bicycling adds a new dimension": Ibid.

357   "molested": [untitled], *NRC Handelsblad*, June 17, 1974.

358   "We wanted a city with fewer": Interview with the author, April 15, 2011.

358   "environment-polluting Mercedes": "Roel van Duijn wil dienstfiets met tien versnellingen," *Leeuwarder Courant*, September 5, 1974.

358   "really too slow for a *wethouder*": Roel van Duijn, *En tranen* (Amsterdam: Meulenhoff, 1976).

359   "I am a free *wethouder*": *Amstelodamum*, 1975.

359   "Phew! It stinks here!": "Op de fiets voor Autovrije Binnenstad," *Het Parool*, October 14, 1974.

359   "A bike is just about nothing": Ibid.

360   "You're working against me": Van Duijn, *En tranen*.

360   "Imagine I'm showing around": Interview with the author, April 15, 2011.

360   "in a fit of craziness": Interview with the author, October 3, 2012.

361   "Our aim is to stimulate people": Paul Kemezis, "Mindful of Oil and Ecology, Dutch Are Returning to Bicycles by the Millions," *New York Times*, November 2, 1975.

361   "My heart has never gone out to the car": Maria C. J. Snethlage, "80 jaar op de fiets," *Vogelvrije Fietser*, no. 1 (1976).

362   "Avoid getting into a wrangle": Flyer distributed to protesters, June 4, 1977.

362   "Bastards!": "Protesterende fietsers legden verkeer stil," *Het Parool*, June 6, 1977.

362   "cycled for their lives": "Amsterdam fietste voor leefbaarder stad," *Amsterdams Stadsblad*, June 8, 1977.

362   "We're ending the pattern": "Verkeer in de knoop door fiets-betogers," *Het Parool*, May 28, 1978.

363   "club of car crazies": "Verkeersplan wordt in fases verwezenlijkt," *Het Parool*, November 23, 1978.

363   "TCP?": *Gemeenteblad van Amsterdam*, Tweede Afdeling III (1978).

364   "In the coming years": *Verkeerscirculatieplan Amsterdam* (Amsterdam: Gemeente Amsterdam, 1979).

20: *It's a Joy to Be on a Bike Again!: The 1980s Onward*

368   "I, too, cycle through red lights": Saar Boerlage and Eric Eljon, "Wel plannen, geen geld," *Gepakte Stad*, no. 9 (March 1985).

368   "a never-ending story": "De Spiegelgracht," *Oek*, no. 1 (1981).

369   "proven to have little more": "Amsterdam fietst weer!!," *Oek*, no. 2 (October 1981).

369   "He's the Indian": Frank Verbeek, "Fietsen als omgekeerde godsdienst," *Nieuw Amsterdams Peil*, September 9, 1981.

370   "executing hundreds of projects": "Bij het opheffen van de Werkgroep Fiets," *Oek*, no. 19 (November 1989).

370   "Oh, oh, oh": Marnix Bruggeman, "Lijn 7 fietsen" *Oek*, no. 19 (November 1989).

371   "It's unbelievable how many people": Albert van der Vliet, "MacBike: 'Gemeente wil fietsen communistisch stallen,'" *Oek*, no. 47 (January 1999).

371   "You can't turn back the clock": "'Afstanden zijn te groot, ook voor de fiets,'" *Het Parool*, June 25, 1971.

371   "It appears as if people think": Peter van den Berg, "'Eigenlijk gedraagt iedereen zich schandalig in het verkeer,'" *De Volkskrant*, October 3, 1992.

372   "crusade against the massive disorderliness": Peter van den Berg, "Politie begint kruistocht tegen massaal wangedrag Amsterdamse fietsers," *De Volkskrant*, October 2, 1992.

372   "gripping": Ibid.

372   "bike accidents with deadly consequences": "Fietsers lopen niet warm voor ongelukkenfilm," *NRC Handelsblad*, October 19, 1992.

372   "I don't need to see": Ibid.

372   "Why should I repair": "Nieuw fietspad gaat gemeente meer kosten," *Het Parool*, November 10, 1992.

373   "Old habits die hard": Ibid.

373   "success": "Actie tegen fietsers zonder licht success," *NRC Handelsblad*, November 10, 1992.

373   "It's a joke!": Bert Steinmetz, "Zonder licht door rood," *Het Parool*, April 1, 1995.

373   "We saw 220 cyclists": "Politie en Stadstoezicht geven kaarten," *Oek*, no. 41 (January 1997).

374   "I don't do it just because": Kurt van Es and Addie Schulte, "Eigenlijk mag je best door rood rijden," *Het Parool*, December 27, 1997.

374   "antisocial cyclists": "Asociale fietsers," *Vogelvrije Fietser*, September/October 2000.

374   "It used to be that the cyclist": Marc van den Eerenbeemt and Weert Schenk, "'Ik vrees dat alles waarin ik geloof, wegsmelt,'" *De Volkskrant*, October 30, 2004.

375   "A bicycle policy doesn't just mean": Jose Onderdenwijngaard, "Amsterdam tegen de auto," *De Waarheid*, June 3, 1989.

375   "Over the past twenty years": Dorien Pels, "Hij staat er nog!," *Trouw*, April 13, 2002.

375   "When people offer to sell me a bike": Jan van Evert, "Halt aan heling," *Oek*, no. 65 (February 2005).

376   "societal acceptance": Projectgroep Fietsendiefstalpreventie, *Werkprogramma Fietsendiefstalpreventie 2002–2006*, February 2002.

376   "We arrested a man who every day": Pels, "Hij staat er nog!"

376   "the cheapest legal bikes in Amsterdam": "Fiets nodig?," *Folia*, September 17, 2010.

377   "The average Amsterdammer": Vera Spaans, "'Ja, u bent uw broeders hoeder,'" *Het Parool*, August 22, 2005.

377   "If you buy a bike for thirty": D.W., "Eerstejaars verwelkomd in Carré," *Folia*, September 3, 2008.

377   "Collectively, these measures": Patrick Meershoek, "Het spel is uit voor de fietsendief," *Het Parool*, March 31, 2005.

379   "With some awkwardness": "Mam, dit is de ware," *De Telegraaf*, September 20, 1999.

379   "Yes, what do you think?": Bert Wagendorp, "Voor het eerst wuivend op de fiets," *De Volkskrant*, September 27, 2001.

379   "Máxima has a good, confident style": Ibid.

380   "There's a fear in this country": Jhim Lamoree, "De navel van de natie," *Het Parool*, August 21, 1999.

380   "None of the architects regarded": Paul Steenhuis, "Fiets in het Rijks," *NRC Handelsblad*, April 6, 2001.

380   "Regarding the discussion": Robbert Roos, "Cruz & Ortiz gaan verder met Cuypers' Rijksmuseum," *Trouw*, April 5, 2001.

380   "In that cathedral": Steenhuis, "Fiets in het Rijks."

381   "one of the wonders of Amsterdam": Van den Berg, "Oermuziek in de passage."

381   "You can . . . breathe": Brita van Oostvoorn, "Actievoerende fietsers geloven stadsdeel niet," *Het Parool*, January 19, 2004.

381   "Many people fear": Xandra van Gelder, "Verbouwing," *De Kunstkrant*, March/April 2004.

382   "ideal image": Ronald Ockhuysen, "Rijksmuseum even weer open," *Het Parool*, July 12, 2008.

382   "chronic parochial commotion": Wierd Duk, "De fiets is heilig," *Elsevier*, November 7, 2009.

382 "Abroad, they laugh about it": Viktor de Kok, "Van fietstunnel naar culturele passage," *De Volkskrant*, August 17, 2011.

382 "When I'm abroad": Duk, "De fiets is heilig."

383 "a prime location": Loes de Fauwe, "'Nooit meer fietsen onder Rijksmuseum,'" *Het Parool*, August 17, 2011.

383 "pig-headed, fundamentalist bicycle lobby": Vincent van Rijn, "Directeur Rijksmuseum woedend om fietstunnel," AT5 Nieuws, June 12, 2012.

383 "The museum is indeed sensitive": Letter from Director Wim Pijbes to Wethouder Eric Wiebes, June 14, 2012.

384 "It's *not* a bike path": Martine Bakker, "Amsterdammers!: Wim Pijbes," AT5, July 4, 2012.

21: Let's Ride: Looking Back and Looking Forward
387 "A guy like that": Bast, "Geheeld voor een geeltje."

388 "Of all antisocial beings": Rob Hoogland, "Chaos," *De Telegraaf*, November 25, 2011.

388 "obvious desire for freedom": Ronald Ockhuysen, "Over de stoep, door rood en dan schelden," *Het Parool*, July 12, 2012.